EMBODYING FORGIVENESS

Embodying Forgiveness

A Theological Analysis

L. Gregory Jones

WILLIAM B. EERDMANS PUBLISHING COMPANY
GRAND RAPIDS, MICHIGAN

© 1995 Wm. B. Eerdmans Publishing Co.
255 Jefferson Ave. S.E., Grand Rapids, Michigan 49503

Printed in the United States of America

00 99 98 97 96 95   7 6 5 4 3 2 1

Library of Congress Cataloging-in-Publication Data

Jones, L. Gregory.
     Embodying forgiveness: a theological analysis / by L. Gregory Jones.
         p.   cm.
     Includes bibliographical references and index.
     ISBN 0-8028-3806 (alk. paper). — ISBN 0-8028-0861-1 (pbk. : alk. paper)
     1. Forgiveness — Religious aspects — Christianity. 2. Reconciliation —
Religious aspects — Christianity. I. Title.
BT795.J66 1995
234'.5 — dc20   95-20782
                                                        CIP

For Susan

Contents

Introduction   xi

PART I

1. The Cost of Forgiveness   3

   Dietrich Bonhoeffer and the Reclamation
   of a Christian Vision and Practice   3

   Rejecting Cheap Grace: God's Forgiveness and the Practices of
   Christian Community   9

   Is Forgiveness Effective? The Struggle against Encroaching
   Darkness   23

2. Therapeutic Forgiveness   35

   The Church's Psychological Captivity in Western Culture   35

   Problems with Forgiveness in Modern Western Culture   37

   The Triumph of the Therapeutic   39

   Therapeutic Forgiveness: Forgiving Hurts We Don't Deserve   47

   The "Revelation" of Judgment   53

   Rethinking Sin   59

   Therapy and the Church's Eschatological Gospel   64

3. Forgiveness Eclipsed   71
   Is Violence the Master of us All?   71

     Forgiven No More   73
     Can Violence Be Unlearned?   77
     Engaging the Pervasiveness of Sin and Evil   83
     Forgiven and Forgiving   91

PART II

4. Characterizing the God Who Forgives   101
   The Triune God and Christian Life   101

     Judaism, Jesus, and Forgiveness   105
     The Father Who Wills Communion   113
     The Advent(s) of Jesus Christ   119
     New Life in the Spirit   129

5. Forgiveness, Repentance, and the Judgment of Grace   135
   The Word That Transfigures Us in the Spirit   135

     The Absence of God's Presence   137
     The Judgment of Grace   145
     The Dynamics of Forgiveness and Repentance   150
     Conclusion: The Woman Who Showed Great Love   160

6. Practicing Forgiveness   163
   Trinitarian Community and the Hope
   for a New Humanity   163

     Baptism: Who Am I?   166
     Eucharist: Remembering the Past in Hope for the Future 175
     Reconciling Forgiveness: Sustaining Permeable Boundaries 182
     Prayer and Healing: Living in the Power of God   197

PART III

7. The Craft of Forgiveness 207

*Traditions, Parables, and Making
and Remaking Responsible Human Life* 207

Whose Forgiveness Is It Anyway? 210

Parables of Christian Forgiveness 219

Crafting Human Forgiveness 225

8. Loving Enemies 241

Living with Others in the Absence of Reconciliation 241

The Moral Significance of Anger, Hatred, and Retribution 243

God's Forgiveness, God's Vengeance, and Ours 251

Loving Enemies on the Path of Christian Forgiveness 262

Punishment and the Politics of Forgiveness 270

9. Is This a Story to Pass On? 279

Forgiveness, Holiness, and the Politics of Memory 279

This is *Not* a Story to *Pass On*:
Simon Wiesenthal's *The Sunflower* 281

This is *Not a Story* to Pass On: Ivan Karamazov's Protest 290

This is *Not* a Story to *Pass* On: Producing Holy People 296

Index 303

Introduction

FORGIVENESS HAS LONG been difficult to embody, even among those committed to its importance. Even the invocation of forgiveness has become rather tricky these days. Some of those one might expect to advocate its importance, particularly people in churches, often are precisely the ones arguing against it (or at least against its abuses). They urge that we need firm punishment and demands for justice, particularly in cases of violence and sexual abuse, not forgiveness. Conversely, some of those who often are taken to be "hard-nosed realists," namely legal scholars and political theorists, have begun to reflect on the possible significance of forgiveness as a means of breaking apart cycles of violence, vengeance, and bitterness — for individuals as well as larger social groups.

Embodying Forgiveness proposes a way in which these sorts of concerns, as well as many others, can be better understood, articulated, and analyzed. It does so, in part, by challenging the terms in which these concerns are developed. For example, while I applaud the resistance to bad understandings of forgiveness and the abuses to which those understandings are often put, and while I challenge the assumption that forgiveness does not involve accountability, I also insist that we can neither make repentance a prerequisite for forgiveness nor separate forgiveness from our understandings of justice. Further, while I applaud the growing conviction — or at least the hope — that forgiveness can become a means of breaking apart cycles of violence, vengeance, and bitterness, I suggest that the issues need to be more carefully situated within the Christian doctrine of the Triune God. Hence, I both draw from and challenge forgiveness's recent critics as well as its recent advocates.

I argue in this book that the overarching context of a Christian account of forgiveness is the God who lives in trinitarian relations of peaceable, self-giving communion and thereby is willing to bear the cost of forgiveness in order to restore humanity to that communion in God's eschatological Kingdom. That is, in the face of human sin and evil, God's love moves toward reconciliation by means of costly forgiveness. In response, human beings are called to become holy by embodying that forgiveness through specific habits and practices that seek to remember the past truthfully, to repair the brokenness, to heal divisions, and to reconcile and renew relationships.

Most fundamentally, then, forgiveness is not so much a word spoken, an action performed, or a feeling felt as it is an embodied way of life in an ever-deepening friendship with the Triune God and with others. As such, a Christian account of forgiveness ought not simply or even primarily be focused on the absolution of guilt; rather, it ought to be focused on the reconciliation of brokenness, the restoration of communion — with God, with one another, and with the whole Creation. Indeed, because of the pervasiveness of sin and evil, Christian forgiveness must be at once an expression of a commitment to a way of life, the cruciform life of holiness in which we seek to "unlearn" sin and learn the ways of God, and a means of seeking reconciliation in the midst of particular sins, specific instances of brokenness.

Further, I argue that forgiveness must be embodied in specific habits and practices of Christian life, paradigmatically as we become part of Christ's Body, the Church. Learning to embody forgiveness involves our commitment to the cultivation of specific habits and practices of the Church. This learning, typically at the hands of exemplars who are more skilled than we are, is similar to the ways in which a person learns to become an excellent physician or an accomplished pianist. Indeed, just as Aristotle emphasized the importance of learning a "craft" for learning how to live, so there is a craft of forgiveness that Christians are called to learn from one another, and particularly from exemplars, as we seek to become holy people.

Hence, the craft of forgiveness involves the ongoing and ever-deepening process of unlearning sin through forgiveness and learning, through specific habits and practices, to live in communion — with the Triune God, with one another, and with the whole Creation. This priority of forgiveness is a sign of the peace of God's original Creation as well as the promised consummation of that Creation in God's Kingdom, and also a sign of the costliness by which such forgiveness is achieved. In this sense, then, forgiveness indicates the ongoing priority of the Church's task to offer the endlessly creative and gratuitous gift of new life in the face of (often horrifying) sin and evil.

The preceding paragraphs invoked several terms crucial to the argument of this book: habits, practices, friendship, craft. I use these terms in this book *not* in the trivial sense in which all people are in favor of, say, friendship, but rather with much stronger (and, in many contemporary circumstances, counter-cultural) force. That is, habits and practices require discipline, patience, and skill, and they are central means for forming people in the virtues necessary for friendship with God; there are no easy techniques, no ways to bypass struggles through self-help manuals. Similarly, when I stress the centrality of friendship with the Triune God (following, among others, Thomas Aquinas), my analysis moves in quite different directions from pious, sentimental affirmations that "Jesus is my friend." By contrast, friendship is a much more formative and transformative relationship than most modern people allow; it requires the cultivation of character through discipline, practice, and time. These are crucial reasons why I suggest that forgiveness involves the lifelong process of learning a craft. There are no shortcuts; and those who genuinely seek to embody Christian forgiveness will find that it involves profoundly disorienting yet life-giving transformations of their life, their world, and their capacity for truthful communion.

Cast most generally, *Embodying Forgiveness* provides a Christian theological analysis of forgiveness. It does so through the development of a stereoscopic vision that seeks to reorient our thinking about the presuppositions and implications of forgiveness. In one sense, the book fills a surprising void, because there have been comparatively few theological discussions of forgiveness in this century. This is so despite the clear significance of forgiveness in crucial Christian texts (e.g., the Bible, the Lord's Prayer, the Apostles' Creed) and despite the prominent concerns about forgiveness in both churches and diverse social contexts. Moreover, over the past fifteen or twenty years the few theological proposals that have been developed have typically been devoted to one or another aspect of forgiveness (e.g., within pastoral care or focused on particular biblical texts) rather than to developing an account that provides several angles of analysis within an overarching theological perspective.

Even so, *Embodying Forgiveness* is not only, or even primarily, for other theologians. This is so for several reasons. In the first place, while I contend that forgiveness is most adequately understood within a Christian theological framework — and more specifically, within the doctrine of the Triune God — the issues raised by a discussion of forgiveness range across the horizons of all of our lives. Hence, the argument of the book needs to be intelligible — and presumably will be of interest — not only to theologians but to people trained in diverse fields. Further, issues of forgiveness are significant not only for professional theologians and other academics, but also for ordinary folk — Christian believers, adherents of other traditions, and nonbelievers alike. That does not mean this is intended to be a "popular" book, or one that is simple to read or understand; but it does mean that the arguments ought to be understandable to anyone willing to take the time and to develop the habits of mind necessary to engage them.

There is a second reason why this book is not intended only, or even primarily, for other theologians: While forgiveness requires a theological analysis, it cannot be confined to a narrow construal of "theology," to one "discipline" of inquiry, or to one "compartment" of our lives. Indeed, one of the primary problems with many contemporary discussions of forgiveness is their willingness either to stay confined within disciplinary barriers or to assume that "we" all know what we are talking about when we invoke language of "forgiveness." To be sure, it is impossible in one book to treat adequately the range of issues and modes of inquiry necessary for a fully comprehensive account of forgiveness. Nonetheless, we cannot afford to let arbitrary disciplinary barriers distort our understandings and embodiments of forgiveness.

By contrast, in *Embodying Forgiveness* I provide a theological analysis that is at the same time social, political, philosophical, cultural, and psychological. That is, this book is "A Theological Analysis" in that it takes the Christian doctrine of the Triune God to be central to the most truthful and comprehensive account of forgiveness; but the subtitle does *not* distinguish the book's argument as "theological" rather than, say, "social" or "political" or other "disciplinary" methods. Indeed, while I do not expect everyone to agree with the account of forgiveness developed here, I do expect that, as a result of my argument, it will become more difficult both for nontheologians to dismiss theological analyses and for theologians to isolate their arguments from Christian practices or other disciplines and analyses.

This is as true of theology as it is of philosophy, psychology, and social and political theory. But our problems are somewhat different. Contemporary theological reflection, particularly about forgiveness, suffers from clichés and from language so abstract that it fails to provide the conceptual clarity necessary for theological claims to carry force. On the other hand, nontheological approaches have tended to provide greater conceptual clarity (e.g., philosophy, social and political theory, psychiatry) or more "effective" deployments of language (e.g., popular psychology) that nonetheless either distort or cheapen an appropriately Christian understanding and embodiment of forgiveness.

These judgments both presuppose and have consequences for the distinctive style and substance of this book's overall argument. In terms of style, I freely draw from, interact with, and criticize diverse arguments, themes, and literary and cinematic works. But I do so in order to develop theological claims, not in order to make points accessible to nontheological audiences. That is, I do not use Flannery O'Connor's short stories, or Clint Eastwood's "Unforgiven," or Toni Morrison's *Beloved,* or Simon Wiesenthal's *The Sunflower* in order to broaden my audience by providing "illustrations" of my arguments; my references to these works are integral elements of my theological arguments. A similar point could be made about my engagement with specific biblical texts, theologians, philosophers, psychologists, social and political theorists, or cultural analysts.

The relative adequacy of the book's style, then, must be judged by the substance of my proposal about how forgiveness ought to be understood and more importantly how it ought to be embodied. My theological proposal, shaped by the overarching context of the Triune God, provides the thematic coherence of the book. Even so, I do not begin fully to develop and defend my constructive proposal until Part II of the book. In the three chapters that comprise Part I, I analyze and confront our tendencies in modernity — both in our churches and in other social and intellectual contexts — to see the world either as "lighter" than it is (hence, trivializing forgiveness by making it "therapeutically" easy) or as "darker" than it is (hence, believing that forgiveness is impossible or ineffective because violence is ultimately the master of us all). My first chapter tells a story of the ways in which Dietrich Bonhoeffer struggled against both tendencies in his thought and, even more, in his life and death at the hands of the Nazis. I then criticize each tendency in successive chapters, focusing on "therapeutic" forgiveness and then on the "eclipse" of forgiveness.

Even though Part I presupposes my overarching theological argument, Parts II and III provide the explication and defense of my constructive theological proposal. The three chapters of Part II explain why a trinitarian identification of God is crucial for an adequate account of forgiveness. I argue that what God is in God's very being — namely, the trinitarian communion of self-giving love — human beings are called to grow into in response to the costly forgiveness of Christ. Such growth occurs through the guidance of the Holy Spirit as Christians unlearn habits and patterns of domination and diminution of others, of sin and evil, and learn to embody habits and practices of Christian communion.

The three chapters of Part III further develop and defend my proposal by analyzing its implications at several junctures of the Church and the world. I show how the craft of forgiveness encompasses people's whole life and how analogues of Christian forgiveness can be found in diverse settings and traditions. I consider the difficult problem of loving enemies, dealing particularly with problems of disparities in power, of impenitent offenders, and the relations between forgiveness, accountability, and punishment. Finally, I explore an issue raised poignantly and painfully by such situations as slavery in the U.S. and the Holocaust in Europe and by such figures as Ivan Karamazov: Are there some situations that are so horrifying in their sin and evil that their perpetrators ought to be designated as "unforgivable"?

As the argument of this book unfolds, it should become clear that the practices of Christian forgiveness are richer and more comprehensive than is often thought. They are richer because forgiveness serves not primarily to absolve guilt but as a reminder, a gracious irritant, of what communion with God and with one another can and should be; and so it should enable and motivate our protest against any situation where people (either ourselves or others) are diminished or destroyed. Forgiveness is an innovative gesture that breaks apart the logic of vengeance and violence, of repression and depression. Further, the practices of forgiveness are more comprehensive because the call to embody forgiveness in the service of holiness is a way of life, a life that carries with it distinctive conceptions of love, confession, power, repentance, justice, punishment, remembrance, and forgetfulness, as well as of community and communion. This does not mean that there are not significant challenges, at both theoretical and practical levels, to a Christian account of the centrality of embodying forgiveness, but I seek here both to confront many of those challenges and to offer, at least in outline, a powerful vision of the gift and task of Christian forgiveness.

A note about Christian traditions and the writing of this book. I write as a United Methodist schooled in the traditions and practices of John and Charles Wesley, and many readers will undoubtedly detect distinctively Wesleyan themes (or, more negatively put, biases) in my argument. This is particularly the case in my discussion of "Practicing Forgiveness" in Chapter 6. However, I have also sought to develop an account that can be shared, or at least should be shared, as broadly as possible across Christian traditions. Indeed, my concern for an ecumenically significant analysis of forgiveness has led me at several places to propose understandings and practices that are not currently a feature of my own Wesleyan tradition. I would argue that this is itself a feature of Wesleyan theology, for at its best it draws on features of the other major Christian traditions: Eastern Orthodox, Roman Catholic, Lutheran, Reformed, Anabaptist, and Anglican.

But an ecumenical focus is not the only characteristic feature of Wesleyan theology; another is a concern for holiness, understood both in personal and more broadly social and political terms. This concern has shaped the perspective of this book in many ways. For I am convinced that unless Christians can learn to understand and, more importantly, embody forgiveness in the context of pursuing such holiness, then there will be little hope that our lives will offer a faithful witness to the Triune God who is, in Word and Spirit, making all things new. And we live in a world, so I suggest, that is in desperate need of a truthful embodiment of costly forgiveness.

It is characteristic of anyone with good sense to express one's gratitude and indebtedness to any and all who have assisted in the writing of a book. In my case this is an almost impossible task because I have been blessed along the way with numerous conversation partners and readers of various drafts of this book. Even so, some have borne more than their share of the burdens of my puzzlements as well as my struggles to embody forgiveness more faithfully. I must first mention James Buckley, Michael Cartwright, Stephen Fowl, and Susan Jones, to whom I am grateful for bearing with me throughout this project; they each read numerous drafts of chapters, engaged me in discussions about both the form of this book and the substance of its arguments, and offered both challenges and support at crucial moments. Their support has been invaluable, their challenges and comments most instructive.

I am also grateful to a diverse company of friends and colleagues who read and commented on an earlier version of part or all of the manuscript: Andrew Adam, Margaret Adam, Kevin Armstrong, Michael Baxter, Rodney Clapp, David Cunningham, Jean Bethke Elshtain, Judith Emerson, Melinda Fowl, Stanley Hauerwas, Reinhard Hütter, Philip Kenneson, Robert Miola, Jonathan Wilson, Ralph Wood, and David Yeago. I am particularly indebted to Peter Ochs, a Jewish colleague and friend who offered many stimulating, incisive, and encouraging comments on an earlier version of the manuscript; his directions to Jewish sources, as well as his own rich reflections on Jewish practices and convictions, were of immense help. I only wish I could have taken more of them into the text of this project.

I am also grateful for the discussion by the members of the Dogmatics Colloquium of the Center for Catholic and Evangelical Theology, who provided a lively and engaging discussion of an earlier version of Chapter 4. In particular, I thank George Lindbeck for a set of comments that greatly clarified the shape of that chapter. Conversations with Clare Mathews and Richard B. Hays were very important to the shape of chapter 4 and more generally in helping me think through implications of the biblical material dealing with forgiveness.

Earlier forms of parts of this book were given as lectures at Wake Forest University, at Allegheny College, at the Sixth International Meeting of the Bonhoeffer Society, at the "Either/Or" Conference in Northfield, Minnesota, and at the Virginia Annual Conference of the United Methodist Church's 1994 Ministers Convocation. I thank the various audiences of these lectures for their questions, criticisms, and thoughtful discussion of difficult issues. I also tried out a number of these ideas on my students at Loyola College in three different versions of the class "Forgiveness and Reconciliation"; I appreciate their patience, goodwill, and the energy that they put into our discussions — including the times they wanted to set their wayward professor straight.

I am fortunate to have received considerable financial support in working on this project. I appreciate the support I have received from several sources at Loyola College: research support from my dean, David Roswell; a Junior Faculty Sabbatical, funded by the Center for the Humanities; and two Summer Research Grants. More generally, Loyola has been an extraordinarily hospitable place in supporting my teaching and research, and I am grateful to have an extraordinary group of colleagues both within the theology department and throughout the college.

I received a year-long fellowship for 1993-94 from the Pew Foundation's Evangelical Scholarship Initiative; that year provided the crucial time for me to complete work on this book. I thank Nathan Hatch and all those who have made such a grant program possible, and particularly Michael Hamilton for his day-to-day handling of the needs of recipients. The Summer Meeting that Pew sponsored so that its fellows could share the fruits of their research with one another also produced a scholarly side-benefit: Conversations with William J. Abraham, J. Deotis Roberts, and Nicholas Wolterstorff were very helpful in shaping some of the final work on the book's argument.

I am deeply grateful to Eerdmans Publishing for bringing this project to completion. That company's commitment to serious theology and the Christian faith is admirable, especially in our current cultural contexts; even more, it has a staff of remarkable and talented people to embody that commitment. In particular, I am grateful for the guidance and friendship of Editor-in-Chief Jon Pott, whose keen editorial and theological acumen has made this a better book. I also appreciate the careful and thoughtful work of John Simpson in seeing the manuscript through to its final form.

My family has provided incredible support in this project. I am particularly grateful to my mother and my stepfather, Bonnie and John Gehweiler, who offered not only their personal support but also the wonderful gift of a computer and a printer to make the production of this book more efficient. My wife and children have been wonderful throughout the writing process, knowing (or at least learning over time) when to leave "daddy" alone and when to offer distractions. I am thankful for the support of Nathan and Benjamin, two boys who have often reminded (and have needed to remind!) their father of the many things more important and more enjoyable than reading and writing theology. During the time this book was in press we celebrated the birth of our daughter Sarah, another sign of God's gracious love.

I also want to thank a host of people whom I cannot mention here by name. These include members of my wider family, teachers, friends, and people in the churches I have been privileged to be a member of as well as, in some cases, to serve as one of their ordained clergy. This communion of saints and of saints-in-the-making has provided me with a rich variety of exemplars, people who by their lives and their interactions have helped me glimpse a bit more clearly what it means to embody Christian forgiveness. My life and this book are richer for their presence and witness.

This book is dedicated to my wife, the Rev. Susan P. Jones. As I mention above, she has read more versions of the chapters of this book than she (or I!) care to recall. Her own passion for theology and for ensuring that theology touches the lives of others is manifested in her rich service as a United Methodist minister. Her comments were crucial, and her insistence on pressing me where I was confused or confusing has helped the book's argument immensely. Further, despite her demanding schedule as a parish minister, Susan often graciously provided the time and space for me to write when the inspiration hit. She did this even though it often meant she was shouldering more of the household and childcare tasks than I had any right to expect. Most centrally, she has provided invaluable guidance, challenge, and support in my struggles to embody forgiveness, both in what she says and in how she lives. I am blessed by her ministry, her friendship, and her love.

PART I

1 The Cost of Forgiveness

Dietrich Bonhoeffer and the Reclamation of a Christian Vision and Practice

"FORGIVING DOESN'T MEAN risk your life." This is the headline in a recent column written by Andrew M. Greeley for Religious News Service. Greeley's focus is domestic violence, more specifically the dangers of Christians telling women that they ought always to forgive their abusers. Greeley writes, "Sure, forgive him because he is not in full control of his own actions. But forgiveness does not require you to risk your own life or that of your children. Quite the contrary, self-esteem and concern for your own selfhood (a gift of God) constrains you to send him on his way before it is too late."[1]

Greeley's advice offers an important corrective to rhetoric about forgiveness that perpetuates and exacerbates problems rather than addresses them. People caught in situations of extreme violence, including abuse, do not need to be told, indeed should not be told, that they should be willing to die, even if this is couched in abstract ideals of forgiveness or of sacrifice or of self-denial. Such observations and injunctions, often grounded in Christians' misreadings of their own Scripture, perpetuate the suffering and prevent the sufferers from being able to respond appropriately.

At the same time, however, Greeley's advice too easily invites continued misunderstandings about forgiveness. For in important ways, Chris-

---

1. Andrew M. Greeley, "Forgiving Doesn't Mean Risk Your Life," *The United Methodist Reporter* 141/8 (July 15, 1994) p. 1.

tian forgiveness *does* require our "death." To be sure, not just any death is required, nor should that requirement result in collusion with those who diminish and destroy human life. But Christian forgiveness requires our death, understood in the specific form and shape of Jesus Christ's dying — and rising. For as we participate in Christ's dying *and* rising, we die to our old selves and find a future not bound by the past. The focus of this dying and rising is the Christian practice of baptism, and it also involves a lifelong practice of living into that baptism, of daily dying to old selves and living into the promise of an embodied new life. This, at least, is the claim Paul makes in his letter to the Romans (6:1-11).

Paul's focus in this passage is not on forgiveness *per se*. Even so, the larger horizon of his argument in Romans suggests that the practice of forgiveness receives its primary intelligibility from Christ's death and resurrection and that Christians learn to embody forgiveness as a baptismal community — indeed, as the Body of Christ. According to Paul, those who have been baptized have entered into the community defined by whomever or whatever they are baptized into; to have been baptized into Christ, as Paul characterizes it in Romans 6:3, is to have entered into the community ruled and defined by Christ — more specifically, by Christ's death and resurrection.[2] According to Paul, baptism is a training in dying — specifically to sin, to the old self — so that people may be raised to newness of life. Further, this new life is given its shape by the Kingdom that Jesus announced and enacted.

That is, as they are initiated into the practices of God's Kingdom, the forgiving grace of Jesus Christ gives people a new perspective on their histories of sin and evil, of their betrayals and their being betrayed, of their vicious cycles of being caught as victimizers and victims, so that they can bear to remember the past well in hope for a new future. But this is not simply a release from the past; it is also freedom for holiness, a holiness that requires prophetic protest and action directed at any situations where people's lives are being diminished or destroyed. Paradigmatically, such forgiveness in the pursuit of holiness is embodied through the practices of Christian community. That is, the new life of holiness signified by baptism is found and lived in communities of God's Kingdom: People learn to embody forgiveness by becoming part of Christ's Body.

The danger in Greeley's advice is that he dissociates forgiveness from any sense of death and new life, specifically that found in the practice of

---

2. For further discussion of this point, see Stephen Fowl, "Some Uses of Story in Moral Discourse: Reflections on Paul's Moral Discourse and Our Own," *Modern Theology* 4 (1988) pp. 293-308.

baptism. Consequently, he diminishes the cost of Christ's forgiveness as well as the hope that is entailed thereby. By situating forgiveness as a largely symbolic gesture (done because "he is not in full control of his own actions"),[3] Greeley fails to grapple with the ways in which Christian forgiveness might provide a more radical critique of situations of abuse and a more radical hope for the future than his perspective allows. It can be so as people embody forgiveness in the specific practices and friendships of God's inbreaking reign.

This suggests that people are mistaken if they think of Christian forgiveness primarily as absolution from guilt; the purpose of forgiveness is the restoration of communion, the reconciliation of brokenness. Neither should forgiveness be confined to a word to be spoken, a feeling to be felt, or an isolated action to be done; rather, it involves a way of life to be lived in fidelity to God's Kingdom. Baptism provides the initiation into God's story of forgiving and reconciling love, definitively embodied in the life, death, and resurrection of Jesus of Nazareth. In response, people are called to embody that forgiveness by unlearning patterns of sin and struggling for reconciliation wherever there is brokenness.

That is, forgiveness is at once an expression of a commitment to a way of life, the cruciform life of holiness in which people cast off their "old" selves and learn to live in communion with God and with one another, and a means of seeking reconciliation in the midst of particular sins, specific instances of brokenness. In its broadest context, forgiveness is the way in which God's love moves to reconciliation in the face of sin. This priority of forgiveness is a sign of the peace of God's original Creation as well as the promised eschatological consummation of that Creation in the Kingdom, and also a sign of the costliness by which such forgiveness is achieved. In this sense, then, forgiveness indicates the ongoing priority of the Church's task to offer the endlessly creative and gratuitous gift of new life in the face of sin and brokenness.

Christian forgiveness involves a high cost, both for God and for those who embody it. It requires the disciplines of dying and rising with Christ, disciplines for which there are no shortcuts, no handy techniques to replace the risk and vulnerability of giving up "possession" of one's self, which is

---

3. Indeed, Greeley's language of forgiving "because he is not in full control of his actions" is bizarre. How does Greeley know that such a person is not in full control of his actions? Further, should people *not* forgive those who *are* in full control of their actions? What role should repentance play? Greeley's formulation reflects, so it seems, both the marginalization of forgiveness and assumptions about its general ineffectiveness as a response to wrongdoing.

done through the practices of forgiveness and repentance. This does not involve self-denial, nor the "death" of selves through annihilation. Rather, it is learning to see one's self and one's life in the context of communion.

Those who embody forgiveness discover that one of the chief obstacles to overcome is the tendency to see one's own life as something to be either possessed or simply given over to another's possession; too often, the result is that people cling to their power or even their powerlessness. Greeley's formulation of forgiveness presupposes this sense of "possession" of the self; by contrast, baptism shows that our selves are given over to God through the Church, and in so doing we receive new life.

That is, the claim that selves are not to be "possessed" receives its shape and focus from a very specific claim about the Triune God, whose character is found in self-giving (and hence self-receiving) communion, and whose Creation and promised Kingdom are also characterized by communion. However, in the face of sin and evil, Christ's costly forgiveness is necessary if communion is to be restored, love realized, reconciliation achieved. For, after all, at the heart of the Christian doctrine of God is the conviction that human beings are created for such communion, for relations of friendship with one another and, most determinatively, with the Other who is God.

Unfortunately, the cost of forgiveness is *too* high for many people. Consequently, they invent and turn to cheaper versions of forgiveness, ones that will enable them to "feel" or "think" better about themselves — or simply to "cope" with their situation — without having to engage in struggles to change or transform the patterns of their relationships. Such versions of cheap, "therapeutic" forgiveness create the illusion of caring about the quality of human relations while simultaneously masking the ways in which people's lives are enmeshed in patterns of destructiveness. Indeed, such versions of forgiveness often exacerbate human destructiveness precisely because their illusions and masking create a moral and political vacuum.

Conversely, others are convinced that the cost of forgiveness cannot be high enough, because forgiveness is at best ineffective and at worst immoral. That is, human sin and evil are such that there can be no effective forgiveness; human beings are enmeshed in violence, and the exercise of violence is the only effective means of coping with life as people experience it. On such a view, the necessity of violence can be either celebrated or mourned; further, people can respond either by seeking to dominate through the deployment of violence, or they can seek to foster community by minimizing the force and effects of violence. But in either case, it is assumed that forgiveness cannot effectively respond to the pervasive darkness that characterizes the world. At most, forgiveness can offer private, personal consolation amid the more pervasive and public necessity of force and violence; any significant politics of forgiveness has been eclipsed by the darkness of the world.

Ironically, these attempts to evade or deny the cost of forgiveness end up incurring other, more deadly costs. They are the costs that animated Greeley's commentary, costs of diminished and annihilated selves, of people afflicting and/or suffering untold physical and emotional violence and destruction. Even so, we do not avoid death by trivializing or denying the cost of forgiveness; rather, the furies of death are thereby unleashed in horrifying ways. We need the schooling provided by the Triune God so that we can learn to envision and to embody costly forgiveness.

Thus far the focus here has been on baptismal death as the context for describing the vocation of dying to old selves and rising to newness of life; however, Christian forgiveness *may* also require of us our death in other ways. Insofar as baptism is a training in dying, it sets us on the course of the discipleship of the cross. In some situations, the struggle to embody Christian forgiveness may cost us our life.

Such was the case with Dietrich Bonhoeffer, a German theologian who struggled against the twin dangers of cheapened forgiveness and the eclipse of forgiveness in the midst of the Nazi terror and the anemic responses to that terror offered by Christians in Germany. His struggles came to mark his life, his thought, and eventually his tragic death at the hands of the Nazis.

Bonhoeffer provided a powerful witness to the cost of forgiveness. He also reclaimed the theological significance of a Christian vision and practice of forgiveness, though his own conceptions were neither fully developed nor wholly adequate. Even so, his witness and reclamation resisted both the false light of a therapeutic forgiveness and also the frightening possibility that pervasive violence and oppression had created a darkness that simply overwhelms.

Given his family background and the time and culture into which he was born, however, it could hardly have been predicted that Bonhoeffer would provide such a powerful witness to the cost of forgiveness. After all, Bonhoeffer was born in 1906 into a comfortable middle-class German family. The family was composed primarily of diverse types of professionals; it was urbane, cultured, and nominally religious. Bonhoeffer's father was a noted psychiatrist and professor at the University of Berlin.

Bonhoeffer was born into a Germany that had been profoundly influenced by the Reformation, by the Enlightenment, and by the liberal Protestant theology of the nineteenth century. Indeed, Adolf von Harnack, one of the primary exponents of liberal theology, was a family friend and neighbor and one of Bonhoeffer's earliest theology teachers. Further, Christian practices and understandings of forgiveness had been fragmented and transmuted by the legacy of the medieval period, the debates of the Reformation, the intellectual challenges of the Enlightenment, and the reformulations of liberal theology. The dawn of the twentieth century was hardly a propitious time for sustaining a coherent Christian account of forgiveness.

Yet Bonhoeffer resisted, and sought to transform, the legacies that he inherited. The man who at the time of Hitler's seizure of power in 1932-33 was seen by many as a bright hope for academic theology was martyred by the Nazis shortly before the collapse of the Third Reich in 1945. Many people know Bonhoeffer best for *Life Together*, his "devotional" book on Christian community, for his polemic against "cheap grace" in *The Cost of Discipleship*, and for his personal martyrdom. Even so, though these books are theologically important and his death is an illuminating example, Bonhoeffer's theological legacy and personal testimony to the cost of Christian forgiveness are not limited to those writings or to the details of his death.

Bonhoeffer sought to reclaim the theological centrality of forgiveness in a world where cheap grace and privatized forgiveness had too often become the norm. As he confronted the Nazis in his life and in his death, he had to face the challenge that forgiveness is ineffective — that only force, and more particularly violence, is effective. So Bonhoeffer also sought to affirm the theological possibility of forgiveness in a world where God's grace had seemingly been eclipsed.

In what follows I neither examine exhaustively Bonhoeffer's theological arguments nor summarize the details of his life. Rather I describe aspects of Bonhoeffer's life and thought in a way that displays his reclamation of a Christian vision and practice of forgiveness, and specifically the costliness of forgiveness, in the face of daunting challenges.[4] To be sure, Bonhoeffer's own life and thought are inextricably linked to his Protestant heritage and commitments; yet they are of ecumenical significance in point-

---

4. Thus my account in this chapter provides an angle of vision on Bonhoeffer's life and thought that overlaps with and builds on the account of Bonhoeffer as a "performer of Scripture" in Stephen Fowl's and my *Reading in Communion* (London: SPCK/Grand Rapids: Eerdmans, 1991). My argument in what follows in this chapter draws on material from a longer essay in which I analyzed Bonhoeffer's account of forgiveness: "The Cost of Forgiveness: Grace, Christian Community, and the Politics of Worldly Discipleship," *Union Seminary Quarterly Review* 46 (1992) pp. 149-169.

The biographical details of Bonhoeffer in this chapter are dependent on Eberhard Bethge's irreplaceable biography, *Dietrich Bonhoeffer*, tr. E. H. Robertson, et al. (London: Collins, 1970).

ing toward the tasks that face us in reconstructing the full theological significance of Christian forgiveness. That is, while Bonhoeffer's struggles, criticisms, and constructive proposals must be understood in the context of his own historical, ecclesial, and political situations, they also point us toward crucial themes and issues that will need to be more fully explicated in the rest of this book.

Rejecting Cheap Grace: God's Forgiveness and the Practices of Christian Community

Bonhoeffer displayed throughout his youth a keen interest in Christianity, and Christian theology in particular. His academic study of theology began in 1923 under several of the great "liberal" theologians, theologians who were convinced that theology takes its cue from human experience, that Jesus' death was significant primarily as a moral example of human relatedness to God, and that forgiveness comes from Jesus' mediation to the Christian community of the intimacy that he himself enjoyed with God. By contrast, as early as 1925, following contact with Karl Barth and Barth's theological project, Bonhoeffer began to challenge the adequacy of this perspective. Bonhoeffer became convinced that Scripture, not personal experience, ought to shape theology, that Jesus' death and resurrection were not simply a moral example, but more determinatively an event of God forgiving humanity of its sin and enabling people to embark on a new life under God's reign, and that God's forgiveness is decisively enacted by Jesus, who is not merely illustrative of a more general human capacity and desire.

During these early years, Bonhoeffer was not only developing his theological perspective through his reading and writing; he also was learning from his travels. He spent a term in Rome (1923), a year in Barcelona as an assistant pastor (1928), and a year as an exchange student at New York's Union Theological Seminary (1930-31). While in New York, Bonhoeffer regularly attended the Abyssinian Baptist Church in Harlem, a prominent African American congregation. He also encountered a French Calvinist named Jean Lasserre, a pacifist whose views had an important impact on Bonhoeffer's thinking about such issues as discipleship and forgiveness. These international travels and ecumenical contacts reinforced Bonhoeffer's longstanding commitment to connecting the doctrines, teachings, and practices of Christianity with the lives that people actually lead.

When he returned to Germany from New York in 1931, Bonhoeffer assumed a position as a lecturer on the theological faculty at the University of Berlin. He also became active in ecumenical work. But perhaps most dramatically, Bonhoeffer's return to Germany brought home the realization that he was a theologian who needed to become a Christian. That is, he discovered the need to engage the Bible more directly, to allow the Bible to challenge him and transform his life as one forgiven by God. As a result, Bonhoeffer's thought became increasingly shaped by his engagements with the texts of Scripture.[5]

At this point Bonhoeffer's challenge to the liberal theology of his teachers became particularly apparent. In a 1932 lecture, "Thy Kingdom Come," Bonhoeffer emphasized the importance of the Kingdom of God for Christian theology, *not* as something that refers primarily to human experience and human activity, but as a petition for God's transformation of the world. This emphasis was particularly urgent given the emergence of Hitler on the stage of German politics. Bonhoeffer wrote, "The petition for the kingdom is not the begging of the anxious soul for its own salvation. It is not Christian trimmings to be used by those who would reform the world. It is rather the petition of the suffering and battling congregation in the world on behalf of the human race, asking that God fully manifest his glory in it."[6] Bonhoeffer shifted the emphasis from a primarily personal and privatized Christian experience to a petition for the coming Reign of God to be embodied, as an eschatological anticipation, within Christian community.

Here, in the context of a discussion of God's Kingdom, Bonhoeffer emphasized the centrality of forgiveness for Christian life and thought. According to Bonhoeffer, the Kingdom of God assumes form in the Church insofar as loneliness is overcome through the "miracle" of confession and forgiveness. He adds,

> This is because in the church, which is the communion of saints created by the resurrection, one person can and should bear the guilt of another, and for this reason the last shackle of loneliness, hatred of others, is removed, and community is established and created anew. It is through the miracle of confession, which is beyond all our understanding, that all hitherto existing community is shown to have been an illusion and is

5. See *Reading in Communion*, pp. 139-149, for further discussion of this shift in Bonhoeffer's own assessment of his engagement with Scripture.

6. Dietrich Bonhoeffer, "Thy Kingdom Come: The Prayer of the Church for God's Kingdom on Earth" (1932) in John D. Godsey, *Preface to Bonhoeffer: The Man and Two of His Shorter Writings* (Philadelphia: Fortress, 1965) p. 38. Bonhoeffer's emphasis on the Kingdom as a call to the Church to be wary of Hitler is even more explicit in his 1933 Introduction to *Creation and Fall*, tr. John C. Fletcher (London: SCM, 1959).

abolished, destroyed, and broken asunder, and that here and now the new congregation of the resurrection world is created.[7]

Several of Bonhoeffer's central themes are sounded here: a concern for authentic community, the importance of the crucified and risen Christ enabling confession and forgiveness, the responsibility to bear the sin of another, and the difference between "illusory" community and Christian community that is empowered by Christ's resurrection and is the concrete presence of Christ.

Underlying Bonhoeffer's perspective on these themes is his understanding of Jesus Christ and, more particularly, his understanding of the relation between Christ and Christian community. That this is the case ought to be clear given Bonhoeffer's own abiding concerns with the centrality of Christ and of who Christ is for us today.[8] Those concerns preceded the rise of Nazi Germany, but they took on particular significance as Bonhoeffer began to recognize the Nazi threat.

In 1933, Bonhoeffer gave a series of lectures, published in English as Christ the Center, in which he developed an account of the centrality of christology and, more particularly, of Christ's relation to Christian community and the world. In so doing, he also emphasized the central significance of Christian forgiveness. Bonhoeffer argued that Jesus Christ forgives sin through his person and work. This is accomplished extra nos (outside us), and as such frees human beings from sin for new life in Christ. But Christ's work is also inextricably pro me (for me): Christ addresses people in their particularity and confronts them with the truth about themselves through forgiveness. Further, Christ is also in nobis (in us). The addressing Word does not come to isolated individuals; it comes, rather, to the community. Christ is present in preaching and in the sacraments, and that presence brings both judgment and forgiveness.[9]

Bonhoeffer insisted on both the theological primacy of christology and its essentially practical significance (claims that will be further unpacked in Part II of this book). He had no place for general or abstract

---

7. Bonhoeffer, "Thy Kingdom Come," p. 41.

8. For further documentation of this point, see Ernst Feil, The Theology of Dietrich Bonhoeffer, tr. Martin Rumscheidt (Philadelphia: Fortress, 1985) pp. 59-96, esp. pp. 95-96. Obviously a full discussion of Bonhoeffer's christology, or even of its relation to Christian community, is beyond the scope of my argument here. A more complete discussion of Bonhoeffer's christology can be found in Charles R. Marsh's Reclaiming Dietrich Bonhoeffer (Oxford: Oxford University, 1994).

9. See Bonhoeffer, Christ the Center, tr. E. H. Robertson (New York: Harper and Row, 1978), esp. pp. 38, 50-51, 57-59.

christologies that are not inextricably linked to the formation and sustenance of Christian communities and, more specifically, Christian discipleship.[10] Among other problems, such christologies could too easily be coopted into the service of Hitler.

Unfortunately, Bonhoeffer discovered as early as 1933 that relatively few Christians understood the significance of Hitler's threat. The vast majority of Protestants swore allegiance to Hitler, forming what became known as the German Christian Church. Bonhoeffer perceived this as a threat to the Church and to the Lordship of Christ; he preached, lectured, and distributed pamphlets trying to counteract the threat. But it did not make an appreciable difference. In the Autumn of 1933, Bonhoeffer told a group of students that "we must now endure in silence, and set the firebrand of truth to all four corners of the proud German Christian edifice so that one day the whole structure may collapse."[11] As a part of that endurance, in October 1933 Bonhoeffer accepted a call to pastor a German congregation in England. During the next two years he would watch and think about how to deal with the gathering storm in Germany.

In 1935 Bonhoeffer returned to Germany to become a theologian/pastor-in-charge of a seminary newly founded by the Confessing Church, that body of Protestant Christians who were united by their opposition to Hitler and to the established Church's support of the Nazis. The seminary, eventually located in Finkenwalde, was founded to train and form clergy to serve churches that would resist the claims of Hitler and the Nazis. Bonhoeffer knew that this would require a revitalization of discipleship learned and lived in Christian community for the sake of service in and to the world.

It was during his years at Finkenwalde that Bonhoeffer wrote *The Cost of Discipleship*; he wrote *Life Together* shortly afterward. Indeed, the latter described the common life around which the activities of Finkenwalde were to be structured. Finkenwalde was a seminary where a group of people was studying for the ministry; but, more importantly, it was also a community of Protestant Christians who fostered a common life together. During this time Bonhoeffer sharpened his polemic against the German Christians, insisting that only a common life grounded in Jesus Christ and embodied

---

10. Note Bonhoeffer's comment from 1937: "An abstract Christology, a doctrinal system, a general religious knowledge on the subject of grace or on the forgiveness of sins, render discipleship superfluous, and in fact they positively exclude any idea of discipleship whatever, and are essentially inimical to the whole conception of following Christ." *The Cost of Discipleship*, tr. R. H. Fuller (New York: Macmillan, 1963) p. 63.

11. Bonhoeffer, cited in Bethge, *Dietrich Bonhoeffer*, p. 252.

in practices of costly forgiveness and reconciliation (including confession), eucharist, prayer, and Bible study would provide a credible Christian witness in the world. That common life, then, would form Christians who could serve in the world *as Christians.* As Bonhoeffer described it, "The aim is not the seclusion of the monastery, but a place of the deepest inward concentration for service outside."[12]

Bonhoeffer recognized, and described in *Life Together,* the centrality of disciplines and practices for Christian life. Christian life is learned and lived through the cultivation of specific habits and practices of forgiveness in the service of holiness that enable us simultaneously to unlearn our habits of sinfulness. But Bonhoeffer knew that cannot be done without embodying forgiveness and other practices that sustain a common life in Christ. Though he did not use the language, Bonhoeffer understood that forgiveness is a craft that must be learned (relying particularly on exemplars) and embodied over time as people seek to become holy in communion with God and one another.

These convictions led Bonhoeffer to polemicize against the trivialization and privatization of Christian life, and specifically Christian forgiveness. These tendencies converged in what Bonhoeffer termed "cheap grace": "the preaching of forgiveness without requiring repentance, baptism without church discipline, Communion without confession, absolution without personal confession." Within such an approach to Christian life, the forgiveness of sins is proclaimed as a general truth, and "my only duty as a Christian is to leave the world for an hour or so on a Sunday morning and go to church to be assured that my sins are all forgiven."[13]

Cheap grace denies any real need for deliverance from sin since it justifies the sin instead of the sinner. As such, cheap grace offers consolation without any change of life, without any sense of either dying or rising in Christ. Indeed, cheap grace does not require any embodiment; Bonhoeffer concluded that "cheap grace therefore amounts to a denial of the living Word of God, in fact, a denial of the Incarnation of the Word of God." Further, he claimed that the Lutheran Church in Germany had been unable to resist Hitler because cheap grace had triumphed: "The price we are having to pay to-day in the shape of the collapse of the organized Church is only the

12. Bonhoeffer, *The Way to Freedom,* tr. Edwin H. Robertson and John Bowden, ed. Edwin H. Robertson (New York: Harper and Row, 1966) p. 31. For similar comments see also Bonhoeffer, *Life Together,* tr. J. W. Doberstein (New York: Harper and Row, 1954) pp. 17-18.

13. Bonhoeffer, *The Cost of Discipleship,* pp. 47, 45, 54.

inevitable consequence of our policy of making grace available to all at too low a cost. We gave away the word and sacraments wholesale, we baptized, confirmed, and absolved a whole nation unasked and without condition." Perhaps most destructively, cheap grace anesthetized people so that they no longer were capable of embodying forgiveness through discipleship; they could not even discern how forgiveness might require of us our death.[14]

In response to this destructive cheap grace, Bonhoeffer emphasized a costly forgiveness. In so doing, he also stressed such themes and practices of Christian community as judgment, repentance, confession, and love for enemies. These are necessary for learning well how to practice (and thereby embody) the craft of forgiveness.

For Bonhoeffer, there is no real grace without judgment. Sin cannot be overlooked or forgotten; it must be confronted and judged in the context of forgiveness. In words recalling Romans 6, Bonhoeffer wrote, "The old man and his sin are judged and condemned, but out of this judgement a new man arises, who has died to the world and to sin."[15]

To be sure, Bonhoeffer was also quite familiar with Matthew 7:1: "Do not judge, so that you may not be judged."[16] But Bonhoeffer insisted that the question was not whether or not judgment should occur. He understood that passage as a critique of the judgment humans tend to exercise, not as a condemnation of Christ's judgment or of judgment *per se*. The prohibition of judgment in Matthew 7:1, according to Bonhoeffer, is a blow directed at sinful humanity, which presumes to play the role of God: " 'Judging' is not a special vice or wickedness of the disunited man; it is his essence, manifesting itself in his speech, his action and his sentiment."[17] Such judgment is closely related to the "self-justification" that Bonhoeffer repeatedly condemned in his writings.[18]

14. *The Cost of Discipleship*, pp. 46, 58-59.

15. *The Cost of Discipleship*, p. 257. On the importance of not overlooking or forgetting sin, see p. 258.

16. See Bonhoeffer, *Ethics*, ed. E. Bethge, tr. N. H. Smith (New York: Macmillan, 1965) p. 30.

17. Bonhoeffer, *Ethics*, pp. 30, 31. See also Bonhoeffer's criticism of Nietzsche on this point (p. 31): "It is not, as Nietzsche supposed, because it arises from these dark motives that judgement is wrongful; judgement is evil because it is itself apostasy, and that is also the reason why it brings forth evil in the human heart. It cannot, of course, be denied that from the psychological point of view extremely noble motives may also be disclosed as determining the thought of the man who judges, but this fact can have no bearing on the character of judgement itself."

18. See Bonhoeffer's comments in *Life Together*, p. 91: "Self-justification and judging others go together, as justification by grace and serving others go together."

Even so, there is also another judgment that, Bonhoeffer noted, is "true activity" of humanity. It is a judgment that "springs from the achievement of union with the origin, with Jesus Christ." This union is accomplished through the work of Christ, the judge whose judgment does not condemn but brings salvation. In Bonhoeffer's terms, God

> does not permit us to classify men and the world according to our own standards and to set ourselves up as judges over them. He leads us *ad absurdum* by Himself becoming a real man and a companion of sinners and thereby compelling us to become the judges of God. God sides with the real man and with the real world against all their accusers. Together with men and with the world He comes before the judges, so that the judges are now made the accused.[19]

Christ's judgment is real. Human sin is forgiven only because it is confronted and judged. But that judgment is wholly in the service of mercy, reconciliation, and new life. "God binds elements together in the breaking, creates community in the separation, grants grace through judgment."[20] Through God's eschatological judgment of grace, human brokenness is overcome and communion is restored.

In order to live in the judgment of reconciliation wrought by Christ, however, we must repent of our sin — more specifically, repent of the judging by which sinful humanity lives. Such judging precludes our ability to see things rightly and to live as holy people. The verses that follow Matthew 7:1 indicate a crucial problem: We so easily judge others while refusing to see our own sin. As Bonhoeffer put it in a sermon on the parable of the unforgiving servant, "That is the whole lesson: the sins of others you see, but your own sin you fail to see. In repentance, recognize God's mercy toward you; in this way alone will you be able to forgive."[21] But repentance, like forgiveness, is not just an attitude or a feeling; it must be practiced and embodied.

Practices of repentance are necessary because of the inescapability of

---

19. Bonhoeffer, *Ethics*, p. 71. Karl Barth develops this christological theme under the heading "The Judge Judged in Our Place." See Barth, *Church Dogmatics* IV/1, tr. G. W. Bromiley (Edinburgh: Clark, 1956), pp. 211-282. I discuss this further in chapter 4.

20. Bonhoeffer, *Life Together*, p. 108.

21. Dietrich Bonhoeffer, "On Forgiveness," in G. B. Kelly and F. B. Nelson (eds.), *A Testament to Freedom* (San Francisco: HarperCollins, 1990) p. 277. See also *The Cost of Discipleship*, p. 206: "By judging others we blind ourselves to our own evil and to the grace that others are just as entitled to as we are."

Christ's judgment, even though that judgment is in the service of (costly) grace. Bonhoeffer noted that "the preaching of grace can only be protected by the preaching of repentance."[22] Even more, there is a mutually reinforcing connection between repentance and forgiveness.

> The prodigal in Luke 15, who knows himself to be lost, is accepted again by the father. That is to say, the one who is ready to repent finds forgiveness. Penitence and forgiveness are so closely tied that one can reverse the principle: only he who is forgiven finds his way to penitence. Only he who is penitent receives the kingdom of heaven, and only because the kingdom of heaven has come near is there repentance.[23]

In one sense repentance prepares us to receive God's grace, but in another, more profound sense we discover through our repentance that God's grace has already found us.

Moreover, the goal of repentance, as with grace, is to lead people into community. The Body of Christ is forged through the dynamic interrelations of repentance and forgiveness. So, referring to Acts 2, Bonhoeffer wrote that Peter "proclaims the full, free grace of God which calls men to action, to repentance, to new life. 'Repent,' in other words, 'Let yourselves be called to the church.' Through grace, on the strength of the call of God, take the step to the community of those who have been visited with grace, the community which has been called out of darkness."[24] Once called to the Church, people become a part of that community whose common life is sustained through such ongoing practices as confession, forgiveness, and loving enemies.

The practice of confession, seen not as self-flagellation but as grace, was at the heart of the Christian community in Finkenwalde.[25] Indeed, confession occasions what Bonhoeffer called "a breakthrough to community."[26] Confession is central to Christian community because it is "the

22. Bonhoeffer, "The Power of the Keys and Church Discipline," in *The Way to Freedom*, p. 151.

23. Bonhoeffer, *Spiritual Care*, tr. J. C. Rochelle (Philadelphia: Fortress, 1985) p. 44.

24. Bonhoeffer, *The Way to Freedom*, p. 47.

25. For the notion that confession *is* grace, see Bonhoeffer, *Spiritual Care*, p. 60. The centrality of confession for Bonhoeffer's understanding of Christian community can be seen by the extensive treatment he gives the topic in *Life Together* and *Spiritual Care* as well as numerous references in his other writings. Even so, there are some enigmatic passages in *Letters and Papers from Prison* that seem to relativize the significance of confession. See my discussion below, pp. 30-32.

26. *Life Together*, p. 112.

God-given remedy for self-deception and self-indulgence," enabling Christians to unlearn our sinful "possession" of our selves through communion with God and one another. Further, through confession Christians are "conformed to the death of Christ," thereby also being empowered in the disciplines of daily dying and rising with Christ.[27]

Bonhoeffer was troubled both by the loss of confession within Protestantism and the reliance on psychotherapy as a secular offshoot once confession was lost as an ecclesiastical institution. The loss of confession, Bonhoeffer thought, opened the door to a Nietzschean critique of Christianity as a religion of pity that abandons responsibility and encourages a self-denying judgmentalism. Both Protestantism and psychotherapy, Bonhoeffer thought, had undermined the centrality of confession for the forgiveness of sin and new life in Christ.

> The most experienced observer of humanity knows less of the human heart than the Christian who lives at the foot of the cross of Christ. No psychology knows that people perish only through sin and are saved only through the cross of Christ. Anyone who has seen the meaning of the cross for but a moment is shocked by the godlessness of the world and by the awesomeness of his own sins; he will no longer be shocked by the sins of his sisters and brothers in Christ. The spirit of judgment is cut off at the roots.[28]

The loss of confession as a genuinely Christian practice, patterned in the cross of Christ, had thus created a vacuum that either denied the costliness of forgiveness or evaded it through other forms of death-dealing godlessness.

By reclaiming the centrality of confession for Lutherans, Bonhoeffer exhibited aspects both of the sacramental character of confession characteristic of Roman Catholics and the emphasis on the practice of "fraternal admonition" characteristic of Anabaptists. He also recovered elements of the pre-Enlightenment Lutheran tradition. In so doing, Bonhoeffer sought to reclaim the insights of the larger Christian tradition, while nonetheless insisting that no single strand of that tradition was wholly adequate.

He argued that through practices of forgiveness, including confession, people are enabled to recognize the Truth of God's judgment of grace and thus learn to embody truthfulness: "Complete truthfulness is only possible

---

27. *The Cost of Discipleship*, p. 325. See also *Spiritual Care*, p. 63: "Confession of sin before another person is an act of discipleship to the cross."

28. *Spiritual Care*, p. 62.

where sin has been uncovered, and forgiven by Jesus. Only those who are in a state of truthfulness through the confession of their sin to Jesus are not ashamed to tell the truth wherever it must be told."[29]

Even so, the question was asked of Bonhoeffer at Finkenwalde: Why must confession be communal? Why should I confess my sin to a brother or sister in Christ? Is confession to God not enough? Bonhoeffer responded that while there is confession to God alone, we also need to bring secret sins to light either now or at the last day. Confession to a brother or sister who also lives by Christ's forgiveness eliminates the danger of that last judgment.[30]

Even more strongly, Bonhoeffer indicated that the certainty of forgiveness occurs only when confession is spoken and heard by fellow believers who have been forgiven and who "stand under the cross": "As the open confession of my sins to a brother insures me against self-deception, so, too, the assurance of forgiveness becomes fully certain to me only when it is spoken by a brother in the name of God. Mutual, brotherly confession is given to us by God in order that we may be sure of divine forgiveness."[31] In our brother or sister, "we find grace before the seat of judgment."[32]

Finally, Bonhoeffer considered confession to another person important in order to break the individual of pride, which is the root of all sin.[33] This may be an important means to forgiveness in some cases, but it is dangerous to presume that all people need "knocking down" in order to be able to appropriate God's forgiveness for new life in Christ — a point that Bonhoeffer himself recognized in his later works, in which he more fully understands the sense in which sin must be seen not only in relation to pride or guilt, but more determinatively in relation to brokenness and ruptures of communion.[34]

---

29. *The Cost of Discipleship*, p. 155.

30. See *Spiritual Care*, pp. 62-63; *Life Together*, p. 116.

31. *Life Together*, pp. 116-117.

32. *The Cost of Discipleship*, p. 146.

33. So *Spiritual Care*, p. 63; *Life Together*, p. 114. Bonhoeffer's reflections in both *Ethics* and *Letters and Papers from Prison* (see n. 34 below) enrich his understanding of sin and challenge this assumed equation of sin and pride. But Bonhoeffer never adequately grapples with the mirror-image of pride, namely self-abnegation. Confession should not be understood simply as an act of humiliating a person's pride because, as will be developed more fully in later chapters, many people come to the Church already having suffered humiliation. For such people who have suffered humiliation, confession becomes a means of gaining a sense of self-worth.

34. *Ethics*, p. 61; *Letters and Papers from Prison*, ed. E. Bethge, tr. R. Fuller, F. Clark, et al. (New York: Macmillan, 1971) pp. 341, 345.

Even so, while Bonhoeffer thought it important to confess to a brother or sister, he did not think that confession is everybody's business. Bonhoeffer stressed the importance of one-to-one confession that respects the secrecy of the confessional seal — which is, Bonhoeffer insisted, a "divine commandment."[35] Otherwise, he feared two different problems. On the one hand, the "act of confession can easily turn into exhibitionism." On the other hand, "gossip is usually the worst evil in a congregation."[36]

But a "general confession of sins" cannot suffice because it is too disconnected from practices of discipleship. When we rely on such general confessions, Bonhoeffer suggested, one of two things happens: Either we despair of genuine forgiveness and so try to substitute forgiveness of ourselves for God's forgiveness, or we feel too secure in the confident knowledge and presumption that "God forgives because that is God's business."[37] As would be expected given Bonhoeffer's polemic against cheap grace, he noted that the second, the temptation to feel too secure, is by far the more dangerous tendency.

Repentance and confession must be practiced in specific and concrete ways, as part of the larger craft of forgiveness, if they are to result in that truthfulness that empowers people for faithful discipleship to Jesus Christ. That is why Bonhoeffer stressed the importance of church discipline and why he insisted that forgiveness cannot be unconditional.

35. It is unclear how Bonhoeffer understands the relation of ordination to the practice of confession in particular and to ecclesiastical discipline more generally. In some places he seems to adopt a rather traditional Lutheran account of the "pastor's" role in these matters (see *Spiritual Care*). In other places, he seems to adopt a more Anabaptist perspective, stressing the responsibility of the whole community (see *Life Together, The Cost of Discipleship*). Finally, in *Ethics* he seems to move more in the direction of a Roman Catholic account (see esp. pp. 292-293). These options are not mutually exclusive, at least in some respects, but Bonhoeffer's overall perspective is clouded by his lack of more explicit reflection on ordination in relation to these issues.

36. *Spiritual Care*, pp. 39-40; see also *Letters and Papers from Prison*, pp. 158-159. This seems to be related also to Bonhoeffer's concern, found later in the letters, about the obsession to make "public" anything that might be understood as part of the realm of the "personal." For example, "Anything clothed, veiled, pure, and chaste is presumed to be deceitful, disguised, and impure . . ." (*Letters and Papers*, p. 345). Of course the contemporary irony is that, just as we seem obsessed with making "public" everything that might be "personal" in some respects, so we also have made "personal" crucial questions that affect our "public" lives together (e.g., for Christians the question of economics).

37. *Spiritual Care*, p. 43. The quotation is from Voltaire.

In other words the preaching of forgiveness must always go hand-in-hand with the preaching of repentance, the preaching of the gospel with the preaching of the law. Nor can the forgiveness of sin be unconditional — sometimes sin must be retained. It is the will of the Lord himself that the gospel should not be given to the dogs. He too held that the only way to safeguard the gospel of forgiveness was by preaching repentance. If the Church refuses to face the stern reality of sin, it will gain no credence when it talks of forgiveness. Such a Church sins against its sacred trust and walks unworthily of the gospel. It is an unholy Church, squandering the precious treasure of the Lord's forgiveness.[38]

Such discipline means that for contingent reasons it may not be possible fully to forgive and be reconciled with other brothers or sisters. In such cases, where people are unwilling to repent and engage in practices of confession, forgiveness, and reconciliation, fellowship may need to be temporarily suspended and the sin retained — but always, Bonhoeffer recognized, "in such a manner that the spirit may be saved in the day of the Lord Jesus (1 Corinthians 5:5)."[39] The aim remains repentance and reconciliation.

That is, Bonhoeffer stressed that even where forgiveness and reconciliation are not fully possible, Christians still must love those who have become "enemies" of Christ's cross. To be sure, there are important differences between those who have been temporarily excluded from Christian fellowship and those who are determinedly opposed to Christ. Not least among such differences is Bonhoeffer's recognition that even those who have been excluded from Christian fellowship remain part of the community of the baptized.[40]

Even so, Bonhoeffer insisted that Christians will have enemies and that we ought to pray for them and love them. Bonhoeffer observed in a 1937 sermon at Finkenwalde:

> So Satan hardens the hearts of those who have to serve him in his struggle against God's kingdom and Word. They are no longer able to hear or

---

38. *The Cost of Discipleship*, p. 324.

39. *Ethics*, p. 33. Bonhoeffer points further to texts such as Galatians 6 and Matthew 18:15ff. for support of this point. See also his discussions in *The Cost of Discipleship*, pp. 324ff., and "The Power of the Keys and Church Discipline in the New Testament," in *The Way to Freedom*, pp. 149-160.

40. See Bonhoeffer, "The Power of the Keys and Church Discipline in the New Testament," in *The Way to Freedom*, p. 152: "Community discipline cannot be exclusion from the community of the baptised; it must always be only from the fellowship of the community of the baptised."

obey. However, because their ears are deaf to the grace of God, their mouths are also mute to the righteousness of God. They are enemies of God and his church. David, Christ, and the church of God recognize them as such.

Even more significant, however, is the sentence that immediately follows: "This realization leads us into prayer."

For what do Christians pray? "We pray in fervent supplication that God may bring all our enemies under the cross of Christ and grant them mercy. We pray with burning desire that the day may soon come when Christ will visibly triumph over all his enemies and establish his kingdom."[41] In so doing, we also plead to God for the sake of those enemies.[42] Why should we pray for, and actually love, our enemies? We are to do so in the imitation of God's action in Christ by the power of the Spirit: As Bonhoeffer put it, "Christ made peace with us while we were yet enemies. He made peace with all our enemies too, on the cross. Let us bear witness to this peace to all."[43]

Prayer is also important in giving us the strength to love our enemies:

> The spirit assents when Jesus bids us love our enemies, but flesh and blood are too strong and prevent our carrying it out. Therefore we have to practise strictest daily discipline; only so can the flesh learn the painful lesson that it has no rights of its own. Regular daily prayer is a great help here, and so is daily meditation on the Word of God, and every kind of bodily discipline and asceticism.[44]

Whereas from the standpoint of forgiveness and reconciliation the love of enemies is the minimum that we can do, Bonhoeffer also recognized the significant and difficult task that is entailed therein. It requires daily disciplines and practices within the craft of forgiveness, for otherwise we will likely find it too difficult to give up desires for vengeance in service to our enemies.

Bonhoeffer identified and explicated a costly forgiveness that acknowledges the importance of judgment, repentance, confession, and love

41. Bonhoeffer, "Vengeance and Deliverance," in *A Testament to Freedom*, pp. 295, 298.

42. *The Cost of Discipleship*, p. 166: "Through the medium of prayer we go to our enemy, stand by his side, and plead for him to God."

43. "Christ's Love and Our Enemies," in *A Testament to Freedom*, p. 302.

44. *The Cost of Discipleship*, p. 189.

for enemies in the context of truthful Christian community marked by God's action in Christ. Bonhoeffer identified such community as a community of the Spirit rather than a community of spirit. That is, a Christian community's ability — empowered by the cross of Christ — to be truthful, to confess, and to love enemies distinguishes it from those illusory communities based on friendliness.[45] As such, Bonhoeffer was convinced that Christians would also be liberated for service to, and more importantly among, the lowly and needy.[46]

Bonhoeffer also recognized, however, that the path of discipleship marked by costly forgiveness might not be widely trodden. It simply costs too much for people who construct their life as a possession and who go to great lengths to avoid or deny death. As he put it in *The Cost of Discipleship*, "To confess and testify to the truth as it is in Jesus, and at the same time to love the enemies of that truth, his enemies and ours, and to love them with the infinite love of Jesus Christ, is indeed a narrow way."[47] The path of discipleship no doubt seemed even more narrow to Bonhoeffer as he observed the collapse of any coherent witness against Hitler, lamented the lack of any legitimate sense of ecclesiastical discipline,[48] and embarked on the resistance that eventually cost him his life.

By the end of 1937 Finkenwalde had been shut down by the Nazis, and by 1940 all of the Confessing Church's seminaries had been shut down. Indeed, the Confessing Church itself was falling apart. Most of Bonhoeffer's seminarians from Finkenwalde had been called into military service. The Nazis had effectively dismantled the Christian community that had formed the backdrop to *The Cost of Discipleship*, had been characterized in *Life Together*, and that seemed so central to the task of embodying forgiveness.

At the same time, however, Bonhoeffer never lost his commitment to the centrality of God's forgiveness as it is discovered in and through the practices and friendships of Christian community. Bonhoeffer's fiancée,

45. See *Life Together*, pp. 31ff.

46. See *Life Together*, p. 94: "The proud throne of the judge no longer lures [the one who has experienced God's mercy]; he wants to be down below with the lowly and the needy, because that is where God found him." See also Bonhoeffer's more pointed reflection on this theme in "After Ten Years," in *Letters and Papers from Prison*, p. 17. Gustavo Gutiérrez has commented on the significance of Bonhoeffer's argument for Latin American liberation theologies in "The Limitations of Modern Theology: On a Letter of Dietrich Bonhoeffer," in his *The Power of the Poor in History*, tr. R. R. Barr (Maryknoll, NY: Orbis, 1983) pp. 222-234.

47. *The Cost of Discipleship*, p. 211.

48. See *Ethics*, p. 302.

Maria von Wedemeyer, reported that toward the end of his life Bonhoeffer indicated to her that the only book "of concern to him at that moment was *Life Together*."[49]

Bonhoeffer was forced to struggle, however, with the dark underside of cheap grace's triumph among the German Christians: it easily transmutes into the conviction that the only effective means of addressing violence, injustice, and evils is through the use of counter-force. As Bonhoeffer found himself increasingly bereft of contexts in which the costly grace of discipleship could be learned, practiced, and sustained in Christian community, he had to confront the issue of whether the encroaching darkness had overwhelmed the light of God's grace. Could forgiveness be effective, or even thinkable, in the midst of Nazi Germany?

Is Forgiveness Effective? The Struggle against Encroaching Darkness

In November 1938 the Nazis unleashed a reign of terror against the Jewish population that came to be known as the "Crystal Night" or the "Night of the Broken Glass." Bonhoeffer had long been concerned with the treatment of the Jews, but he began to see more clearly the urgency of action to help them. Bonhoeffer insisted that "only he who cries out for the Jews may sing Gregorian chants."[50]

In 1939 Bonhoeffer went to England for two months and then on to America for what was to be a year. At least part of his motivation was to avoid military service. However, shortly after arriving in America he decided to return to Germany. He did so because he felt the need to bear responsibility and accept guilt for his church, his nation, and his class.[51]

Thus Bonhoeffer returned in 1939 to a Germany where Christian community had largely been eclipsed by the Nazis, where the cries of the Jews needed to be heard, and where he believed he needed to bear responsibility for what was happening.[52] The darkness of violence and oppression threatened the possibility of any meaningful future.

49. Cited in *Letters and Papers from Prison*, p. 416.

50. Cited in Bethge, *Dietrich Bonhoeffer*, p. 512.

51. See Bonhoeffer's letter to Reinhold Niebuhr in Bethge, *Dietrich Bonhoeffer*, p. 559.

52. This paragraph and the following one have been adapted from *Reading in Communion*, p. 151.

It was in this context that Bonhoeffer went to work for the *Abwehr*, the German army's counterintelligence organization. He became a spy and thereby could remain in Germany without having to become a soldier. But he was more than a spy for the *Abwehr*: he was a "double agent" (at least from the Gestapo's perspective) who assisted Jews in escaping Germany, who let the Allies know of several events developing in Germany, and who engaged in an ill-fated plot to assassinate Hitler. Bonhoeffer had always been involved in the world, but by 1940 he had become intensely and intimately involved with the issues of his contemporary world, his place, and his time.

From 1940 to 1943, while working as a double agent, Bonhoeffer sketched a number of fragments for a book on ethics that he thought would be his life work. Unfortunately, he would never be able to complete the *Ethics*.[53] In 1943 he was arrested by the Gestapo and imprisoned for questioning. It was only later, after the plot to assassinate Hitler failed in July 1944, that Bonhoeffer himself was implicated in the resistance. In prison, he kept up a clandestine yet vigorous correspondence with various people, particularly his close friend and former Finkenwalde student Eberhard Bethge. That correspondence contains Bonhoeffer's last theological reflections, later edited and published by Bethge as *Letters and Papers from Prison*. Bonhoeffer was transferred to a concentration camp in Buchenwald, where he remained until April 9, 1945. On that day, he was hanged by the Nazis as a traitor; more determinatively, for Christians he was hanged as a martyr whose life was in God's hands and who thereby accepted the cost of forgiveness, of discipleship, even unto death.

It was in 1939 to 1945 that Bonhoeffer's thought focused increasingly on "the world."[54] But he continued to struggle with Scripture and with themes that had been prominent throughout his life and particularly during his time in Finkenwalde.[55] For example, as far back as *The Cost of Discipleship* Bonhoeffer had insisted that Christians must be willing to suffer by bearing the burdens of others through forgiveness:

> The law of Christ, which it is our duty to fulfil, is the bearing of the cross. My brother's burden which I must bear is not only his outward lot, his natural characteristics and gifts, but quite literally his sin. And the only

53. The fragments came to be compiled and edited by Eberhard Bethge and published as Bonhoeffer's *Ethics*.

54. For extensive discussion of Bonhoeffer's reflections on "the world," see Feil, *The Theology of Dietrich Bonhoeffer*, passim.

55. See *Reading in Communion*, pp. 149-157, for a more extensive discussion of the ways Bonhoeffer continued to struggle with Scripture in the last years of his life.

way to bear that sin is by forgiving it in the power of the cross of Christ in which I now share. Thus the call to follow Christ always means a call to share the work of forgiving men their sins. Forgiveness is the Christlike suffering which it is the Christian's duty to bear.[56]

In one sense, such a passage clearly points to Bonhoeffer's conception of a christologically grounded confession and forgiveness in disciplined Christian community. After all, a section of *Life Together* is devoted to "The Ministry of Bearing."[57]

But in *The Cost of Discipleship* passage, it is not clear that the call to "Christlike suffering" in bearing the burden of others is primarily focused in Christian community. The primary focus is discipleship in the imitation of Christ and as such points to the importance of discerning Christ's significance in both the Church and the world.[58] Bonhoeffer's *Ethics* and *Letters and Papers from Prison* reveal a continuing desire to understand the cost of forgiveness, now at the juncture between Christian community and the world and in the midst of a horrifyingly violent social situation.

Bonhoeffer was convinced that *if* Christians are to offer a witness to the world capable of resisting the encroaching darkness, it cannot be through either cheap grace or a refusal to face our complicity in the world's sinfulness. Bonhoeffer emphasized the disciplines of Christian community as a way to combat the seductiveness of cheap grace. He also stressed the need to confess the Church's complicity in "the apostasy of the western world from Jesus Christ." Bonhoeffer saw it as the task of the Church in the midst of Nazi Germany both to confess its guilt and, in the imitation of Christ, to bear the burden of it.

> The Church today is that community of men which is gripped by the power of the grace of Christ so that, recognizing as guilt towards Jesus Christ both its own personal sin and the apostasy of the western world from Jesus Christ, it confesses this guilt and accepts the burden of it. It

56. *The Cost of Discipleship*, p. 100.
57. *Life Together*, pp. 100-103.
58. Such a point only reinforces the importance of Feil's argument about *The Cost of Discipleship* generally: "This book is of no little significance for the study of Bonhoeffer's christology. Not much attention has been paid to this fact; indeed, the book is regarded much more as a contribution to his ecclesiology. The central concern of the work is determined by christology; at its center is the Sermon on the Mount, in relation to which the reality of discipleship is determined." *The Theology of Dietrich Bonhoeffer*, p. 78.

is in her that Jesus realizes His form in the midst of the world. That is why the Church alone can be the place of personal and collective rebirth and renewal.[59]

Such confession leads, Bonhoeffer suggested, to the "re-attainment of the form of Jesus Christ who bore the sin of the world." Through submitting to, and reattaining, the form of Jesus Christ, the Church is justified and renewed. Further, Bonhoeffer indicated that in the internal and external political struggle of the nations, "there is something in the nature of forgiveness, though it be only a faint shadow of the forgiveness which Jesus Christ vouchsafes to faith." That is, secular parables of God's forgiveness can sometimes be found among those who do not locate it in relation to Christ. More pointedly, however, Bonhoeffer also argued that forgiveness could not become relevant in the life of the nations *at that time* until "justice, order and peace" had been restored, until "reprisals" had ceased, and until the Church of Jesus Christ — as "the fountain-head of all forgiveness, justification, and renewal" — was given room to do its work among the nations.[60]

In one sense, Bonhoeffer thought the violence of Nazi Germany was so pervasive that forgiveness perhaps could no longer be effective. He knew that forgiveness could be effective when grounded in the disciplines of Christian community, but the virtual collapse of such communities perhaps also meant the virtual collapse of forgiveness. However, Bonhoeffer knew that such a claim would abandon the very heart of the Christian gospel, conceding that violence and death are more powerful and determinative than God's gracious forgiveness.

Bonhoeffer dealt with this issue by emphasizing the eschatological significance of Christian life.[61] For Bonhoeffer, God's forgiveness is both the first and the final word of Christian life; in this time between the times of Christ's first and second advents, however, we must also respond to God's forgiveness by "preparing the way" for the final, ultimate word of God's forgiveness. Preparing the way means concrete, social acts in response to God's forgiveness that are designed to enable people to hear — and thus also to be able to receive — the ultimate word of God's forgiving and reconciling grace. Such acts range from silence with the bereaved to feeding the hungry and resisting other forms of injustice. Even so, such acts are not

59. See *Ethics*, pp. 111, 112-116.

60. See the discussion in *Ethics*, pp. 116-119.

61. Bonhoeffer developed this argument most completely in his discussion of the relations between the "ultimate" and the "penultimate." See *Ethics*, Part I, chapter 4.

simply a program of social reform, as liberal theologians might have emphasized. They are preparing the way for the coming of Christ.

> It is quite certain that the preparation of the way is a matter of concrete interventions in the visible world, and it is certain that hunger and satisfaction of hunger are concrete and visible matters; yet everything depends on this activity being a spiritual reality, precisely because ultimately it is not indeed a question of the reform of earthly conditions, but it is a question of the coming of Christ.

More determinatively, these visible actions in response to God's action must involve practices of repentance. "Preparation of the way means repentance (Matt. 3:1ff.). But repentance means a concrete turning back; repentance demands action."[62]

Bonhoeffer recognized, particularly though not exclusively in his struggle against the Nazis, that it is difficult to discern precisely how Christians ought to embody practices of forgiveness and repentance in specific social and political circumstances. Such discernment involves the work of the Holy Spirit, particularly as the Spirit guides Christian communities in their practices. Christians learn how to practice this discernment well from exemplars, particularly saints, whose holy lives testify to their craft of forgiveness. Unfortunately, Bonhoeffer tragically found such Christian community and such exemplars largely absent in the crucial period of 1938 to 1940, when he was trying to discern the shape of his own commitments, and this made it more difficult for him to avoid being enmeshed in the sin and evil he was so ardently struggling to resist.[63]

Perhaps because of the very absence of such Christian community, Bonhoeffer concluded that there are times of "extraordinary necessity" — like the predicament posed by Nazi Germany — in which it is unclear what ought, or even can, be done to resist the encroaching darkness. In such situations, the "ultimate question remains open and must be kept open, for in either case man becomes guilty and in either case he can live only by the grace of God and by forgiveness."[64]

---

62. *Ethics,* p. 138. See also Bonhoeffer's comment in one of his circular letters of 1938, found in *A Testament to Freedom,* p. 463: "Without penitence, i.e., unless the church struggle itself becomes our penitence, we shall never receive back the gift we have lost, the church struggle as gospel."

63. See Bonhoeffer's letter to Bishop Bell in England during this time, cited in Bethge, *Dietrich Bonhoeffer,* p. 541.

64. *Ethics,* p. 240.

The individual person is left to engage in "responsible action," which takes its form and shape in Jesus Christ: "If it is responsible action, if it is action which is concerned solely and entirely with the other man, if it arises from selfless love for the real man who is our brother, then, precisely because this is so, it cannot wish to shun the fellowship of human guilt."[65] Such fellowship and willingness to accept guilt are significant. Indeed, they are crucial to recognizing that forgiveness is concerned with the world's brokenness, not just with my own history.

Even when "responsible action" is justified by "necessity," however, Bonhoeffer contended that the Christian is not freed from his or her relation to and need for God's forgiveness: "Before other men the man of free responsibility is justified by necessity; before himself he is acquitted by his conscience; but before God he hopes only for mercy."[66] The person "hopes" for God's mercy; he or she cannot presume it.[67] If it becomes a presumption rather than something that must be hoped and prayed for under the reality of God's judgment, then the action loses its quality of repentance and becomes a cheap and venal grace. This is how Bonhoeffer understood his own involvement in the resistance and in the plot to assassinate Hitler.

Thus even in the midst of situations of "extraordinary necessity" where "responsible action" is required, there still remains the guiding significance of Bonhoeffer's account of God's forgiveness and Christian community. Such terms as "confession," "repentance," and even "forgiveness" were extended, and in some sense revised or transformed, but they continued to structure the overall shape of Bonhoeffer's argument and his life.

This is even more the case in his enigmatic references to the "arcane discipline" in *Letters and Papers from Prison*.[68] Most generally, it refers to a practice in the early church whereby the "*mysteries* of the Christian faith" were "protected against profanation." Those who were not full members of the Church were permitted to observe part of the community's worship, but were not permitted to observe or participate in the central practices of the Church (e.g., baptism and the eucharist). Those practices would occur "in secret,"

---

65. *Ethics*, p. 241.

66. *Ethics*, p. 248.

67. Though it must be admitted that in "After Ten Years," a reflection addressed to his closest friends in the resistance, Bonhoeffer used somewhat stronger language, referring to God's promise of forgiveness. See *Letters and Papers from Prison*, p. 6: Free responsibility "depends on a God who demands responsible action in a bold venture of faith, and who promises forgiveness and consolation to the man who becomes a sinner in that venture."

68. The significance of the term far exceeds the two brief places where Bonhoeffer used it in the *Letters*. See Bonhoeffer, *Letters and Papers from Prison*, pp. 281, 286.

from which the Christian would emerge for service in the world. The aim of a recovery of this discipline would be to provide the space for, and to enable, the Christian formation and discernment necessary for appropriate eschatological activity in the world.[69]

Even more important, however, is the way in which a conception of the "arcane discipline" should change the ways in which Christians use theological language and embody practices of forgiveness so that they can be more effective against the encroaching darkness. Bonhoeffer thought that Christian language and practices had become cheapened, trivialized, and abstract so that they had lost their significance in the world. A famous passage from *Letters and Papers from Prison* is worth quoting at length:

> Reconciliation and redemption, regeneration and the Holy Spirit, love of our enemies, cross and resurrection, life in Christ and Christian discipleship — all these things are so difficult and so remote that we hardly venture any more to speak of them. In the traditional words and acts we suspect that there may be something quite new and revolutionary, though we cannot as yet grasp or express it. That is our own fault. Our church, which has been fighting in these years only for its self-preservation, as though that were an end in itself, is incapable of taking the word of reconciliation and redemption to mankind and the world. Our earlier words are therefore bound to lose their force and cease, and our being Christians today will be limited to two things: prayer and righteous action among men. . . . It is not for us to prophesy the day (though the day will come) when men will once more be called so to utter the word of God that the world will be changed and renewed by it. It will be a new language, perhaps quite non-religious, but liberating and redeeming — as was Jesus' language; it will shock people and yet overcome them by its power; it will be the language of a new righteousness and truth, proclaiming God's peace with men and the coming of his kingdom. "They shall fear and tremble because of all the good and all the prosperity

---

69. See Bonhoeffer's language in *Ethics*, p. 297: "The cross of atonement is the setting free for life before God in the midst of the godless world; it is the setting free for life in genuine worldliness."

It should be noted that this conception of the arcane discipline is not entirely new. As cited earlier, Bonhoeffer noted that the aim of the seminary at Finkenwalde "is not the seclusion of a monastery, but a place of the deepest inward concentration for service outside." See *The Way to Freedom*, p. 31. Bethge also notes that at Finkenwalde Bonhoeffer made explicit reference to early church practice in his call for the shaping of their communal life together. See Bethge, *Dietrich Bonhoeffer*, p. 784.

I provide for it" (Jer. 33:9). Till then the Christian cause will be a silent and hidden affair, but there will be those who pray and do right and wait for God's own time.[70]

This passage reflects Bonhoeffer's own passionate struggle to understand the integrity of Christian witness in a world of horrifying violence where Christian language and practices had become impoverished, if not entirely coopted.

Bonhoeffer was troubled that Christians had been unable to resist the Nazis and had failed to communicate the gospel of reconciliation and redemption to the world. He therefore thought that the "silence" and "hiddenness" of the arcane discipline would enable Christian language and practices to be purified and renewed so as to provide a more effective witness to the power of forgiveness.[71] This would involve practices of worship as well as other practices of discipleship, including "righteous action" in response to God's action in Christ.[72]

Bonhoeffer thought that the practice of confession certainly needed to be purified and renewed — if, that is, there was to be a place for it at all. His doubt about the practice's importance occurred primarily because of his altered conception of the problem of sin. In the *Letters* Bonhoeffer no longer thought that people absolutely need to confess the sin of pride. Rather, he focused on the new life to which people are called: "When Jesus blessed sinners, they were real sinners, but Jesus did not make everyone a sinner first. He called them away from their sin, not into their sin. . . . Jesus claims for himself and the Kingdom of God the whole of human life in all its manifestations."[73] Or, even more strongly,

---

70. *Letters and Papers from Prison*, pp. 299-300.

71. This is in contrast to those interpreters (particularly in the 1960s) who thought Bonhoeffer's "new" language meant the invention of new terms and the displacement of traditional Christian language. Bonhoeffer's own language, even in the closing letters, is thoroughly theological and biblical — even in the letter calling for a "new language." Hence the language is not so much "new" as it is radically purified and renewed through the arcane discipline.

72. Bonhoeffer's reference to "prayer" in the passage ought to be read in expansive rather than restrictive terms, referring to the range of practices of the worshiping community. That would cohere with the reference to the early Church's practice of the arcane discipline, and it also coheres with the larger horizons of Bonhoeffer's thought. See, for example, Bethge's comment in *Dietrich Bonhoeffer*, p. 785: "The discipline of prayer, meditation, worship and coming together ('in genuine worship') is as essential — though of course, reformable — as daily food and drink. But it is also as much an 'arcane' affair as the central events of life, which are not amenable to a missionary demonstration."

73. *Letters and Papers from Prison*, pp. 341-342; see also pp. 345-346.

It is not the religious act that makes the Christian, but participation in the sufferings of God in the secular life. That is *metanoia*: not in the first place thinking about one's own needs, problems, sins, and fears, but allowing oneself to be caught up into the way of Jesus Christ, into the messianic event, thus fulfilling Isa. 53. . . . This being caught up into the messianic sufferings of God in Jesus Christ takes a variety of forms in the New Testament.

Bonhoeffer mentioned some of that variety: among others, there is the act of the woman who was a sinner in Luke 7 — an act, he notes, that she performed "without any confession of sin"; there is also the centurion of Capernaum, held up as a model of faith even though he "makes no confession of sin." The only thing that diverse forms of discipleship have in common is "their sharing in the suffering of God in Christ."[74] Bonhoeffer suggested that practices of repentance occur not so much through confession as through discipleship.

Bonhoeffer's criticism of the practice of confession was based primarily on its narcissistic and individualistic tendencies (note his consistent and polemical critiques of psychology); in so doing, he emphasized the new life of discipleship.[75] That is, the problem with the confession of sin, even within the Christian community of the arcane discipline, is that it is typically too "methodical" and insufficiently attentive to the social and political circumstances of people's lives. Hence, a truly personal yet communal confession of sin along the lines of *Life Together* (though with a transformed conception of the sin that needs to be confessed) might still be important in enabling the life of discipleship. However, as I suggested above, it is not insignificant that in *Life Together* Bonhoeffer discusses several other practices of Christian community before turning to confession. In this light, Bonhoeffer's critical comments in *Letters and Papers from Prison* about confession are an indictment of the impoverished practices of Christian community and thus also an expression of a fear that the adoption of corporate confession without such correlative practices would be destructive because it would invite self-righteous judgment rather than form truthful community.

74. *Letters and Papers from Prison*, pp. 361-362. In such cases as Bonhoeffer adduces here, as in Luke's Gospel more generally, it is discipleship that occasions repentance.

75. Although Bonhoeffer is certainly right to criticize many aspects of psychology, therapy, and psychotherapy, his polemic does not acknowledge some important contributions of psychotherapy. For an instructive treatment of Bonhoeffer's views on psychotherapy, see Clifford Green, "Two Bonhoeffers on Psychoanalysis," in A. J. Klassen (ed.), *A Bonhoeffer Legacy* (Grand Rapids: Eerdmans, 1981) pp. 58-75.

Overall it seems that Bonhoeffer thought the arcane discipline, if it were practiced, would serve a crucial role in resisting the encroaching darkness and embodying the cost of forgiveness through holy living. It would preserve the mysteries of the faith from profanation, purifying and renewing the Church's language and practices so it could once again communicate the costly grace of God's forgiveness and enable Christians to learn to see the world "from the perspective of those who suffer," or as he also put it, "from below."[76] In such a way, Bonhoeffer sought to embody forgiveness through holy living on behalf of any and all who suffer the pains of brokenness and injustice.

The tragedy of Bonhoeffer's life and death is that he had to embody the cost of forgiveness in relative isolation from the Body of Christ, a Body that had been largely unable to sustain the disciplines of Christian life, whether in hidden or public contexts.[77] For Bonhoeffer had spent much of his life, and his writing, seeking to foster communities capable of embodying God's forgiveness through specific habits and practices. Yet the twin dangers of therapeutic forgiveness and the tendency for forgiveness to become eclipsed by sin and evil, and more specifically by violence, had conspired to marginalize and undermine such communities.

Bonhoeffer understood his participation in the resistance as an act of repentance for the guilt of his church, his nation, and his class. He thought that Christians needed to act because of their complicity in helping give rise to Hitler and the Nazis. But it is worth pondering whether Christian communities schooled in the habits and practices of forgiveness, seeking to live as holy people, might have provided Bonhoeffer and others with more potent resources to resist the Nazis than his (admittedly failed) "act of repentance."

Even so, amid the tragedy of Bonhoeffer's untimely death, we are left with a powerful witness — in both thought and deed — to the cost of forgiveness. He sought to reclaim the gospel's eschatological focus on a forgiveness that is not simply a word to be spoken but a way of life to be embodied in fidelity to God's inbreaking Kingdom. He vigorously attacked the "lightness" of a therapeutic forgiveness while also seeking ways to resist the encroaching darkness of the Nazi terror.

Further, Bonhoeffer cultivated habits and practices through which

76. See *Letters and Papers from Prison*, p. 17.

77. This is similar to the conclusion reached by J. W. McClendon in his account of Bonhoeffer. See his *Ethics: Systematic Theology Vol. I* (Nashville: Abingdon, 1986) chapter 7.

God's forgiveness becomes embodied in the Body of Christ and in holy lives. Throughout his life and in his death Bonhoeffer refused to understand his life as his own possession. He lived it in communion with God and with others. He was an exemplary practitioner of the craft of forgiveness. He sought not only to understand its significance, but to embody it through a sanctified life. However one evaluates the wisdom of any specific decisions in his life, it can hardly be doubted that Bonhoeffer consistently sought to discern God's call — even recognizing, at an early point in his life, that the theologian needed to become a Christian. Bonhoeffer thought even his decision to assassinate Hitler, while perhaps justifiable (though certainly controversial both then and in later generations' assessments), was an act of repentance for which he would pray to God for forgiveness.[78] His understanding of this complex dynamic was shaped by his conviction that it was a time of "extraordinary necessity"; Bonhoeffer concluded that he had to take on guilt by acting (in repentance for his complicity in how things had come to be so dark), but in doing so could rely on nothing else than the *hope* of God's forgiveness.

To be sure, Bonhoeffer's account of forgiveness was never fully or systematically developed.[79] This is not surprising, given the struggles in which he was engaged and the urgent crises that he addressed. Even so, he not only pointed toward a more adequate conception of forgiveness in his theological reflection, one grounded in the work of the Triune God and in specific habits and practices of Christian community. He also embodied the power and cost of forgiveness in his life and in his death.

Alas, while there is much to be learned from Bonhoeffer in developing a constructive account of forgiveness, we — like Bonhoeffer — still have to struggle with the twin dangers of a cheap therapeutic forgiveness on the one hand and the eclipse of forgiveness by encroaching darkness on the other. So before developing a constructive account of God's forgiveness and its implications for human life, I need first to explore more fully those dangers — and the ways in which they have resulted in distorted and impoverished conceptions and embodiments of forgiveness.

---

78. See the discussion in *Reading in Communion*, p. 158, with references to various sources for Bonhoeffer's own assessment of his actions.

79. One crucial difficulty with Bonhoeffer's thought is his failure adequately to articulate the work of the Holy Spirit in guiding, judging, and consoling the Church as it seeks to discern how to appropriate Christ's forgiveness in and through specific practices in diverse social and political circumstances. See the conclusion of my essay "The Cost of Forgiveness" for further reflection on this aspect of Bonhoeffer's thought. I develop the constructive argument in Part II of this book.

2 Therapeutic Forgiveness

The Church's Psychological Captivity in Western Culture

PSYCHIATRIST Robert Coles tells of a friend, a devout Roman Catholic, who was hospitalized with cancer.[1] On one of Coles's visits to the hospital, he found his friend quite angry. A priest had recently been to visit and had wanted to know how the patient was managing to "cope." The priest proceeded in what Coles calls a "relentless kind of psychological inquiry." How was the patient "feeling"? How was he "managing," in view of the "stress" he had to "confront"? The friend was enraged by such questions; he wanted to talk with the priest about God and God's ways, about Christ's life and death, about Luke's Gospel (a particular favorite), about Heaven and Hell — only to be approached repeatedly with words and phrases drawn from the vocabulary of popular psychology. As the friend characterized it to Coles: "He comes here with a Roman collar, and offers me psychological banalities as God's word!"

The friend commented that he was prepared for the priest's next visit. Among other things, he was going to ask the priest to read Psalm 69. Coles cites one part of that psalm: "Save me, O God; for the waters are come into my soul. I sink in deep mire,where there is no standing: I am come into deprivation, where the floods overflow me." Coles concludes by com-

---

1. The story is told in "Psychiatric Stations of the Cross," in Robert Coles, *Harvard Diary* (New York: Crossroad, 1988) pp. 10-12. All references will be to this version of the story.

35

menting: "There are, of course, many kinds of burdens in this life. I wonder whether the deepest mire, the deepest waters, for many of America's clergy, not to mention us laymen, may be found in the dreary solipsistic world so many of us have learned to find so interesting: the mind's moods, the various 'stages' and 'phases' of 'human development' or of 'dying,' all dwelt upon (God save us!) as if Stations of the Cross."

When a psychiatrist criticizes our culture, and particularly our Church, for being overly therapeutic and solipsistic, people — especially Christians — ought to be concerned. Such language helps to suggest, I think, what would otherwise be a rather odd circumstance: a Christian theologian suggesting that we need to reassess the place of forgiveness within Christian theology and Christian life. After all, if there is any topic that seems assured not only of a place, but of a central place, in Christian theology, it would be forgiveness. It is at the heart of Jesus' life and of the apostle Paul, it is featured in both the Lord's Prayer and the Apostles' Creed, it is central to the Church's celebration of baptism and eucharist, and it is a unifying feature among doctrines of God, Christ, the Church, and ethics and politics.

Yet, several decades after Bonhoeffer sought to reclaim the cost of forgiveness through his critique of "cheap grace" and his own life and death, Coles's story reveals the dominance in the Church of nontheological modes of thinking, feeling, and acting. These modes have become too deeply embedded in "Christian" life and discourse, particularly in our practices and conceptions of forgiveness. It seems as though Christian forgiveness is too costly for many people; consequently, they seek a cheap, therapeutic forgiveness in its place.

To be sure, many people have needed to turn to therapies as ways to put their lives back together in the midst of great tragedies and horrifying evils — not least because of failures of the Church to embody faithfully the gospel of reconciliation. There is an abiding importance for psychological explorations and practices in our world, and particularly in Christian life. However, Christians have allowed therapies — and, more generally, a therapeutic mindset — to overtake Christian claims and Christian practices. As a result, Christians have failed to appropriate psychological insights *critically,* all too often adopting distorting and reductionistic practices and beliefs that trivialize those central Christian claims and practices.

Therefore in this chapter I analyze the trivialization of forgiveness specifically by attending to the ways in which a "therapeutic" conception has overtaken and marginalized Christian practices and understandings of forgiveness. I do so in six steps: first, by identifying several problems with forgiveness in modern Western culture; second, by describing the triumph of the therapeutic; third, by analyzing specific themes of therapeutic forgiveness; fourth, by challenging such therapeutic notions with the importance of judgment in forgiveness; fifth, by suggesting that Christians nonetheless need to rethink conceptions of sin; and sixth, by proposing that the most important task is for the Church to reclaim the eschatological significance of the gospel.

Problems with Forgiveness in Modern Western Culture

I want to identify briefly four particular problems that have impoverished contemporary understandings and practices of forgiveness in modern Western culture. These are problems that have helped provide the soil in which therapeutic conceptions of forgiveness have taken root.

First and most generally, forgiveness has become an increasingly marginal notion. Modernity's emphasis on such themes as individual autonomy, isolated acts rather than character, inevitable progress rather than repentance, and the fascination with technique have all helped to undermine practices of forgiveness and to marginalize conceptions of it.

If all that ultimately matters is individual autonomy, then forgiveness and reconciliation — which are designed to foster and maintain community — are of little importance. If all that we evaluate are isolated acts rather than people's character, then forgiveness — which enacts and reflects a quality of character and thus cannot be confined to an "act" that people do — is relatively insignificant. If we are on a path of inevitable progress, then there is little need — as forgiveness requires — to reflect on the past and attempt to reclaim it through repentance. If what ultimately matters is the successful use of technique, then we will only deploy forgiveness if it is useful to further control and is easily quantifiable — perhaps through a series of easily identified "steps."

Hence, there are cultural reasons why practices and understandings of forgiveness have been undermined and marginalized in contemporary thought and life. Even so, Western Christians cannot simply blame the Enlightenment or modernity for our contemporary predicament. A primary reason for the marginalization of forgiveness in modernity and for the undermining of its practices is Christianity's ambiguous legacy. That is, although Christians have been among those who have most clearly stressed the centrality of forgiveness, our history also reflects ways in which we have trivialized it as well.

This is the second problem that has impoverished our understandings and practices of forgiveness. Christianity's ambiguous legacy is the result of transformations within our own practices and conceptions of forgiveness. Forgiveness was theologically crucial for both the people of Israel and the early Christians. Indeed, for the early Christians a set of communal practices necessary for rightly characterizing and witnessing to the eschatological salvation wrought by the Triune God was crucial to the "grammar" of forgiveness.

But as Christianity increasingly distanced itself from its Jewish roots and became the established religion in the fourth century, practices and conceptions of forgiveness began to take different shapes. This was only intensified by schisms in the eleventh and sixteenth centuries, which led to divergent practices among diverse traditions. While I cannot in any sense do justice to the complex social, historical, and theological factors leading to these different shapes, it is nonetheless important to note that conceptions and practices of forgiveness were significantly altered. For example, in Western Christianity the confession of sin, which was in its origins primarily — though not exclusively — a communal practice, moved from the community to individualized and increasingly privatized contexts. Further, Christian piety turned increasingly inward; God's forgiveness became principally an individual transaction between God and a particular person, largely devoid of its eschatological context and with virtually no consequences for either Christian community or social and political life.

Hence in contemporary Christian theology and life, while the *rhetoric* of forgiveness remains a part of our worship, the conceptions and practices of forgiveness have been radically transmuted. Such transmutations, I will suggest later, have helped to contribute to the separation of our understanding of Christ from our doctrines of God, the Church, and ethics and politics. Thus Christian failures, through trivialized rhetoric, to embody our own best insights concerning forgiveness and practices of forgiveness have resulted in an ambiguous legacy.

A third problem, one explicitly noted by Coles, is that as Christians we have increasingly secularized our own language. Outside worship, and sometimes even in worship, we have tended to adopt nontheological language to describe Christian theology and Christian life. For example, instead of baptism, we talk of "getting the baby done." Instead of sin and grace, we talk about "accepting that you are accepted." And instead of practices of reconciliation, we talk about "managing conflict" or "coping with difficult people." Indeed, it would seem as if Christians — laypeople, clergy, and theologians — have become immunized against the use of theological language for characterizing our lives in general, and forgiveness in particular.

Unfortunately, we have not been as effectively immunized against "therapeutic" language. The grammar of Christian forgiveness has been largely co-opted by a therapeutic grammar. Theodore Jennings has characterized our culture as being caught by "mental health moralism and therapeutic narcissism."[2] When forgiveness is seen in primarily individualistic and privatistic terms, we lose sight of its central role in establishing a way of life — not only with our "inner" selves but also in our relations with others.

This contrast may seem to be only a matter of emphasis, with "therapeutic" language emphasizing the *intra*personal dimension and what I have been calling "theological" language the *inter*personal dimension. Both of them, it might be argued, are theological in that they are ultimately concerned with right relation to God. Further, the argument might continue by *rightly* emphasizing that Christian forgiveness *needs* to be attentive to and in dialogue with psychological and psychoanalytic concerns if people are to become holy. If degrees of emphasis were the only issue or even the primary issue, then there would hardly be cause for alarm or even concern.

But "therapeutic" language has increasingly distorted the grammar of Christian forgiveness. Despite the fact that elements of "therapeutic" forgiveness can be incorporated into a Christian account, there are crucial differences between them. Unfortunately, we Christians have failed to diagnose those differences adequately because psychological language and practices have become more powerful than the language and practices of the gospel, not only in the whole culture but even in the Church. In Bonhoeffer's terms, we have substituted cheap grace for the costly grace of discipleship. In order to understand how Christian practices and understandings of forgiveness have been replaced with therapeutic simulacra, it is important to see how the therapeutic has triumphed in our culture and Church.

The Triumph of the Therapeutic

In his book *After Virtue*, Alasdair MacIntyre argues that every culture has within it a stock of "characters" — types that furnish people with a cultural and moral ideal and that morally legitimize a mode of social existence.

2. Theodore Jennings, *The Liturgy of Liberation* (Nashville: Abingdon, 1988) p. 23.

MacIntyre argues that in modern Western societies there are three such "characters": the Manager, the Rich Aesthete, and the Therapist. The Manager represents the collectivist realm of bureaucratic rationality, while the Rich Aesthete and the Therapist represent the individualist realm of private feelings and values.

> The bifurcation of the contemporary social world into a realm of the organizational in which ends are taken to be given and are not available for rational scrutiny and a realm of the personal in which judgment and debate about values are central factors, but in which no rational social resolution of issues is available, finds its internalization, its inner representation in the relation of the individual self to the roles and *characters* of social life.[3]

In such a view two modes of social life are available to us: one in which the free choices of individuals are sovereign and one in which the bureaucracy is sovereign precisely so that it may limit the free choices of individuals.[4]

Ironically, while in some respects therapeutic and bureaucratic mindsets are antagonistic to each other, they collude to undermine the Christian gospel and the ecclesial practices in which the gospel is embodied. Examples of this can be found in the therapeutic and bureaucratic preoccupation with techniques without any evaluation of the ends toward which the techniques are developed; in the ways in which they regulate and discipline behaviors, attitudes, and feelings judged "inappropriate" or "aberrant"; and in the ways in which they perpetuate the privatization of forgiveness, specifically by producing pale imitations of Christian notions of community, of sin, and of compassion.

Both therapists and managers see ends as given or, worse, as arbitrary, subjective, and made up. Hence, ends are beyond the realm of their competence; they are concerned only with technique. "Good" therapists or managers can do their work independently of the convictions or practices of the people with whom they are working. Consequently, they fail to see how their putatively "neutral" techniques reshape the ends toward which their languages and their practices are directed.

A notable instance of this is the extensive popularity, particularly within churches, of the Myers-Briggs Type Indicator. It combines the techniques of the therapist and the manager, purporting to be a neutral tool

3. Alasdair MacIntyre, *After Virtue* (second ed., Notre Dame: University of Notre Dame, 1984) p. 34.

4. MacIntyre, *After Virtue*, p. 35.

that identifies my "personality type" (e.g., "I'm an EFNP") within manageable categories that can be used to differentiate those with whom I am compatible from those with whom I am not. Even more, bureaucratic structures in churches are increasingly mandating that such inventories become a primary means of determining whether someone is or is not fit for leadership in the Church. Thomas Long aptly reveals the dangers of the Myers-Briggs in a short piece entitled "Myers-Briggs and Other Modern Astrologies." He writes,

> In short, the MBTI profiles read like horoscopes from Camelot. Taken too seriously, they can be perilously close to fortune cookies for the human potential movement. In contrast, running through the Christian theological tradition is a view of humanity that is far more complex, at once far more sober about human failings, far more truly hopeful about the human prospect, and far more infused with mystery, featuring a landscape of exhilarating peaks of communion with the holy and also valleys of tragic denial of our humanity.[5]

The Myers-Briggs is not simply a neutral technique for evaluating personality types and managing people; rather, it is an instrument predicated both on modernity's bifurcation of ends and means and on its construction of the self as an enduring, discrete entity that is impervious to cultural, moral, and theological shapes.

Further, bureaucratic structures (and their managers) collude with therapeutic structures (and their therapists) to produce similar techniques for regulating and disciplining behaviors, attitudes, and feelings judged "inappropriate" or "aberrant." For example, a judge in Baltimore whose decision in a rape trial showed egregious misogyny was not removed from office or called on to repent; rather, he was sent off for counseling. Within Church structures, clergy who are found guilty of sexual or financial misconduct are typically *not* asked to engage in concrete practices of forgiveness and reconciliation either with those they have offended or with the Church; rather, they are sent off for counseling, at the conclusion of which they are presumed to be "cured" without engaging in the difficult and costly embodiment of forgiveness and reconciliation.[6]

---

5. Thomas G. Long, "Myers-Briggs and Other Modern Astrologies," *Theology Today* 49/3 (October 1992) p. 294.

6. To be sure, that they are sent off for counseling is actually more than used to happen, at least in many cases. One of the sad features of the Church's life has been its failure to take seriously sexual and financial misconduct among the clergy. But I intend

That is, these techniques, bureaucratically mandated and implemented through therapy, are focused on particular individuals and their actions, attitudes, and feelings. But, divorced from the ends toward which those actions, attitudes, and feelings *ought* to be directed (namely, communion with God and one another embodied in Christian practice), the techniques only short-circuit the more difficult and more hopeful aim of reconciliation. This is particularly the case since bureaucratic and therapeutic techniques fail to see how their languages and their practices are immunized against evaluation. Any individuals can criticize particular disciplines, or be criticized for their failure to conform to those disciplines, without there being any clear context for the argument.

So, for example, clergy who ask how the Myers-Briggs inventory coheres with the Christian doctrine of God are looked at quizzically; they are presumed to have made a category mistake. More perniciously, so are people who claim that costly practices of forgiveness and reconciliation whose aim is the restoration of communion with God and one another are significantly different from those counseling techniques that focus on an individual's ability to cope with his or her feelings or to alter his or her behavior to conform to unexamined standards.

Counseling may have an important role to play in Christian life, but only if it is understood in relation to the ends toward which Christian practices of costly forgiveness and reconciliation are directed. After all, there are important and substantive issues pertaining to the relationship between psychology and theology. The gospel does not provide a full account of human psychology, and people need to attend to the complexities of the human psyche and human life. For example, at its best therapy can help people understand the ways in which human lives are enmeshed in complex intrapersonal, interpersonal, and more broadly political relations. Further, it can help people discern and disentangle those issues — particularly in relation to the many horrifying tragedies that happen to specific people. But at its worst, and particularly in popular American culture, therapy has become a substitute for the gospel. As such, it has perpetuated privatized notions of forgiveness and produced pale imitations of Christian notions of community, of sin, and of compassion for victims.

Philip Rieff published *The Triumph of the Therapeutic* in 1967. The

---

to suggest here that sending them off to counseling is more likely to be a capitulation to a therapeutic culture than an engagement in the costly practices of forgiveness and reconciliation, which includes specific practices of repentance and the aim of which is restoration of communion.

book has made a significant impact, particularly because of its prophetic critique of an emerging cultural shape in American life. Unfortunately, the subsequent twenty-five years has dulled neither its insight nor its prophetic relevance. With remarkable prescience, Rieff predicted that in a therapeutic culture there would not be less of an emphasis on spirituality, but *more*.

> In the emergent culture, a wider range of people will have "spiritual" concerns and engage in "spiritual" pursuits. There will be more singing and more listening. People will continue to genuflect and read the Bible, which has long achieved the status of great literature; but no prophet will denounce the rich attire or stop the dancing. There will be more theater, not less, and no Puritan will denounce the stage and draw its curtains. On the contrary, I expect that modern society will mount psychodramas far more frequently than its ancestors mounted miracle plays, with patient-analysts acting out their inner lives, after which they could extemporize the final act as interpretation.

But according to Rieff the effect of this psychodramatic interest in spirituality will not be a return to classical Judaism or Christianity, in which human life is shaped and transformed in relation to sound doctrines and teachings; it will consist, rather, in a consumerist desire to pick and choose one's own spirituality through broad experimentation. In Rieff's words, "The wisdom of the next social order, as I imagine it, would not reside in right doctrine, administered by the right [people], who must be found, but rather in doctrines amounting to permission for each [person] to live an experimental life."[7]

This description fits not only our culture's fascination with New Age spirituality and other faddish trends; alas, it also increasingly characterizes the life of the Church in the United States. Ironically, at the same time that we have privatized Christian practices and understandings, we have made public that which ought to remain private. Take, for example, the ways people parade themselves before television talk-shows, self-help groups, and even "church" groups in order to "share" with the world intimate and outlandish details of their "stories." This includes testimonies that will someday combine into one account of "codependent cross-dressing adult children of alcoholics who have had strange encounters with extraterrestrial aliens." People sit transfixed, and titillated, by such stories. But (as MacIn-

7. Philip Rieff, *The Triumph of the Therapeutic* (Chicago: University of Chicago, 1967) p. 26.

tyre's analysis suggests) we have no means to exercise discriminating judgment about these stories, because we lack criteria for their evaluation. Further, we are told that such judgment might harm the storytellers' ability to cope and hinder the development of their "self-esteem" or their attempts at "self-realization." As Christopher Lasch has recently suggested, "The only thing forbidden in our culture of exposure is the inclination to forbid — to set limits on disclosure."[8]

Such behavior creates an aura of "community," but too often what transpires does not reflect the bonds of friendship. It is rather a pale, synthetic substitute, a simulacrum of Christian community: strangers bound together by a "common" dysfunction or a common desire to "feel better" speaking *at* one another. Rather than substantial discussion and debate, conversation is reduced to competition for airtime, a kind of "dueling autobiographies." Indeed, this actually bypasses any need for the substantive friendships and practices of community.

Regrettably, such therapeutic notions may have arisen at least partly because of the lack of substantive Christian communities marked by forgiving love. The rise of therapy cannot be understood without simultaneously recognizing both the complicity of the Church and its failures to embody practices of love, forgiveness, and reconciliation. Even so, the task for Christians ought to be to reform and re-create such communities, to (re-)learn to embody the gospel; but these therapeutic simulacra of Christian communities actually undermine the possibility of authentic and genuine communion.

In a recent, extensive survey, Robert Wuthnow found that almost two-thirds of the "support groups" in the United States are focused on Bible study.[9] But while he characterized such groups as part of "America's New Quest for Community" (the subtitle of his book), his description of their activities reveals them to be providing simulacra of Christian community. Persons join and participate primarily to "feel better about yourself," which ranked first in a list of reasons for belonging, while "feeling closer to God" — itself still a therapeutic description — only ranked eighth. More ominously, the groups tend to produce not better or wiser readers of the Bible (indeed, they seem not even to increase their adherents' knowledge of the content of the Bible); rather the people are inclined to use it as a self-help book, a book that is true because it works (e.g., "the Bible is true because

8. Christopher Lasch, "For Shame," *The New Republic* (August 10, 1992) p. 29.
9. See Robert Wuthnow, *Sharing the Journey: Support Groups and America's New Quest for Community* (New York: The Free Press, 1994).

it helped me get a job"). And, perhaps reflecting the primary desire to "feel better about yourself," the groups are asked to offer support to people — but never to challenge them to repent or to change their life. Indeed, Wuthnow found that if such a group makes demands on people's lives, suggesting specific disciplines and practices, members will leave to find another, more supportive and less challenging group.

Hence, though "Bible study" groups are ostensibly gatherings of Christians seeking to become holy people through the study of Scripture, the ways in which too many of these groups are organized and structured actually perpetuate a therapeutic culture. Not only do they fail to engage in the practices of Christian community that form people capable of embodying forgiveness in the pursuit of holiness; they also fail to recognize that, whenever people insist on verbally exposing themselves to one another, the result is a collusion with sin's destructiveness. As Rowan Williams has suggested, "Since the Fall, concealment is necessary and good in the sense that there is plenty in human thought, feeling, and experience that *should not* be part of shared discourse. We are alienated, divided, and corrupted; but to bring this into speech (and to assume we thereby tell a better or fuller truth) is to collude with sin."[10]

Further, the self-absorbed "testifying" characteristic of many of these groups implicitly carries with it a distinctive sense of sin: there is plenty of sin to be found (though rarely named as such), but it almost always lies with others. It is society, or my parents, or my disease, or all three, and more, that are responsible for the way I am; so I am encouraged to abdicate responsibility for my own actions. This emoting and "passing the buck" also trivializes important issues; when virtually *any* parental mistakes become "child abuse" — as has been suggested by extravagant claims about "dysfunctional" families and the origins of "codependency" — then it is impossible to distinguish the inconsequential from the serious. As a result, people are often numbed to the point where we fail to respond adequately to, to repent for, or to take action against the serious violence and abuse that are inflicted on people both near and far.

This numbing of our capacity for compassion is increasingly addressed by a discourse of victimization. If any person can claim the status

10. Rowan Williams, "The Suspicion of Suspicion: Wittgenstein and Bonhoeffer," in Richard H. Bell (ed.), *The Grammar of the Heart* (San Francisco: Harper and Row, 1988) p. 44. See also similar remarks offered by Dietrich Bonhoeffer, both in his *Letters and Papers from Prison*, ed. E. Bethge, tr. R. Fuller, F. Clark, et al. (New York: Macmillan, 1971) pp. 344-346, and in his fragment "What is Meant by 'Telling the Truth,'" in *Ethics*, ed. E. Bethge, tr. N. H. Smith (New York: Macmillan, 1965) pp. 363-372.

of a victim, then that person has recourse to people's attention regardless of how numb they are. As a result, the very discourse of "victimization" has become a commodity by which people attempt to purchase compassion. As such, the language of the therapeutic has created a cult of the "victim." The modern American *cogito* might be better phrased "I am a victim, therefore I am." Whoever can claim the status of victim with greater authority wins, because that status projects an image of innocence over against which all others are somehow guilty. This competition becomes a means of deflecting attention from the serious issues that confront us; when public figures seek to deflect their own misogyny or domestic violence by appealing to ways in which they, too, are "victims," the discourse actually exacerbates social problems rather than addressing them.[11]

Further, the status of victim not only purchases compassion; it also is used to gain cultural and ecclesial power. The results of this are devastating. Lasch's comments are instructive: policies based on a therapeutic culture have

> given rise to a cult of the victim in which entitlements are based on the display of accumulated injuries inflicted by an uncaring society. The politics of "compassion" degrades both the victims, by reducing them to objects of pity, and their would-be benefactors, who find it easier to pity their fellow citizens than to hold them up to impersonal standards, the attainment of which would make them respected. Compassion has become the human face of contempt.[12]

Therapeutic mind-sets have triumphed in both culture and Church. This is so despite the corrosive effects of such mind-sets in separating means from ends, in producing disciplinary techniques antithetical to Christian practices, and in producing pale and distorting imitations of Christian community, of sin, and of compassion for victims. Regrettably, the therapeutic focus appears sufficiently like the gospel to seduce Christians into imagining that therapeutic language and categories are simply a translation of the gospel. In so doing, however, Christians fail to recognize their cancerous effects on the Body of Christ. This becomes particularly troubling when one examines how this therapeutic captivity has affected discussions of forgiveness in Western cultures and churches.

---

11. In recent years, the United States has seen this discourse used all too effectively by Senator Robert Packwood and O. J. Simpson.

12. Lasch, "For Shame," p. 34.

Therapeutic Forgiveness:
Forgiving Hurts We Don't Deserve

Though forgiveness should be at the heart both of Christian theology and the practices of Christian community and life, it has largely been co-opted by the therapeutic grammar of modern Western life. Wuthnow's surveys of what people are looking for in their "new quest for community" reveal that many people desire to become "more forgiving" when they join such groups. But the forgiveness they want to learn is separated from such practices as baptism and eucharist (including the elements of judgment entailed therein), much less practices of repentance or love for enemies. Such groups tend to offer cheap grace, when grace is offered at all; rarely are they sustained by the costly grace of discipleship.

To be sure, there is a crying, urgent need for people in general, and more specifically in the Church, to learn to become more forgiving in their relations with one another. But for Christians this can only happen when we simultaneously learn to embody what it means to be *forgiven* — by God and by one another. At the center of Christian forgiveness is the proclamation of God's Kingdom and the call to repentance so that we can live as forgiven and reconciled people with God and with one another. We learn to become more forgiving as an integral feature of our life in God's Kingdom, precisely as we are also unlearning our deeply entrenched habits of sin — whether that sin is manifest in prideful self-assertion or in shameful self-diffusion, or perhaps elements of both.

The invitation to God's Kingdom, the call to conversion and new life, is an invitation to discover our selves, not as something to be "possessed" or obsessively concerned about, but as people called into communion through forgiving and reconciling love. We are called out of our obsession with ourselves by the One who invites us to friendship with God and with one another in Christian community. Such friendship is not the trivial "Jesus is my friend," but rather substantive and enduring relationships characterized by a continual giving and receiving of life with others and the Other.[13] On this understanding, it is as difficult to learn to accept forgiveness from God or from another as it is to offer it; but such invitations to friendship are far more likely to enable people to see the world and themselves truthfully than are calls for us simply to will

---

13. For further discussion of this notion of friendship with both God and others, see my *Transformed Judgment: Toward a Trinitarian Account of the Moral Life* (Notre Dame: University of Notre Dame, 1989).

ourselves to be "more forgiving" as an emotional quality of an isolated individual's life.

But if particular people have learned to see themselves primarily (if not exclusively) in terms of what others have done *to* them — that is, to see themselves as victims — then the focus will, inevitably, be almost exclusively on the difficulty of forgiving others as a challenge to the emotional will. There will be little sense of the dynamics of being forgiven and forgiving, much less of the need to *embody* that forgiveness in specific practices and friendships of community. But such are the problems of therapeutic forgiveness in the culture and, more perniciously, in the Church.

One example of this focus is Lewis Smedes's remarkably popular book *Forgive and Forget: Healing the Hurts We Don't Deserve,* which is an example of a genre of books on forgiveness that have emerged out of popular psychology and pastoral counseling. Smedes is an evangelical Christian who taught for many years at Fuller Theological Seminary, and in this book he seems to be articulating a Christian perspective.[14] After all, he indicates that forgiveness is "God's invention"; God began it "by forgiving us, and he invites us all to forgive each other."[15] Further, Smedes rightly is concerned with the ways in which people's lives are often destroyed by a refusal to forgive and by the need to distinguish carefully what forgiveness does and does not entail. As he develops his account of the importance of forgiving through four parts — The Four Stages of Forgiving, Forgiving People Who Are Hard to Forgive, How People Forgive, and Why Forgive? — Smedes distinguishes forgiveness from other things that some people confuse with forgiving, he defends forgiveness from the charge that it is too soft on morally evil acts, and he explores some difficulties people encounter in learning to forgive.

In this sense Smedes is dealing with several issues whose critical importance in people's lives is impossible to deny. Moreover, there is no doubt that many people find consolation and encouragement from reading books such as Smedes's. Unfortunately, despite its intermittent insights and its author's good intentions, the book's overarching shape and perspective

---

14. Smedes explicitly indicates in his reply to Robert C. Roberts's review article that this is what he is doing. See *The Reformed Journal* (July 1986) pp. 23-24. Interestingly, Roberts's review article is entitled "Forgiveness as Therapy" (see pp. 19-23 of the same issue).

15. Lewis B. Smedes, *Forgive and Forget: Healing the Hurts We Don't Deserve* (New York: Harper and Row, 1984) pp. xi-xii. Further citations to this book will be given parenthetically in the text.

represent an anemic attempt to explicate the significance of forgiveness. It replicates some of the worst features of a therapeutic mind-set and ignores — or, at best, seriously underplays — central practices and themes of Christian forgiveness.[16] As a result, Smedes's argument provides an illuminating example of how and why practices and conceptions of Christian forgiveness are radically transmuted and distorted in a therapeutic context — even when well-meaning Christians are the ones doing the transmuting and distorting.

Most generally, Smedes's analysis oversimplifies the very description of why forgiveness is necessary. He describes forgiveness as necessary for "coming to terms with a world in which, despite their best intentions, people are unfair to each other and hurt each other deeply" (pp. xi-xii). There is no doubt that people are unfair to each other and hurt each other deeply in the world in which we live. However, this is not typically "despite" people's "best intentions."

Such a description significantly underplays the Christian claim that forgiveness is necessary because of our *culpable* complicity both in specific breaches of relationship — what might be characterized as sin*s* (in the plural) — and in a pervasive reality of always-already brokenness and diminution — what might be characterized as sin (in the singular). Further, for Christians this forgiveness must be embodied in a way of life, a life marked by specific practices that enable us to unlearn patterns of sin, to repent for specific sins, and to foster habits of holy living. By contrast, Smedes's description internalizes and privatizes forgiveness so that there is little need for its embodiment in specific practices; it also virtually ignores issues of culpability and repentance, thus separating forgiveness from any sense of sin. Forgiveness becomes a means of being "healed of your hate," of which Smedes argues people have a *right* to be healed.

Smedes internalizes and privatizes forgiveness by making it primarily an activity that goes on within individual persons' hearts and minds.[17] It

---

16. As will become clear in what follows, my sympathies are clearly with Roberts in his exchange with Smedes, though my reasons for criticizing Smedes's perspective are somewhat different from those of Roberts. See also Roberts's more extensive engagement with Smedes's thought in his "Therapies and the Grammar of a Virtue," in Bell (ed.), *The Grammar of the Heart*, pp. 149-170.

17. Indeed, in Smedes's reply to Roberts, he describes his aims as follows: "In short, I took a long look at what actually goes on in a person's *heart* and *mind* when he or she forgives another human being and then set it down in a book" (p. 23, emphasis added).

is neither a way of life for people who must unlearn entrenched habits through specific practices (hence dealing with the always-already pervasiveness of ruptures of communion), nor is it an activity in which people must struggle *together* to overcome brokenness. Indeed, Smedes indicates that the purpose of forgiving is "for our own sakes" and is focused on specific actions in which people "hurt us unfairly, even if their intentions were pure" (pp. 12-13). Even more, Smedes's "four steps" of forgiveness (note the use of a handy technique) suggests that we must "heal ourselves" — the third step — before we "come together." But forgiveness, at least as Christians ought to understand and embody it, is not about "healing ourselves"; it is about being healed *by God and by others* in and through specific practices of forgiveness. Smedes's description only makes sense within an internalized and privatized conception of forgiveness beholden to a therapeutic culture.

This internalization is further reflected in Smedes's almost exclusive preoccupation with forgiving rather than being forgiven. There is no sense in which we are obligated, or even encouraged, to go to those whom we have wronged and seek forgiveness. Indeed, the one place where Smedes does acknowledge a person's need to be forgiven only reinforces this internalization: Smedes thinks that persons need to be forgiven as they forgive themselves. As he puts it, "To forgive yourself is to act out the mystery of one person who is both forgiver and forgiven. You judge yourself; this is the division within you. You forgive yourself: this is the healing of the split" (p. 77). Smedes seems to think that all that is needed is a kind of therapeutic will: I think I can forgive myself, so I can. But what if, as the Christian doctrine of sin at its best suggests, one of humanity's most intractable problems is self-deception? And what if, as the Christian practice of embodying forgiveness suggests, we find forgiveness not by looking within our selves but by being restored to communion with God and with one another in and through specific practices of forgiveness, thus embodying that forgiveness as a way of life?

Underlying Smedes's internalization and privatization of forgiveness is its preoccupation with individual feelings and thoughts at the expense of analyses of culpability, responsibility, and repentance. The unrelenting focus on isolated individuals suggests that forgiveness is important because of its effects on my feelings (see p. 56), not because of a need to discern whether there are tragic misunderstandings or culpable wrongdoing and brokenness that need to be dealt with through practices of forgiveness and repentance. Smedes does not attend to whether there is anything to be forgiven or whether it is clear that another person ought either to forgive or to be forgiven. Take, for example, a story Smedes tells from his own life (p. 9):

A colleague of mine once wrote a private letter to my board to accuse me of some theological delinquencies. His letter was unfair to me, and it caused me a lot of trouble. I believe that my colleague meant to be fair. But what he meant and what I experienced were two different things. It *was* unfair, no matter if he *meant* it to be fair. And the unfairness of it threw me into a crisis: did I want to let it fester in my memory, or would I use the "magic eyes" and be healed?

Smedes does not ask whether the colleague had done anything for which he should be held culpable; correlatively, questions about repentance are absent from Smedes's description. Even more, Smedes does not address whether, on his reading, it would be possible for anybody to criticize or judge anybody else without being labeled "unfair." Rather, the question is wholly internalized: I should forgive him because I need to heal this hurt that *I* feel I did not deserve.

Smedes urges us to put on "magic eyes" that will enable us to see things differently. But what are we to see through such eyes? Are we to see our own relationship to the God of Jesus Christ, our own capacity for sin as well as our need of costly grace? Are we to see the importance of a judgment oriented toward grace, of the call of God's Reign, which invites us to new life through repentance? Are we to see that the God of Jesus Christ calls us, through the power of the Spirit, to the practices and friend-ships of Christian communities that, as forgiven and reconciled, are in mission to the larger world of God's good Creation?

No, we are to "see" that the "deepest truth" about human beings is that we are "weak, needy, and fallible." This is not surprising, given the extent to which Smedes divorces his conception of forgiveness from the Christian practices and doctrines that originally gave them their intelligi-bility. Further, the context turns quickly from a claim that everybody (in-cluding me!) might be a sinner — or at least a "weak, needy, and fallible" human being — to a view that the faults lie with others. Indeed (p. 27),

> they were people before they hurt us and they are people after they hurt us. They were needy and weak before they hurt us and they were weak and needy after they hurt us. They needed our help, our support, our comfort before they did us wrong; and they need it still. They are not *only* people who hurt us; this is not the deepest truth about them.

Smedes does not explicitly discuss sin, but his implicit account is one in which the fault typically lies with others. Even worse, he trivializes sin by suggesting that the "hurts" and "unfairness" that need forgiveness happen despite our "best intentions" (p. xii). There is no sense of the bondage of the will here, no identification of the pervasiveness of webs of sin in which all of humanity finds itself caught apart from the gospel. We are fundamentally well-intentioned people who nonetheless periodically — almost accidentally — are unfair to others and hurt them. Such a shallow, therapeutic conception is a long way from an appropriately Christian understanding of sin and forgiveness.

Even worse, Smedes virtually ignores any prior sense in which any of us needs to be forgiven (except as we forgive ourselves) and thus need to repent. There is little sense in his discussion that sin is a complex reality that requires us to recognize that we are not only those on whom hurts are inflicted; we are also people capable of horrifying sin and evil, including the violence that nailed, and nails, Jesus Christ to the cross. Unless we are able to acknowledge our own complicity in various dimensions of sin and to recognize when the issues involve tragic misunderstandings or simply accidents (and thus require responses other than acts of forgiveness), forgiveness becomes a catchall for making myself feel better about life's hurts and unfairness.

Smedes's therapeutic forgiveness, manifested both in its excessive internalization and its bypassing of issues of sin and culpability, finds its *reductio ad absurdum* when he suggests that we not only can but indeed ought to forgive God. It does not matter that God is not culpable; what matters are my own feelings and health. "Would it bother God too much if we found our peace by forgiving him for the wrongs we suffer? What if we found a way to forgive him without blaming him? A special sort of forgiving for a special sort of relationship. Would he mind?" (p. 83).

Once one makes the move to a therapeutic mind-set, it becomes mind-numbingly difficult to explain why God "would mind." It hardly needs noting, however, that this is a god very different from the God who answers Job out of the whirlwind, the God to whom Jesus appeals in Gethsemane and again on the cross, the God in whose service Bonhoeffer accepted his own tragic death.

By this point it should not be difficult to discern the overall picture that emerges from Smedes's book. His seemingly "helpful" therapeutic account is actually a frighteningly shallow perspective that trivializes and undermines central Christian practices and understandings of forgiveness. On Smedes's account, therapeutic forgiveness is divorced from Christian practices and doctrine; an individual's psychic health replaces the goal of substantive Christian community lived in faithfulness to the Triune God; sin — though not named as such — is something others do to me (typically "despite their best intentions") rather than a more complex reality that pervades our lives and relations as well as afflicting specific behaviors; and a false compassion without attention to repentance and culpability reflects a failure to exercise a discerning judgment oriented toward graceful reconciliation.

Ironically, one of the more prescient diagnoses of the effect of this therapeutic cancer on the body of Christ was offered by the novelist Flannery O'Connor a generation before Smedes. O'Connor presents a scathing indictment of the ways in which Christians have abandoned the richer contexts of forgiveness. Her short story "Revelation" is — or at least ought to be — a revelation to Christians trapped by a therapeutic culture.[18]

The "Revelation" of Judgment

Mrs. Ruby Turpin, a "very large," respectable, and church-going Southern woman with a self-deprecating sense of humor, has brought her husband Claud to the doctor's office to be treated for a leg ailment. The doctor's small waiting room is almost full when they arrive. As gospel music plays softly in the background, Ruby takes center stage among the people there. Indeed, both her physical size and her personal presence virtually overtake the room. Full of self-certainty about her own goodness, she begins making mental observations about the other people in the room — even classifying them by the shoes they wear. Ruby has a habit of classifying others; when she has trouble falling asleep at night, she calms herself by imagining all the classes of people.

> On the bottom of the heap were most colored people, not the kind she would have been if she had been one, but most of them; then next to them — not above, just away from — were the white trash; then above them were the home-owners, and above them the home-and-land owners, to which she and Claud belonged. Above she and Claud were people with a lot of money and much bigger houses and much more land.

Ironically, in the midst of this classification of others, Ruby runs into trouble.

18. "Revelation," in *The Complete Stories of Flannery O'Connor* (New York: Farrar, Straus, and Giroux, 1977) pp. 488-509. Further references will be to this edition and will be given parenthetically in the text.

But here the complexity of it would begin to bear in on her, for some of the people with a lot money were common and ought to be below she and Claud and some of the people who had good blood had lost their money and had to rent and then there were colored people who owned their homes and land as well. There was a colored dentist in town who had two red Lincolns and a swimming pool and a farm with registered white face cattle on it. Usually by the time she had fallen asleep all the classes of people were moiling and roiling around in her head, and she would dream they were all crammed together in a box car, being ridden off to be put in a gas oven. (pp. 491-492)

This is one way of making a totalitarian mind. As Ralph Wood has suggested, "O'Connor uncovers the real terror of evil by showing how it begins guilelessly enough but how, by a strange mutation, it is transformed into something heinously destructive. . . . The world's refusal to conform to Mrs. Turpin's idea of it poisons her imagination."[19] Once we begin classifying people, whether in the way Ruby does or by saying that sin is what others do, we have lapsed into the kinds of bifurcations that easily lead to destructive — indeed potentially totalitarian — behavior.

Perhaps because of this poisoning of her imagination, Ruby is not simply content to classify people in the context of her own smug self-contentment. She begins to hurl well-mannered comments, really carefully disguised sharply-barbed insults, even observing that her pigs are cleaner than some children she has seen. Ruby's arrogance is based on a self-righteous judgment in which faults consistently lie with others, not herself. Indeed, her philosophy of life is "to help anybody out that needed it." She is grateful that Jesus "had not made her a nigger or white-trash or ugly! He had made her herself and given her a little of everything. Jesus, thank you! she said. Thank you thank you thank you! Whenever she counted her blessings she felt as buoyant as if she weighed one hundred and twenty-five pounds instead of one hundred and eighty" (p. 497).

There is one college girl in the room, however, that Ruby is not able to dismiss as easily as the rest of them. Mary Grace is home from Wellesley and sits in the doctor's waiting room reading a book entitled *Human Development*. Ruby notices how ugly the girl is, that she wears Girl Scout shoes, and that she seems to be filled with contempt for just about everybody — including, unfortunately, Ruby. "All at once the ugly girl turned

---

19. Ralph C. Wood, *The Comedy of Redemption* (Notre Dame: University of Notre Dame, 1988) p. 127. I am greatly indebted to Wood in my reading of O'Connor's story.

her lips inside out again. Her eyes fixed like two drills on Mrs. Turpin. This time there was no mistaking that there was something urgent behind them" (p. 497). Indeed, Mary Grace's expressions are most vivid when Ruby says something that Mary Grace knows Ruby does not believe.

Ruby tries to deflect attention away from Mary Grace, turning to talk with Mary Grace's mother about the importance of gratitude. As Ruby is in the midst of replicating her chorus of thanksgiving to Jesus for "making everything the way it is," Mary Grace strikes Ruby just over the left eye with the book *Human Development*. Before Ruby can utter a sound, Mary Grace wrestles Ruby to the floor. Ruby looks into Mary Grace's fiercely maniacal eyes with "no doubt in her mind that the girl did know her, knew her in some intense and personal way, beyond time and place and condition." It was this knowledge that made Mary Grace's judgment, and her final words to Ruby, even more severe: "Go back to hell where you came from, you old wart hog" (p. 500).

Even so, Ruby has the possibility of transcendent hope, if only because she recognizes that she has met a transcendent judgment.[20] When Ruby and Claud return home, she looks out the window suspiciously: "She would not have been startled to see a burnt wound between two blackened chimneys" (p. 502). Even so, it takes her a while to accept the judgment. She begins with a rather lame denial that she is a wart hog. From hell. But being unable to repudiate the message herself, she looks to Claud and then to her black workers for consolation. But instead, she gets a false consolation from the workers, complete with the ironic subversions of polite words loaded with sarcasm. They tell her, "You the sweetest white lady I know" (p. 505).

Dissatisfied with the lack of consolation, Ruby heads off to the pig parlor. There she encounters an old pregnant sow lying on her side and grunting contentedly. But Ruby herself is far from content. " 'What do you send me a message like that for?' she said in a low fierce voice, barely above a whisper but with the force of a shout in its concentrated fury. 'How am I a hog and me both? How am I saved and from hell too?' " (p. 506). As she continues to struggle with the judgment, she returns to her old system of justifying herself by judging others. But even that fails, and her protests take on an almost comic quality as she discovers that perhaps God is not simply a therapeutic nice guy who asks only that we be nice too. Finally, in a surge of fury, she roars, "Who do you think you are?" (p. 507).

With that question, Ruby finally begins to acknowledge with clarity

---

20. I owe this way of formulating the contrast to Wood's discussion in *The Comedy of Redemption*.

precisely who she is. The narrator tells us that the "color of everything, field and crimson sky, burned for a moment with a transparent intensity. The question carried over the pasture and across the highway and the cotton field and returned to her clearly like an answer from beyond the wood. She opened her mouth but no sound came out of it" (pp. 507-508). Ruby, that talkative woman from the waiting room, eager to classify and judge, has now been left speechless. She recognizes that her self-righteousness has been a false way of being upright; "like a monumental statue coming to life, she bent her head slowly and gazed, as if through the very heart of mystery, down into the pig parlor at the hogs" (p. 508). There she discovers the old sow nourishing others with what seems to be "a secret life."

As she looks up, Ruby discovers that the scathing judgment she has received has been nothing less than God's redeeming grace. She sees a purple streak in the sky leading into the descending dusk.

> A visionary light settled in her eyes. She saw the streak as a vast swinging bridge extending upward from the earth through a field of living fire. Upon it a vast horde of souls were rumbling toward heaven. There were whole companies of white-trash, clean for the first time in their lives, and bands of black niggers in white robes, and battalions of freaks and lunatics shouting and clapping and leaping like frogs. And bringing up the end of the procession was a tribe of people whom she recognized at once as those who, like herself and Claud, had always had a little of everything and the God-given wit to use it right. She leaned forward to observe them closer. They were marching behind the others with great dignity, accountable as they had always been for good order and common sense and respectable behavior. They alone were on key. Yet she could see by their shocked and altered faces that even their virtues were being burned away. (p. 508)

Ruby's vision of those transformed by God now includes herself. Further, she is no longer either the judge of others nor even the "first" among people; people like her are among the last to move through the field of living fire, and even then their virtues are being burned away.

The context of Ruby's vision of the Kingdom is clear; none of us can escape divine judgment. Yet, as Ralph Wood has rightly pointed out, here "divine wrath is couched wholly in terms of divine mercy. It is a mercy that is like a refiner's fire — cleansing rather than consuming."[21] The transformation is not, as with a therapeutic culture, a move from condemnation

21. Wood, *The Comedy of Redemption*, p. 131.

to a cheap consolation in which judgment is rendered innocuous; but neither is it an acceptance of some "dialectical interplay" between condemnation and consolation, as if we could be content to be both people and pigs at the same time.[22] Rather, the transformation occurs through a judgment of grace, a judgment of God that enables new life by the power of the Holy Spirit.

It is this purifying, sanctifying character of the "living fire" of God's Holy Spirit that makes Ruby's vision a sign of God's grace rather than simply a consuming destruction. But despite the clarity of Ruby's eschatological vision, the story does not simply end there. She returns to her house along a "darkening path." As her sight fades, she notices that invisible cricket choruses have struck up; but what she hears are "the voices of the souls climbing upward into the starry field and shouting hallelujah" (p. 509). Here the story ends, reminding us that though our vision of God's Kingdom is important and indeed central, we must nevertheless learn to live in this time between the times as "through a glass darkly" (1 Corinthians 13:12).

O'Connor's story represents a stark contrast to therapeutic mind-sets in general, and therapeutic forgiveness in particular. Ruby Turpin might have been very willing to forgive others in particular instances, and perhaps even to forget. After all, she considered herself a very "religious" person. But analyses like Smedes's would simply have reinforced Ruby's own self-certainty and self-righteousness. Ruby is absolutely convinced of the truthfulness of her observations, all the while standing in self-righteous judgment of others. And Smedes, who suggests that a person's feelings are valid because they are what you feel, offers Ruby no resources for coming to terms with her own self-deception.

Furthermore, when Ruby does learn to see things differently, it is not by putting on the "magic eyes" of seeing ourselves simply as "weak, needy, and fallible." Rather, she learns to see differently through an encounter with the purifying fire of God's judgment of grace, a fire that forces Ruby to acknowledge her own sin and need of grace. It is not a question of forgiving herself, or even of forgiving God. Ruby could not forgive herself because one of the identifying features of her character is self-deception. That is, she fails to see herself as she really is until she has to come to terms with the judgment of God as found in Mary Grace. And though Ruby might have found it psychologically comforting to forgive God for this hurt she

---

22. I am indebted to my colleague Jim Buckley for this way of putting the matter. See his wonderful essay "A Field of Living Fire: Karl Barth on the Spirit and the Church," *Modern Theology* 10/1 (January 1994) pp. 81-102.

has received, it would have been thoroughly inadequate. For what Ruby really needs is not the psychological comfort of forgiving God for hurts she feels she does not deserve (and wondering if God would mind!), but rather the encounter with God's judgment of grace, which enables her to see herself and her world more truthfully.

Ruby's story alludes to the parable of Jesus that is often identified as the Parable of the Prodigal Son (Luke 15:11-32).[23] In that parable, the younger son asks for and receives his share of his father's inheritance. He then takes his possessions, travels to a far country, and there squanders those possessions in dissolute living. As a result, he finds himself in great need and has to hire himself out to a farmer who sends him to feed his pigs. But then he comes to himself (v. 17) and discovers that even the pigs are in better shape than he is. He resolves to go home and repent, asking to be taken back as one of his father's hired servants.

But as he gets near home, but while he is "still far off," his father sees him and is "filled with compassion." He runs and puts his arms around his son and kisses him. The son responds with a confession of his sin, indicating that he is no longer worthy to be called his father's son. But his father does not respond by asking for sackcloth and ashes; he calls his servants to get festal garments for his son, to slay the fatted calf, and to prepare for a party celebrating his son's return. After all, "my son was dead and is alive again; he was lost and is now found!" (v. 24).

The elder son, however, is not as thrilled as his father to see the younger son return. Indeed, he is filled with self-righteous indignation. Doesn't a proper sense of fairness, of justice, demand equal treatment? The elder son has always been faithful, has never been disobedient, yet his father has never provided him with even a young goat, much less a fatted calf, for a party. The nerve of the father! But the father's response is not simply to leave the elder son to stew in his juices; he goes out and seeks this son as well, and he responds to the son's indignation by saying, "Son, you are always with me. Everything that is mine is yours. But we had to celebrate and rejoice because your brother was dead and has come back to life. He was lost and has been found" (vv. 31-32).

Like Ruby, the younger son only comes to himself by comparing his own existence to that of contented pigs. He has deceived himself by thinking that life and the self are things to be possessed. In the pigsty he realizes that

23. It is better identified as the Parable of the Forgiving Father. The focus is not so much on either of the ungrateful sons as on the character of the Father who joyously forgives and receives both of his children back into his fellowship.

his life has been dissipated in an attempt at control. But in that recognition he also discovers that the father gives and *forgives* him. He does not forgive himself; indeed, he is prepared to punish himself by becoming one of his father's hired workers. Nor does he forgive his father; he realizes that the father has not done anything for which he would be culpable. But he does discover his father's prior forgiveness, which celebrates his return and creates a changed context for his future.

But the older son is no better off. He also sees life in terms of possession, and he is outraged at the breach of fairness and justice. While he has not squandered his inheritance, he assumes that he possesses a righteousness based on his fidelity. But, like Ruby Turpin, his is a false way of being upright, a stance that is unable to bend the body in gestures of love, to acknowledge the gift that others, including the Other who is God, offer to him. The father does not see human life as the sons see it: They see it as a possession, but he sees it as a gift that must be continually given — even through the cost of forgiveness.[24]

The revelation of the judgment of grace that comes to Ruby, like the revelations that the two sons receive in Jesus' parable, suggests that forgiveness is a free gift and that its purpose is the restoration of communion with God and with others in Christian community and the re-creation of human life with holiness as its destiny. But this forgiveness is inseparable both from the judgment that challenges human self-deception and from the repentance that becomes possible as we learn to see ourselves more clearly.

Why, then, have accounts of forgiveness such as Smedes's struck such a chord with so many people in our culture? Is it *only* because we are trapped in a therapeutic culture and because it has corrupted our thinking and our living? Or is there some other reason, perhaps grounded in the ambiguous legacy that Christians have left concerning forgiveness? Modern Christians have too often and too easily assumed that the primary problem that afflicts individuals is prideful rebellion against God. But what if the sin that afflicts many people is not simply pride but other forces of diminution?

Rethinking Sin

Often underlying therapeutic accounts of forgiveness is a sense that many people find it difficult to overcome a sense of helplessness. Stories about

24. For further discussion of this point see Jean-Luc Marion, *God without Being*, tr. Thomas A. Carlson (Chicago: University of Chicago, 1991) p. 99.

Ruby Turpin are all well and good, it might be suggested, to skewer those who are afflicted with pride and self-righteousness. But what about those people who are afflicted with the loss or diminishment of a sense of self, people for whom the problem is not pride but self-abnegation?

There has been a tendency in Christian thought and life to emphasize the sin of pride so much that other dynamics of sin are lost. To be sure, many people have been damaged both (on the one hand) by oversimplified and/or destructive notions of sin and (on the other hand) by the social and political contexts legitimated by such destructive notions. Smedes's discussion, at its best, is attentive to these issues.[25] Yet we make a serious mistake when we respond to distortions in our thinking about sin by abandoning the notion or by falling prey to a therapeutic conception that reduces sin to what others do to us. The solution is to formulate, or better to rediscover, theologically richer and more faithful articulations of what is at stake in the Christian doctrine of sin. We need to find ways of thinking about sin — and thus also about forgiveness — that are attentive to the complexity both of the issues involved and of our ways of analyzing and struggling against sin by embodying forgiveness.

In recent years a number of feminist theologians have rightly emphasized that sin is too complex to be identified with pride.[26] They have rightly focused attention on the dynamics of sin as self-abnegation or "hiding." This is an important insight, reminding Christians that sin can be both prideful self-assertion and shameful self-diffusion, and people often have to struggle with both.[27] Even so, our rethinking of sin needs to be developed in more clearly theological terms, drawing on the rich resources of the

25. See also Smedes's *Shame and Grace: Healing the Shame We Don't Deserve* (San Francisco: HarperSanFrancisco, 1993). It has many of the same weaknesses as *Forgive and Forget*, yet it also is helpfully attentive to some of the ways in which Christianity's ambiguous legacy has actually compounded the problems.

26. For example, Valerie Saiving Goldstein, "The Human Situation: A Feminine View," *Journal of Religion* 40 (1960) pp. 100-112; Judith Plaskow, *Sex, Sin, and Grace: Women's Experience and the Theologies of Reinhold Niebuhr and Paul Tillich* (Washington: University Press of America, 1980); Susan Nelson Dunfee, "The Sin of Hiding: A Feminist Critique of Reinhold Niebuhr's Account of the Sin of Pride," *Soundings* 65 (1982) pp. 316-327; and Mary Potter Engel, "Evil, Sin, and Violation of the Vulnerable," in Susan Brooks Thistlethwaite and Mary Potter Engel (eds.), *Lift Every Voice: Constructing Theologies from the Underside* (San Francisco: Harper and Row, 1990) pp. 152-164.

27. For an instructive analysis of each of these temptations drawing on Kierkegaard's analysis, see William J. Cahoy, "One Species or Two? Kierkegaard's Anthropology and the Feminist Critique of the Concept of Sin," *Modern Theology* 11/4 (October 1995).

Christian tradition in so doing. A first step in doing so requires that I describe, if only briefly, a Christian understanding of the nature and purpose of human life in relation to the Triune God.[28]

The Triune God is characterized by self-giving love; further, God loves those whom God has created. God wills communion with Creation, and so creates human beings in the divine image and likeness. So human beings are created for loving communion — with God, with one another, and with the whole Creation; we are not made to live as isolated or self-enclosed individuals. Hence, we can only fulfill our purpose and destiny when we fulfill our God-given capacity to love, to live as a part of the pattern of God's Creation. In an analogous fashion to God's self-giving life among Father, Son, and Spirit, we find our life in self-giving love with others.[29] The "deepest truth" about ourselves is neither that we are self-sufficient nor that are weak, needy, and fallible; it is that we are created for communion with God, with one another, and with the whole Creation. We need God and others both to discover who and whose we are and also because it is only through our life together that we can fulfill our destiny for communion in God's Kingdom.

Yet human beings have persistently rejected, and continue to reject, that communion. We find it difficult to accept our creatureliness, following a will-to-power, a will-to-self-obliteration, or perhaps despairing amid the struggle to sustain identities in the face of awesome forces of annihilation. In each case, however, the reality of communion collapses into a series of isolated and divided individuals obsessively concerned with preserving or sustaining a sense of "self." As a result, the musical harmony of God's self-giving communion is transmuted into the cacophony of self-asserting or self-abnegating selves unable to hear one another. This not only has

---

28. This will, of course, be further developed in Part II.

29. Recent critiques, particularly (but not exclusively) among feminists, have raised issues and problems about addressing God as "Father." The issues range from whether Christians are *obligated* to use the term "Father" (because, on this view, "Father, Son, and Holy Spirit" is the name of God) to whether Christians or others should *ever* call God "Father" (because, on this view, the term is hopelessly sexist). There are a number of mediating positions and a variety of proposed ways of dealing with issues of God language. My own view is that, while there are certainly varieties of ways to image and identify God, the identification "Father, Son, and Holy Spirit," understood in the light of a long tradition of creedal and conciliar commentary, has provided a shared way of naming and articulating the relations among the "persons" of the Godhead. Hence, in this book I rely on the traditional appellations while also acknowledging that further reflection, conversation, and argument are needed.

happened, it continues to happen; and its effects have histories that we cannot truthfully deny or evade.

People are not culpable for those histories in the abstract, as if — for example — I am somehow "guilty" for the enslavement of African Americans in the seventeenth to nineteenth centuries; but I am culpable for that history in the sense that the effects of slavery continue to mar my relations with others, making me complicit in the continuing racism of the culture into which I was born. I can either remain complicit in that racism, thereby perpetuating it in ways for which I am also culpable; or I can struggle against it, seeking to mitigate its effects through faithful discipleship. But there is no one who can claim only to be a victim of others' histories; though levels of culpability certainly vary, sometimes immensely, we are all enmeshed in various histories and circumstances, and the result is that we cannot evade the truth that we all invariably diminish and destroy others in the ways in which we live.

This always-already brokenness is the fundamental condition of Sin. But this fundamental situation of fragmentation and brokenness also manifests itself in particular and specific sins. Such sins include both things that human beings do *to* one another (such as violence, adultery, lying, and racist actions or comments) and things that they *fail* to do *for* one another (such as abandoning those who suffer, neglecting the physical or emotional needs of others, or refusing to act justly or truthfully). In either case, we not only diminish the other(s); we diminish ourselves.

Even worse, this pervasiveness of sin — embodied both in Sin and in sins — has the force of habit that is difficult to unlearn. Indeed, the habit of sinfulness eventually takes on the force of necessity. As a result, we find it increasingly difficult — if not impossible — not only to escape sinfulness, but even to *desire* to escape it. Augustine frames the matter well in his *Confessions:* "The enemy held fast my will, and had made of it a chain, and had bound me tight with it. For out of the perverse will come lust, and the service of lust ended in habit, and habit, not resisted, became necessity. By these links, as it were, forged together — which is why I call it 'a chain' — a hard bondage held me in slavery."[30] In Augustine's view, people become habituated to sin and, more specifically, to wicked behavior, so that it is no longer a struggle that we worry about; indeed, in the case of some sins such as lust, we actually perversely learn to "delight" in doing such a sin. But even if it is not delight, the habit of sin creates positions of security and

---

30. Augustine, *Confessions,* tr. and ed. Albert C. Outler (Library of Christian Classics; Philadelphia: Westminster, 1955) p. 165 (8.5.10).

possession to which we want to cling; even if the sin destroys others (or oneself), the habit is reassuring because it is how we have learned to negotiate our relations in ways that reinforce a secure position. Rather than being turned outward in self-giving love *with* others, the self turns inward on itself.

So sin and forgiveness have to do with more than pride and with more than my "individual" guilt. They have to do with the pervasive brokenness for which we are all, in some measure, culpable and with specific instances and habits of culpable wrongdoing that undermine not only my communion but *our* communion with God, with one another, and with the whole Creation. Hence forgiveness must involve an unlearning of the habits of sin as we seek to become holy people capable of living in communion. As Jon Sobrino rightly insists, "the purpose of forgiveness is not simply to heal the guilt of the sinner but the purpose of all love: to come into communion."[31]

These descriptions of sin and forgiveness present a sharp challenge to therapeutic notions of human life and of sin and forgiveness. A Christian account ought to insist on the ongoing difficulty of learning to narrate our lives in relation to the God from whom we have become estranged by habits of sin — albeit habits we recognize primarily by the gracious forgiveness of being known by God. As Rowan Williams describes it,

> The "authentic" self is what I acknowledge as already, non-negotiably, caught up in continuing encounter with or response to divine action; and the acknowledgment is inseparable from converted behaviour. The person who knows him- or herself is manifest as such in the practice of prayer and almsgiving. Or, in short, the meaning of self-knowledge here is displayed in the performing of acts intelligible as the acts of a finite being responding to an initiative of generosity from beyond itself, an initiative wholly unconditioned by any past history on the self's part of oblivion or betrayal.[32]

That is, we discover our "selves" in relation to the friendships and practices of the Church, through which we receive God's grace. Because of the pervasiveness of sin, healing brokenness and unlearning sinful habits is an unfinished and *unfinishable* task. Williams continues, "Truthful self-knowl-

31. Jon Sobrino, "Latin America: Place of Sin and Place of Forgiveness," *Concilium* 184 (1986) p. 51.

32. Rowan Williams, " 'Know Thyself': What Kind of an Injunction?" in Michael McGhee (ed.), *Philosophy, Religion and the Spiritual Life* (Cambridge: Cambridge University, 1992) p. 219.

edge thus entails a constantly self-critical autobiographical project, striving to construct the narrative least unfaithful to the divine perspective."[33]

In this sense, then, we need to resituate our conceptions of the self, of sin and forgiveness, and of the call to holiness, in their larger context of God's inbreaking Kingdom. These notions are significantly different in their assumptions and implications when they are removed from a therapeutic context and placed in the context of God's Kingdom. Ruby Turpin's vision, and even her hearing in the midst of her darkness, was of God's eschatological salvation and the reconfiguration of personal, social, and political relations that salvation brings about. And the prodigal son's forgiveness and repentance are signified by a party, indeed a banquet, emblematic of God's messianic Kingdom. If Christian life is fundamentally oriented toward the coming fullness of God's eschatological reign, then so should be our practices and understandings of Christian forgiveness.

Therapy and the Church's Eschatological Gospel

An eschatological account of forgiveness, situated in the context of the doctrine of the Triune God, stands in stark contrast to a therapeutic culture that sees forgiveness as an internalized process of healing ourselves of our hate. But though it might be comforting for Christians to imagine that we are the "victims" of other people's reduction of the gospel to therapy, we must take the log out of our own eyes before we become preoccupied with the specks in our brothers' and sisters' eyes (cf. Matthew 7:1-5). The triumph of the therapeutic was not simply an invasion by external forces upon an otherwise healthy Body; we Christians had prepared the Body for the therapeutic cancer through our own distorted and distorting ecclesial practices. Most specifically, we have been unable consistently to embody Christian forgiveness because we have failed to situate the Church's proclamation of the gospel in relation to God's eschatological Kingdom. This has left us in a significantly weakened and impoverished state. Only by reclaiming the centrality of God's already-established but yet-to-come Kingdom will we be able to understand Christian forgiveness properly and, more importantly, to *practice* Christian forgiveness properly.

Speaking of the predicament of Protestant liberalism (though that is a phenomenon by no means limited to heirs of the Reformation) is one way to identify the reasons for the Church's weakened immune system. The

---

33. Williams, "Know Thyself," p. 221.

familiar story rightly notes that Protestant liberals evacuated the gospel of eschatological content, deprived it of its ability to interrogate us, and transmuted it into (at most) banal truisms such as "God loves you." Once these transformations occurred, the Church had few defenses against the introduction of alien forces such as a therapeutic mind-set. Or, more strongly put, the Church no longer realized that there was something it needed to defend against.[34]

But there are nagging passages in the Bible that seem to run counter to Protestant liberalism's therapeutic gospel, passages that seem oriented toward Christian life embodied in eschatological community. Take, for example, the Sermon on the Mount. Richard Lischer has noted that not only does the Sermon rarely appear in discussions of pastoral care, psychiatrists also often turn to examples in the Sermon when discussing those features of Christianity that are "most toxic to the mental health of their patients." For psychiatrists

> the Sermon's tone violates the moral neutrality necessary for self-acceptance and change. Its obsession with purity gives free reign to the tyranny of the super-ego. The main objection to its message is that those who take it too seriously move away from the median ranges of mental health, our culture's translation of *salvus*. Far from a set of helpful guidelines for living the happy life, the Beatitudes detail the disjunction of blessedness from happiness, and salvation from health. In a society that celebrates "the narcissism of similarity" the Sermon disappoints repeatedly. What someone said of the characters in the stories of Flannery O'Connor applies to the adherents of the Sermon: "You shall know the truth, and the truth shall make you odd." The psychiatrists have a point. Theirs is no small indictment to bring against a religious program that so thoroughly dis-accommodates its adherents for a well-balanced life in a technological and therapeutic society.[35]

Lischer rightly argues that the Sermon on the Mount is an eschatological document, an expression of God's "radical pastoral care," that "can only be 'interpreted' as communities of Christians attempt to live it."[36]

---

34. Unfortunately, while "Protestant liberalism" may have contributed mightily to the Church's predicament, this attitude also infects and afflicts many accounts of Christian life offered by evangelicals (such as Smedes) and Roman Catholics.

35. Richard Lischer, "The Sermon on the Mount as Radical Pastoral Care," *Interpretation* 41/2 (April 1987) p. 164. The internal reference is to Robert Bellah, et al., *Habits of the Heart* (New York: Harper and Row, 1985) p. 72.

36. Lischer, "The Sermon on the Mount as Radical Pastoral Care," p. 169.

The Church could claim the power of the gospel, and we could begin to be healed of our therapeutic cancer, if Christians would learn to embody such a radical pastoral care. This is particularly important if we are to reclaim the centrality of Christian forgiveness. If we are to do so, we will need to abandon the pervasive and, unfortunately, still hegemonic culture of Protestant liberalism, specifically its correlative therapeutic conception of forgiveness. Therapeutic mind-sets and practices have overrun the contemporary Church, infecting our parishes, our seminaries, our ministerial workshops, our processes of considering candidates for ordination, even our dominant conceptions of spirituality and the spiritual life. We will not be able to reclaim the significance of forgiveness for Christian life or Christian theology unless we abandon the therapeutic mind-set and begin the difficult yet more hopeful task of *embodying* forgiveness in specific habits and practices.

Further, we will need to return to the eschatological focus of both the Sermon on the Mount and the gospel as a whole in order to understand what such embodiment entails. Doing so involves emphasizing the formation and transformation of our lives through an ever-deepening friendship with the Triune God. This formation and transformation occurs by the power of the Holy Spirit as Christians are conformed to the image and likeness of Christ. As such, this involves unlearning habits and practices of sin and learning to cultivate habits and practices of holiness in communion with God, with one another, and with the whole Creation.[37]

We also need an eschatological understanding of Christian forgiveness. Christian forgiveness is not simply a word of acquittal; nor is it something that merely refers backward.[38] Rather, Christian forgiveness — and, more specifically, forgiven-ness — is a way of life, a fidelity to a relationship of friendship, that must be learned and relearned on our journey toward holiness in God's eschatological Kingdom. It is a way of life that requires the ever-deepening and ever-widening sense of what friendship with God and God's creatures entails. It is ever-deepening and ever-

37. The themes of this paragraph are more fully developed in my *Transformed Judgment*.

38. Unfortunately, once justification was taken by Protestants to be *the* central theological category for Christian life, forgiveness often became merely a subcategory of justification and one that refers only backward, as acquittal. Such descriptions not only fail adequately to deal with the New Testament accounts of forgiveness, but more importantly they detach "personal" forgiveness from larger ecclesial, ethical, and political issues. For an example of one who construes forgiveness as a subcategory of justification, see Paul Lehmann, *Forgiveness: Decisive Issue in Protestant Thought* (New York: Harper and Brothers, 1940).

widening precisely because we must continually find ways — in communion with God, one another, and the whole Creation — to unmask our deceptions of our selves, of others, and of the world through lives of forgiven-ness. As Wanda Warren Berry has suggested, "Forgiveness is truth when it is lived and because it can be lived transparently, without self-deception."[39]

God's Spirit is at work forgiving, healing, and re-creating us in the likeness of Christ for life in God's Kingdom. Further, that Spirit is at work in the ways we are learning to forgive and be forgiven, to heal and be healed, to re-create and be re-created, in our life with others. In this light it becomes apparent that Christian forgiveness is not so much a word to be spoken as a life to be lived in fidelity to the eschatological salvation of the Triune God.

But, it might be suggested, this sense in which forgiveness is eschatological points to the very importance of therapy. After all, the "friendships and practices" of the Church that are supposed to embody that ever-deepening and ever-widening sense of forgiveness often not only are impoverished, they also have been the occasion of colluding in the oppression and victimization of others. That is one of the reasons why Christians sometimes *need* psychotherapy, not because of a desire to recover the tradition but to recover *from* some aspect of it. This is true both in personal dimensions of sin and on larger historical and structural levels of evil and oppression.

So, the interlocutor might continue, "Am I not suggesting part of the problem as the solution?" The Church's complicity in sin and evil is, at one level, undeniably true. Regrettably, there have been — and continue to be — impoverished and distorted convictions, practices, and communities that have gone by the name "Christian." That should not be surprising, particularly given the recognition that churches will inevitably be — on this side of the fullness of God's reign — holy *and* sinful communities. But what ought to be surprising is the tendency to self-deception, to a lack of penitence.

For this reason alone, there is a place for substantive psychological and psychotherapeutic theories and practices that help provide a check against tendencies to deceit and self-deception. Even more, there are insights and wisdom to be gained from such theories and practices if they

---

39. Wanda Warren Berry, "Finally Forgiveness: Kierkegaard as a 'Springboard' for a Feminist Theology of Reform," in George B. Connell and C. Stephen Evans (eds.), *Foundations of Kierkegaard's Vision of Community* (Atlantic Highlands: Humanities, 1992) p. 206.

are detached from ossified therapeutic mind-sets. This is particularly the case since several of these theories have moved away from focusing on isolated individuals to deal with larger social, cultural, and political contexts. The gospel should not be captured by therapy; nor should the two simply coexist. But that is not to say that Christians cannot critically appropriate and learn from the insights of psychology and psychotherapy, particularly as we seek to learn the complexities of human sin and evil and the ways in which forgiveness needs to be embodied and understood.

The great danger of therapeutic conceptions of forgiveness is that they overlap with Christian forgiveness just enough to distort our understandings of their differences. And, in particular, conceptions of forgiveness such as Smedes's seduce us into thinking that the world is filled with more light than it really is. After all, we people do a lot of things that do not reflect our "best intentions." Christians may believe that Christ has decisively defeated sin and evil on the cross; but no serious Christian account of that defeat would suggest that, on this side of the fullness of the Kingdom, sin and evil have lost their force, threat, and consequences.

Indeed, simply reading the newspaper, watching the news, or reflecting on human history — including especially on what we Christians ourselves have often done — might actually tempt us to believe that darkness has snuffed out the light. Is the world, truthfully acknowledged, really a place of persistent darkness? Nicholas Lash has observed that, "bombarded by the fables spun by salesmen and politicians, knowing how easily we succumb to fantasies that make us 'feel good,' the narratives that we secretly suspect are true are those that intimate that force, the human face of which is violence, is the one effective agency in a nightmare of absurd unmeaning."[40]

Tragically, some people really do seem to believe, or at least pretend to believe, the naively optimistic narratives that suggest that everything and everybody are basically okay. After all, there is a great temptation to be optimistic and thereby either to trivialize or to ignore sin. This is true whether the sin occurs far away or in our own backyard; people inside and outside Germany and the former Soviet nations have effectively ignored or deflected the horrifying realities of genocidal practices carried out by the Nazi German and Soviet Stalinist states, just as we might deal thus with the harsh persistence of domestic violence in our own neighborhoods and communities. Such optimism consistently evades the reality of sin and the costliness of forgiveness.

40. Nicholas Lash, *Believing Three Ways in One God* (Notre Dame: University of Notre Dame, 1992) pp. 66-67.

But perhaps others of us, all too aware of our capacity for massive evil and injustice, have been seduced by therapeutic forgiveness *precisely because,* deep down, we fear that the only effective agency in the world is force, the human face of which is violence — and we do not want to admit that the world is as dark as that. This is the sense in which therapeutic forgiveness easily lapses into totalitarian violence. Can even costly forgiveness be effective? Or is violence the master of us all?[41]

41. This final question, which also serves as the subtitle to the next chapter, is from John Milbank, *Theology and Social Theory* (Oxford: Blackwell, 1990) p. 276. I am indebted to Milbank for much of the framework of my argument about the relationships among peace, violence, and forgiveness.

3 Forgiveness Eclipsed

Is Violence the Master of Us All?

I T IS NOT surprising that human beings typically reap the consequences of sin that we ourselves sow; though we may sometimes think we can "get away" with telling a small lie or giving in to a single lustful desire, for example, we also at least are dimly aware of the ways in which those single acts are woven into larger patterns and practices of sin. Regrettably, we often fail adequately to recognize the effects of the sinful patterns and practices that each of us has sown until they have become entrenched habits that we find difficult, if not apparently impossible, to unlearn and to break the hold of. We find it difficult because we often do not really want to unlearn sin and to break habits because they create secure positions in which we take either a perverse delight or at least a masochistic self-satisfaction. But even if we do want to unlearn and break the habits of sin, it is difficult because they are so entrenched in the patterns and practices of our lives.

However, it is also the case that we human beings often sow the consequences of sin that we ourselves reap.[1] It is now well-established that people who are physically abused are, regrettably, often likely to become abusers. Peoples who have been terrorized are often filled with a righteous indignation and anger that all too easily is transformed into terrorizing patterns of vengeance. People who have been beaten down or violated often

---

1. I owe this distinction of reaping what we sow and sowing what we reap to Cornelius Plantinga, Jr.'s *Not the Way It's Supposed to Be: A Breviary of Sin* (Grand Rapids: Eerdmans, 1994) pp. 69-70.

internalize the effects of those actions, making those people increasingly unable to love or trust. Sometimes, it even makes them unable to desire love or trust because the wounds go too deep. It is exceedingly difficult for people who have suffered greatly to escape these cycles, for one of the horrifying effects accomplished by those who dominate, oppress, and abuse others is the sufferers' diminished capacity to act or to take responsibility for their lives. More pointedly, those who ought to repent and take this responsibility for stopping the cycles, namely the offenders, are typically those least likely either to want or to be willing to do so.[2]

These patterns of sin, of reaping what we sow and sowing what we reap, are enmeshed with one another throughout the world in which we live. That is, these habits have histories not only in individual lives and social contexts but also in institutional structures; indeed, we often find ourselves caught in the traps of these habits before we are able to recognize them or even to decide whether or not we want to participate in them. This is then compounded by people's willful accumulation of patterns and practices of sin, specific acts and habits of commission or omission that deepen the darkness and thus make our predicament in this world seem ever more hopeless.

Hence, we see how habits of sin can begin to seem overwhelming. Perhaps human beings are already so habituated to sinful patterns and practices that those patterns and practices are inescapable. They cannot be unlearned. And perhaps that is why many people are tempted to believe that brute force, the human face of which is violence, is the only effective force in coping with the darkness of our world. In this sense, perhaps our only "hope" lies in having the skill and the power to utilize violence more effectively and justly than anyone else. For the alternative would seem to be to internalize the effects of others' violence, an internalization that easily leads to despair, melancholy, or perhaps even suicide.

The pervasiveness of sin and evil is such that we are compelled, over and over again, to wonder whether the darkness has indeed eclipsed the light. There would seem to be no way to avoid the vortex of violence as it sucks people into its destructiveness so that they either kill or are killed, dominate or are dominated. On this view, even costly forgiveness makes the world seem lighter than it is; violence must be met with counter-violence, injustice with force. By contrast to forgiveness, which even as a craft seems unable adequately to respond to the power of darkness, violence

---

2. I take up these issues again, particularly in relation to the difficulty of envisioning the forgiveness of unrepentant sinners, in chapters 8 and 9.

provides a "counter-craft" whose habits and institutions are deeply ingrained in the world and in our lives. Violence may not be as hopeful as forgiveness, but it seems more realistic and more effective — and, perhaps, more truthful about the way the world really is.

These are powerful claims, and their significance must be confronted if a coherent account of forgiveness is to be adequately articulated and defended. Further, it is also urgent to explore whether there are ways to unlearn and break habits of sin, to stop the cycles of violence and vengeance, to cultivate a politics of holiness. The difficult question that haunts us is whether there are so many people who are unforgiven precisely because there is something deep in us that makes our lives unforgivable.

The argument of this chapter proceeds through four steps. First, I briefly consider a recent film, "Unforgiven," which poses in stark fashion the question of whether violence is the master of us all. Second, I distinguish different ways of construing the issue of whether violence can be unlearned, whether violence is inescapable. Third, I reposition questions about violence within a theological context, suggesting that a Christian account can both confront the pervasiveness of sin and evil *and* sustain a coherent account of forgiveness. Fourth and finally I display a specific example of a person who embodied Christian forgiveness in the midst of a situation of horrifying evil. As with Bonhoeffer, this person understood and embodied the cost of forgiveness, but he did so precisely by showing forth the power of God's peace.

Forgiven No More

Clint Eastwood's 1992 Academy Award–winning film "Unforgiven" is an extraordinarily powerful and unrelenting depiction of a world where forgiveness is assumed to be impossible or, at most, ineffective. Habits of sin, and more specifically of violence, are inescapable; they cannot be unlearned. Violence is the inescapable reality that persistently tears at the fabric of people's lives until everyone is diminished, if not destroyed, by it.

Set in the 1880s, primarily in Wyoming and neighboring states, the film's main character is William Munny. He was "a known thief and murderer, a man of notoriously vicious and intemperate disposition" before he married his wife. But she helped reform him of drinking and wickedness. Since her death from smallpox, he has turned to working a farm in the

Kansas countryside and taking care of his two small children. He seems content to live a relatively isolated life.

He is startled one day by the arrival of a stranger. He initially denies who he is to the young man, fearing that the man has come to kill him for something he did "in the old days." The young man, calling himself "The Schofield Kid," has been told that Munny was "cold as the snow, with no weak nerve, no fear." The Kid wants Munny to join him as a partner in claiming a bounty. The bounty of $1000 has been offered by some prostitutes to anyone who would come to Big Whiskey, Wyoming, and kill — and thus bring vengeance on — two cowboys who have attacked and severely cut one of them.

Munny tells the Kid "I ain't like that any more." His wife has changed his life. The Kid tells him that if he should change his mind, he can catch up with him on the western trail. After the Kid leaves, Munny gives the offer some thought while working with his pigs. He pulls out his guns and begins practicing his shooting. Ironically, Munny in a sense "comes to himself" — like the prodigal son — in the midst of pigs; but it is his violent self that he begins to recover. As Munny struggles to recover his aim, his young children look on in disbelief. Unaware of their father's past, the little girl wonders to her brother, "Did pa used to kill folks?"

Munny decides to go, explaining that he needs the money to feed his kids because his pigs are dying. Before he departs, he takes some flowers over to his wife's grave. He tells his children that he will be home in a couple weeks, and he leaves instructions about where they should go if they need assistance. But his departure is slowed by his inability to get back into the saddle with gun in hand; evidently Munny finds it more difficult to return to his violent habits than he thought. Indeed, he observes out loud that "the horse is getting even with me for the sins of my youth"; but he also tells his children that "your ma showed me the error of my ways."

On his way, Munny struggles with the acknowledgment that, in some sense, there is no need for violence; he can unlearn his habits of violence and learn to live a forgiven and forgiving life. Further, he insists — to himself as much as to an old friend, a black man named Ned, who goes with him — that going on this killing is not a reversion to old habits; he is simply doing it for the money, for the sake of his children.

Just before Munny, Ned, and the Kid arrive, the madam in Big Whiskey despairs that nobody will provide vengeance for the attack. But their arrival gives the women a hopeful glimpse that "justice" will be served. Indeed, the three men enter into a shoot-out with several cowboys from the Bar-T as they seek to kill the two cowboys who have attacked the prostitute. After a few shots, it is clear that Ned's heart is not in it anymore. So Munny takes control and shoots and kills the accomplice to the attack on the prostitute. In the meantime, Ned announces that he is heading back to Kansas and promises to look in on Munny's children. And Munny promises to bring Ned his share of the bounty.

A short while later, the prostitute who has been attacked is grieved when she hears that one of her victimizers has actually been killed. The sheriff has a quite different response when he hears about the killing. He forms a posse to look for the assassins. Before they depart, however, the sheriff is notified that people from the Bar-T have caught Ned. The sheriff brings Ned to the jail for questioning and a whipping. But when Ned is caught lying about the names of his two partners, the whippings become even more severe.

At daybreak, the Kid kills the other cowboy in the Bar-T's outhouse while Munny covers for him. After they flee to the sound of gunshots, they find themselves in a calm setting on a mountainside. As they drink whiskey together, the Kid asks Munny if that was what it was like in the old days. Munny can't remember the old days; he was drunk most of the time. The Kid, retelling the killing of the cowboy between shots of whiskey and amid tears, admits that — contrary to earlier bravado about being a "killer" — this was the first person he has ever killed. He plaintively observes, "It doesn't seem right. He'll never breathe again. . . . All on account of pulling a trigger." Munny's response is poignant, though delivered matter-of-factly: "It's a hell of a thing, killing a man." The Kid finally explains it to himself by saying, "I guess he had it coming." To which Munny responds, "We all have it coming." For Munny, there are no easy divisions between good guys and bad, between victimizers and victims. The world, and human lives, are far murkier than an ability to salve consciences by saying that someone or some group "had it coming."

As Munny and the Kid are talking, one of the prostitutes brings them the bounty. She also reports that Ned was killed by the sheriff, perhaps accidentally; further, she indicates that his body is on display in front of the saloon with a sign indicating that this is what happens to assassins. As she recalls what she heard Ned confessing about his and Munny's past, Munny begins to chug the whiskey — perhaps to stiffen his resolve, perhaps to try to forget once again his past, perhaps to stiffen his resolve precisely by forgetting his complex past of both violence and glimpses of peaceableness.

But the Kid will not join Munny on this killing. "I ain't like you, Will," he tells Munny. And so he gives Munny his gun. As Munny returns to town, he throws away the now empty whiskey bottle. He enters the crowded saloon, where the sheriff is congratulating the posse on its performance. Munny kills the saloon owner for decorating his saloon with Ned. As he points his rifle at several other men, the sheriff, Little Bill, tells him: "You're William Munny, from out of Missouri, killed women and children." To which Munny responds, "That's right. I killed women and children. I've killed just about everything that walked or crawled at one time or another. And I'm here to kill you, Little Bill, for what you did to Ned."

Munny then kills five men in rapid succession and wounds the sheriff; he clears the rest of the people out the back. As Munny stares over the wounded sheriff, the sheriff tells him, "I don't deserve this. To die like this. I was building a house." Munny responds, " 'Deserve' got nothing to do with this." The sheriff defiantly asserts, "I'll see you in hell, William Munny." "Yea," Munny agrees, as he kills him. As Munny leaves town, he yells to any and all people that they had better give Ned a proper burial, or else he'll come back and kill them all. As he rides out of town, and as the film ends, there is very little life left; the prostitutes and a few of the townspeople watch with lifeless horror.

Despite the horrifying violence in the film, it does not glorify violence the way many westerns do. It is far too morally serious for such a depiction. Rather, it suggests that human beings are filled with both the possibility of goodness and the capacity for great destruction. In this sense there is no stable *self* that can be presumed to be fundamentally good or fundamentally evil; rather, our selves are battlefields in which we can never claim complete control. Either we are constrained by the forces of sin and evil, the habits of death, or we learn to be constrained by the very practices of forgiveness and reconciliation through which God's peace is communicated.

Further, the story shows the fragility of our commitments to unlearn and break our habits of sin, even when there is a desire to do so. If such commitments are to be sustained, they require supportive friendships, practices, and institutions that enable the unlearning of destructive habits and the cultivation of holy ones. The film suggests that those friendships, practices, and institutions are absent precisely because of their fragility in the face of violence and vengeance. It takes only a moment to destroy lives through violence, but it takes lifetimes to cultivate alternative patterns and practices of forgiveness, of trust, of love.

In what sense, then, is this a depiction of a world "unforgiven"? Or, more precisely, who is unforgiven and why? In one sense, the answer is clearly William Munny. Though he had briefly glimpsed forgiveness as a new life with his wife and children, he eventually returns in the wake of his wife's death to the unforgiven world of violence and vengeance — albeit initially by self-deceptively attributing his motives solely to getting some money for his children. But the film also suggests a more extensive and complex picture of who is unforgiven and why.

In this context it is not only William Munny who is unforgiven; so also are the rest of the characters. At times the film suggests the rather extreme picture that we are all unforgiven because we are all unforgivable. From this perspective, forgiveness simply has no place in a world of violence; violence must be met with counter-violence, injustice with force. Even those who seek to avoid the use of violence all too easily become its casualties. But this equation of being unforgiven with being unforgivable is not the film's dominant perspective.

That is, the film does not necessarily suggest that violence is somehow "natural" to people, or that we are biologically or ontologically doomed to violence. After all, the Schofield Kid finds it extremely difficult to live with the consequences of having killed someone. Even Will Munny has to drink heavily to sustain his impulse to wreak vengeance. But the film does suggest that violence is an extremely difficult, indeed perhaps impossible, habit to unlearn and break once we are formed into it. The darkest aspect of the film is its suggestion that we are so habituated to violence that we are now — historically, socially, and politically — incapable of unlearning it.

So the film leaves us with the haunting fear that perhaps violence is indeed the master of us all. And anyone who reflects seriously about either the history of human life or the contemporary realities of abuse, violence, and destructiveness cannot but be haunted by the possibility. But before we succumb to such a despairing, though possibly accurate, judgment, we need to distinguish different ways in which to construe the seeming inescapability of violence, to construe our inability to unlearn violent patterns and practices.

Can Violence Be Unlearned?

It may be impossible to unlearn violence because it is inscribed in the way things are, in the very nature of the world. From such a perspective, the only way people can escape violence is by denying the reality of who we are as human beings and the reality of how the world is constructed. In this sense we are ontologically determined by violence.

To be sure, there are different premises that might lead to such an argument, even (or especially) beyond the gut-level political judgments embodied in the view that "whoever has the most guns wins." For example, the argument might be predicated on sociobiological judgments about the genetically and biologically determined character of human nature drawn from analogies with the violence and aggression seen in the animal kingdom.[3] Or the argument might be predicated on a hypothetically constructed theory about the original "state of nature" of human beings in intensive conflict before the development of political and social arrangements.[4] Or the argument might be predicated on metaphysical judgments about the relations between "presence" and "absence" in language and the bearing of language on human life, relations that suggest the impossibility of ever escaping patterns of violence.[5]

Such examples are not exhaustive, nor are they meant to suggest that the various positions are entirely compatible in their judgments about what people can or should do in the face of the inescapability of violence. Indeed, there are sometimes sharp oppositions in their readings of how, precisely, we are to understand the inescapability of violence. Even so, such positions do share the view that violence is inscribed, in one way or another, in the way things are and that we are compelled to acknowledge the inescapability of violence in our personal, social, and political lives. This acknowledgment can lead to a variety of normative judgments, ranging from a glorification of aggression and violence (and hence a celebration of martial "virtues") to an ethical refusal to endorse violence, seeking to minimize — but never escape — the violence that determines the world and our existence in it.

Friedrich Nietzsche represents a controversial and important example of the position that violence is inescapable because it is inscribed in the way things are, in the very nature of the world. While Nietzsche does not develop his arguments in precisely the same way as any of the examples offered above, his views overlap with each of them. Further, his normative judgments about what people should do in the face of this inescapability of violence also overlap — or at least can be read as overlapping — with a range of responses that might be offered.

3. See, for example, the arguments of sociobiologist Edward O. Wilson in *On Human Nature* (Cambridge: Harvard University, 1978).

4. See, for example, Thomas Hobbes, *Leviathan,* and the political theories (and accounts of international relations) that depend on Hobbes's basic picture.

5. See, for example, the essay by Jacques Derrida, "Violence and Metaphysics," in his *Writing and Difference,* tr. A. Bass (Chicago: University of Chicago, 1978). For an important exposition of the ethical possibilities of Nietzsche's and Derrida's position, see Romand Coles, "Storied Others and Possibilities of *Caritas*: Milbank and Neo-Nietzschean Ethics," *Modern Theology* 8/4 (October 1992) pp. 331-351.

Nietzsche's ideas are difficult to summarize, partly because of their complexity and partly because of the intentionally elliptical way in which he thought and wrote. But his overall perspective is marked by a clear recognition of the inescapability of violence. Though he does not posit genetically or biologically determined accounts of human nature, he does deploy arguments drawn from analogies with the animal kingdom.[6] Though he does not posit a "state of nature" in which people were in conflict and sought to kill each other prior to the emergence of political arrangements, he does deploy a "genealogy" of morals that begins with a "master morality" in which the strong "naturally" ruled over the weak. Though he does not explicitly posit a metaphysics of "presence" and "absence" in language and its bearing on human life, he does deploy arguments that suggest that our very uses of language involve struggles for power and the use of violence. In the beginning, suggests Nietzsche, was violence, and so it has been ever since.

It is, however, a complex question whether Nietzsche celebrates that violence, the predatory strength of masters over their weak and weakened prey. Nietzsche certainly wants to "unwrite" the Christian narrative, which, he thinks, glorifies weakness and dulls people's will to power and drains away true heroic excellence.[7] From such a perspective, forgiveness is genuinely immoral because it glorifies weakness; Christianity is, in

6. Note the following quotation from the First Essay of Nietzsche's *On the Genealogy of Morals* (tr. Walter Kaufman and R. J. Hollingdale, ed. Walter Kaufman [New York: Vintage, 1989] section 13, pp. 44-45):

> That lambs dislike great birds of prey does not seem strange: only it gives no ground for reproaching these birds of prey for bearing off little lambs. And if the lambs say among themselves: "these birds of prey are evil; and whoever is least like a bird of prey, but rather its opposite, a lamb — would he not be good?" there is no reason to find fault with this institution of an ideal, except perhaps that the birds of prey might view it a little ironically and say: "*we* don't dislike them at all, these good little lambs; we even love them; nothing is more tasty than a tender lamb." To demand of strength that it should *not* be a desire to overcome, a desire to throw down, a desire to become master, a thirst for enemies and resistances and triumphs, is just as absurd as to demand of weakness that it should express itself as strength.

7. See John Milbank, *Theology and Social Theory* (Oxford: Blackwell, 1990) p. 389, where he rightly suggests that Nietzsche's *Genealogy of Morals* is an attempt to counter the narrative told by Augustine in *The City of God*. Augustine emphasizes the priority of God's gift of peaceableness in Creation, but Nietzsche wants to subvert that by stressing that in the beginning was violence, not peace.

Nietzsche's eyes, a "religion of pity," one that undermines that which is truly admirable about human beings. There is no place for forgiveness in a world of predatory conquest, survival of the fittest, and sustained power through the willingness to use violence.

Such a reading of Nietzsche, at least in some of his writings, is not implausible. Indeed, that is the Nietzsche that was attractive to the Nazis in the construction of their political outlook and practices. It is not, however, the only account of Nietzsche's thought, nor even, on balance, the most persuasive one. For while Nietzsche wants to stress the inescapability of violence, the importance of the will to power, and the dangers of a weak-willed celebration of pity, he also emphasizes in several places the significance of gift-giving.[8] Indeed, he calls gift-giving the "highest virtue." Nietzsche recognizes that gift-giving is inextricably bound up with questions of power and violence, and he criticizes those whose talk about gift-giving and receiving ignore these questions.

Nietzsche's account of gift-giving is significant in its distinction of power from violence.[9] Gift-giving uses the strength of power as a way of minimizing, though never escaping, the reality of violence. From such a perspective, life is sustained by the effective utilization of power, which requires a recognition that violence is inescapably part of how things really are in the world; even so, we ought also to recognize that gift-giving can be a power that is generous in its very being. This reading of Nietzsche moves away from the Nazi glorification of predatory violence to a more sustained ethical and political concern.[10]

In this sense, there is a great deal to be said for Nietzsche's account. After all, he rightly notes how easily notions such as forgiveness can be turned into a glorification of weakness. One hardly needs much imagination to see how therapeutic claims that humans are "weak, needy, and fallible" are susceptible to Nietzsche's critique. Further, Nietzsche takes with great seriousness the pervasiveness of power and violence and, at least in some places, suggests ethical and political ways of living amidst that pervasiveness.

8. See in particular Nietzsche's *Thus Spoke Zarathustra*.

9. As Nicholas Lash has rightly emphasized, a failure properly to distinguish power and violence besets Milbank's account of Nietzsche in *Theology and Social Theory*. For Lash's argument, see "Not Quite Politics or Power?" *Modern Theology* 8/4 (October 1992) pp. 353-364.

10. Such a concern can also be found in Derrida's essay "Violence and Metaphysics."

Even so, Nietzsche and his heirs, along with fellow travelers who might disavow connections to Nietzsche, remain convinced that violence cannot be unlearned because it is inscribed in the way things are, in the very nature of the world. But there is another way to construe the seeming inescapability of violence, a construal that both acknowledges the ways in which human beings are trapped in webs of violence (and so is not susceptible to criticism for pretending that the world is all light) *and* refuses to concede that this is the way reality either *necessarily* is or ought to be (and so is not convinced that the world ultimately is darkness). But this construal is difficult to sustain. Iris Murdoch has posed the problem well: "How is one to connect the realism which must involve a clear-eyed contemplation of the misery and evil of the world with a sense of an uncorrupted good without the latter idea becoming the merest consolatory dream? (I think this puts a central problem in moral philosophy.)"[11]

One version of such a connection would suggest that peace is logically and ontologically prior to violence, friendship prior to conflict, goodness prior to sin. Rather than asserting the fundamental character of violence, which makes cooperation and peace the task that must be explained, this construal insists that peace, friendship, and goodness are both the beginning from which the world was — and more specifically humans were — created and the *telos* toward which all things are — or at least ought to be — striving. But it would also involve a clear-eyed contemplation of the very real misery, evil, and violence that afflicts us in this world. Perhaps unsurprisingly (though as yet unpersuasively to a thinker such as Murdoch), such a construal is grounded in the Christian doctrine of the Triune God.

But, it might easily be asked, on what grounds could such a suggestion be made? Does it not involve special pleading, the introduction of God as a solution just when the going gets tough? Or, to change the metaphor, does such a claim involve a flight of fancy, escaping a genuine confrontation with the way the world really is?

Such questions have considerable force, and it must be acknowledged that people — including, perhaps especially, Christians — have sometimes invoked God and notions of peace, friendship, and goodness as a way of denying the horrifying reality and the seeming inescapability of the violence and destructiveness that mark our world. Nietzsche's critique of Christianity as a "religion of pity" is biting, at least as it is directed to the ways in which Christianity has often been understood and practiced in modernity.[12]

11. Iris Murdoch, *The Sovereignty of Good* (New York: Schocken, 1971) p. 61.
12. This is a point that has been nicely developed by Merold Westphal. Westphal

But whether those questions are finally persuasive has to do with our reading of "the way the world really is." For there is no single determinative argument that could resolve whether "what is" ought to be understood ultimately in terms of peace or violence. We have competing narratives of the way the world is. Depending on which narrative one subscribes to and seeks to live in, one will have either problems understanding "goodness" (e.g., How is it that there seem to be peaceable people and communities living in a determinatively violent world?) or problems understanding "evil" (e.g., How is it that evil and violence seem so pervasive in a world created by the Triune God's gift of peaceful love and harmony?). Violence is not the only form that evil takes, but it is certainly one of the most destructive and pervasive forces of evil. Those who are convinced that violence *is* incapable of being unlearned have the former problem, whereas those who believe that violence is neither the beginning nor the end of our existence have the latter problem. Put differently, what anyone takes to be evil depends on beliefs about what the world is ultimately like. Hence, there will be sharp divergences about the potential significance of forgiveness between those whose convictions are grounded in the Triune God and those who are convinced that — for whatever reason — violence is the fundamental reality of the world that creatures inhabit.

To be sure, even those who believe that peace is prior to violence and that forgiveness is a central practice for bringing healing and reconciliation into the midst of violence may continue to feel the force of the question: Is violence the master of us all? This is particularly true for those who have suffered the effects of violence far more often, and with far greater severity, than those who have typically been the "masters" of the violence. Gustavo Gutiérrez, at the end of a sustained reflection on the Book of Job, writes:

> It needs to be realized, however, that for us Latin Americans the question is not precisely "How are we to do theology after Auschwitz?" The reason is that in Latin America we are still experiencing every day the violation of human rights, murder, and the torture that we find so blameworthy in the Jewish holocaust of World War II. Our task here is to find the

---

argues that Nietzsche's critique is a prophetic indictment of the practices of Christianity structurally analogous to the criticisms offered by the biblical prophets (including the prophet Jesus). To be sure, and as Westphal clearly knows, this is not all there is to Nietzsche's project; but Westphal's primary point is crucial. See his *Suspicion and Faith* (Grand Rapids: Eerdmans, 1992). I discuss Nietzsche's argument further, and particularly the significance of his account of revenge, in chapter 8.

words with which to talk about God in the midst of the starvation of millions, the humiliation of races regarded as inferior, discrimination against women, especially women who are poor, systematic social injustice, a persistent high rate of infant mortality, those who simply "disappear" or are deprived of their freedom, the sufferings of peoples who are struggling for their right to live, the exiles and the refugees, terrorism of every kind, and the corpse-filled common graves of Ayacucho. What we must deal with is not the past but, unfortunately, a cruel present and a dark tunnel with no apparent end.[13]

Violence seems inescapable because of the personal, social, and political conditions in which people are forced to live. Amid such massive suffering, it no doubt seems almost unthinkable, and even more unlivable, that there are ways of escaping or unlearning violence.

Almost. Yet violence only *seems* inescapable, because Gutiérrez, and countless others like him, continue to cling to the hope found in the story of the Triune God whose Creation comes by way of a peaceable gift, whose redemption through costly forgiveness inaugurates God's peaceable Kingdom, and whose promised consummation of that Kingdom sustains people in the midst of both joys and griefs, loves and losses. That is to say that Gutiérrez would, I think, share the conviction that violence and vengeance are not "natural" to us creatures, that they are neither our beginning nor (or so we hope) our *telos*. But then, the question might rightly be asked, how have sin and evil — and, more specifically, violence — become so pervasive? And have Christians provided — or, more radically, *can* Christians provide — a theological perspective that accounts for this pervasiveness?

Engaging the Pervasiveness of Sin and Evil

A prior question, however, also emerges. Before sin and evil can become pervasive, they have to be possible. And, so the familiar question goes, *if* Creation emerges from the gracious and peaceable self-gift of the Triune God, whence came evil and violence? Though numerous attempts through the ages have struggled with this question, with varying degrees of success and failure, there is no adequate "solution" — nor is there simply one

13. Gustavo Gutiérrez, *On Job: God-Talk and the Suffering of the Innocent*, tr. Matthew J. O'Connell (Maryknoll: Orbis, 1987) p. 102.

"problem" of evil. The notion that there is *one* problem of evil only arrives with the Enlightenment and its correlative assumption that the real issues are theism and atheism.[14] Christian theology ought to have little stake in that debate, for Christians are not concerned primarily with theism (i.e., the notion that there is a general object of ultimate concern, a divinity); we are concerned, rather, to narrate the doctrine of God's Trinity. The Christian affirmation of the Trinity is not a notion "added to" a theistic affirmation; it *is* the primary affirmation about the God Christians worship.

Hence Christians should not seek fully to "explain" the problem of evil in relation to a philosophically postulated concept of divinity. Rather, Christians seek to narrate the Triune God's peaceable gift of Creation, God's presence in and through Israel and the life, death, and resurrection of Jesus of Nazareth, and God's promise to bring about the consummation of Creation in the Kingdom. It is in relation to this narrative of the Triune God that Christians ought to situate sin and evil, of which violence is a crucial specification. In this context, problems of sin and evil arise *as problems* precisely because of their incompatibility with Christian claims about the gracious character of God's love, forgiveness, and peaceableness. As Kenneth Surin has suggested, "In an identifiably Christian context, the 'problem of evil' arises (at least in part) when *particular* narratives of events of pain, dereliction, anguish, oppression, torture, humiliation, degradation, injustice, hunger, godforsakenness, and so on, come into collision with the Christian community's narratives, which are inextricably bound up with the redeeming reality of the triune God."[15] These collisions of narratives require that Christians engage problems of sin and evil, but it requires them to do so within the context of the narrative of the Triune God's work of creating, redeeming, and sustaining the world.

That is, although I cannot offer a historically causal account of the pervasiveness of sin and evil (particularly since the Christian doctrine of Creation is not about historical causation in these sorts of ways), it is nonetheless important to grapple with the empirical realities of sin and evil that have afflicted and continue to afflict so many people. Those afflictions give rise to the painfully authentic cries of Gustavo Gutiérrez and of many

14. For impressive historical and conceptual arguments that this is the case, see, for example, Michael J. Buckley, *At the Origins of Modern Atheism* (New Haven: Yale University, 1987); Kenneth Surin, *Theology and the Problem of Evil* (Oxford: Basil Blackwell, 1986); and Terrence J. Tilley, *The Evils of Theodicy* (Washington: Georgetown University, 1991).

15. Kenneth Surin, *Theology and the Problem of Evil*, p. 27.

nameless people who suffer and die in conditions of outrageous violence and degradation.

I have already identified several ways in which habits of sin become entrenched in our lives and, further, ways in which those habits can produce reified positions of either victimizers or victims. These entrenched habits are particularly pernicious in situations of violence and abuse, where they become so ingrained that one wonders whether they even *can* be unlearned, regardless of what we might desire. As William Munny discovered, in some sense to his own regret, violence easily becomes a habit that is difficult — if not impossible — to break. That is true both for the perpetrators of violence and for those who suffer from its effects. People become trapped in habits that create vicious cycles of violence and vengeance. As Thomas Aquinas rightly insisted, habits can be formed not only by what we do but by what is done to us.

These habits, particularly in relation to violence, are even further entrenched because they get inscribed in our bodies and, indeed, even in our souls. So Simon Harak has instructively suggested that, for Aquinas, "the habits of the soul are caused by our capacity to be moved by another. When we combine that insight with what we have already seen [about the effects of violence], we can understand that the soul is affected through embodiment, and learns mainly through touch. Habits are in the body, but principally in the soul. These habits of the soul and the body are acquired by repeated acts, through the agency of another, and mainly through touch."[16] This is so because, contrary to popular bifurcations of "body" and "soul" or "body" and "spirit," human beings are embodied spirits, ensouled bodies. Such a perspective helps to explain why the effects of violence, and more particularly severe physical or emotional abuse, perdure through time even after — and sometimes long after — the actual attacks have stopped.

Indeed, the effects of this violence are pervasive beyond the actual willed intention of individual persons or even of groups. They perdure through time in our bodies and in our souls, and also in the lived realities of larger institutional structures. As a result, we human beings find ourselves in relations — personal and systemic — that are always already marked by the effects of violence and destruction. Further, these effects are unequally distributed among human beings. Rowan Williams puts the matter well:

> We are all of us, in some measure, shut off from each other: our own individual options for violence fade into a world where there is *already*

16. Simon Harak, "Abuse and Embodiment," *Modern Theology* 11/3 (July 1995) pp. 315-340.

a history of oppression and victimization: our moral and spiritual growth does not occur in a vacuum. And so, before we can be conscious of it, the system of oppressor-victim relations absorbs us. It is this "already" which theology (sometimes rather unhelpfully) refers to as original sin — the sense of primordial "diminution" from which we all suffer before ever we are capable of understanding or choice.[17]

Original sin thus denotes not simply *my* tendency or *another's* tendency to will sinful acts; more pervasively, it reflects the inescapable networks of violence and diminution that separate us from one another and, most determinatively, from God.

The crucial question, then, becomes how we learn to cope with and respond to the sin and evil — the violence, the diminution — that perdures in our bodies and in our souls. One corrupting response, embodied quite powerfully in William Munny, is the assertion of brute force. If one can gain access to sufficient force, then it is possible to destroy or incapacitate others through violence, through the threat of violence, or through the continuation of those systems that enable the maintenance of dominance over the other(s). Hence we end up with a slightly rewritten "survival of the fittest." Violence may be the master of us all, and we all may get it in the end; in the meantime, however, it is better to be the master, dominant over others. Given the appeal of this perspective to many people, it is not surprising to find so frequently the lure of wars of conquest, of torture, of abuse, of cold-blooded murder, and of the desire to maintain systems of dominance — so long as "I" am the one who is conquering, torturing, abusing, murdering, and dominating.

But there is also a second problematic response, one that offers a mirror-image of the first. This is the internalization of the effects of violence through what the ancients called *melancholia*. To be sure, there are diverse causes of melancholy and of what we often call depression, and some of these causes have only recently been discovered and treated. For example, depression may occur through various biological and chemical reactions in the brain, reactions that require the countervailing forces of a salt such as lithium.

Even so, a melancholic outlook or severe depression can also be a reflection of a violence internalized, of a refusal or an inability to return violence for violence. Thus depression may occur because of psychological reasons related to the perdurance in the soul of habits of violence and abuse, or it may occur because of moral misgivings about the inappropriateness of responding to violence with more violence. It may also occur because

17. Rowan Williams, *Resurrection* (New York: Pilgrim, 1982) p. 24.

the disparities of power are so great that there cannot be an adequate response to violence except through internalizing its effects. Or it may occur among Christians as a by-product of reductive or corrupt understandings or practices of forgiveness.

Whatever its causes, the effects of a melancholic perspective or of severe depression are highly destructive. William Styron, a writer who survived an episode of such depression, describes their effects in this way:

> Sometimes, though not every often, such a disturbed mind will turn to violent thoughts regarding others. But with their minds turned agonizingly inward, people with depression are usually dangerous only to themselves. The madness of depression is, generally speaking, the antithesis of violence. It is a storm indeed, but a storm of murk. Soon evident are the slowed-down responses, near paralysis, psychic energy throttled back close to zero. Ultimately, the body is affected and feels sapped, drained.[18]

This description is not of the bare assertion of force and violence, but rather of its mirror image: the contraction of the self into a narrower and smaller world, until one feels so helpless — and indeed hopeless — that it becomes impossible to imagine how to go on. On occasion such depression erupts into a brief but violently destructive act (the "final" act of grandeur, a shooting spree, or a car bomb, etc.); but it might also, and more typically, simply result in the disappearance of the self through suicide.[19] Julia Kristeva has characterized the effects of such a contraction of the self as "Merely an abyssal suffering that does not succeed in signifying itself and, having lost meaning, loses life."[20]

---

18. William Styron, *Darkness Visible: A Memoir of Madness* (New York: Random House, 1990) p. 47.

19. It is important that I not be misunderstood here. There is no single cause of suicide, nor should there be any single moral evaluation of suicide. As Styron rightly insists, in some cases suicide may be the result of the unbearability of pain. He writes, "the pain of severe depression is quite unimaginable to those who have not suffered it, and it kills in many instances because its anguish can no longer be borne. The prevention of many suicides will continue to be hindered until there is a general awareness of the nature of this pain" (*Darkness Visible*, p. 33). There are also, to be sure, acts of suicide that are defiant acts of abandonment. My point in this context is not a moral evaluation of this or that act of suicide; rather it is the ways in which the "always already" character of violence in our world, and in our lives, may lead people to feel that there is no option other than recourse to violence or internalization of violence.

20. Julia Kristeva, *Black Sun*, tr. Leon Roudiez (New York: Columbia University, 1989) p. 189.

Kristeva goes on to suggest that forgiveness, understood in the light of the crucified and risen Christ, is the only solution to the alternative mirror-images of murder and depression. Such forgiveness provides the possibility of new life, of escaping the dance of death produced by sin and evil.[21] From such a perspective forgiveness cannot merely refer backward, as if only to the cancellation of some past action. It also points forward, to a refusal to be trapped in cycles of violence and thus also to be trapped by the conviction that we are all ultimately condemned to death and destruction. If forgiveness entails such a refusal, then forgiven-ness becomes a lifelong process of un-learning habits and patterns of sin and evil and learning the habits and patterns of God's peaceful charity and the promise of new life.

Hence Christians should not deny the darkness of sin and evil in general or of violence (afflicted or internalized) in particular. But neither should we to seek to explain it in some reductive sense. Rather we ought to seek to counteract that darkness through induction into, and a lifelong process of learning to live in, the light of the Triune God. As John Milbank has suggested,

> How does it help though (one might protest) to imagine a state of total peace, when we are locked in a world of deep-seated conflict which it would be folly to deny or evade? It helps, because it allows us to unthink the necessity of violence, and exposes the manner in which the assumption of an inhibition of an always prior violence helps to preserve violence in motion. But it helps more, because it indicates that there is a way to act in a violent world which assumes the ontological priority of non-violence, and this way is called "forgiveness of sins."[22]

In this context, it becomes clearer why forgiveness is a notion, and more importantly an embodied way of life, at the very heart of Christian theology. But even more, it also becomes clearer how and why many objections to Christianity are objections to one or another aspect of Christian forgiveness; they object to the claim that forgiveness might be either possible or effective in a world whose darkness is such that evil cannot be avoided or violence unlearned. Such objections are found, for example, in Nietzsche and his heirs, as well as in Ivan Karamazov.[23] However, as Kristeva notes,

21. See Kristeva, *Black Sun*, p. 192.

22. Milbank, *Theology and Social Theory*, p. 411. Of course the real task is not simply to "unthink" the necessity of violence, but to *live* differently.

23. I return to Ivan's protest and to the force of these objections after developing my own constructive proposal. See the discussion of Ivan in chapter 9.

the forgiveness that is objected to — understood as connivance with degradation, moral softening, and refusal of power — is perhaps "only the
image one has of decadent Christianity."[24]

To be sure, such a "decadent" Christianity is imaged not only by
the objections of Nietzsche and others; it is also, regrettably, embodied
in too many modern Christian accounts themselves — particularly as
found in accounts of "therapeutic" forgiveness. But even those who do
not want to evade the darkness of our world can remain beset by the
legacy of a truncated conception of Christian forgiveness. For example,
Marie Fortune, who has done a great deal to bring situations of family
violence and sexual abuse to public attention, particularly within Christian contexts, nonetheless thinks of forgiveness as a "last step" that requires justice as a prerequisite.[25] Her perspective is certainly understandable as a protest against the "cheap grace" so characteristic of many
Christian churches, pastors, and laypeople. There has been a tendency to
make forgiveness so easy as to deny the reality of the suffering of those
who have been sinned against. Even so, to turn forgiveness·into a "final
step" is to concede that it is ultimately a psychological category for
coping, whereas what we really need are more *forceful* mechanisms designed to produce justice.[26]

Justice is important; even so, there is a significant difference between
a conception of "justice" understood as a means of inhibiting violence
through structured processes of resolution and a conception that is understood as virtuous habits and patterns of relationship contextualized
within a wider account of the forgiveness wrought by the Triune God.[27]
For Christians, forgiveness is not a first or even a final "step"; it is rather
an embodied way of life. Christians cannot be content with standards of
justice found in a political constitution, much less in popular therapeutic
currency; rather, Christians learn the fullness of what justice *is,* and what
it entails, precisely by participating in such Christian practices as baptism,
eucharist, and interpreting Scripture. Unsurprisingly, these are also ex-

24. Kristeva, *Black Sun,* p. 190.

25. Marie M. Fortune, "Forgiveness: The Last Step," in Anne L. Horton and Judith
A. Williamson (eds.), *Abuse and Religion: When Praying Isn't Enough* (New York: Lex-
ington, 1988) pp. 215-220.

26. See below, chapter 8, for a more extensive critique of this bifurcation of
forgiveness (as a personal, private act) and justice (as a political, public act).

27. See the comments of John Paul II in his encyclical "Dives in Misericordia,"
Origins 10/26 (December 11, 1980), esp. p. 414. There he notes that "True mercy is, so
to speak, the most profound source of justice."

amples of practices through which Christians learn what forgiveness is and what it entails.[28]

Even so, in some sense, the force of the original question remains: Is violence the master of us all? I might have been able to suggest some theoretical and, more specifically, theological resources for rejecting the claim that violence is our master — resources that, to be sure, will require much more conceptual elucidation in Parts II and III. But is that so much theorizing in the wind? Can we unlearn habits of sin and evil, break apart the cycles of violence, in practice? After all, the concerns of people such as Smedes and Fortune, no less than of William Munny and Nietzsche, are about how people actually can live and should live. So, in some sense, the answer to the question cannot remain at the level of theory; it also has to be displayed, if possible, in the lives of particular people and communities.

For Christians, this involves bringing God's reconciling action in Jesus Christ to bear, through both word and deed, in the concrete situations in which people find themselves. In some situations this may require heroic action and suffering, whereas in other situations this may involve more prosaic patterns of reconstruction. But in whatever situations we find ourselves, responding to sin and evil — and particularly to situations of violence — will involve us in seeing forgiveness as an innovative gesture, patterned in Christ, that breaks apart those habits and forces that diminish and destroy. In this sense, forgiveness is an invitation to imagine and embody a future, a future revealed in God's Kingdom that is not bound by the past or condemned to repeat it.[29]

In later chapters I will explore situations of forgiveness in more "ordinary" circumstances of life. However, if part of the charge against Christian forgiveness is that the world simply is too dark to enable forgiveness to be effective, then it is instructive to return to one of the darkest times of human history: Nazi Germany. There is a danger in doing so, for sometimes we have so demonized Nazi Germany as to make it seem that this is the only time when destructive violence has been systematically perpetrated. It was neither the first nor the last. But Dietrich Bonhoeffer's story shows that, despite the terror of death and destruction unleashed by Nazi

---

28. See below, particularly chapter 6, for further discussion of Christian practices of forgiveness and their links to justice.

29. This point is emphasized by Hannah Arendt, *The Human Condition* (Chicago: University of Chicago, 1958) pp. 236-243. Arendt's perspective offers some rich resources, though her own reading of the Gospel narratives on forgiveness is problematic.

Germany, it was also a time that produced some eloquent witnesses to the costly yet enlivening shape of God's forgiveness.

Therefore I conclude this chapter with a brief explication of another life that embodies the light of Christian forgiveness in the midst of Nazi Germany's darkness. The life is Ian MacMillan's fictionalized yet accurate portrait of the true story of Maximilian Kolbe in his novel *Orbit of Darkness*. Kolbe was a Roman Catholic priest who gave up his life in a Nazi concentration camp so that another person, a Jew, might live. From some standpoints, the story does not and cannot make "sense." A Christian way of making sense of the story, and showing that it indeed makes perfect sense, will only become fully apparent in later chapters of this book. This is because Kolbe's life and death are inextricably situated in the larger story of God's self-gift in Jesus Christ and the practices of Christian life through which that story is embodied.

Forgiven and Forgiving

Orbit of Darkness begins in Auschwitz on July 30, 1941, in Roll Call Square, Block 14A.[30] One of the prisoners, Szweda, number 8616, marvels at the camp deputy commandant's absolute freedom to do whatever he wants in the camp. Szweda watches with admiration as the commandant begins a selection process that is a reprisal for an escape. Ten prisoners will die by starvation. One man, initially chosen for the selection, pleads with the commandant that he be spared for the sake of his family. At that point a man emerges from the lineup, and Szweda observes that it is "that little priest," the one people talk about because "he holds services and sometimes gives away his rations" (p. 4). The priest's action startles the camp guards, who draw their rifles and machine pistols into ready position. As the priest speaks, the deputy commandant becomes momentarily flustered. Szweda wonders "what the priest could have said that would crack the exterior of superiority and absolute power" (p. 5). The priest has asked to take the other man's place. The deputy commandant assumes the priest is insane, while Szweda wonders why he had not committed suicide by throwing himself onto the electric wire. As the selection ends, the priest is taken away with nine other men. Szweda has "the image of the priest's face burned into

---

30. Ian MacMillan, *Orbit of Darkness* (New York: Harcourt Brace Jovanovich, 1991). All page references to quotations in this novel will be given parenthetically in the text.

his mind" (p. 5) because there is something so different about the priest's character. But Szweda goes to sleep imagining ways in which he can collaborate with his captors, for he is impressed with their displays of brute strength.

The novel moves from this selection to the first of several vignettes of World War II, told over a period of several years in a variety of voices and from different perspectives. We are taken in alternating chapters to these diverse perspectives and then repeatedly returned in the other chapters to the agonizingly slow pace of time in the concentration camp. Whereas the vignettes move from 1939 to the end of the war in 1945, the tale of the priest's fate happens in a span of little more than two weeks in 1941.

The vignettes of World War II show people trying to survive, doing whatever it takes to resist the darkness. But in many cases, their own beliefs undermine their capacity to offer effective resistance. So one man, who believes that humans are basically nothing better than animals, ends up being hanged by the Nazis in a brute contest of domination. A woman who believes in God and trusts that prayer alone is sufficient ends up having to prostitute her body as a way to survive — until she is used, discarded, and sent off to die. An artist is haunted by his own acts of resistance that have caused others to die, and he fears that there is to be no forgiveness for his action. Others become part of a resistance group that kills Nazis without mercy or emotion, for mercy "plays into the hands of the enemy" (p. 157). The various vignettes display optimists and pessimists, pragmatists and realists, people stimulated by murder and people who must learn to cope with it; but they share the conviction that the violence is inescapable and cannot be unlearned.

When returned in the intervening chapters to Auschwitz, however, we discover people who simply cannot make sense of the priest's action — yet are also haunted by him. The Germans have tried in the past to get to him through beatings, but nothing has been effective. In the starvation cells, one of the guards, a man named Vierck, becomes bothered by singing and praying led by the priest. He even concludes that the singing is coming not only from the men but is now actually "in the bricks" (p. 65). Such singing and praying are examples of the Christian practices that have animated the priest's life and his embodiment of the gospel.

Eventually Nehring, a representative from the deputy commandant's staff, comes to test the priest by offering him a bite of cheese. Nehring mockingly asks where the "saint" is to be found. Nehring is convinced that the priest embodies "the smug self-righteousness of victims, especially those who have given up. They act superior to everything" (p. 85). When Nehring offers the priest the cheese, he notices a "sudden twinge of shocked desire in the priest's face" (pp. 85-86); but then the expression vanishes, and the priest asks that the cheese be given to the other men in the starvation cell. The priest consistently refuses to accept the cheese for himself, and so Nehring leaves with the cheese. But he is satisfied, for he has gotten to the priest — if only for a moment. As Nehring notes, "Did you see his face? I got to him. He's human after all. . . . The way I heard it the little shit had the whole camp wrapped around his finger. . . . The word got round — that this man had somehow made this part of the camp grind to a halt or something, just by volunteering" (p. 86). Even though Nehring is satisfied, however, the guard Vierck is still bothered by the priest's countenance.

Seven days after the priest has entered the starvation cell, his effect on other prisoners continues to be profound. But so also is his effect on some of the guards. As they take a dead prisoner from the cell, the guards are troubled by the priest looking at them. So they command him to look at the floor, not at them. The guards seem to know that the priest's eyes "seared their flesh." Another prisoner observes that the guards are afraid of the priest; they fear him so much that his stare is a curse. The prisoner "laughs at the strange simplicity of it — the priest overcame their excess of power with an excess of selfless love" (p. 103).

By the ninth day, the priest has truly gotten to the guard Vierck, so much so that one of his comrades has considered reporting him so that he can be transferred. But this comrade, a guard named Guerber, also is bothered by the priest. He considers the priest a "nerveless automaton," a "superhuman machine of a priest"; he also recognizes that the priest's act "had no other motivation than a spiritual one" (p. 127). He wonders to himself about the priest: "What, after all, would possess a man to go to the extremes he did? Clearly his doing it in the manner he did was in a way a revolutionary act, because of the way he called such attention to himself. Martyrdom was usually imposed and later made to look like more than it was. But this act was a matter of choice" (pp. 128-129). Guerber is baffled and troubled by the priest; even so, he offers a toast to his comrades in honor of the priest's survival beyond expectations, for "we must honor toughness wherever we find it" (p. 129). The others agree, though Nehring reminds them that he had gotten to the priest by offering him the cheese.

On day eleven, the guard Vierck requests of Nehring that they "do away with" the priest, for the priest is having too great an effect on "the men." It soon becomes apparent that Vierck himself is one of the men who has been affected — particularly by the priest's eyes. Nehring angrily scolds

Vierck, telling him that the priest has "made self-sacrifice a virtue, and by doing that he's fogging our certainty, don't you see? He's using himself as an example to make men out of vermin. Don't you see it in these prisoners' eyes? . . . Now they all walk around acting as if there's some sort of virtue in martyrdom, and all because of this one little man" (p. 173). Further, Nehring thinks that as soon as the priest dies, he will be forgotten. But Vierck is not so sure, for indeed Vierck is listening to something — perhaps the singing in the bricks? — that Nehring cannot hear.

On day twelve, we are reintroduced to the prisoner Szweda, who is hauling away corpses with another prisoner, a young boy. Szweda is now becoming more fearful that he will not be able to collaborate with the Nazis, that his fate may be to become another of the corpses that surround him. The boy, for his part, says that he had thought of committing suicide by throwing himself on the fence; but the priest told him not to, that he needed to live (p. 198). Neither murder nor suicide is an option in the priest's world. Szweda thinks suicide would have been a preferable option, and he is clearly bothered by what the priest is doing. It just does not make any sense.

The thirteenth day opens with the priest praying, "Behold, O Lord, this dreaming skeleton in its feast of the spirit." He remembers to pray for "those who torture us, pray tenfold for the masters of this empire." At the same time, "He feels a throbbing numbness, one of few sensations left to a moribund body that is the sleeve of a mind that has doggedly held its hands cupped under the water of peace. He thinks, that man who offered me cheese — bless him in his trek toward the light" (p. 218). The priest ponders the simplicity of the words "I thirst," clearly reflecting his own tragic circumstances while also evoking another man who uttered those words while hanging from a cross. With the little voice left in his throat, the priest says to a guard peering through the window, "I forgive you." When the guard asks him if he regrets having taken the other man's place, the priest responds, "no." Neither his suffering nor his impending death prevents the priest from continuing his course, refusing the violence that surrounds him and forgiving others in both word and deed.

The fourteenth day in Auschwitz turns to a conversation between Szweda and a group of prisoners who have taken the priest's example to heart. The group has learned to share what they have with one another — the priest has instructed them to "pray over the dead and work to keep the living alive" (p. 237). Szweda is appalled by this behavior and even mocks the intimations that such actions may involve "holiness." As Szweda notes, "when it comes to saving myself in the dark, I couldn't care less who or what it costs. It takes a sense of self-preservation to keep from becoming smoke" (p. 237). In response, one of the other prisoners notes that indeed it is the priest's self-giving that has changed things. Because of the priest, he tells Szweda, "we are no longer the same and the Germans are no longer the same" (p. 238). Further, the prisoner notes that men like Szweda "don't last." He invites Szweda to become a part of their little group that seeks to emulate the priest. When Szweda asks "what group?" the prisoner responds, "The human race" (p. 239). It is as if the priest's lonely yet powerful example glimpses what the human race is truly called and destined to be — even if, perhaps, we find it terribly difficult to be human in that way.

It happens on the fifteenth day. Not yet the priest's death; rather, it is the suicide of the guard Vierck. He cannot bear any longer the pressure of the priest's presence, of the priest's eyes, of the voices and singing. He recognizes in the priest's life, the priest's forgiveness, a call for his own conversion. But he cannot bear the confrontation of his evil with the priest's goodness. And so he hurls himself onto the fence.

Such an action horrifies Nehring. He announces that anyone who mentions the priest's name will be beaten to death. Further, he instructs the guards to "watch for people helping each other or for people giving food away — it is obvious that this lessens their own ability to work, self-sacrificial benevolence notwithstanding. When these acts are observed both parties shall be beaten to death, do you understand?" (p. 261). He thinks this self-sacrificial benevolence is making people smug, and he will have none of it.

Underneath his fury about Vierck's weakness, however, Nehring also recognizes the priest's profound threat to the Nazis simply by his refusal to submit to, and thus reproduce, a world of violence. He recognizes the power that particular lives and practices can have in breaking the cycle of violence. Nehring knows that

> the priest has compromised the stability of a good system. He has lulled these vermin into being convinced that they are men. The horrible fact is that if every one of them were magnetized by the example of his extreme, willful selflessness, then the system would topple. . . . He understands the worst of it now — what the priest has done is a profound secret that is hidden only because it is so obvious, and it is Nehring's job to see that the secret is kept. (p. 262)

The priest embodies a forgiveness that restores the communion of self-giving love, a forgiveness whose origin and purpose are found in the life-giving communion of the God of Jesus Christ. The priest's embodiment of forgiveness, his witness to the power of the crucified and risen Christ, challenges both the inevitability of violence and the security of that violence. It is a secret that is hidden only because it is so obvious.

On the sixteenth day, the Nazis decide to kill the priest more directly through an injection of carbolic acid into his body. People throughout the camp realize that something is going to happen today to their "hero" and "martyr." That realization creates "a kind of spiritual rebellion in the physical deportment of each man" (p. 277). After the priest is killed, one of the prisoners requests that he be buried rather than cremated like everybody else. The request is denied. The guard Guerber knows, however, that the priest's death does not mean it is over. Indeed, as he walks away from the starvation cell, "he is aware that his feet do not feel right on the ground under him, that just a little way beyond the limits of his understanding there is something obviously wrong, although he cannot define it. His best instincts tell him that to protect himself he must avoid thinking about it, as if carefully walking past whatever it is and forcing himself not to look" (p. 280). He knows that in order to cope with what has been done he can neither remember nor look; he must repress both his memory and his vision.

As the priest's body is carried out, several prisoners defy the camp rules and take off their hats in a gesture of respect. Guerber actually intervenes to prevent a young boy from being beaten for having his hat off, though he also feels vaguely embarrassed at the thought of intervening on the boy's behalf. No sooner does the priest's body get taken to the crematorium, however, than two more prisoners are taken to the starvation cells for having been caught stealing. As two guards take the prisoners into the cells, Guerber is left standing at the base of the steps. The novel ends with Guerber watching "the heavy smoke coming from the crematorium chimney" (p. 305).

The Nazis were neither the first nor, regrettably, the last people to engage in systematic oppression and killing. But they did succeed in creating a world of almost total darkness, a world in which violence seemed to be the master of us all, where violence seemed to be inescapable and unlearnable. Yet the rather simple action of a rather simple priest turned the Nazis' world upside down. In his refusal to submit to their violence and thus to reproduce it, and in his refusal to give up hope by throwing himself on the electric wire, the priest pointed toward — indeed embodied — a holiness that is as compelling as it is seemingly nonsensical.

That he did so was the result of his own acknowledgment of what it means to be forgiven and forgiving people, people whose forgiven-ness by the God of Jesus Christ sets us free from the destructive patterns that divide, separate, and kill. The priest's life and death only make sense within the story of a God whose judgment is gracious, whose will is ever directed toward the mercy that brings new life.

The vignettes that surround the story of the priest are a stirring reminder of precisely how dark our world often is. People there were reduced to trying to survive, even if it involved cannibalism, or murder, or prostitution, or to developing patterns of escapist fantasy. But tragically their attempts were often linked to ideologies that presumed the inescapability (or perhaps even the desirability) of violence.

In one vignette, however, two people who have been brought together as resistance fighters are transformed by the birth of a baby. As fighters, they have become preoccupied with questions of killing and being killed: "This past year he finally understood that they would kill until they were killed, and like moths, or grubs, or mosquitoes, they would have fulfilled their mindless, obsessive reason for existing and gone back to the earth. Like the reverse of procreation, their function was to serve the cause of discontinuing the species" (p. 228). In the midst of death and destruction, however, a baby is born to the woman. There they encounter the possibility of new life. The birth gives them a glimpse of hope, suggesting the power of a single person — or even a single birth — to transfigure the future.[31]

Ironically, there was nothing more powerful than the priest's refusal to submit to the Nazis' power. In one of the vignettes of the war, a character says, "Those who give up their lives, at least in principle, become more dangerous to the Germans than planes or tanks. They become the ultimate weapon" (p. 249). This weapon suggests that we need an account of forgiveness that represents not a distorted and distorting weakness (as Nietzsche thought and as Christians have too often actually embodied) but an alternative form of power, a forgiveness whose power is found in Christ's cross and resurrection, a pattern to which the priest's life and death bears witness. For it is this power that breaks apart the cycles of violence and offers a re-turning of the announcement of God's peace. This power shows that violence is neither inescapable nor unlearnable. Nor is it the master of us all. The priest's embodiment of the gospel of Jesus Christ offers a contrast to *Unforgiven*, to William Munny, and to anyone's convictions or fears that violence is the first or final or fundamental reality. We are not condemned to "all get it" either in the end or in the beginning.

31. See also Hannah Arendt's rich reflections on the power of "natality" in *The Human Condition*, esp. pp. 177-178.

There is a way of unlearning sin and evil in general, and violence in particular; it is found in embodying habits and practices of forgiveness in the service of holiness. That way is costly, and, as such, may require a willingness to give up our lives. Perhaps Bonhoeffer was right that the costly character of forgiveness means that the way will not be widely trodden; yet, as the priest so clearly saw, the alternative to embodying forgiveness is not less death, but more horrifying death and destruction, more frightening terror. Further, embodying forgiveness is the way that offers new life and a hopeful future to those who suffer *and* to those who inflict suffering. And, perhaps, if Christians were to embody the habits and practices of forgiveness more faithfully, there would be less need for heroic examples of martyrdom. Or so the lessons of the rise and fall of Nazi Germany would suggest, lessons that we have as yet failed to learn well.

That is, we Christians have too often failed to embody our own best insights and practices concerning forgiveness. We need to relocate our practices and understandings of forgiveness in the work of the Triune God because that context enables us to make sense of the extraordinary lives and deaths of people whose embodiment of forgiveness shines forth the light of God's love in the midst of a world darkened by sin and evil. That is to say, if we are to sustain practices and understandings of forgiveness that are neither co-opted by a "therapeutic" lightness nor undermined by violent and sinful darkness, then we need to explicate more fully the theological context in which such forgiveness is announced and embodied. Such is the task of Part II.

PART II

4 Characterizing the God Who Forgives

The Triune God and Christian Life

PART I PRESUPPOSED, but did not fully develop, the relationship between claims about God's forgiveness and claims about human forgiveness. How should claims about God's forgiveness be understood? The claim *that* God forgives is, at least for Jews and Christians, neither novel nor problematic. But how to characterize the God who forgives, and that forgiveness, is potentially more problematic — and certainly more complex than is often assumed. So the nature of the forgiving God and of God's forgiveness will be the focus of the three chapters that comprise Part II.

The difficulties in characterizing the God who forgives can be illustrated by briefly examining the Gospel of Luke's linkage of God's forgiveness to the life, death, and resurrection of Jesus of Nazareth. According to (some versions of) Luke, the first words Jesus uttered from the cross were "Father, forgive them, because they do not know what they are doing" (Luke 23:34).[1] These words provide a focal point in Luke's account of Jesus and more particularly in Luke's claim that God's forgiveness is most decisively proclaimed and enacted in and through Jesus' life, death, and resurrection: Jesus' cry recalls his announcement and embodiment of forgiveness

---

1. Many important early manuscripts of Luke's Gospel do not include these words. Even so, while the textual evidence may not enable us to identify the "original" reading, the passage fits narratively and logically into the larger perspective of Luke-Acts concerning Jesus' forgiveness.

in his ministry, it reflects the significance of his death for forgiveness, and it points forward to the disciples' proclamation and embodiment of forgiveness after his resurrection.

Jesus' ministry is shaped by his proclamation and enactment of God's inbreaking Kingdom; and central to that proclamation and enactment is the forgiveness of sins. In one sense, this is not surprising; Israel knew a gracious God, and the promise of God's forgiveness is found throughout the Hebrew Bible. Further, significant movements within Israel looked forward to the dawn of the messianic age as a time when forgiveness and repentance would become pivotal signs of God's salvation.

Even so, the forgiveness that Jesus proclaimed and enacted was controversial, primarily because he seemed to diverge from Israel's understandings and practices in crucial ways. For example, he both claimed divine authority to forgive sins and offered forgiveness without necessarily presuming prior repentance. According to Luke's account, Jesus offers forgiveness early in his ministry to a paralytic (Luke 5:17-26); yet the immediate response from scribes and Pharisees is "Who is this who is speaking blasphemies? Who but God can forgive sins?" In response, Jesus heals the paralytic to show that "the Son of Man has authority on earth to forgive sins." Later in his ministry, Jesus tells the stories of the lost sheep, the lost coin, and the lost son in response to charges that he welcomes sinners and eats with them without requiring repentance (15:1-32). He also calls Zacchaeus down from his tree, offering him forgiveness and new life by going to stay and eat with him at his house (19:1-10).[2]

We thus see in Luke's Gospel how controversial Jesus' proclamation and enactment of forgiveness is by the time he is nailed to the cross, where he utters his cry for God to forgive his crucifiers. Jesus' cry echoes Israel's practice of sacrifice for unintentional sin (see Numbers 15:27-31) and thus intensifies and extends the horizons of forgiveness by locating his death as an enactment of divine forgiveness — as a sacrifice, a judgment, that brings salvation through forgiveness. This forgiveness is offered even though the people are "ignorant" of what they are doing, though no less culpable for it (see also the proclamations in Acts 3:17; 7:25). As such, Jesus' death takes on a salvific significance that comes to be recognized by Christians as a definitive, once-for-all sacrifice and judgment of grace. Not surprisingly, this claim diverges from at least some segments of first-century Judaism's

---

2. To be sure, the relationship between forgiveness and repentance in the Zacchaeus story is complex. Even so, the scandal is that Jesus offers to go to Zacchaeus's house before Zacchaeus repents.

practices and understandings of God's forgiveness, as well as those of the Judaism of our day.

According to Luke, Jesus' proclamation and enactment of God's forgiveness is confirmed by his resurrection. Indeed, the resurrected Jesus returns to his disciples with offers of hospitality and forgiveness, with a judgment that does not condemn but offers new life. Further, he explains to them how his forgiveness fulfills Israel's scriptures, and he calls and authorizes the disciples to go to the nations proclaiming a gospel of repentance for the forgiveness of sins (see Luke 24:47; Acts 2:38; 5:31; 10:43; 13:38; 26:18). According to Acts, this proclamation provides the Church's mission and also points to some of the contexts and practices through which Jewish and Christian understandings of God and of forgiveness will ultimately diverge.

Overall, Luke's account suggests that, through Jesus, God's Kingdom has been inaugurated and forgiveness enacted in ways that are both continuous and discontinuous with Israel's understandings and practices. A crucial discontinuity is provided by the Christian claim that Jesus' inauguration of God's Kingdom is the determinative context in which we are called to embody forgiveness, a context that reflects the fullness of God's triune communion. That is, Christians seek to provide a faithful witness to God's Kingdom by embodying the forgiveness wrought by Jesus in the power of the Holy Spirit.

This all too brief survey needs to be developed more fully in this chapter and later chapters. Even so, it should already be apparent that though Jews and Christians hold in common the view *that* God forgives, they have diverse and sometimes overlapping conceptions of the *specific* character of the God who forgives. Hence, though both traditions also hold that people are called to forgive as God forgives,[3] they have diverse and sometimes overlapping conceptions of the shape of the call to imitate God's forgiveness.

These claims raise issues that go back to the origins of Christianity as a movement that emerged, over an extended period of time in the first and second centuries, out of the matrix of Judaism. They also press issues in quite specific ways in the present — not least when assessing issues related to the Holocaust and the future of Jewish-Christian relations.

---

3. For examples of this claim in each tradition, see (for Christians) Ephesians 4:32 and (for Jews) the Babylonian Talmud, *Shabbat* 133b, cited in Elliot N. Dorff, "Individual and Communal Forgiveness," in Daniel H. Frank (ed.), *Autonomy and Judaism* (Albany: SUNY, 1992) p. 197.

Indeed, some of the most vigorous published disagreements between Jews and Christians have been over the nature and scope of forgiveness.[4]

Emmanuel Levinas has eloquently stated one version of a Jewish objection to a Christian understanding of forgiveness: "Jewish wisdom teaches that He Who has created and Who supports the whole universe cannot support or pardon the crime that man commits against man. . . . No one, not even God, can substitute himself for the victim. The world in which pardon is all-powerful becomes inhuman."[5] Such a world becomes inhuman because too little attention is paid to the victim. By contrast, Levinas insists that there is a "horizontal" dimension to forgiveness among human beings that must precede, or is at least indispensable to, any "vertical" forgiveness from God. Put most sharply, Levinas's Judaism would insist that only victims can forgive offenses committed against them.

There is also another, in some ways equally powerful, objection that mirrors Levinas's formulation: A world in which pardon is all-powerful might actually encourage an abdication of responsibility by creating a culture of victims, one in which people simply wallow in the notion that we are "weak, needy, and fallible" human beings in desperate need of Jesus Christ's all-powerful forgiveness. Indeed, people may even be able to achieve social power by trading on their status as victims, thus immersing themselves in their victimization.

Yet Christians claim that, in some sense, a world in which pardon is all-powerful is dramatically announced and embodied in the life, death, and resurrection of Jesus of Nazareth. Despite Bonhoeffer's and Kolbe's noble witness to the cost of forgiveness, the question still needs to be pressed in relation to the Christian doctrine of God: Do Christian convictions about the God of Jesus Christ entail a "cheap grace" whereby human beings can abdicate responsibility for offenses and crimes that they commit against one another?

Christians ought to acknowledge the practical force of these objections. As I have already suggested in Part I, people have too often interpreted the forgiveness announced and enacted by Jesus Christ in ways that trivial-

---

4. See, for example, the exchanges in *Sh'ma* 10/198 (October 3, 1980) and 11/202 (November 28, 1980); *European Judaism* 19/2 (Spring 1985); *Christian-Jewish Relations* 19/1 (March 1986); and the symposium following Simon Wiesenthal's story in *The Sunflower* (New York: Schocken, 1976). On Wiesenthal's story, see also my discussion in chapter 9.

5. Emmanuel Levinas, *Difficult Freedom: Essays on Judaism*, tr. Sean Hand (Baltimore: Johns Hopkins University, 1990) p. 20.

ize victimization, either by ignoring the claims of victims or by seeing virtually everyone as a victim. So the question that Jews such as Levinas press on Christians is urgent: Can, or should, Christians claim both that God forgives and that this forgiveness requires lives of forgiven-ness that take seriously the offenses and crimes that human beings commit against one another? If so, how should that claim be understood in relation both to the doctrine of God and to the vocation of Christian life?

If, as I take it, there is little point to being a Christian unless the answer to the first of these questions is Yes, then adequately addressing the second question becomes the crucial task. That is, I need to offer an account of Christian claims about the character of the God who forgives, of the cor-relative implications about the nature and purpose of relationships among human beings and of humans with God, and of the predicament of sinful-ness, namely, that human beings seem unable to live in faithful relationships with God, with one another, and with God's Creation.

Such an account, however, cannot bypass the crucial issues that re-volve around Jews' and Christians' overlapping yet divergent conceptions about the God who forgives and the nature of that forgiveness. These issues deal with such problems as the relationship between forgiveness and re-pentance; who has the authority to forgive whom; the relationship between God's forgiveness and the dynamics of interhuman forgiveness; the context of messianic expectation and the proclamation of an already-but-not-yet Kingdom of God; and whether there are thus some events that are, or ought to be, understood as unforgivable. Not surprisingly, these issues continually return to disputes over Jesus' forgiveness and the Christian claim that Jesus is Israel's Messiah and, indeed, the One whose incarnation, life, death, and resurrection reveal the identity of the Triune God.

Hence an adequate characterization of the Christian God who for-gives involves both developing constructive claims about the Triune God and returning — if even only sketchily and briefly — to the specific con-texts of the first century, when some of Christianity's pivotal claims about forgiveness came to be articulated and slowly differentiated from Judaism. I begin with the latter issues.

Judaism, Jesus, and Forgiveness

Jesus was born a Jew. As such, he would have been raised within a Jewish culture that, despite its internal diversity, knew that God is gracious and forgiving. God's forgiveness is manifest throughout the Hebrew Bible (i.e., what Christians call the Old Testament). Despite attempts down through the centuries by people as different as the second-century thinker Marcion and the eighteenth-century philosopher Hegel to drive a wedge between the God of the Hebrew Bible (as a "God of wrath") and the God of the New Testament (as a "God of love"), it is clear that God is characterized throughout both testaments as a God of judgment *and* grace, divine justice *and* merciful forgiveness.

Further, too many depictions of Jesus' ministry, death, and resurrection operate with a logic that works backward from contemporary assumptions.[6] First, in these depictions it is (rightly) assumed that forgiveness is at the heart of Christian theology and Christian life. Secondly, it is then (wrongly) assumed that if forgiveness characterizes Christianity, then it could not have been present in the religion from which Christianity came. After all, if Jesus' cross provides a decisive forgiveness through his atonement, then presumably — or at least so the argument goes — the only way to explain why Jesus had to be nailed to a cross is that he offered and embodied a forgiveness that was thoroughly unknown in Judaism.

But that God forgives, and more specifically that forgiveness is always available to those who return to the way of the Lord, would have been familiar and assumed not only by Jesus but by any typical first-century Jew.[7] After all, the people of Israel knew that God had created the world and had called them to be God's people in covenantal love. Further, they had repeatedly experienced God's forgiveness as a people, albeit a forgiveness accompanied by divine judgment. In the Torah, God renews the covenant with Israel even after Israel has broken it immediately after the exodus (and after a pointed exchange in which Moses intercedes on Israel's behalf, calling on God to forgive): "YHWH, YHWH, a merciful and gracious God, who is slow to anger, with great and continual love and faithfulness, who keeps continual love for the thousandth generation, and who forgives iniquity, transgression, and sin — but who by no means acquits the guilty, but brings the iniquity of parents on children and grandchildren to the third and the fourth generations" (Exodus 34:6-7).

Further, God's forgiveness of the people of Israel is dramatically illustrated in Hosea 11:1-9. Since the exodus, and even before, Israel had struggled — and often failed — in its attempts to be faithful to the covenant

---

6. See E. P. Sanders, *Jesus and Judaism* (Philadelphia: Fortress, 1985) pp. 38-40, 200-207, for a more extended account of this problem, particularly in relation to New Testament scholarship.

7. See Sanders, *Jesus and Judaism*, p. 202.

with God. Indeed, Israel's stubborn and persistent sinfulness, its infidelity to the covenant, cries out for God's judgment — perhaps even God's wrathful condemnation. God is filled with fierce and righteous anger; but it is the anger of a parent struggling over her wayward child. "When Israel was a child, I loved him. I called him out of Egypt. The more I called them, the more they ran from me. They kept sacrificing to the Baals and offering incense to idols" (11:1-2). Israel strayed even though God has nurtured Israel and has led its people "with cords of human kindness" (v. 4). So God will punish Israel by sending the people into exile (vv. 5-7).

Even so, condemnation is neither God's first nor God's final word. The God who created and called Israel remains the God who seeks a reconciling, covenantal relation with God's people. So God's compassion grows warm and tender, and God's mercy once again overcomes human sinfulness. For, as God says, "I am God and not a mortal, the Holy One in your midst, and I will not come in wrath" (11:9b). Mortals may think that violence and vengeance are the masters of us all; but the God of Israel knows better. God's judgment and righteous anger are real, as is God's punishment; but they are in the service of a reconciling, covenantal love (see also Jeremiah 3:12; Isaiah 54:8).

Jews of the first century c.e. knew that God can forgive particular transgressions of the people against God. This would be the case both for the people of Israel corporately and for particular individuals. This forgiveness from God is most clearly formalized in the ritual of Yom Kippur, the Day of Atonement. On that day, the priest enacts an atonement for the priests and for all the people, and sins — intentional as well as unintentional — are forgiven (see Leviticus 16:29-34).

A prominent theme in God's forgiveness of individuals is that God forgives particular transgressions of individuals if they repent and accept culpability. This is seen dramatically in Psalm 51, linked to David after Nathan had confronted him about his adulterous relationship with Bathsheba. The psalmist asks to be cleansed from sin, to be washed thoroughly (vv. 1-2), and for God to create in him a clean heart (v. 10). If God restores to him the joy of God's salvation, the psalmist promises to teach transgressors God's ways (v. 13). He acknowledges his wrongdoing, and reminds God of God's willingness to receive and forgive a broken and contrite heart (v. 17).

God does forgive particular transgressions if the individuals repent. Even so, there is nonetheless a presumption that such transgressions would occur typically because the person acted out of ignorance or unintentionally, that the person did not intend to commit a sin but did so out of a lack of information or because the consequences could not be foreseen. A ritual

of sacrificial offerings was developed for the forgiveness of such unintentional sin (see Leviticus 4:22-31; Numbers 15:27-29). However, as David
Daube rightly points out, there is a second sense in which someone could
act out of ignorance, a deeper blindness to the full import of one's own
actions because of one's ignorance of the true Good, which is God.[8] That
deeper blindness is the gist of a more serious charge, one in which the
possibility of forgiveness was more dubious (see Numbers 15:30-31).

But even here, God's forgiveness is not completely precluded. God's
concluding words to Jonah concerning Nineveh reveal God's forgiveness
despite the people's deeper blindness: "Should I be unconcerned about
Nineveh, a great city in which there are more than a hundred and twenty
thousand people who do not know their right hand from their left, and
also many animals?" (Jonah 4:11). Daube's comments on this passage are
instructive:

> "They do not know" does not here signify lack of information, the wicked
> Ninevites had not been acting from ignorance in the ordinary sense, the
> phrase refers to their basic ignorance as weak, shortsighted creatures, not
> much wiser than their beasts, they are spared because they did not know
> in this deeper sense what they were doing. What makes this particular
> passage relevant to an investigation of Judaism in New Testament times
> is the fact that, almost certainly, the Book of Jonah was then as today
> used as a lesson from the Prophets on the Day of Atonement — this
> year's reading is still fresh in our memories.[9]

Indeed, Daube suggests that the entire service of the Day of Atonement is
placed under the *motif* of forgiveness on the ground of deeper ignorance
(and cites the first-century rabbi Eliezer the Great's comment on Numbers
15:25 as a source for this teaching).

Thus, it would be clear to most first-century Jews that God forgives.
It would also be clear that this forgiveness is open to anyone who returns
to the way of the Lord (see Ezekiel 18:25-32). Such returning would require
repentance; it would also require restitution for wrongs committed against
other human beings (see Leviticus 6:1-7; Numbers 5:5-7). Individuals must
go to the person they have wronged and seek forgiveness; such forgiveness
ought to involve a willingness to rectify the wrong.[10] God forgives the

---

8. See David Daube, *Sin, Ignorance and Forgiveness in the Bible* (London: Liberal
Jewish Synagogue, 1960) p. 20.

9. Daube, *Sin, Ignorance and Forgiveness in the Bible*, p. 24.

10. However, it is important to remember that the obligation for the wrongdoer

person only after such interhuman forgiveness has taken place. Or, more precisely, seeking forgiveness from the offended person is also, at the same time, a first step in seeking forgiveness from God, which would be enacted in a sacrificial atonement.[11] Hence the importance of being reconciled with those whom you have offended and doing so before, and in anticipation of, the service of Yom Kippur.

At the same time, however, first-century Israel also longed for a messianic forgiveness; it hoped for the restoration of the corporate identity of God's people (see Isaiah 65:17-25; Jeremiah 31:31-34). The sacrificial system included not only the individuals' remedy for sin but also the reaffirmation of political, social, and religious hope. As N. T. Wright has suggested,

> Partly, no doubt, [the sacrifices] were seen as simply the appointed worship of the one true god, whom to celebrate (in thank-offerings, peace-offerings, etc.) was in itself to reaffirm Israel's monotheism and election and hence her national identity and hope. Partly, though, there was most likely a sense that the sacrificial ritual itself dramatically enacted the movement of judgment and salvation, exile and restoration, death and resurrection for which Israel longed.[12]

It was in the context of this Jewish hope, as well as the firm conviction that God's judgment is in the service of a forgiving, reconciling love that makes that hope a reality, that Jesus was born.

Even from this brief sketch of first-century Judaism's beliefs and practices, then, it ought to be clear that, for Israel, God's forgiveness makes a difference in the world of human relationships. Indeed, God's forgiveness could not be used as an excuse for bypassing situations of human wrong-doing. To turn to the one whom an individual has wronged is precisely also to take the first step toward re-turning to God.

As will become clear below, Jesus' ministry is marked by this same insistence on the difference that God's forgiveness makes. So resituating

---

is to ask only three times; if the offended one still refuses to grant forgiveness, then the wrongdoer has nonethess fulfilled his or her obligation. This is important in a world where bitterness can persist on both sides of wrongdoing.

11. See also the discussion in Louis E. Newman, "The Quality of Mercy: On the Duty to Forgive in the Judaic Tradition," *Journal of Religious Ethics* 15/2 (Fall 1987) p. 168, where he contextualizes these issues in relation to developments in Judaism beyond the first century.

12. N. T. Wright, *The New Testament and the People of God* (Minneapolis: Fortress, 1992) p. 277.

Jesus within the context of Israel's beliefs and practices already goes a long way toward overcoming abstract and lifeless depictions of God's forgiveness. But we are still faced with the problem of its mirror image; Judaism protected, and protects, against forgiveness making *too much* difference by its assumption of the prior requirement of repentance. Does Jesus, in his teachings and his actions concerning such issues as repentance, teach and embody a forgiveness that makes too much difference? Is Levinas's protest that Christianity's all-powerful forgiveness is inhuman ultimately decisive and persuasive? Perhaps.

Or perhaps the gospel calls for a transformation of what we take to be "human." It seems clear that Jesus' proclamation of the Kingdom transforms the relationship between repentance and forgiveness by stressing the gracious priority of forgiveness. As E. P. Sanders has suggested, Jesus seems to have invited people into the Kingdom without requiring them to repent in the way that repentance was understood within Judaism — that is, without requirements of restitution, sacrifice, and obedience to the law.[13]

However, that does not mean — as Sanders sometimes seems to imply — that Jesus' message abandoned repentance. Indeed, in the Synoptic Gospels Jesus' ministry is inaugurated with his announcement of the Kingdom and his call to repentance (see, for example, Matthew 4:17). But it does suggest that Jesus' message and actions implied, and sometimes explicitly claimed, a transformed understanding of the relationship between forgiveness and repentance — a repentance contextualized within the announcement of God's inbreaking Kingdom. Thus repentance comes to be situated within Jesus' overall announcement and enactment of God's costly forgiveness.

Further, Jesus claims and enacts — at least so the Gospel narratives suggest — divine authority to forgive sins, an authority that Israel assumed belonged ultimately to God alone (see Mark 2:1-12; Luke 5:17-26).[14] Such a claim of authority, particularly when linked to Jesus' conferral of that authority on his disciples, shifts the focus of forgiveness in early Christianity

---

13. Sanders, *Jesus and Judaism*, p. 207.

14. I am not persuaded by the arguments of such scholars as Sanders and J. D. G. Dunn that the story of the paralytic in Mark 2:1-12 is *not* about Jesus claiming God's authority to forgive sins. To be sure, they are focusing on the historical context of the passage; nonetheless, within the context of Mark's Gospel, it seems clear that the dispute is not only over Jesus' proclamation of forgiveness of sins outside the cultic obligations of the Temple (as Dunn suggests); it is also a sign of Jesus' divinity that he has the divine authority to forgive sins. For the discussions, see Sanders, *Jesus and Judaism*, p. 273; Dunn, *The Partings of the Ways* (Philadelphia: Trinity, 1991) pp. 44-46.

from the Temple and its sacrificial system to communities of disciples that are authorized and obligated to forgive in God's name (see Matthew 16:19; 18:18; John 20:23).

Jesus' proclamation and embodiment of the Kingdom's inauguration is, in some sense, the proclamation and embodiment of a world in which "pardon is all-powerful." This is particularly focused in his crucifixion and resurrection. Further, Christians claim that the God of Israel, the God in whose name Jesus announces the coming of the Kingdom, is the one who raised the crucified Jesus from the dead and has exalted him as Lord. And, even more audaciously, from their earliest days as a movement Christians claimed that the God of Israel is inseparably united with Jesus in a unique relationship that definitively identifies and characterizes them both.[15]

For example, this claim is made in the famous "Christ hymn" in Philippians 2:5-11. The passage echoes Isaiah 45:21-24, where God declares that "all will bend the knee to me, and every tongue will swear by me, saying, 'In YHWH alone are saving justice and strength,' until all who used to rage at him come to him in shame." That same passage also has God earlier declaring that "There is no other god except me, no saving God, no Saviour except me!" But the Philippians passage begins by narrating that, though Jesus Christ was "in the form of God," he "emptied himself, taking the form of a slave, being born in human likeness." He was "obedient to the point of death — even death on a cross." Therefore, the passage concludes, "God also highly exalted him and gave him the name that is above every name, so that at the name of Jesus every knee should bend, in heaven and on earth and under the earth, and every tongue should confess that Jesus Christ is Lord, to the glory of God the Father."

There are only a few conceptual possibilities for relating the God of Israel to Jesus in this passage. As N. T. Wright summarizes them,

> For consider: if the God who will not share his glory with another has now shared it with Jesus (the position asserted in 2:9ff.), then there are only three possible conclusions that can be drawn. It might be the case that there are now two Gods. Or Jesus — who up until then had been a man and nothing but a man — might now have been totally absorbed into the one God without remainder (so to speak). Or there might be a sense — requiring fuller investigation, exploration, and clarification, no doubt — in which Jesus, in being exalted to the rank described in 2:9ff.,

15. I am indebted for the formulation of this sentence, as well as several of the ideas that follow, to David S. Yeago's unpublished essay "The New Testament as Witness to the Triune God."

is receiving no more than that which was always, from before the beginning of time, his by right.[16]

Since neither of the first two options was credible in relation to both Isaiah and the logic of Jesus' name continuing to be "above every name," the Church confessed — and continues to confess — that the relationship between YHWH and Jesus must always have been intrinsic to God's identity (see, for example, Romans 1:3).

Further, the early Christians identified the crucified and risen Jesus with YHWH by the power of the Holy Spirit (see 1 Corinthians12:3), who is also intrinsic to God's identity. As David Yeago nicely formulates the claim,

> Thus just as turning to the God of Israel means, for the New Testament, turning to the *Kurios* [Lord] whom he has raised from the dead, so too this turning means being caught up in the working of the *Pneuma* [Spirit] which God has poured out on his Anointed. The *subject* of the eschatological worship of the New Testament is always a subject-in-the-Spirit.[17]

The object of early Christian worship was the crucified and risen Christ, who is praised to the glory of God the Father, and the means by which Christ is worshiped is the subject of the gathered Christian community *in the Spirit.*

From this perspective it should be apparent that the doctrine of the Trinity is not simply a later addition to Christian confession that emerges only in the encounter with Greek and Roman philosophical ideas. It is rather the means by which, from the very beginning of their worship in the wake of Jesus' life, death, and resurrection, Christians have characterized the God who forgives and the nature of that forgiveness.

That is to say, while Jesus' forgiveness must be understood in relation to the Judaism out of which his ministry emerges and in the light of which his death and resurrection are interpreted, we can only adequately assess the difference that (Christians claim) God's forgiveness makes by situating Jesus' life, death, and resurrection within a deeper understanding of the mystery of the Triune God. Hence, we cannot adequately respond to Levinas's objection until we provide a more careful Christian characterization of the God who forgives and the nature of that forgiveness.

For at the heart of the Christian doctrine of God is the conviction that God lives as the loving friendships, the self-giving relationships, of Father, Son, and Holy Spirit. Further, that giving of self becomes manifest

16. N. T. Wright, *The Climax of the Covenant* (Minneapolis: Fortress, 1991) p. 94.
17. Yeago, "The New Testament as Witness to the Triune God."

in God's outpouring in Creation. The Father creates through the Son in the power of the Spirit. As such, God creates *ex nihilo* ("out of nothing"). There is nothing prior to or outside of God's creative initiative. As the first creation story in Genesis suggests, God creates not by conquest but by speech — as John 1 puts it, by God's *Word*.

But that Word is none other than the One who is, as a result of human sin and evil, nailed to the cross. In the slaying and raising of Jesus of Nazareth, God overcomes our propensity for violence by binding it up into God's own trinitarian life. That is to say, in the face of human sin and evil God's love moves toward reconciliation by means of costly forgiveness.

However, as I suggested in chapters 2 and 3, we are tempted either to trivialize that forgiveness by individualizing it so that it leaves our relations with others essentially untouched, or to despair of forgiveness, secretly believing that violence is primary and peace a folly for the naive. But the Christian doctrine of the Triune God avoids both of these temptations. Indeed, the Prologue to John's Gospel does not state that everything is light; it specifies that the darkness has not overcome the light. Hence it is a mistake to construe the Christian gospel in such a way that we either deny the existence of the darkness (by individualizing my relationship with God so that I can live in the happy consciousness of being justified) or assume that the darkness is determinative (by giving priority to violence rather than peace).

Forgiveness, specifically the forgiveness offered and enacted by the Triune God, offers the Christian response to the threat of darkness and the promise of reconciliation. So it is to a characterization of the Triune God who forgives and of the nature of that forgiveness that I now turn.

The Father Who Wills Communion

Like the Jewish affirmation of a covenantal God, the Christian claim is that God is not simply a Being who responds to situations and actions in the world. Rather, God lives, so Christians affirm, as the trinitarian relations of Father, Son, and Holy Spirit, which manifest eternal and perfect communion. That is to say, God is constituted by the trinitarian relations, relations marked by the continuous positing of harmonic difference. As John Milbank suggests, "The harmony of the Trinity is therefore not the harmony of a finished totality but a 'musical' harmony of infinity."[18] God is God as the endless and ever new self-giving among Father, Son, and Spirit.

18. John Milbank, *Theology and Social Theory* (Oxford: Blackwell, 1990) p. 424.

This self-giving is linked to the claim that God's communion is characterized by love. In the "begetting" of the Son and the "breathing out" of the Spirit, the Father wills a life of eternal, loving communion.[19] As such, the Triune God is identified not as a "being" that can be possessed or objectified but as the self-giving relations of love.[20] God loves and remains God in that love, a love that continually gives all to the Other(s) in God.

Not only is God love, but God loves those whom God has created. As I suggested in chapter 2, God wills communion with Creation and so creates human beings in the divine image and likeness. More specifically, human beings are made in the image and likeness of the Triune God, a God characterized by perfect communion. So also human beings are created for loving communion with God, with one another, and with the whole Creation. As Gregory of Nyssa suggested in the fourth century, our destiny is eternal communion with God that manifests the endless self-giving relations of love. Thus human beings are not made to live as isolated or self-enclosed individuals. We can only fulfill our purpose and destiny as human beings when we fulfill our God-given capacity for loving communion, for living as a part of the pattern of God's Creation. We can glimpse the significance of this communion in many ways, but Christians (re-)learn it most centrally through such practices as baptism, eucharist, and hospitality.

Even so, human beings have persistently rejected, and continue to reject, that communion. We do so in myriad ways, refusing our creatureliness and our call to communion in a world where we always-already diminish and destroy others, ourselves, and God's good Creation. We do so when we believe that violence and domination or being dominated, not communion, is our only destiny; we do so when we evade or deny our complicity in habits and histories of sin and evil; we do so when we pretend that those habits and histories are not really so bad after all; and we do so when we even interpret our status as creatures *not* as a sign of communion with our Creator but as a sign of our victimization. After all, none of us has been able to "choose" our particular social or political background, our genetic makeup, or the circumstances that come to shape our lives.

As a result, the musical harmony of God's self-giving communion is

---

19. Note John Zizioulas's similar claim: "The life of God is eternal because it is personal, that is to say, it is realized as an expression of free communion, as love." *Being as Communion* (Crestwood: St. Vladimir's Seminary, 1985) p. 49.

20. See also Jean-Luc Marion, *God Without Being*, tr. Thomas A. Carlson (Chicago: University of Chicago, 1991).

transmuted into a cacophony of voices competing with one another for access to power, to material resources, and to a self-validating identity. Despite our created destiny for communion, we human beings do not typically give and receive freely with one another, and certainly not with any trusting expectation; rather, we seek to secure our lives at the expense of others. Our discourses are built not on the trinitarian surplus of self-giving and self-receiving communion, but rather on the competitive desires of individuals whose life is sought at the expense of others.[21] Within this cacophony, it becomes increasingly difficult to discern the legitimate claims of those who have been and continue to be denied access to power, material resources, and selves. We are now the heirs of histories and habits of sin and evil that make it difficult, if not impossible, to break out of the cycles of violence and counterviolence, of diminishing and being diminished.

It is often difficult because people refuse to acknowledge these cycles, or to acknowledge them as problems that require or permit a personal response. One response is to refuse to acknowledge them through moral anesthesia; once anesthetized, people accept that these cycles are either inevitable or the way things are supposed to be. For example, people who suffer from domestic violence often become unable to act against their offenders, becoming numbed to the point where they accept it without further questioning. But another form of moral anesthesia exists in bureaucrats who observe such cycles with chilling detachment. Hannah Arendt has described with chilling power the rule-bound rigidity and moral emptiness of Adolf Eichmann;[22] similarly, many people are tempted to believe and live as if moral responsibility can be limited to the ability to follow specific, personally defined rules. So people can be horrified by stories of the Nazis, or of Stalinesque repression, or of domestic violence, while nonetheless failing to recognize their own responsibility to respond in appropriate ways. Indeed, one of the ironies of ideologies of progress is the conviction that "we" who are "progressive" or "civilized" have learned how to live without diminishing or destroying other people. Hence "we" conclude that the solution to all problems is for others to become like "us," all the while masking the ways in which our own "progress" is built on the backs of others as they are destroyed.

However, people can also be paralyzed by taking *too much* responsi-

---

21. Michael Ignatieff poignantly reflects on the tragic character of this competition in his *The Needs of Strangers* (New York: Penguin, 1984).

22. *Eichmann in Jerusalem: A Report on the Banality of Evil* (New York: Penguin, 1963).

bility and wallowing in guilt or shame. People can become convicted by the recognition of complicity in evil and paralyzed by that guilt from continuing to make discriminating judgments. When this happens, people typically end up rebelling against their temporary obsession with guilt and return to the desire to destroy victims precisely for being victims. Hence, we see the difficult relations between racial groups, where, for example, in the U.S. "white guilt" is now producing a backlash of renewed racism. The positions of "victimizer" and "victim" become entrenched, and both moral anesthesia and obsessive guilt make it virtually impossible to break the cycles whereby people diminish and destroy one another, themselves, and Creation.

Indeed, the attempt to divide the world into tidy categories of oppressor and oppressed or victimizer and victim oversimplifies the more complex realities of histories and habits of sin and evil. While it is undeniably true that many people have suffered — and continue to suffer — immensely through exploitation and violence, systemic and otherwise — none of us is free from the trap of being *both* victimizer and victim. In one and the same relationship, I may be both oppressor and victim (though obviously to different degrees). For example, some people who have undeniably suffered and have been exploited at the hands of others may also use that exploitation as a means to play on the guilt of others. As Roberta Bondi has suggested, "if we identify ourselves as victim, or place most of the blame for our condition outside ourselves, we also take away from ourselves our own ability to affect what happens to us."[23]

Further, identifying oneself exclusively as a victim masks the ways in which each of us victimizes others. In the complex webs that constitute human relations, it is inevitable that we human beings find ourselves as both oppressors and victims — though obviously, once again, to different degrees and in different situations. We cannot let ourselves or others off the hook for patterns of victimizing others; nor ought we or others blame the victims as if they were somehow perversely responsible for their own suffering. At the same time, however, we must also resist the temptation to trade on secure positions of victimization — either as victims or victimizers — as a means of gaining power, rather than responsibly seeking to reconstruct human relationships as forgiven and forgiving people. In the midst of habits and histories of sin and evil, claiming the exclusive status of a victim carries with it an invitation (particularly seductive in therapeutic cultures) to the power that comes with remaining immersed in the stories

23. Roberta C. Bondi, *To Pray and to Love* (Minneapolis: Augsburg Fortress, 1991) p. 82.

of one's own — or one's people's own — victimization.[24] This is the result *both* of the Church's conceptual failure to recognize the ways in which "victimization" language continues to undermine the capacity for forgiveness, and hence communion, *and* of the practical failure to respond appropriately to those who are suffering, so that they must resort to the languages of victimization in order to be heard.[25]

Despite the fact that we are created for communion with the Triune God, human beings continue to be trapped in histories and habits of sin and evil. Indeed, the Christian doctrine of original sin conveys the conviction that none of us can escape the "always-already" character of the fragmentation and brokenness in which we find ourselves. Walter Kasper describes a "universal situation of disaster" in which "every attempt to alter this situation is itself subject to the conditions created by the disaster. The result is an unending satanic cycle of guilt and revenge, violence and counterviolence."[26] Though Jews typically have rejected the Christian notion of original sin, their messianic hope — articulated with such power by the prophets — nonetheless includes an acute awareness of this pervasive disaster.

Christians claim that this fundamental condition of Sin manifests itself in particular and specific sins, sins that are often difficult to learn to identify and name in one's own life and in the lives of others. Forgiveness is necessary for such sins, as Israel well knew. And repentance is necessary for such sins to be forgiven. This is so whether the offense is against God or is the inevitable damage that we human beings inflict on one another, on ourselves, and on the whole Creation.

But if we confine ourselves to sin*s*, as Christian cultures have sometimes tended to do, we will lose sight of the more determinative condition of Sin in which we find ourselves and for which we also need forgiveness. The crisis of the human condition is not simply *my* individual guilt, but rather the evil, suffering, and brokenness — the "universal situation of disaster" — that undermines not only my communion with God but *our* communion with God and with one another. But given the universal situation of disaster and the ways in which habits of sin and evil become

24. For a powerful account of this problem, see Ellen Charry's essay "Literature as Scripture: Privileged Reading in Current Religious Reflection," *Soundings* 74/1-2 (Spring/Summer 1991) pp. 65-99.

25. I am indebted to my colleague Stephen Fowl for this way of putting the issues.

26. Walter Kasper, *The God of Jesus Christ*, tr. Matthew J. O'Connell (New York: Crossroad, 1984) p. 160.

secure positions from which we have difficulty extricating ourselves, the restoration of *our* communion with God requires something beyond my repentance, beyond my initiative or any human initiative — but not beyond God the Father's gracious will for communion with Creation.

A "new beginning" is needed, a breakthrough by God that transcends not only the human tendency to commit sin*s* but also the fundamental reality of sin. As Kasper puts it,

> If hope is to be at all possible in the face of the universal situation of suffering and disaster, if in the face of injustice that cries out to heaven human beings are not to surrender their dignity, then a new beginning must be possible that cannot be derived from the conditions present in our situation, and there must be a final authority that is above all injustice and will have the last word to say at the end of history.[27]

As I suggested above, within the Hebrew Bible Israel knows that God forgives not only in response to repentance, enacted through the Temple and its sacrificial practices, but because of God's own gracious initiative. God's self-giving, God's condescension, to Creation — and more specifically, to Israel — in gracious forgiveness is found throughout the Hebrew Bible. But the promise of a "new beginning" remains for Israel an eschatological hope.[28]

Christians claim, however, that this new beginning has already occurred in the journey of God's Son "into the far country." Here God's self-giving, condescending love finds its decisive focus and its costly climax. In Karl Barth's terms, "God shows Himself to be the great and true God in the fact that He can and will let His grace bear this cost, that He is capable and willing and ready for this condescension, this act of extravagance, this far journey."[29] In and through the "far journey" of the life, death, and

27. Kasper, *The God of Jesus Christ*, p. 161.

28. To be sure, that eschatological hope also finds performative embodiment in Israel's practices, specifically in God's daily renewal of Creation. In a profound sense, Judaism is born in the renewal of its biblical practice *after* the utter destruction of the Temple and the people in 70 c.e. In this sense, "new beginnings" occur again and again as the people and the faith are transformatively renewed after wholesale destructions. At the same time, however, Israel continued and continues to hope for an eschatological transformation. I am indebted to Peter Ochs for helping me to see these points.

29. Karl Barth, *Church Dogmatics* IV/1, tr. G. W. Bromiley (Edinburgh: Clark, 1956) p. 159. More generally, Barth deploys the image of "going into the far country," taken from the parable of the "forgiving father" (also known as the parable of the "prodigal son") in Luke 15, as a way to frame his christological perspective in this portion of the *Dogmatics*.

resurrection of Jesus Christ, Christians claim that God brings the Kingdom, which is marked by a definitive forgiveness restoring human beings' communion with God and with one another. The decisive difference between Judaism and Jesus, and ultimately Judaism and Christianity, is whether God's Kingdom has genuinely been inaugurated in this man Jesus. For it is a Kingdom that also provides a shift in understanding the purpose and scope of God's forgiveness, a shift signaled by Christianity's vision of the Judge judged for us (or, in terms of the Temple, of Christ as the perfect Sacrifice). In order to understand why, we need to turn to a theological explication of the Son's journey into the far country.

The Advent(s) of Jesus Christ

The very notion of a "journey" into a "far country" implies that something precedes the human birth of Jesus Christ. What is at stake in the doctrine of the incarnation is the affirmation that the self-giving love of God manifested in Jesus is neither different from God's creative and forgiving love nor unrelated to the communion of God's own life. Through the incarnation, the whole history of the created order is taken up into the life of God. As Barth describes it, "God reveals and increases His own glory in the world in the incarnation of His Son by taking to Himself the radical neediness of the world, i.e., by undertaking to do Himself what the world cannot do, arresting and reversing its course to the abyss."[30] God's desire for communion with Creation leads God, as a sign of mercy, to draw human history into God's life.

So there is a sense in which the incarnation ought to be understood as *theosis*, as the "deification" of humanity. In Athanasius's classic formulation, Christ "assumed humanity so that we might be made God."[31] Through the action of the Son of God we are invited to become like God through God's grace and acceptance. Thus, from one angle, Christ becomes human to draw us into the life of God's communion and to embody for us the shape of human communion.

But there is also a correlative movement in the incarnation signified by Christ's *kenosis*, Christ's self-emptying for the sake of obedience to the Father's will for humanity's salvation. Paul Valliere offers a counterpart to Athanasius's

30. Barth, *Church Dogmatics* IV/1, p. 213.
31. Athanasius, *On the Incarnation* (Crestwood: St. Vladimir's Seminary, 1982) p. 93.

statement: "God became a human being so that nothing truly human should be deemed alien to God's being, mercy and love."[32] Such a *kenosis* occurs not only in Christ's birth but throughout his ministry, culminating in the events of Good Friday and Holy Saturday. As Rowan Williams puts it,

> Our distance from God is itself taken into God, finds place in God; by the Spirit of adoption we enter the relation between Father and Son, the relation of exchange and mutuality. In the Incarnation, God distances himself from himself: the divine, intra-Trinitarian love is enacted and realized in the world by the descent of Christ into Hell. And the separation between Father and Son is bridged by the Spirit, who is the common will and love of Father and Son. The inconceivable self-emptying of God in the events of Good Friday and Holy Saturday is no arbitrary expression of the nature of God: this is what the life of the Trinity is, translated into the world.[33]

Hence from another, complementary angle, Christ's incarnation signifies his openness to the whole range of human experiences. And his redemption encompasses that range as well.

That is to say, in the incarnation Christ becomes vulnerable to the world of human beings. He becomes vulnerable not only to our capacity for created goodness and forgiveness and love and joy but also, and more determinatively, to the manifold ways in which people inevitably diminish, betray, oppress, abandon, and kill one another. But though he is vulnerable to them, he does not allow himself or us to be defined by them. Rather, Jesus' refusal to participate in those cycles of betrayal, vengeance, and violence judges all of humanity in its sin.

Christ's ministry is marked by a persistent breaking down of barriers, declaring that God's forgiveness is present for all. Indeed, Christ judges others in the righteousness of God precisely by embodying forgiveness as a way of life. In the midst of the brokenness of human community occasioned by the universal and ongoing disaster of both personal and structural sin, Christ draws others into communion with himself and with one another, and the sign of that communion is self-giving love.

32. Paul Valliere, "The Humanity of God in Liberal Orthodox Theology," *Modern Theology* 9/1 (January 1993) p. 57.

33. Rowan Williams, "Barth on the Triune God," in S. W. Sykes (ed.), *Karl Barth: Studies of His Theological Method* (Oxford: Clarendon, 1979) p. 177. Williams is discussing these themes with reference to Hans Urs von Balthasar's reflections on the life and death of Christ.

Jesus' forgiveness does not entail an abdication of responsibility or accountability to other people. Rebecca Chopp rightly insists that "In Jesus, history is not escaped, but made anew, changed, reordered, transformed."[34] Those who are forgiven by Jesus are called to embody that forgiven-ness in the new life signified by communion with Jesus and with other disciples. Indeed, that forgiven-ness calls believers to live *penitent* lives that seek to reconstruct human relationships in the service of holiness of heart and life. For Jesus, forgiveness cannot be earned, whether through repentance or by any other means. But our repentance is the only adequate response to God's forgiveness. This shifts the emphasis from Judaism's assumption that repentance precedes human forgiveness to an assumption that repentance will become an indispensable component of the habit of forgiveness. Indeed, Jesus tells the parable of the Unforgiving Servant (Matthew 18:23-35) as a warning and judgment for those who would presume to receive God's forgiveness without thereby embodying that forgiveness in new life. Such people exclude themselves from communion by their refusal to acknowledge forgiveness as the way of life for Jesus' disciples.

Jesus enacts forgiveness in diverse ways, perhaps most clearly in his table fellowship with tax collectors and sinners. Table fellowship was seen as a sign not only of communion among people but also of communion in the sight of God. Thus because the cultically impure were welcomed at Jesus' table, they were implicitly included in a relationship of communion with God. And when Jesus is attacked for his behavior toward sinners in Luke 15:2, he responds by telling the parables of the Lost Sheep, the Lost Coin, and the Lost Son. Each of these stories presses the issue of inclusion within the realm of God's communion, particularly with reference to Gentiles and those who were the "lost" within Israel. Further, each of those stories, particularly the final account of the prodigal son and the ungrateful son, are ultimately stories of God's forgiving love.

As his ministry progresses, Jesus is attacked in ways that are both more persistent and more threatening. The attacks come from those who are comfortable with things as they are and do not want their own role as self-righteous judges to be subverted by this One whose judgment seems wholly in the service of forgiveness and new life. As a result of these threats, Jesus seems to realize the urgency of his proclamation and ministry, but also its costliness. Williams's comments are instructive:

[Jesus] must sustain the urgent and transfiguring vision of an ultimate

34. Rebecca Chopp, *The Power to Speak* (New York: Crossroad, 1989) p. 57.

mercy at last made plain and the knowledge that he cannot make it so plain that all will see it. His irony, his imagination, his anger, his despair, his many-layered and even anarchic wit, all of them stem from the struggle to make visible to all what is to him so visible that it needs no description; and when he cries out against the obstinate stupidity of his hearers, it is because he has exhausted the resources of language and picture to no avail in trying to communicate to people what lies in front of their noses. He is at once eloquent and inarticulate; and at last, confronted with the rational politics of Caiaphas, he falls silent. "If I tell you, you will not believe; and if I ask you, you will not answer" (Luke 22:67-68).[35]

Christ's ministry is marked by his attempts to break the cycles of guilt and revenge, of violence and counterviolence, of victimizer and victim, through his own sinless life.

But that sinlessness should not be understood as an ahistorical miracle imported from another world. Rather, it is Christ's refusal to be drawn into the sinfulness of human beings trying to play God as unrepentant judges. Adam and Eve provide an archetype for our tendency to justify ourselves, to play the role of judge by identifying others as those in need of repentance and ourselves as either righteous ones or helpless victims (which carries with it its own tendency toward self-righteousness). In Barth's terms, the human

> unwillingness to repent is the constant renewal of his sin. The sinlessness of Jesus Christ consists in the fact that He does not take part in this game. He was a man as we are. His condition was no different from ours. He took our flesh, the nature of man as he comes from the fall. In this nature He is exposed every moment to the temptation to a renewal of sin — the temptation of impenitent being and thinking and speaking and action. His sinlessness was not therefore His condition. It was the act of His being in which He defeated temptation in His condition which is ours, in the flesh.[36]

Put differently, Jesus' sinlessness consists in his ability to suffer human evil, particularly the human tendency toward destructive judgment, and to absorb it without passing it on.

But human beings are unable to accept the announcement and em-

---

35. Rowan Williams, *The Truce of God* (New York: Pilgrim, 1983) pp. 67-68.
36. Barth, *Church Dogmatics* IV/1, pp. 258-259.

bodiment of Christ's forgiveness. Rather than bringing us to repentance, Jesus' ministry only heightens our desire to be the judges. So we judge him. We inflict suffering on Jesus as a reflection of our judgment of him. In Bonhoeffer's terms, God "lets himself be pushed out of the world onto the cross."[37] Having created free human beings, God then submits to our judgment, to our freedom to reject God. In this sense, Jesus is sent to the cross as the One judged *by* humanity, the One rejected by humanity, the One killed by humanity.

More comprehensively, Jesus goes to the cross as the One who accomplishes the judgment of the world such that he bears our sin, our judgment, in order to bear it away. The cross is the scene of a contest of judgments. We judge Christ, but in so doing God also judges us — precisely by allowing the Judge to be judged. As Barth has so magnificently characterized and summarized it, Christ is "The Judge Judged in Our Place." By that, Barth means that "[Christ] took our place as judge. He took our place as the judged. He was judged in our place. And he acted justly in our place."[38]

Christ takes our place as the judge because only by doing so can he be the Savior who judges our judgment and even judges our fear of judgment. The Father judges the world in Jesus Christ to accomplish our salvation. As Barth describes it, God judges the world "In order to judge it in the exercise of His kingly freedom to show His grace in the execution of His judgment, to pronounce us free in passing sentence, to free us by imprisoning us, to ground our life on our death, to redeem and save us by our destruction. That is how God has actually judged in Jesus Christ."[39] The character of that judgment is even more striking. The Father allows Jesus to be the judge who is judged by us. Jesus bears our judgment by being willing to be pushed out of the world onto the cross. "What took place is that the Son of God fulfilled the righteous judgment on us men by Himself taking our place as man and in our place undergoing the judgment under which we had passed." As such, he is the judge judged *for us*. He does not do it "with" us, in the sense that we might be able to claim any contribution to Jesus' action that must be, because of his willingness to bear our judgment, his passion. Rather, Jesus is the judge whose judgment is for us while it is accomplished without us (except in the sense of our complicity

37. Dietrich Bonhoeffer, *Letters and Papers from Prison*, ed. E. Bethge, tr. R. Fuller, F. Clark, et al. (New York: Macmillan, 1971) p. 360.

38. Barth, *Church Dogmatics* IV/1, p. 273.

39. Barth, *Church Dogmatics* IV/1, p. 222.

in nailing him to the cross). "Discipleship, the being of the Christian with Him, rests on the presupposition and can be carried through only on the presupposition that Jesus Christ is in Himself 'for us' — without our being with Him, without any fulfilment of our being either with or after Him — on the contrary (Rom. 5:6f.), even when we were without strength, godless, and enemies."[40] Jesus' willingness to be the Judge judged for us, however, is not only the burden of bearing this negative judgment on our lives. It is also the fulfillment of God's own righteousness, a forgiving love that seeks communion with God's Creation. "Jesus Christ has to be the Judge, the judged and in His own person the fulfilment of the judgment; His decisive work and word has to be His suffering and dying. But that is only the negative form of the fulness of a positive divine righteousness, which itself and as such is identical with the free love of God effectively interposing between our enmity and Himself, the work and word of His grace."[41] As such, Jesus Christ embodies the decisive change from the old age to the new. That change begins with his incarnation and in his ministry, but it finds its fulfillment in the judgment of the grace of God enacted on the cross.

Jesus' announcement and enactment of the inauguration of God's Kingdom, a Kingdom that requires social embodiment, provides not only a continuous relationship with the gracious and forgiving God of Israel; it also reveals the scope and costliness of the judgment that is in the service of that grace and forgiveness. Jesus' mission does not introduce a forgiveness unknown to Israel; but it does announce the costliness of God's forgiveness, focused on the restoration of all human beings to communion — with God, with one another, and with the whole Creation.

If the cross provides the judgment of God's grace, the resurrection provides the grace of that judgment. Through the resurrection, the contest of judgments reaches a decisive and transforming climax that reveals God's grace. The world judges Jesus by pushing him onto the cross, and God judges the world in that judgment; God issues a vindicating judgment of Jesus in the resurrection. This ensures that our judgment of Jesus and God's judgment of us are not the final word; God's forgiving grace transforms the contest of judgments into the possibility of new life for God's Creation. Thus Christ's resurrection is the Father's verdict, by the power of the Holy Spirit, confirming the efficacy of the cross as a judgment that brings a forgiving grace that we do not deserve and cannot earn.

40. Barth, *Church Dogmatics* IV/1, p. 229.
41. Barth, *Church Dogmatics* IV/1, p. 257.

The Father's verdict in the resurrection does not simply cancel the judgment of the cross. There is a world of difference between Christ "uncrucified" and Christ crucified and risen.[42] The risen Christ continues to bear the wounds of the crucified Jesus. As I will describe in the next two chapters, the gracious work of the Holy Spirit can re-create for the sake of a renewed future, but the Spirit cannot undo the past.

The resurrection is thus God's eschatological event, a sign by the power of the Spirit that human beings need not remain trapped in the judgment that fuels cycles of guilt and revenge, violence and counterviolence. Through baptism, Christians are inducted into God's eschatological Kingdom through the pattern of Christ's death and resurrection (see Romans 6:1-11). As such, the resurrection of the Crucified One calls people to a baptismal repentance, a daily living into our baptism that occasions the transformation of relationships. Such transformed relationships break the cycles of violence and vengeance. The risen Christ — the Judge judged for us, the pure Victim sacrificed for us — returns to us his judges with a judgment that does not condemn but calls us to new life. As Williams has argued,

> it is the pure victim alone who is capable of creative action, the transformation of the human world, the release from the pendulum swing of attack and revenge. The victim as "pure" victim is more than victim: when God receives and approves the condemned Jesus and returns him to his judges through the preaching of the Church, he transcends the world of oppressor-oppressed relations to create a new humanity, capable of other kinds of relation — between human beings, and between humanity and the Father.[43]

The crucified and risen Christ thus fulfills the work of his ministry and definitively reveals the gracious character of the God who forgives to reestablish communion. In Geoffrey Wainwright's terms, "From the side of humanity, Christ's total surrender of himself in love towards God and towards friend, neighbour and enemy ('Father, forgive them') defines a movement into which we may enter — and must, if we are to fulfill the human vocation to communion with God and among ourselves."[44]

We can enter such a movement, however, only if we recognize in our

42. See Rowan Williams, *Resurrection* (New York: Pilgrim, 1982) p. 89.

43. Williams, *Resurrection*, p. 15.

44. Geoffrey Wainwright, *Doxology: The Praise of God in Worship, Doctrine, and Life* (New York: Oxford University, 1980) p. 79.

rejection of Jesus, in our willingness to push God onto the cross, our own complicity in Sin. We must recognize ourselves as neither self-righteous judges nor as helpless victims. Such pictures invite the distortions in which all justice is only on one side, in which the lines of oppressor and oppressed are very clearly drawn. But such divisions only encourage the repetitive logic whereby those who were oppressed tend to become oppressors once they gain power. In response, as Christian Duquoc has suggested, "What is required is an attitude that is not determined by what has already been done, an innovative, a creative gesture. Otherwise enclosure within a repetitive logic is inevitable, and the term of this logic is the exclusion or the death of at least one of the parties. It is forgiveness that represents this innovative gesture."[45] That innovative gesture of forgiveness is definitively embodied in Jesus Christ; only the crucified and risen Christ is the just Judge, the pure Victim.

Thus it is by steadily keeping our eyes set on the crucified and risen Jesus, the "pure" Victim, that we can accept responsibility for our own complicity in the universal disaster of sinful brokenness. Accepting responsibility will vary according to the ways in which we have afflicted ourselves with, and been afflicted by, histories and habits of sin and evil. This undoubtedly calls for far greater repentance from those who have been more the perpetrators of sin than those who have suffered more; but none of us can escape the struggle to acknowledge our own capacity for and complicity in histories and habits that oppress and destroy. Whatever the particularities of our situation may be, we are enabled to accept responsibility because Christ's forgiveness breaks apart and transcends the reversals of roles that trap us as oppressors and oppressed, as victimizers and victims. We are invited to become a part of the new, eschatological community whose practices of forgiveness and reconciliation signify the restoration of communion — with God, with one another, and with the whole Creation.

I need at this point to return to Levinas's objection to ask whether, and if so how, it is addressed by my account of Christ's forgiveness. Levinas objected that a world where God substitutes himself for the victim, a world where pardon is all-powerful, is inhuman. I suggested that Christians claim that such a world is embodied in the life, death, and resurrection of Jesus of Nazareth. Is such a world "inhuman"? No, though an adequate response requires unpacking both sides of the objection. On the cross, God enfleshed in Jesus Christ is the substitute for all of the world's victims, bearing the

45. Christian Duquoc, "The Forgiveness of God," *Concilium* 184 (April 1986) p. 40.

judgment of the world's brokenness — its universal situation of disaster — so as to bear it away. But God does so in a way that does not ignore, but actually *requires,* the conversion of victimizers through a turning to their particular victims to seek forgiveness and reconciliation.[46] As Williams has suggested, our hope is that God is to be found "as we return to our victims seeking reconciliation, seeking to find in renewed encounter with them the merciful and transforming judgement of Jesus, the 'absolute' victim."[47]

That is why the "all-powerful pardon" that Jesus unleashes does not create an inhuman world, but actually signifies the hope for a more human world that approximates the fully human vocation to communion with God embodied in practices of God's Kingdom. For our conversion is a turning from our own judgment and our complicity in relations that diminish and oppress to a forgiven life that, by Christ's work in the power of the Holy Spirit, frees us and requires us to return to our particular victims seeking forgiveness and reconciliation. Again Williams's comments are instructive:

> God does not shoulder aside the victim to pronounce an empty and formal acquittal to the oppressor (what right has anyone to forgive on behalf of another? What right has any Gentile to "forgive" those who organized the Holocaust? What right has a non-worldly, discarnate, God to forgive any human being?): he is not to be found, his grace and mercy are not to be found, anywhere but in the past of human violence. God as gracious "occurs," is manifest, only in the resurrection of the crucified.[48]

Jesus' pardon is all-powerful precisely because it calls us — as those who have been forgiven — to seek forgiveness from those we have sinned against and to offer forgiveness to those who have sinned against us. Such forgiveness does not abandon the importance of reparation for the former or justice for the latter, but it does transform the context in which they are to be understood and embodied.[49]

In engaging in such practices of forgiveness, people learn to follow the crucified and risen Christ in overcoming and transcending the destruc-

---

46. This may include turning to myself as well, insofar as I may be both a victimizer and a victim in relation to my own life.

47. Williams, *Resurrection,* p. 16.

48. Williams, *Resurrection,* p. 22.

49. These are obviously difficult issues, and I unpack them in greater detail in chapters 8 and 9.

tive patterns of relationship in which we are enmeshed. Indeed, it is learning from Abba Anthony that "Our life and our death is with our neighbour."[50] It is learning to "love my neighbor as myself," discovering that my very identity is bound up with others — including those whom I have sinned against and those who have sinned against me.[51] Such a process may be slow, it may be painful, and it may be laborious, but it is also necessary and ultimately a sign of the triumph of God's grace.

That the process of learning to appropriate and embody Christ's forgiveness is slow, painful, and laborious is a reminder that we live in a time between the first and the second advents of Christ. It is a time when suffering and death still exist, a time when a regrettably large number of people refuse — or suffer from others' refusal — to embody God's forgiveness and so remain trapped in histories and habits of sin and evil.[52] It is a time analogous to that of Holy Saturday, that "puzzling interval" between the two great acts of God's judgment of grace.[53]

Thus, though the all-powerful pardon of Jesus Christ has been decisively embodied and pronounced in the cross and the resurrection, its full power has not yet been disclosed to us. For that, we still await the consummation of God's Kingdom in the second advent of Christ. This eschatological transformation of the world, for which we wait and to which we witness, is the work of the Holy Spirit because it is the Spirit who renews life in the newness of Jesus Christ.

50. Anthony 9, in *The Sayings of the Desert Fathers: The Alphabetical Collection,* tr. Benedicta Ward (Oxford: Mowbrays, 1981) p. 3.

51. The second part of the twofold Great Commandment does not say "Love your neighbor as *you love* yourself." The passage does not support the view that "healthy self-esteem" is necessary in order to be able to have something to give to others. Such a perspective would only invite the continuing self-absorption manifest in the self-help and self-esteem movements so prevalent in U.S. popular culture. To be sure, we must have a self that is capable of loving; and the heart of the gospel is that Jesus returns to each of us our self through the power of the resurrection. But the injunction to love the neighbor *as yourself* indicates that we must see our own lives as inextricably bound up with our neighbors' lives. And, of course, the parable of the Good Samaritan indicates the expansiveness of the neighbor's potential identity.

52. How Christians ought to deal with such people who refuse to seek lives of forgiveness is a complex problem that I take up in chapter 8, "Loving Enemies."

53. See Barth, *Church Dogmatics* IV/1, pp. 323-324 for the invocation of the "puzzling interval" as a description both of Holy Saturday and the time of the Church.

New Life in the Spirit

According to John's Gospel, as Jesus faces his imminent betrayal and likely death, he promises his disciples that he will not leave them orphaned. He promises to send an Advocate to abide with them as God's presence in the world, teaching them everything and reminding them of all that he has said to them (see John 14:15-21, 26). Indeed, this Advocate is none other than the Holy Spirit, the Spirit of truth, who comes from the Father, will testify on Jesus' behalf, and will guide the disciples into all the truth (15:26-27; 16:13). Hence, Jesus promises to send the Spirit to be God's abiding presence, enabling the continuing embodiment of the truthful, forgiving communion announced and enacted by Jesus. In so doing, Jesus also leaves the disciples with the assurance of peace — not as the world gives, but the peace of Christ.

Further, when the resurrected Christ returns to his frightened and bewildered disciples, he again says "Peace be with you." Then he breathes on them and says, "Receive the Holy Spirit. If you forgive anyone's sins, they are forgiven. If you retain anyone's sins, they are retained" (John 20:21-23). There is thus an inextricable relation between receiving the Holy Spirit and engaging in practices of forgiveness.

Indeed, the Spirit works both to turn and re-turn people to the power of Christ's forgiveness and to embody that forgiveness in relations with others. One cannot be had without the other. As Rowan Williams describes it,

> Truthfulness given to human beings and "sustained" in them, as a constant self-critical, alert, prayerful and receptive turning-back to Jesus, is the gift of the indwelling Spirit. And as given in the resurrection experience, it is also the empowerment to preach and realize the grace of Christ (John 20:22, 23). If we search for the bridge connecting our forgiven-ness with the commission to forgive, it is to be found in the presence with believers of the Spirit, given for recollection of Jesus *and* witness to Jesus.[54]

The Spirit enables those who have been forgiven by Christ also to become those who forgive, seeking to restore communion with others in analogous fashion to the ways it has been restored to them.

Prior to Christ's ascension, John's Gospel provides examples of the risen Christ conjoining this turning and re-turning to Christ with the

54. Williams, *Resurrection*, p. 42.

commission to witness to Jesus in relations with others. Indeed, these examples, especially the encounters with Mary Magdalene and Peter in chapters 20 and 21, illustrate the diverse ways in which forgiveness applies to the irreducible particularities of people's histories and habits.

Mary Magdalene was a follower of Jesus who had been forgiven and had shown the promise of new life during Jesus' ministry. But in John 20, it is early on Easter morning, and she is weeping outside the tomb. Unlike Peter and the other disciples, she had not deserted Jesus; rather, she felt deserted and disconsolate herself. In response to a question from two angels, Mary says she is weeping "because they have taken away my Lord, and I do not know where they have laid him" (John 20:13).

Mary is crying not simply because someone has carried away a body. The body that has been carried away is the Lord's body, the body of the One who has loved and affirmed Mary's humanity. So in a very real sense Mary has also been "carried away." Her sense of a diminished and even lost self is almost overwhelming. Jesus' death has brought not only the loss of identity but also the loss of hope. But then Mary hears the voice of Jesus call her by name. The risen Christ "names" Mary and thus calls her to a renewed sense of her own identity, precisely by restoring communion (20:15-16). Mary is now able to see this stranger as none other than the One who has forgiven her, loved her, and given her life. She is enabled to recognize her self precisely as she also recognizes God.[55]

The risen Lord responds to Mary's loss with a forgiving love that restores her to resurrected communion. The Jesus who was her friend now returns to her and once again befriends her. But she cannot cling to her past relationship with Jesus; she must go forward and embody her new life in mission to others (20:17-18). The risen Christ's appearance to Mary enables her to embody forgiveness in the promise of a new life that she, just a few verses earlier, had thought would be impossible. It is a new life that, presumably, would entail a willingness to proclaim and embody Christ's forgiveness in relations with others.

In contrast to Mary, Peter *had* very clearly betrayed Jesus. Indeed, after Jesus' arrest Peter had three times publicly denied any connection to Jesus, while standing by a charcoal fire. In chapter 21 of John's Gospel, the resurrected Christ appears to Peter and the other disciples on a beach in Galilee. There is again a charcoal fire, and Christ serves the disciples break-

---

55. See also the discussion in Williams, *Resurrection,* pp. 43-47, who has some extraordinary reflections on the significance of this passage for the task of restoring hope to people who have such a sense of diminished selves.

fast. Christ asks Peter three times, "Do you love me?" Each time, Peter responds, "Lord, you know that I love you." After the third time, the risen Christ gives the forgiven and reconciled Peter a mission to "feed my sheep" (21:15-17). Just as Peter had denied Jesus three times, so Jesus asks Peter about his love for Jesus three times. Yet even as he recalls Peter's sin, he communicates his forgiveness and reconciliation by giving Peter a renewed mission.

Just as the forgiveness and new life that Mary and Peter receive in their encounters with the risen Christ are patterned in irreducibly particular ways, so, after Christ's ascension, it is the work of the Holy Spirit to guide people in learning how to embody Christ's forgiveness in relation to the diverse, irreducibly particular histories, habits, and situations of specific people's lives. In this time between the times of Christ's first and second advents, it is often not clear what Christ's forgiveness entails in those specific situations — especially in instances, or perhaps long-standing trajectories, of horrifying evil and destructiveness. The Spirit listens, judges, and guides believers as we deliberate about the new life of Christ's forgiveness and seek to embody it through specific practices in irreducibly diverse circumstances.

The Spirit not only makes particular the universal significance of Christ's forgiveness; the Spirit also takes the particular identity of Christ and makes it universal through the practices and friendships of the Body of Christ, the Church. Jesus authorizes and obligates his disciples to forgive and be forgiven in God's name; more precisely, the disciples are called and enabled to do so by the power of the Holy Spirit, the Spirit of Truth. Indeed, as Christians engage in practices of forgiveness, we learn from the Spirit to name truthfully the Sin and the sins that have created habits and histories of sin and evil. Hence practices of forgiveness genuinely guided by the Holy Spirit enable us to begin the slow, difficult process of unlearning those habits of sin and evil — habits reinforced by attempts to justify ourselves or deceive ourselves or hate ourselves for those habits — and learning to hear and embody the Truth. But this Truth, including the painful and affirming truth about ourselves, comes to us inevitably as a judgment of grace, a forgiving and reconciling love that offers us the new life of communion and gives us a new perspective on our histories.

As such, the Spirit is the consoler and critic of the Church, judging and guiding Christians as we aim to be faithful to our eschatological vocation as forgiven and forgiving people seeking communion with God, with others, and with the whole Creation. In so doing, the Spirit enables the Church to become a "carrier" of the forgiving truthfulness of Jesus. As Williams describes the situation,

The believer who lives in the furnace of this truth is being made a witness to the rest of humanity of the possibility of living with truth — burning, but not consumed; and thus he or she becomes part of God's act of giving back to the world its memory. In the Spirit, we are not only the recipients but the transmitters of hope, and our new identity is bound up with that destiny to transmit hope, to "preach the gospel."[56]

In a similar fashion, James Buckley (borrowing a phrase from Flannery O'Connor) identifies the Church as "A Field of Living Fire," the fire that refines and purifies rather than consumes. The Spirit universalizes Christ's work by bringing the Church to a judgment in which "condemnation becomes purifying, cleansing, life giving, embodying anger but mostly joy (and its earthly parable, humor)."[57]

As such, the Spirit of Christ is at work in human life, bringing people to judgment and forgiveness so that our lives can once again be marked by communion. As John Zizioulas has described it, "The Spirit as 'power' or 'giver of life' opens up our existence to become relational, so that he may at the same time be 'communion' (koinonia, cf. 2 Corinthians 13:13)."[58] Indeed, the Spirit is at work throughout God's Creation, seeking to open up spaces where forgiveness can interrupt our tendencies toward self-destructive judgment and thereby create space for communion. Thomas Hopko rightly suggests that "people who are not believers in God, by the fact they are made in God's image, can have the sense that reconciliation is better than allowing the evil to go on."[59] Where the reconciliation is an authentic sign of God's judgment of grace, there we can say that the Spirit of Christ is at work.

In the next chapter I will explore in greater detail the ways in which the Spirit makes particular the universality of the Father's forgiveness in Christ. Then in chapter 6 I will explore the ways in which the Spirit makes universal, through specific practices of the Church, the particularity of the Father's forgiveness in Christ. In Part III, especially in chapter 7, I will consider the possibilities of finding the Spirit's work in diverse settings and lives in God's Creation.

56. Williams, Resurrection, p. 43.

57. James J. Buckley, "A Field of Living Fire: Karl Barth on the Spirit and the Church," Modern Theology 10/1 (January 1994) p. 96.

58. Zizioulas, Being as Communion, p. 112.

59. Thomas Hopko, "Living in Communion," Parabola 12/3 (August 1987) p. 51. See also chapter 7 below for further exploration of this theme.

What I have done thus far is to characterize the God who forgives and the nature of that forgiveness. The primary context of a Christian account of forgiveness is the God who lives in trinitarian relations of self-giving communion and thereby is willing to bear the cost of forgiveness in order to restore humanity to that communion. I have suggested that Christians claim that God's forgiveness is decisively pronounced in the life, death, and resurrection of the Jew Jesus. In the "far journey" of Jesus of Nazareth, God inaugurates a Kingdom marked by the definitive forgiveness that restores human beings' communion with God, with one another, and with the whole Creation. Christians need to recognize that this forgiveness is not unknown in Israel; Judaism knew and knows a gracious God, and embodies practices of repentance and forgiveness in relation to God and among human relationships. The decisive difference between Judaism and Jesus, and ultimately Judaism and Christianity, is whether God's Kingdom has genuinely been inaugurated in this man Jesus. For it is a Kingdom that also provides a shift in understanding the purpose and scope of God's forgiveness, a shift signaled by Christianity's vision of the Judge judged for us (or, in terms of the Temple, of Jesus as the perfect Sacrifice).

Even though Christians claim that this definitive forgiveness has been inaugurated in the Jew Jesus, we also recognize that the coming of the Kingdom in its fullness awaits the eschatological work of the Spirit, who is renewing our lives in the newness of Jesus Christ. And that takes time, the time of the Spirit's consoling, judging guidance in the Church and, perhaps, in other settings and lives in God's Creation. Nicholas Lash puts the matter eloquently when he suggests that there does not seem

> good reason to suppose that God's forgiveness, laborious donation of the Spirit of the Crucified through human hearts and practices, will ever finally transform, definitively overcome, our strenuous resistance to reality before the finishing of Paradise, the end of time, the "appearance" of the Lamb whose coming "takes away the sin of the world." Thus, the forgiveness of "original" sin is, as we would expect, the finishing of God's creation.[60]

God's love moves to reconciliation in the face of sin by means of forgiveness. So such forgiveness is a sign of the hoped for and promised coming of God's New Heaven and New Earth (see Revelation 21:1-5a).

To claim, as I have, not only that God forgives but that this forgiveness

---

60. Nicholas Lash, *Believing Three Ways in One God* (Notre Dame: University of Notre Dame, 1992) p. 116. Lash is referring to John 1:29.

is at the heart of the Triune God's creative and re-creative work in restoring humanity to communion with God, with one another, and with the whole Creation, opens up further questions and difficulties. It undoubtedly makes the task of understanding and embodying forgiveness more complex, even if it also makes the human prospect more hopeful. But such a claim, in all of its complexities, is also necessary if we are to bear faithful witness to the Father who forgives and recreates humanity in Jesus Christ by the power of the Spirit. So it is to a further specification and elaboration of this claim that I now turn.

5 Forgiveness, Repentance, and the Judgment of Grace

The Word That Transfigures Us in the Spirit

GOD'S FORGIVENESS in Christ is universal in scope, but it cannot be general or abstract. It needs to be made particular; that is, it must continually be re-presented in the diverse, irreducibly particular lives and situations in which we find ourselves. This is true both diachronically (in the movement historically through time) and synchronically (in the movement contemporaneously through place). Christians believe that the Holy Spirit enables this diachronic and synchronic re-presentation of the universal significance of Christ in particular lives and situations.

To some, invoking the Holy Spirit seems to be little more than using pious language that adds little to the discussion. That sometimes occurs, particularly if we fail to recognize the Spirit's work in enabling the specific friendships and practices of Christian community. Even so, the consequences of failing to recognize the Spirit's work can be considerable. For (as we shall see) when Jesus' name is invoked or, more specifically, his forgiveness proclaimed apart from the enlivening work of the Spirit, the invocation of "Jesus" and "his" forgiveness can destroy people's lives as easily as it can redeem them.

Further, if it is the work of the Spirit to bring people to holiness through specific habits and practices, then we need to attend to the dynamic relations between judgment and grace, repentance and forgiveness. For it is all too easy to have either grace without judgment or judgment without grace, to have forgiveness without repentance or repentance without forgiveness. As I will suggest in this chapter and the next, the Spirit is the One who enables human transformation by making Christ's universally significant judgment of grace particular by inducing our repentance as a component of God's forgiveness; in so doing, the Spirit guides us — so I will argue in the next chapter — in our habits and practices as we seek to discern how to appropriate and re-present Christ in the particularities of our lives and in the situations we face.

This chapter focuses on the relationships between judgment and grace, between forgiveness and repentance. For if a grace without judgment becomes simply "cheap grace" that occasions no transformation, a judgment without grace becomes the means for holding others accountable such that cycles of violence can easily go unbroken and even escalate. Similarly, if forgiveness without repentance invites the perpetuation of sin and the condoning of wrongdoing, repentance without forgiveness can easily lead to despair and self-destructive nihilism. How, then, does the Spirit work to hold together the priority of grace and forgiveness while nonetheless taking judgment and repentance seriously?

I will argue that God's forgiveness, enacted decisively in the slaying and raising of Jesus Christ, is a judgment of grace that requires and enables our repentance. Further, our repentance itself includes the centrality of a judgment of grace on ourselves and on others. This movement arises out of the priority of God's eschatological Kingdom. That is, the notions of judgment and grace, forgiveness and repentance, must be placed within the context of the ends (and more comprehensively the eschatological End) toward which they are directed. For Christians, judgment aims at grace, and grace is a form of judgment. This judgment of grace, a specification of God's forgiveness, aims at transformation — a transformation that the recipients of forgiveness consent to and that therefore calls for repentance. But this repentance aims not at itself — for when this happens, the result is either a self-righteousness of works or despair — but at the responsive and mutual love of communion in God's Kingdom. Put concisely, I will argue that the *particularity* of God's forgiveness, of God's judgment of grace, requires and enables lives of repentance in the context of the communion of God's inbreaking Kingdom.

Unfortunately, when we fail to see and embody this forgiveness in relation to particular lives, specific situations, and concrete practices, we too easily transmute the notions of judgment and grace, forgiveness and repentance into abstractions that destroy rather than give life. Hence, the chapter begins with an exploration of the destructive consequences of proclaiming Jesus' forgiveness only in general and abstract terms. Flannery O'Connor's novel *Wise Blood* shows how certain understandings of God, and more specifically of God's forgiveness, actually distort our notions of judgment and repentance, grace and forgiveness. As a result, asserting Jesus' forgiveness only in general and abstract terms might actually lead not to new life but further "inhuman" destruction and all-too-human death.

Following the discussion of *Wise Blood,* I turn to an exploration of the relationship between judgment and grace, focusing on the implications of claiming that we cannot avoid engaging in judgment, but that God's forgiveness transforms that judgment into a judgment of grace. Then I focus on issues of repentance and forgiveness, specifically by addressing the objections — using Richard Swinburne's account as an example — that repentance must be prior to forgiveness if we are to take Sin and sins seriously. Finally, I conclude by briefly examining a story in Luke's Gospel that suggests the transformative difference God's forgiveness in Christ can indeed make.

The Absence of God's Presence

Hazel Motes, the central character of *Wise Blood,* is the son and grandson of southern evangelical preachers, preachers who traveled the southern U.S. preaching in tents, from the tops of automobiles, and out in the open fields. His grandfather would urgently insist that his hearers repent, for they had the character of stones. But, "Jesus had died to redeem them! Jesus was so soul-hungry that He had died, one death for all, but He would have died every soul's death for one! Did they understand that? Did they understand that for each stone soul, He would have died ten million deaths, had His arms and legs stretched on the cross and nailed ten million times for one of them?"[1]

After one episode as a small child, when Hazel had snuck into a circus tent and seen a naked woman, he had recognized that he, too, needed to repent of his sin. But when his mother told him that Jesus died to redeem him, Hazel responded that "I never ast him." Instead, he put rocks in his

---

1. Flannery O'Connor, *Wise Blood,* in *3 By Flannery O'Connor* (New York: Signet, 1962) p. 16. Further citations will be of this edition and will be given parenthetically in the text. In this discussion I am indebted to conversations with Michael Cartwright in the shaping of my understanding of the novel and its bearing on forgiveness.

shoes, hoping to satisfy Jesus of the guilt he felt — though he never received a sign that it did satisfy him.[2] Here was a repentance for its own sake.

Even so, Hazel knew by the time he was twelve that he was going to be a preacher. While still a youth, he "saw Jesus move from tree to tree in the back of his mind, a wild ragged figure motioning him to turn around and come off into the dark where he was not sure of his footing, where he might be walking on the water and not know it and then suddenly know it and drown" (p. 16). As a young man going off to serve in the Army, Hazel had a strong confidence in his ability to resist evil; the Bible was the only book he read.

He comes back from the Army, however, a changed man. He reads no book at all now, though he keeps the Bible because it came from home. Hazel does not return to his family home, for the members of his family have died. So he sets off to a nearby town where he does not know anyone. His first stop in the new town is to go to a hooker. When the cabbie taking him there comments on the oddity of a preacher going to such an establishment, Hazel responds "I ain't any preacher" and insists that "I don't believe in anything" (p. 21).

The next day Hazel goes into town, and there he encounters a blind preacher named Asa Hawks and his daughter Sabbath Lily. Asa insists to Hazel that "you can't run away from Jesus" and urges him to "Repent." Hazel protests, "I don't believe in sin." When Asa responds with several invocations of "Jesus loves you," Hazel says that "Nothing matters but that Jesus don't exist" (pp. 32-33). Asa tells Hazel to distribute some religious tracts to people leaving a building. Instead Hazel begins preaching a different message:

> I want to tell you people something. Maybe you think you're not clean because you don't believe. Well you are clean, let me tell you that. Every one of you people are clean and let me tell you why if you think it's because of Jesus Christ Crucified you're wrong. I don't say he wasn't crucified but I say it wasn't for you. Listen here, I'm a preacher myself and I preach the truth. . . . I'm going to preach a new church — the church of truth without Jesus Christ Crucified. (p. 34)

Hazel then turns to a young man that he has met named Enoch Emery and observes "I don't need Jesus." Yet a short while later, as Enoch is unsuccess-

---

2. See p. 39. This story appears as a flashback later in the novel, though chronologically it takes place when Hazel is a young child.

fully trying to make friends with Hazel, he finally tells Hazel, "I knew when I first seen you you didn't have nobody nor nothing but Jesus. I seen you and I knew it" (p. 36).

Enoch Emery is a loner whose life is characterized by ritualized daily routines and an almost mystical sense of when things are going to happen. Further, he is obsessed with material objects, most of all a small statue that he has seen in the museum that he visits each afternoon. He is eager to show it to someone, and senses that this person will arrive on a particular day. And, when Hazel drives his new car (purchased for forty dollars) to the park and finds Enoch, Enoch thinks that Hazel is the one. Hazel simply wants Asa and Sabbath's address, but Enoch promises to give it to him only if he first goes to see this little statue. But they can only get to the statue by going through Enoch's full rituals, including a stop at a local diner. There Hazel blurts out to the waitress, "I AM clean. . . . If Jesus existed, I wouldn't be clean" (p. 53).

Hazel may not believe in Jesus, or even that Jesus exists, but he cannot avoid becoming a preacher. "Well, I preach the Church Without Christ. I'm member and preacher to the church where the blind don't see and the lame don't walk and what's dead stays that way. Ask me about that church and I'll tell you it's the church that the blood of Jesus don't foul with redemption" (p. 60). And when Asa and Sabbath's landlady asks whether this church is Protestant or something foreign, Hazel responds unhesitatingly "Protestant" (p. 61). He rents a room from the landlady, and then goes to see Asa and Sabbath. He has decided to seduce Sabbath, because he thinks that when Asa sees his daughter ruined, it will prove that Hazel is serious about preaching The Church Without Christ. Further, having women is a way of showing that "he didn't believe in sin since he practiced what was called it" (p. 63).[3] So Hazel slips Sabbath a piece of paper indicating his interest in her.

Asa tells Hazel, "You still have a chance to save yourself if you repent," adding that "I can't save you but you can save yourself." Hazel responds that he has already saved himself, and "without the repenting" (p. 64). In turn, Asa hands Hazel a newspaper clipping with the headline EVANGELIST PROMISES TO BLIND SELF. The news story itself indicates that Asa Hawks promised to blind himself with lime "to justify his belief that Christ Jesus had redeemed him." But Hazel insists that "nobody with a good car needs to be

---

3. Or, as Hazel had earlier indicated, if there is sin, it is much deeper and precedes acts of whoremongering or blaspheming. See pp. 44-45. Even there, however, Hazel says that "I don't have to run from anything because I don't believe in anything."

justified" (p. 64), and Hazel has such a car — or so he thinks. After Hazel leaves, Sabbath reminds Asa that he did not show Hazel the other clipping, the one headlined EVANGELIST'S NERVE FAILS. Asa is a fake.

Hazel continues to preach The Church Without Christ, a church where there is no forgiveness because there is no redemption or any need for it. And any talk of redemption, such as it is, does not make any real difference for specific friendships or practices. Hazel proclaims,

> If Jesus had redeemed you, what difference would it make to you? You wouldn't do nothing about it. Your faces wouldn't move, neither this way nor that, and if it was three crosses there and Him hung on the middle one, that wouldn't mean no more to you and me than the other two. Listen here. What you need is something to take the place of Jesus, something that would speak plain. The Church Without Christ don't have a Jesus but it needs one! It needs a new jesus! It needs one that's all man, without blood to waste, and it needs one that don't look like any other man so you'll look at him. Give me such a jesus, you people. Give me such a new jesus and you'll see how far the Church Without Christ can go! (p. 78)

Enoch Emery, listening to Hazel preach, suddenly realizes that the new jesus that Hazel needs is none other than the statue hidden in the museum. He heads off to steal it for Hazel.

Hazel's preaching attracts another preacher, Onnie Jay Holy, who finds Hazel's message compelling but in need of some refinement. Onnie Jay insists that the Church Without Christ is trustworthy because there is nothing foreign in it and because it is based on the Bible — more specifically, "it's based on your own personal interpitation of the Bible" (p. 84). But Hazel is distrustful of Onnie Jay, and he becomes perturbed when Onnie Jay calls the church "The Holy Church of Christ Without Christ." When Hazel corrects him, Onnie Jay says, "It don't make any difference how many Christs you add to the name if you don't add none to the meaning, friend." And, Onnie Jay adds, "If you want to get anywheres in religion, you got to keep it sweet. You got good idears but what you need is an artist-type to work with you" (pp. 86-87). Onnie Jay knows how successful the creation of a "sweet jesus" constructed in our own image can be.

Even so, Hazel rejects the advice. He remains committed to the truth that there is no truth. As he preaches the next day,

> I preach there are all kinds of truth, your truth and somebody else's, but behind all of them, there's only one truth and that is that there's no

truth. . . . No truth behind all truths is what I and this church preach! Where you come from is gone, where you thought you were going to never was there, and where you are is no good unless you can get away from it. Where is there a place for you to be? No place. (p. 90)

When he returns to his room from preaching, Sabbath is waiting for him in his bed. The night before, Hazel had snuck into their apartment, lit a match in front of Asa's eyes, and thereby had uncovered Asa's deception. Now Sabbath tells Hazel that she's not going to leave Hazel no matter what. After all, she tells him, "There's no place for me to go. [Asa's] run off on me and it was you who run him off. I was watching last night and I seen you come in and hold that match to his face. I thought anybody would have seen what he was before that without having to strike a match. He's just a crook. He ain't even a big crook, just a little one, and when he gets tired of that, he begs on the street" (p. 92). Sabbath then indicates that she is filthy, just as she takes Hazel to be, the only difference being that she likes it. She offers to teach Hazel to like it too, and they end up having sex.

Enoch brings the stolen new jesus to Hazel's apartment and gives it to Sabbath. However, when Hazel sees the statue he smashes it against the wall and sweeps the pieces out the window. Sabbath is furious; she says, "I knew when I first seen you you were mean and evil," adding that "I seen you wouldn't let nobody have nothing. I seen you were mean enough to slam a baby against a wall. I seen you wouldn't never have no fun or let anybody else because you didn't want nothing but Jesus!" Hazel shouts back, "I don't want nothing but the truth" (pp. 102-103).

Indeed, he has such a passion for the "truth" (that is, the truth that there is no truth) that he kills a man that Onnie Jay Holy has hooked up with to preach another new jesus. Hazel thinks this other prophet believes in Jesus and so cannot be true in his preaching about a new jesus. After Hazel runs the man over with his car, he walks up to him and observes, "Two things I can't stand . . . — a man that ain't true and one that mocks what is" (p. 111).

The next day, Hazel goes to a filling station to get his car checked out and filled with gas for a trip to a new city, another place where he can preach The Church Without Christ. He tells the boy who is tending to the car that

it was not right to believe anything you couldn't see or hold in your hands or test with your teeth. He said he had only a few days ago believed in blasphemy as the way to salvation, but that you couldn't even believe in that because then you were believing in something to blaspheme. As for the Jesus who was reported to have been born at Bethlehem and crucified on Calvary for man's sins, Haze said, He was too foul a notion for a sane person to carry in his head, and he picked up the boy's water bucket and bammed it on the concrete pavement to emphasize what he was saying. (p. 112)

As he proceeds out of town, Hazel is pulled over by a policeman. He does not have a driver's license, so he is in a vulnerable position. Further, the policeman tells Hazel that he just doesn't like his face — not a chargeable offense, but it compounds Hazel's problems. So the policeman sends the car, Hazel's security and simulacrum of salvation (a man with a good car don't need to be justified!), over an embankment. The policeman then asks him whether he is going anywhere, to which Hazel replies "No" (p. 114).

Hazel makes his way back into town, buys a bucket and some quick-lime from a supply store, and returns to his apartment to blind himself. His landlady does not understand this action: Why would he destroy his eyes, yet save himself from death? To be blind was to be as good as dead. "She imagined it was like you were walking in a tunnel and all you could see was a pin point of light. She had to imagine the pin point of light; she couldn't think of it at all without that. She saw it as some kind of a star, like the star on Christmas cards. She saw him going backwards to Bethlehem and she had to laugh" (p. 119).

Hazel also walks now with rocks in his shoes and wraps pieces of barbed wire around his chest. When his landlady asks him why, he says "To pay." And when she asks him "Pay for what?" he says, "It don't make any difference for what." A few minutes later, he observes to her, "If there's no bottom in your eyes, they hold more" (p. 121). Hazel has begun to see something, perhaps only that he is not clean (p. 122). Yet the landlady still cannot see, understanding only the link between blindness and death (p. 125).

Hazel sets out from the apartment, despite the landlady's protestations. When he doesn't return after two days, the landlady asks the police to find him and return him to pay his rent. Two policemen find him almost unconscious, lying in a drainage ditch. He protests that "I want to go on where I am going" (p. 126), perhaps the first time that Hazel genuinely has a sense of direction, of an orientation to his life. But the policemen plan to return him to the landlady, and one of them knocks him on the head with a billy club.

Hazel dies in the squad car, but the policemen do not notice and take him back to the landlady. There she observes his now composed face.

> She shut her eyes and saw the pin point of light but so far away that she could not hold it steady in her mind. She felt as if she were blocked at the entrance of something. She sat staring with her eyes shut, into his eyes, and felt as if she had finally got to the beginning of something she couldn't begin, and she saw him moving farther and farther away, farther and farther into the darkness until he was the pin point of light. (p. 126)

And there the story ends.

Wise Blood presents a stark critique of a world in which God's forgiveness, if there is such, makes virtually no difference — or at least no transformative difference — in people's lives. "Jesus" hovers throughout the novel, but it is a Jesus whose presence is endlessly deferred by a more decisive absence. The name seems to refer to an abstract and general, perhaps even all-powerful, redeemer. But Jesus, and such notions as sin and redemption and repentance, are abstracted from the gospel narratives and practices, which give them their intelligibility. As a result, the ever-present invocation of the name is inextricably tied to the ever-absent narratives and practices that tell us who this Jesus is and what his work does and does not accomplish.

Hazel represents a Protestantism evacuated of its substance, left only with a lingering rhetoric of justification — now transmuted into vain and ultimately self-destructive attempts at self-justification, finally through repentance — and hackneyed (and finally meaningless) claims about Jesus' redemption. That is why Hazel believes that his Church Without Christ is not foreign but Protestant.

Conversely, Enoch Emery represents a Catholicism that insists on the importance of the material world and of ritual. But whereas such convictions ought to be contextualized within a sacramental mediation by the Holy Spirit of God's presence in Jesus, they are detached in Enoch's life from the narratives and practices that invoke Jesus' presence. As a result, Enoch's sacramental sensibility is transmuted into confused and twisted attempts to provide a material character to God's presence — even if it means stealing a new jesus from the museum.

Indeed, *Wise Blood* creates a world in which God's forgiveness, represented by the ever-present invocational Jesus, is taken to be all-powerful — for individuals and for the world. Yet it makes no transformative difference in people's lives, because there is no means to actualize that forgiveness in the dynamics of human relationships. Consequently, the difference that it makes is often a destructive one, as the illusions of either a cheap grace or an ineffective redemption wreak havoc and even death on particular people's lives and relationships. There is no material work of the Holy Spirit transforming our habits and practices as we appropriate Christ's forgiveness in the particularities of our lives. There is no grace, nor any promise of a new or renewed community.

In fact, the invocation of an endlessly deferred presence of Jesus makes too much of a difference in the world, creating a paralysis of judgment and repentance coupled with a desperate longing for the grace and forgiveness that creates new life. We are left either with the self-satisfied smugness of Onnie Jay Holy or the desperate attempts by Asa Hawks (who fails) and Hazel Motes (who in some sense succeeds) at *proving* their earnest interest in justification through acts of self-immolation. But even Hazel admits that it "don't make any difference" what his payment is for. There is no end for his repentance. The characters are looking for signs of presence, signs of hope; but unfortunately there is no signifier. We are left with the absence of God's forgiving presence: judgment without grace, repentance without forgiveness.

At the same time, however, the language of a more authentic gospel of God's forgiveness continues to haunt Hazel Motes in particular, and it hovers over the novel generally. In the preface to the second edition of *Wise Blood*, Flannery O'Connor makes the following observation: "That belief in Christ is to some a matter of life and death has been a stumbling block for readers who would prefer to think it a matter of no great consequence. For them Hazel Motes' integrity lies in his trying with such vigor to get rid of the ragged figure who moves from tree to tree in the back of his mind. For the author Hazel's integrity lies in his not being able to" (p. 8). Hazel cannot escape the sense that Jesus might truly be the One who redeems and, in that redemption, offers the promise of new life. Indeed, at the end of the novel, even in the destructive act of blinding himself, Hazel begins to see; rather than the nihilistic aimlessness that has characterized so much of his life, he is given a sense of direction. After all, the landlady sees that pin point of light taking him backward to Bethlehem — and presumably also forward to a clearer glimpse of God's inbreaking Kingdom.

That light signifies the Holy Spirit's illumination of both Christ's life and our lives, a light that enables us to *see* Christ's judgment not as condemnation but as grace. It is a light that overcomes our blindness, our captivity to the darkness, by enabling us to recognize and reclaim the particularity of the universal significance of Jesus Christ. It is a light that enables us to repent *as a response to* God's forgiveness, not in a self-destructive (and often other-destructive!) repentance that seeks to *earn* God's forgiveness.

If O'Connor is right in satirizing both a Church Without Christ and the destructiveness of an abstract, all-powerful Christ, then we need to reconnect the invocation of Jesus Christ's name with the Holy Spirit's animation of the narratives, friendships, and practices that give intelligibility and specificity to Christ's forgiveness. O'Connor herself provides a cue toward that reconnection in the very name of "Hazel Motes." One need not treat *Wise Blood* as an allegory to note how Hazel's name indicates the problem of a lack of vision and judgment. Hazel is a standard description for a particular eye color; further, he is often called "Haze," suggesting a lack of clear vision. Even more, the last name "Motes" evokes (particularly for Southerners at the time O'Connor was writing) the King James translation of Matthew 7:1-5. There people are criticized for being preoccupied with seeing "motes" (that is, specks) in their brothers' and sisters' eyes while failing to recognize the "beams" in their own eye. This suggests Hazel's preoccupation with judging others self-righteously, with seeing the motes in their eyes, while failing to recognize his own culpability, his own need of judgment — a judgment of grace.

The passage in Matthew's Gospel is situated within the narratives and practices of Jesus' life, death, and resurrection. The Gospel presents Jesus' challenges to our self-righteous judgment (which ultimately nails Jesus to the cross), culminating with the crucified and risen Jesus' judgment of grace. That judgment of grace transforms the human situation. This is a reminder that while Christ's forgiveness was accomplished *extra nos* (outside us), it also carries with it the central benefit of being *pro nobis* (for us). That is, we need to return to some of the themes developed in the last chapter to see more specifically what Christ's judgment of grace, mediated through the Holy Spirit, means *for each of us* in our particularity and for our understanding of the relationship between judgment and grace. In so doing, we will also become better prepared to understand the complex relationships between repentance and forgiveness.

The Judgment of Grace

We have already seen in Chapter 1 how Dietrich Bonhoeffer challenged the "therapeutic" interpretation of Matthew 7:1 ("Do not judge so that you will not be judged"). Bonhoeffer rightly recognized that the choice is not whether we judge; the question is *how* we are to judge. We are to give up that judgmental*ism* by which we sit in self-righteous condemnation of others. We need to learn, by the power of the Holy Spirit, how to receive and offer a discerning judgment that occasions and enhances new life rather than destruction.

Such learning requires us to remember and proclaim, as I suggested in Chapter 4, that the "journey of the Son into the far country" is a judgment of grace. Or, more directly put, Christ's forgiveness must be received by us simultaneously as a judgment on the destructiveness of our lives — whether it be our own self-destruction or the ways in which we destroy one another. God's forgiveness does not come apart from an acknowledgment of, and confrontation with, human sin and evil. God does not "overlook" or "ignore" our destructiveness.[4] If that were the case, Christ's journey would not have taken the shape that it inevitably did. Rather, God confronts sin and evil in all of its awfulness. In so doing, God exposes our wounds, both those that have been inflicted on us and those we have inflicted on others and on ourselves.

However, God's confrontation with sin and evil is *not* for the purpose of condemning us. Indeed, it is for the explicit purpose of forgiving us and healing our — and the world's — wounds (see John 3:16-21). It is a judgment *of grace*. As I have already suggested, there is nothing we can do to *earn* God's forgiveness, God's healing. This is one of the mistakes that afflicts the characters throughout *Wise Blood*. God's forgiveness, God's healing, has been accomplished *extra nos* through the slaying and raising of Christ. Thus forgiveness and healing come to us as a free gift of grace. It is in this sense that we rightly speak of God's *un*conditional forgiveness and healing as signs of God's Kingdom.

Even so, while there are no conditions for God forgiving us, we must engage in practices of repentance in order to appropriate that forgiveness. That is to say, God's forgiveness becomes available to us as we learn to see both the reality of the world under judgment and our participation in that fallenness. As Hans Urs von Balthasar puts it, "God forgives through free grace and not on the basis of acts of penance, but . . . this forgiveness cannot become effective unless there is an expiatory conversion of the person."[5] Our conversion comes about as we recognize that we can confront our past, understood in personal, social, and cosmic terms, because we are no longer

4. This is the problem with John Milbank's formulation, according to which Christian forgiveness and reconciliation involve acting "as if [people's] sin was not there." By contrast, it is only by acknowledging that their sin *is* there, but dealing with it through a judgment of grace, that we can genuinely achieve reconciliation. See Milbank, *Theology and Social Theory* (Oxford: Blackwell, 1990) p. 411.

5. Hans Urs von Balthasar, "Jesus and Forgiveness," *Communio* 11/4 (1984) p. 322.

in bondage to it. We have been judged, and thus we acknowledge our sinfulness; but that judgment is wholly in the service of grace, healing, and holiness.

Judgment is important, because no matter how much we may try to forget the past and our history of sinfulness, unconfronted sin and bitterness find ways to influence our lives. That is why it is largely a mistake to say "forgive and forget." Rather, the judgment of grace enables us, through the power of the Holy Spirit, to remember well. When God promises to "blot out [Israel's] transgressions" and "not remember [Israel's] sins" (Isaiah 43:25; see also Jeremiah 31:34), God is not simply letting bygones be bygones. Rather, God is testifying to God's own gracious faithfulness. Moreover, such forgiveness provides a way to narrate the history of Israel's sinfulness within the context of God's covenant of grace. To be sure, such a narration makes it possible, and even necessary, to forget the sin. But the past itself, the history, is and needs to be remembered so that a new and renewed future becomes possible.

The judgment of grace, a judgment that enables the recovery of memory, involves moving initially from a third person stance of *holding* people (or oneself) responsible to a first person stance of *accepting* responsibility.[6] The third person stance invites a judgmental stance that destroys others (particularly when exercised self-righteously) and also oneself (particularly when exercised as self-condemnation). The first person stance invites us to accept responsibility; and that occurs through a forgiving love that redraws the boundaries of our identity. Indeed, Ruby Turpin's conversion in O'Connor's "Revelation" (see chapter 2 above) occurs as she moves from a judgmental, third person stance to a first person stance of accepting responsibility. Love draws us into relationship, enabling and inviting us to remember and claim the past as our own.

Paradigmatically, Christians believe that this occurs through God's forgiving love. If, as I suggested in the last chapter, we have been created for *communion,* then we are called back into that communion through love. Because of the manifold ways in which we — all of us — engage in the diminution and destruction of our selves and those of others, that restoration of communion must ultimately be accomplished by a messianic, forgiving love. But it must also be a forgiving love empowered by the Holy Spirit and enacted in the habits and practices of specific people and in specific situations — in and through all of their particularity.

6. See Jonathan Lear, *Love and Its Place in Nature: A Philosophical Interpretation of Freudian Psychoanalysis* (New York: Farrar, Straus, and Giroux, 1990) pp. 175ff., for an insightful discussion of this contrast in relation to psychoanalysis.

This is why the fundamental orientation of Christian life is that we are forgiven. As Stanley Hauerwas has suggested, more important than our learning to forgive is our learning to be forgiven.[7] For in many situations, the possibility of reconciliation has been eliminated because both parties (or all the parties) have come prepared to forgive and are completely unprepared to be forgiven. We cannot trade on our ability to forgive or on our own self-righteousness and power. Conversely, we also cannot trade on our *in*ability to forgive or on our own self-degradation and our lack of power. We must have an ironic relationship to our own acts of forgiving, recognizing the prior need for us always to examine the ways in which we need to be forgiven for either our self-righteousness or our self-degradation (or both). We are fundamentally people who are forgiven sinners. Indeed, in the Gospel of Luke the people most able to respond to Jesus' forgiving love are those who see themselves as sinners (for example, Peter, the woman "who showed great love" in ch. 7, Zacchaeus, and the tax collector in ch. 18). Through the cleansing of our eyes (see Luke 11:33-36), we are enabled to respond to Jesus by seeing God, ourselves, and others more clearly. Such an ironic posture to our own forgiving, so the Gospel suggests, takes us out of the realm of thinking in terms primarily of domination and control (or of being dominated and controlled). We are enabled by Jesus' forgiving love to forgive others because we learn to understand ourselves as sinners who have been forgiven.

This is a reminder that forgiveness inevitably involves power and the dynamics of power-relations. The granting or withholding of forgiveness entails an exercise of power; but if the understanding of forgiveness begins with an acknowledgment that we are all in *need* of God's forgiveness, then this alters the dynamics of power and creates new possibilities for community. As Rowan Williams has characterized the importance of learning to be forgiven,

> So to live a "forgiven" life is not simply to live in a happy consciousness of being absolved. Forgiveness is precisely the deep and abiding sense of what relation — with God or with other human beings — can and should be; and so it is itself a stimulus, an irritant, necessarily provoking protest at impoverished versions of social and personal relations. Once we grasp that forgiveness occurs not by a word of acquittal but by a transformation of the world of persons, we are not likely to regard it as something which merely refers backwards.[8]

7. Stanley Hauerwas, *The Peaceable Kingdom* (Notre Dame: University of Notre Dame, 1983) p. 89.

8. Rowan Williams, *Resurrection* (New York: Pilgrim, 1982) p. 52.

Forgiven-ness provides a new context for us to understand our lives in relation to God, one another, and the whole Creation and to discern more clearly God's purposes from the act of creation to the promised eschatological consummation of Creation. That is, learning to be forgiven also provides the context for our journey toward holiness, toward the consummation of my and our friendship with God (and thereby also with one another) in God's Kingdom.

If we understand forgiven-ness not only as a freeing of the burdens of the past but also as "the deep and abiding sense of what relation — with God or with other human beings — can and should be," then we can only learn to embody that forgiven-ness in habits and practices that attend to the particularities of each of our lives and situations. Just as there is no one way in which social and personal relations have become impoverished and continue to be impoverished (and also no one way in which people are victimizers and victims), so there is no one way of appropriating Christ's forgiveness by the power of the Spirit. Such appropriation invites us not to forget the past, but to remember it well so that we can envision and embody a future different from the past. In that sense, we need the Spirit both to return to us our memories and also to enliven our imaginations.

I will suggest in the next chapter that Christians learn to appropriate Christ's forgiveness as the Spirit guides, judges, and consoles us in and through specific practices and friendships of Christian communities. Before doing so, however, I need to identify four interrelated objections to the account of Christ's judgment of grace I have offered thus far. First, by stressing Christ's judgment of grace for people, am I not overplaying the "vertical" dimension (of God's forgiveness) at the expense of the "horizontal" dimension (of interhuman forgiveness)? Second, have I not obscured the difference between Sin (as estrangement from God, one another, and ourselves) and sins (as specific acts or failures to act appropriately, specific thoughts or failures to discern well, specific passions or failures to be properly affected)? Third, in my emphasis on the sense in which we all need to be forgiven, have I not unfairly collapsed the differences among various people's culpability and accountability — or, put more sharply, am I not letting those who have done horrifying things off the hook too easily by an oversimplifying equivalence that "we all need forgiveness"? And fourth, by making repentance an integral component of, but not a prerequisite for, forgiveness, am I not opening the door to the abuse of forgiveness by people who have no intention of repenting or even of stopping their most destructive behavior?

Obviously, I cannot adequately address all the implications of these objections in this chapter; later chapters will take them up as well. But I need to begin responding to them here because they expose uncomfortable questions often glossed by Christians both in theoretical discussions of forgiveness and in practical situations. I do so by focusing our attention on the complex dynamics of forgiveness and repentance in Christian life.

The Dynamics of Forgiveness and Repentance

I suggested in the last chapter that one of the crucial differences between Jesus and the Judaism of his day was Jesus' willingness to forgive in God's name without requiring prior repentance and, more determinatively, his authorization for his disciples to do likewise. That he does so, however, is linked to his proclamation and enactment of God's inbreaking eschatological Kingdom through his life, death, and resurrection. Hence, if we are rightly to attend to the complex relations between Christian forgiveness and repentance and to the distinctions between Sin and sins and between the vertical and horizontal dimensions of forgiveness, we also need to situate those relations and distinctions in the context of God's inbreaking Kingdom and its implications for specific people and specific situations.

Yet this is precisely what is missing in many modern discussions of forgiveness and repentance. These discussions have tended to focus on the importance of repentance, partly as a way of seeking to avoid or overcome "cheap grace" and partly as a way of grappling with the horrifying and often persistent violence that turns forgiveness-without-repentance into a weapon used by the powerful to subjugate the powerless. In such circumstances, unfortunately all too familiar in many situations of (for example) domestic abuse, the wrongdoer can persist in the physical abuse, knowing that afterward he can presume that the victim(s) will offer unconditional forgiveness.

To be sure, emphasizing the centrality of repentance is a way to guarantee that people take questions of culpability and accountability seriously and that they not lose sight of the particular sins that they have committed not only against God but against one another. However, it is unfortunately all too often a way to guarantee that we will either (at best) oversimplify issues of forgiveness and repentance or (at worst, and more likely) distort a Christian understanding of forgiveness by making repentance a prerequisite for forgiveness.

This is often true in popular treatments of forgiveness, as also in everyday life. But it is no less true in sophisticated philosophical and theological analyses. For example, Immanuel Kant offers a classic account of this position in *Religion within the Limits of Reason Alone*. Kant argues that the union of an atonement (for example, reparation for debt, redemption, reconciliation with God) and a good course of life in the future can only be comprehended by assuming that one can be *derived* from the other. Further, Kant thinks that it must be the forgiveness of a "transcendent atonement" that must be derivative from repentance. So, he concludes, a person "must believe that he must first improve his way of life, so far as improvement lies in his power, if he is to have even the slightest ground for hope of such a higher gain [from a transcendent atonement]."[9]

More recently, the prominent and influential British philosopher Richard Swinburne has extended the logic of Kant's argument for the prior requirement of repentance to forgiveness in his book *Responsibility and Atonement*. Swinburne's argument is remarkably clear and straightforward, and it merits careful examination in order to show both how common is the modern assumption of a causal priority for repentance to forgiveness and why that assumption carries with it such deleterious consequences for practices of Christian theology and life.

Swinburne argues that reparation, repentance, apology, and penance to the victim(s) are all necessary prerequisites for a person to remove his or her guilt and to make atonement for the past. He indicates that, following these other four actions, "The final act belongs to the victim — to forgive."[10] Further, Swinburne adds that a victim's "disowning of a hurtful act is *only* to be called forgiveness when it is in *response* to at least some minimal attempt at atonement such as an apology."[11]

On one level, Swinburne expresses an important claim, designed to take seriously the ways in which people diminish and destroy one another and to emphasize that only those to whom the wrong has been done are in a position to forgive. But on a second level, Swinburne's argument, cast with the precision of a gifted analytic philosopher, fails to articulate ade-

9. Immanuel Kant, *Religion within the Limits of Reason Alone*, tr. T. M. Green and H. H. Hudson (New York: Harper and Row, 1960) pp. 106-107. I cannot explain here the larger context of Kant's account of "forgiveness" in its relation to his claims about freedom and the moral law. But it is worth noting that John R. Silber contends in his Introduction to *Religion within the Limits of Reason Alone* that "If Kant had consistently held to his theory of unqualified freedom, he would have followed the line of argument taken by Ivan Karamazov" with respect to the possibilities of forgiveness (p. cxxxiii).

10. Richard Swinburne, *Responsibility and Atonement* (Oxford: Clarendon, 1989) p. 84.

11. Swinburne, *Responsibility and Atonement*, p. 87 (emphasis added).

quately the theological issues involved in repentance and forgiveness. Consequently, his argument actually distorts a properly Christian understanding of their relationship. Contra Swinburne, Christian forgiveness is not "the final act," nor does it *necessarily* follow that a "disowning of a hurtful act" *only* becomes identified as forgiveness when it is in "response" to at least some minimal attempt at atonement. But in order to see why Swinburne makes these judgments, we need to turn briefly to his articulation of "redemption" later in the same book.

In his chapter on redemption Swinburne describes several "theories" of the atonement. After surveying several of the "standard" options, he suggests that the "most satisfactory biblical model for what was effected by the life and death of Christ is the model of sacrifice."[12] But, he goes on to note, the sacrifice model has to be "somewhat transformed" because "in so far as Christ is God himself, he cannot offer a sacrifice to himself." Hence, he suggests that "God *makes available* the sacrifice (of himself), but it is *we* who have to *offer* it." He adds, somewhat surprisingly, that "on this model Christ's death has *no* efficacy until men choose to plead it in atonement for their sins." Further, "the sinner has to *use* Christ's death to *get* forgiveness."[13]

Swinburne seems to have a twofold rationale for these formulations. First, he argues that the only way to take sin seriously is to claim that we are involved in the process of removing it. So he observes that it seems "quite contrary to the spirit of the New Testament to suppose that men's sins are removed without their being involved in the process of removal — this would be overlooking sin rather than taking it seriously." Secondly, and closely related, he contends that our forgiveness could not happen independently of our knowledge of it; hence the importance of repentance and baptism. In Swinburne's terms, "If the sinner could be forgiven as a result of Christ's death, without using it to secure forgiveness, we could be forgiven by God as a result of what had happened on Calvary independently of our knowing about it; and that seems a suggestion very distant from the New Testament. Forgiveness is available through 'repentance and baptism in the name of Jesus Christ.'"[14]

Once again, there is something right about Swinburne's insistence that the New Testament emphasizes repentance, that we are somehow involved in "the process of removal" of sin, and that sin is not "overlooked"

12. Swinburne, *Responsibility and Atonement,* p. 152.
13. Swinburne, *Responsibility and Atonement,* p. 153 (emphasis added).
14. Swinburne, *Responsibility and Atonement,* p. 153. Swinburne quotes Acts 2:38.

but is indeed taken seriously. Yet there is something profoundly wrong about the wider implications of Swinburne's formulations and of his insistence on the priority of repentance. We can make considerable progress toward responding to the objections above by identifying precisely what is wrong with Swinburne's account.

First, we need to recognize the logical and theological priority of God's forgiveness to various dimensions of human forgiveness. In terms of method, this would suggest that for a Christian account we can only know how to understand appropriately the relationship between forgiveness and repentance in the dynamics of interhuman forgiveness if we *first* understand their relationship in God's forgiveness (and, consequently, how God's forgiveness changes the various social contexts of our lives). After all, we are called to forgive as God forgives, to love as God loves, to be holy as God is holy, to be perfect as God is perfect.[15] So we ought to focus our attention *in the first instance* on who God is and how God is involved in the world.

Swinburne does not do this, at least rhetorically. Instead, he first seeks to explain the relationship of repentance and forgiveness philosophically, then turns to a theological account of the nature and function of Christ's person and work. Indeed, the titles of the two sections of his book are revealing of his method: "Responsibility" is the first, and then "Its Theological Consequences." However, Swinburne might respond that his presentation is *only* a matter of rhetorical judgment, and that his philosophical account in Part I presupposes that he has already (in the first instance!) focused his attention on judgments about who God is and how God is involved in the world. That is, he might contend that people — and philosophers more specifically — are more likely to be persuaded by the truth of the Gospel if they are first presented with a general account of responsibility. Fair enough. But then the burden falls on the person to show that the general account adequately presupposes the theological perspective. Swinburne's argument, I think, fails to do this.

The overarching problem with Swinburne's argument is that it fails to situate God's forgiveness in relation to Jesus' announcement and enactment of the Kingdom through his life, death, and resurrection, and more precisely, it fails to recognize the Kingdom as a new social reality where we can unlearn Sin as well as deal with the problem of ongoing sins. An

---

15. Of course, important qualifications need to be made because God is God and we are not. Even so, it is clear that for the Bible and for the Christian tradition, God's forgiveness provides the paradigm for how we are to understand our own vocation to be forgiven and forgiving people.

example is seen in his chapter on "Guilt, Atonement, and Forgiveness" (in the philosophical section of the book, Part I), where Swinburne considers the important question of what to do if a person fails to forgive another even after the wrongdoer makes due amends, giving a serious apology with due reparation and penance.[16] His analysis is insufficiently complex.

His primary question is whether, if the victim fails to forgive, the guilt still remains. But for Christians, that is neither the only nor even the primary question. For those who have accepted forgiveness of Sin by God and have thereby been initiated into God's inbreaking Kingdom, failure either to forgive *or to repent* — including seeking forgiveness from those whom we have sinned against — are equally scandalous. The first question for Christians is not whether the guilt remains but how such a scandalous thing could happen among those who have been forgiven by God. Further, our primary focus is not on the individual's *guilt*, but on how to engage as individuals in communal practices of forgiveness and reconciliation that most clearly reflect the character of God's reconciliation in Jesus Christ. As I will suggest in the next chapter, these are practices of God's Kingdom, practices that situate forgiveness and repentance as an embodied way of life that enables us to become holy people.

Within this new social reality, there are important questions to deal with in terms of guilt and culpability, forgiveness and repentance. Further, these issues become more complex when we reflect on the possibilities and limits of forgiveness and repentance, reconciliation and accountability outside the sphere of Christian communities committed to these practices — whether it be through breakdowns in Christian communities, interactions of Christians with others in the world, or attempts to diagnose and respond to various situations in the world itself.

I will address these complexities in subsequent chapters of this book. At this point, my argument is that if we follow Swinburne in focusing *only*, or even primarily, on individual acts of wrongdoing (that is, on sin*s*) without setting them in the context of a lifelong Christian commitment to habits and practices of forgiven-ness and repentance in response to the priority of God's eschatological forgiveness (and thereby our redemption from Sin through being conformed to Christ as Christ's Body, the Church, by the power of the Holy Spirit), we unnecessarily constrict the scope of forgiveness as well as distort a proper focus on the restoration of communion rather than the elimination of individual guilt.

It should be clear that my disagreement with Swinburne is not only

16. See the discussion in Swinburne, *Responsibility and Atonement*, pp. 87f.

methodological but also theological. In part, this has to do with different ways of construing the Christian gospel. But, more fundamentally, I would argue that Swinburne makes several crucial mistakes in christology and pneumatology that lead to distortions in his account of forgiveness and repentance.

The most serious mistake is that Swinburne's understanding of forgiveness and repentance collapses Jesus' life, death, and resurrection into an account of the atonement. In so doing, he loses the integral significance of Jesus' proclamation and enactment of the Kingdom in its relation to Judaism as well as its invocation and embodiment of a transformed way of being community; of how and why Jesus' nonviolent, forgiving love leads him to the cross; of the Father's vindication of Jesus' life and death through raising him from the dead and how that transforms our understanding of the relationships of forgiveness and repentance. He loses the larger and more complex horizons of the claim that Christian forgiveness is the way God's love moves toward reconciliation and the restoration of communion in the wake of Sin.

As I have repeatedly insisted, we are all in need of forgiveness from Sin, from the pervasive reality that causes us invariably to diminish and destroy one another. This is as true for those who have suffered horrifying evils at the hands of oppressors as it is for those who have inflicted suffering. We all need to be freed from the death-dealing realm of Sin (see, for example, 1 John 1:5-10). But this should not lead us to an easy acquiescence to current social conditions. Indeed, it ought to induce a profound repentance, a repentance that seeks to turn and re-turn to any person or people that we have victimized. It ought also to lead us to clearer-eyed diagnoses and prophetic indictments of people and situations where pervasive or systemic sins are being perpetuated without any repentance or accountability.

From this perspective, Christians ought to be people who, precisely because of the forgiveness of Sin that Christ has already announced and enacted, seek to become holy people through embodied practices of forgiven-ness and repentance. As I will argue in greater detail in the next chapter, those who have been forgiven by God in Jesus Christ ought to be people whose repentance is never in question, who understand that holiness of heart and life can only be achieved through the unique conjunction of forgiveness, repentance, and hope found in turning and re-turning to God *and* to those against whom we have sinned. This is as true for those whose repentance involves confronting our own pride and violence as for those whose repentance involves confronting our own self-abnegation and despair.

So Christians ought to insist more than anyone else on the importance of accountability and culpability — but they should do so within a context in which the judgment *of grace* is the determinatively prior aim and where eschatological holiness is the ultimate goal. It ought to make us acutely aware of and sensitive to the haunting effects of being sinned against, and not only of Sin *per se*. It ought also to inspire a passionate concern for the cultivation of communities where human destructiveness can be transformed into new life, where despair can be transformed into hope. Unfortunately, Swinburne's exclusive focus on the cross and his insistence on the causal priority of repentance preclude him from adequately articulating the ways in which the priority of God's forgiveness actually creates new social contexts for repentance (and hence ongoing forgiveness of sins) to occur.

Swinburne's first mistake is closely related to another, namely that he collapses the important distinction between what Christ has done outside us *(extra nos)*, what Christ does for us *(pro nobis)*, and what Christ does in us as the Body of Christ *(in nobis)*. As Bonhoeffer emphasized (see chapter 1 above), we need first to recognize *who* does the work of forgiving our sin without our participation if we are to be rightly freed for new life. That is, "I am met in his work as one who cannot possibly do the work he does. It is through his work that I recognize the gracious God. My sin is forgiven, I am no longer in death, but in life."[17] It is not the case, as Swinburne suggests, either that Christ only "makes available" the sacrifice of himself, which we have to "offer," or that Christ's death has "no efficacy" until we "choose to plead it in atonement" for our sin.

To be sure, Swinburne is right to recognize the importance of our being involved in the removal of our sin. Christians are called to holiness learned and lived as the Church, to lifelong habits and practices of forgiveness and repentance in God's Kingdom.[18] But we can only be involved in the removal of our sin if we first stress what Christ's work accomplishes *outside* us. That emphasis rightly preserves the priority both of God's forgiveness to human forgiveness and of forgiveness to repentance. If the emphasis on Christ's work "outside us" is to ensure the irreducible singularity of the subject in the phrase "Jesus Christ is there for us," Swinburne's collapse of the distinction effectively inverts the sentence into "We are there

17. Dietrich Bonhoeffer, *Christ the Center,* tr. Edwin H. Robertson (San Francisco: Harper and Row, 1978) p. 38.

18. Though Swinburne does not develop the centrality of forgivenness as a way of life, he does briefly note the connection of forgiveness to such practices as baptism and eucharist. See *Responsibility and Atonement,* pp. 153-154, 161.

for Jesus Christ." In some significant ways, Swinburne's argument suggests that it is by *our* atonement, *our* sacrifice, *our* penance that we are forgiven of our sin. This is why he mistakenly concludes that repentance is prior to forgiveness.

Indeed, Swinburne's insistence that the sacrifice of Christ's death has *no* efficacy until we plead it in atonement for our sins bears a striking resemblance to Hazel Motes's predicament in *Wise Blood*. Both Swinburne and Hazel have abstracted the significance of Christ's work from the gospel narratives that tell the full story and form the practices of God's Kingdom enacted in Christian community. As a result, both conclude that human efforts at repentance are causally prior to any offers of, or (at least in Hazel's case) attempts to earn, forgiveness. Further, like Hazel Motes, Swinburne's account is of an all-powerful Christ who offers the decisive sacrifice for our forgiveness but does little himself to effect any transformation of people's lives.

Neither Motes nor Swinburne has an adequate understanding of the relationship between the name of Jesus and the narratives and practices associated with that name. But there is a further problem; neither one has an adequate sense of the Spirit who makes Christ's forgiveness audible to each of us in our particularity. The Spirit is the one who guides, judges, and consoles us as we seek to appropriate Christ's forgiveness in diverse lives and situations (see, for example, the story of Cornelius's conversion in Acts 10 and 11). That forgiveness cannot be pronounced in the abstract; it must be made particular. If we do not recognize the Holy Spirit's work in re-presenting Christ in diverse situations and lives, we run the risk of proclaiming a forgiveness that merely comforts the comfortable and afflicts the afflicted — rather than the Christian gospel's forgiveness, which comforts the afflicted and afflicts the comfortable.[19]

That is, while recognizing the priority of God's forgiveness to our repentance, we also need to be guided, judged, and consoled by the Spirit as we seek to discern what that forgiveness means, and what repentance is called for, in relation to the narratives of our own and each others' lives, the situations we and others have faced and continue to face. As St. Paul reminds us, the Spirit transforms our past (and the world's past) for the sake of new life in the future (see in particular Romans 8). Further, because our forgiveness involves a recovery and redemption of the past, not its obliteration, we face the *ongoing task* of cultivating habits and practices that

19. The second half of this formulation comes from H. Richard Niebuhr's famous dictum.

enable us to discern, in the Spirit, how we should appropriate Christ's forgiveness — and understand our ongoing call to daily repentance — in our particular lives and situations.[20]

Therefore, Swinburne's account of the relationship between forgiveness and repentance fails to articulate adequately the significance of either Christ or the Spirit, much less their interrelations. We need to develop the habits and practices that enable us to see and embody the ways in which Christ's judgment of grace is re-presented by the Spirit in the irreducible particularities of our lives and the situations in which we find ourselves. A crucial part of our difficulty in articulating the relationship between forgiveness and repentance, I am suggesting, lies in our failure to articulate the work of the Spirit in and through our habits and practices. This is so both in terms of appropriating Christ's forgiveness and in understanding the importance and shape of our repentance throughout our lives, as we seek to become — by the power of the Holy Spirit — holy people.

I have spent considerable space addressing and responding to several problems in Swinburne's account of forgiveness and repentance. I have done so to diagnose the consequences in both theory and life of failing to situate our account of forgiveness and repentance in relation to God's Kingdom, and more precisely, in terms of the work of Christ and Spirit in inaugurating that Kingdom and, eventually, bringing it to completion. In so doing, I have also been responding to the four questions identified at the close of the previous section of this chapter.

That is, my account of God's forgiveness requires an intensified search for and embodiment of interhuman forgiveness. Indeed, my account not only requires recognition of and engagement with the pervasive disaster of Sin; it also requires the cultivation of concrete habits and practices that enable people to discern, confront, and forgive one another for particular sins. Further, these distinctions enable us both to emphasize that "we all need forgiveness" and to attend to the complex differences in culpability and accountability of people who have committed particular sins against God, others, or themselves.

But at this point I need to return to the fourth question, only now with two slightly different issues in mind. The question was: By making repentance an integral component of, but not a prerequisite for, forgive-

---

20. I develop this account of the Spirit's work in more detail in chapter 3 of *Transformed Judgment: Toward a Trinitarian Account of the Moral Life* (Notre Dame: University of Notre Dame, 1989). See also chapter 6 below.

ness, am I not opening the door to the abuse of forgiveness by people who have no intention of repenting or even of stopping their most destructive behavior? I have responded to that question by suggesting that, at least within the context of the announcement and enactment of God's Kingdom, it is scandalous — and, for the early Christians, virtually unthinkable — that God's forgiveness would not induce lifelong repentance. To be forgiven by God, to be initiated into life in God's Kingdom, is to be transferred from one narrative — the narrative of death-dealing sin — to the narrative of God's reconciliation in Christ. And in that latter narrative we are forgiven of our sin so that we can learn to become holy through lifelong repentance and forgiveness. That is why, in 1 John, we see an emphasis both that "Those who have been born of God do not sin because God's seed abides in them" (3:9a) and that "If we confess our sins, he who is faithful and just will forgive us our sins and cleanse us from all unrighteousness. If we say that we have not sinned, we make him a liar, and his word is not in us" (1:9-10).

But, we need to add, what seems to be virtually unthinkable — namely, to find unrepentant Christians, who assume that God's forgiveness can be received without any cost — has happened and continues to happen all too frequently. In one sense, the notion of "unrepentant Christians" is an oxymoron — as is its correlative notion of "cheap grace." Yet, it might be objected, particularly by our Jewish brothers and sisters, this is precisely what an all-powerful forgiveness really does. Indeed, Christians could do well to (re-)learn from Jews the importance of repentance for life with God.[21] Indeed, Christians would be better off with Judaism's account of repentance and forgiveness than with temptations either to "cheap grace" or to self-destructive and other-destructive attempts to *replace* a lost hope for forgiveness with a nihilistic penance (as found, for example, in Hazel Motes).

Still, the fully Christian vocation is to embody lifelong habits and practices of forgiveness and repentance, understood in their dynamic interrelations, within the larger horizons of the saving forgiveness wrought

---

21. See, for example, the arguments in Maimonides' *Laws of Repentance* or, in contemporary contexts, those of Joseph B. Soloveitchik in Pinchas H. Peli's *Soloveitchik on Repentance* (New York: Paulist, 1984), particularly the latter's comment about repentance as a task that takes time: "Repentance is not a function of a single, decisive act, but grows and gains in size slowly and gradually, until the penitent undergoes a complete metamorphosis, and then, after becoming a new person, and only then, does repentance take place" (p. 76).

by Jesus' announcement and enactment of God's Kingdom. Those habits and practices invite us, and require us, to turn and re-turn both to God and to those whom we have sinned against. If, and insofar as, we fail to do both of these things, we also provide a scandal to the Christian claim that the Messiah has come and the Kingdom has been inaugurated in the life, death, and resurrection of Jesus of Nazareth.

There is, of course, a second problem. How should we understand the failure of people to repent — particularly by returning to their victims and seeking forgiveness — as an integral component of having been forgiven? As I have noted above, this is particularly a problem in situations of persistent abuse and recurring violence. In part, this requires us to reclaim the significance of "loving enemies" as an indispensable feature of the craft of Christian forgiveness. That is, Christians should not confront this perplexing and troubling reality by failing to continue to insist on the priority of God's forgiveness to our forgiven-ness and repentance. But if, and insofar as, people fail to respond to forgiveness with repentance, then perhaps the best that can be done is to acknowledge that they are enemies of the cross of Christ — but enemies whom we are nonetheless called to learn to love. These are difficult and complex matters, and they will be discussed further in subsequent chapters, particularly in relation to the eighteenth chapter of Matthew's Gospel. But a discussion of God's Kingdom and the dynamic interrelations of forgiveness and repentance would be incomplete if we did not at least note in this context the troubling difficulties that do in fact arise in the case of unrepentant sinners.

Conclusion: The Woman Who Showed Great Love

In the seventh chapter of Luke's Gospel, there is a story about a woman, identified as a sinner, who encounters Jesus and shows him great love. The story has sometimes been taken as an indication that people can earn forgiveness through repentance. But on closer examination, it shows that God's forgiveness induces her repentance of showing extravagant love.

The story begins in verse 36, where Jesus is a guest at a meal given by a Pharisee named Simon. The woman arrives with a jar of ointment and stands at Jesus' feet, bathing them with her tears, drying them with her hair, kissing them, and anointing them with her ointment. Simon is upset that Jesus would allow such activity from one who is so obviously a sinner. Jesus responds by telling Simon a story: There were two debtors, one of whom was released from a large debt, the other from a small debt. Now, says Jesus, which of them will love the creditor more? Simon answers that it would be the one for whom the greater debt was canceled. Jesus indicates that Simon has judged rightly.

The consequences of the story become immediately apparent. Simon has shown Jesus only minimal hospitality, whereas the woman has shown extravagant love. Hence, she must have been forgiven much, and the Pharisee only a little. But verse 47 seems to move in a different direction, particularly as that verse has sometimes been translated into English. Jesus says, "Therefore, I tell you, her sins, which were many, have been forgiven, *hoti* she has shown great love." The Greek word *hoti* can be translated as "because" or, as the New English Bible and the Revised Standard Version have it, with the more ambiguous "for." In either case, it would seem that Jesus is saying that the woman's sins have been forgiven on account of the fact that she showed great love. This would indicate that her forgiveness is occasioned by her repentance, manifested by her love. Indeed, this reading would seem to be supported by Jesus' declaration to the woman in verse 48, "Your sins are forgiven." There would still seem to be an inconsistency between Jesus' story and his statement to the woman, but that could be explained by the difference between Jesus' story and the Evangelist Luke's commentary on the story.[22]

But there is another, more satisfactory way to translate the passage. The *hoti* might relate to "tell" rather than to "show," suggesting that Jesus is saying something like "The reason that I [am able to] tell you that her many sins are forgiven is the fact that she is showing so much love."[23] The New Revised Standard Version handles it by translating *hoti* as "hence." In either case, the point becomes clear. The woman shows so much love because she has known such great forgiveness. In this account, Jesus' comment in verse 48, "Your sins are forgiven," simply reaffirms a fact that has already been shown by the woman's love. She has not earned her forgiveness through the repentance of extravagant love; because she has been forgiven, she is able to repent by showing such love.

Such a reading also reinforces a point found elsewhere in the New

---

22. This is the conclusion reached by, for example, Claude Montefiore in his commentary on this passage. See the discussion of Montefiore's exegesis, along with a much more satisfactory reading of the passage, in C. F. D. Moule, "'. . . As We Forgive . . .': A Note on the Distinction between Deserts and Capacity in the Understanding of Forgiveness," in E. Bammel, C. K. Barrett, and W. D. Davies (eds.), *Donum Gentilicum* (Oxford: Clarendon, 1978) pp. 68-77, esp. pp. 72-74.

23. This formulation is from Moule, "'. . . As We Forgive . . . ,'" p. 74.

Testament, notably in Matthew's telling of the parable of the Unforgiving Servant (Matthew 18:23-35). Both stories communicate the same reality: Those who are forgiven by God must be transformed by that forgiveness into people who embody forgiveness and repentance throughout their lives. In the one story the sign of forgiven-ness is the ability to show great love; in the other the failure to forgive others heightens the judgment to which the person is subject. In both cases, it is assumed that God's forgiveness should occasion a repentance, a turning, that marks people's new life with and in Christ and results in their showing love to others.

Indeed, the woman's extravagant love shows both the transformative power of forgiveness and the specific patterns of repentance enabled by that forgiveness. In direct contrast to Hazel Motes in *Wise Blood*, the woman who showed great love had a site — the body of Christ — where her forgiveness and repentance could be practiced in specific, life-giving ways. She could recognize the judgment on her life as a judgment of grace, enabling her forgiveness and repentance to be directed toward the ends of God's Kingdom.

Christians believe that the Holy Spirit transforms human life by re-presenting Christ's judgment of grace, God's forgiveness, to us in all our particularities. The Spirit does so by enabling our repentance, by shaping in us new habits and practices of forgiven-ness and repentance as we seek to be transfigured into holy people. Further, the Spirit does so both by focusing on the particularities of each person's narrative, offered as a gift to others within Christian community, and by binding people together in communities that proclaim and embody habits and practices of forgiveness. Hence it is to a discussion of "Practicing Forgiveness" that I now turn.

6 Practicing Forgiveness

Trinitarian Community and the Hope for a New Humanity

FOR CHRISTIANS, forgiveness is not simply an action, an emotional judgment, or a declarative utterance — though Christian forgiveness includes all those dimensions. Rather, forgiveness is a habit that must be practiced over time within the disciplines of Christian community. This is so because, as I have been suggesting, in the face of sin and evil God's love moves toward reconciliation by means of forgiveness. Forgiveness aims to restore communion on the part of humans with God, with one another, and with the whole Creation. This forgiveness is costly, since it involves acknowledging and experiencing the painful truth of human sin and evil at its worst. In the midst of such brokenness, God's forgiveness aims at healing people's lives and re-creating communion in God's eschatological Kingdom.

Even so, such healing and re-creating is not God acting wholly without us. They also invite, and require, our practices, which — by the guiding, judging, and consoling work of the Holy Spirit — enable us to witness to God's forgiving, re-creating work and to be transformed into holy people. To be involved in such practices is to engage the narrative of the Triune God's creative and re-creative work as Father, Son, and Spirit; likewise, to believe faithfully in the Triune God is to have our lives formed and transformed through participation in Christian practices. These practices involve attending to the particularities of each person's life story and fostering disciplined, Christian community, the horizons of which are (at least potentially) the whole world. It is in this sense that Christian life calls us to practice forgiveness.[1]

The practice of forgiveness entails unlearning all those things that divide and destroy communion and learning to see and live as forgiven and forgiving people. The goal of this unlearning and learning is the holiness of communion — with God, with others, and with the whole Creation. We are called to do this most specifically, though by no means exclusively, among those who seek to live in truthful communion with God and with one another in Christian community.

More broadly, the practice of forgiveness calls us to develop habits that enable this unlearning and learning to occur. Learning the Christian life is not only a matter of acquiring the right kind of knowledge or cultivating the appropriate sorts of passions or acting in particular ways, though it involves these things; more fundamentally, it requires our full participation in practices whose disciplines of the body are necessary for the transformation of our souls and minds.[2] If, as Augustine and Aquinas rightly insist, individuals become habituated to wickedness so that it is both no longer a struggle that we worry about and also something in which we

1. The notion of "practices" has been developed in a particularly interesting way by Alasdair MacIntyre in *After Virtue* (second ed., Notre Dame: University of Notre Dame, 1984). His description is as follows (p. 187): "By a 'practice' I am going to mean any coherent and complex form of socially established cooperative human activity through which goods internal to that form of activity are realized in the course of trying to achieve those standards of excellence that are appropriate to, and partially definitive of, that form of activity, with the result that human powers to achieve excellence, and human conceptions of the ends and goods involved, are systematically extended." MacIntyre further suggests that his notion of practices must be situated within the narrative order of a single human life, and within traditions.

My use of "practices" in this chapter is indebted to, though not identical with, MacIntyre's account. For example, I think MacIntyre underplays issues of power in the formation and sustenance of practices. In addition, his account underplays the centrality of friendship in the formation and sustenance of community. Perhaps most significantly, however, I am less interested in developing a theory about practices (or, more broadly, virtue) than I am in articulating the theological and ethical significance of a specific set of practices — namely, those involving forgiveness. For further discussion and analysis of MacIntyre's account of practices, see my *Transformed Judgment: Toward a Trinitarian Account of the Moral Life* (Notre Dame: University of Notre Dame, 1989), especially chapter 2.

2. For an instructive discussion of this issue in relation to medieval Christian monasticism, see Talal Asad, *Genealogies of Religion* (Baltimore: Johns Hopkins University, 1993) pp. 125-167.

actually, perversely, learn to "delight" in doing, then forgiveness needs to become a habit that transforms — by God's gracious love — our sin and evil into signs of communion with God, with one another, and with the whole Creation.

Further, Christian forgiveness is a set of habits that occasion and require prophetic criticism of all those situations and lives where communion is undermined. This is not an easy task, for God's forgiveness requires us to confront our tendencies to see the world either as "lighter" than it is (hence engaging in cheap grace) or as "darker" than it is (hence believing that forgiveness is impossible or ineffective). It calls us to learn to see the world and our lives truthfully, and we do so in the context of Christian communities whose ultimate hope is sustained in the practice of reconciling forgiveness. As John Milbank has argued, "the real refuge provided by the Church" is "the forgiveness of sins." He continues, "Instead of a peace 'achieved' through the abandonment of the losers, the subordination of potential rivals and resistance to enemies, the Church provides a genuine peace by its memory of all the victims, its equal concern for all its citizens and its self-exposed offering of reconciliation to enemies."[3] Practicing forgiveness in Christian community — that eschatological community called into being by the Father, identified by the Son, and sustained, judged, and guided by the Spirit — enables us to be sustained in our hope for a new humanity, for the New Heaven and the New Earth to appear in its fullness (see Revelation 21:1-5).

As I will argue in this chapter, the practice of forgiveness is closely related to, and partially learned in the context of, other practices. That is, forgiveness both describes a practice of Christian life (bound up with such notions as confession, repentance, and reconciliation) and involves the sustenance of a set of practices (which have purposes that include, but are not limited to, forgiveness). We need to understand both dimensions in order to learn and embody God's forgiveness as we seek to become holy people. However, in the order of exposition, forgiveness as a specific practice will be discussed only after we characterize the central significance of baptism and eucharist in the formation and sustenance of Christian community. The reason for this is that — as Bonhoeffer suggested in Life Together — other practices of Christian community need to be in relatively good order if the specific practice of reconciling forgiveness is to be edifying rather than destroying. So I begin with an exposition of how forgiveness is practiced in the context of baptism and eucharist. I then turn to the practice

3. Milbank, Theology and Social Theory (Oxford: Blackwell, 1990) p. 392.

of reconciling forgiveness as it is bound up in Christian community with confession, repentance, and excommunication. Finally, I explore the relationship of forgiveness to practices of prayer and of healing.

Baptism: Who Am I?

Baptism is the sacrament that signifies our forgiveness of sin by God. More generally, baptism into Christ's death and resurrection signifies our transition from one world — a world marked by sin, destruction, and death — to the world of God's Kingdom, a world marked by forgiveness, love, and new life. In baptism, we are cleansed of sin and identified as heirs of God's Kingdom. This signifies both our new birth and the initiation of our journey into Christian forgiveness as citizens of God's eschatological Kingdom, indeed as friends of God.[4]

Baptism thus has a twofold focus: It is at once a sacramental action of the Church *and* an ongoing process of "living into your baptism," of learning to appropriate God's forgiveness through that repentance and discipleship that make us holy people. This dual emphasis is central to Paul's letters, and it receives perhaps its paradigmatic formulation in Romans 6:1ff. According to Paul, those who have been baptized have entered into the community defined by whomever or whatever they are baptized into; to have been baptized into Christ, as Paul characterizes it in Romans 6:3, is to have entered into the community ruled and defined by Christ — more specifically, by Christ's death and resurrection.[5] The pattern of our forgiven-ness, and hence our discipleship as forgiven and forgiving people, is none other than the pattern we find in Christ.

As such, the baptized are now defined by the forgiveness that Christ announced and enacted. It means a death of the old self and the creation of a new self "alive to God in Christ Jesus" (6:11). The death of the old self is signified by the renunciation of the power of sin and evil at the beginning of the baptismal liturgy. Baptism signifies that, by the grace of Jesus Christ, people are set free from patterns of sin and evil, of betrayals and of being betrayed, of vicious cycles of being caught as victimizers and victims, so that they can bear

---

4. For a further discussion of baptism in relation to the notion of becoming friends of God, see my *Transformed Judgment*, esp. pp. 137-141. My discussion here builds on the arguments developed throughout chapter 3 of that book.

5. For further discussion of this point, see Stephen Fowl, "Some Uses of Story in Moral Discourse," *Modern Theology* 4 (1988) pp. 293-308.

to remember the past in hope for the future. They can do so because they are given a new perspective on that past, the perspective of forgiveness.

Even so, this "setting free" for a new life that "can bear to remember the past in hope" is not easy to embody. Indeed, given the often horrifying effects of the sin and evil that mark our world, it may seem an insuperable task to envision such a "new life." And apart from God's grace working by the Holy Spirit, it *is* insuperable. But baptized believers, those who are learning in the context of God's Kingdom to name the sin and evil that destroy and the forgiving love and friendship that edify, are enabled by God to envision and increasingly embody such a new life. In so doing, they testify not so much to their own abilities, virtues, or strengths as to the gracious forgiveness of God manifested in the crucified *and risen* Christ. To be sure, "living into your baptism" is a lifelong task and struggle to appropriate God's forgiveness; but not only is it not an insuperable task, it is the Spirit's gift that is received precisely in and through the struggles.

This gift and these struggles are not lived alone. For the conferral of a new self by God's Spirit is definitively found in, and lived in, communities of God's Kingdom. The Church is the community that enables the baptism to take place and to be lived through. As Robert Jenson puts it, the Holy Spirit invoked in the liturgy "*is* the new life that baptism grants, and the bond of the community into which baptism inducts."[6] Baptism is not the formation of new, isolated selves; it is, rather, the formation of a new people, the Body of Christ, by the power of the Spirit. As such, baptized believers are becoming holy by learning to live together as forgiven and forgiving people in mission to the world. That is, baptism signifies the transformation of individual selves through their initiation into the friendships and practices of eschatological Christian community, the horizons of which are ever-expanding.

In baptism, then, we receive a new life in the Spirit, a new self, that is found and lived most definitively in the context of Christian community. It is not, however, a generically new life; it remains profoundly particular. The community of the Holy Spirit does not obliterate the particularities of people's lives; rather it enables the sustenance of common life through them. As Paul's vision of the diversity of the Spirit's gifts suggests (1 Corinthians 12), being initiated into a common life is not an initiation into homogeneity. Communities of the Spirit not only permit difference in heritage and vocation: They actually require such difference. Just as Mary Magdalene's narrative was different from Peter's, and both of them from

6. Robert W. Jenson, *Visible Words* (Philadelphia: Fortress, 1978) pp. 157-158.

Paul's, so also Christian community is sustained through the crafting of our particular stories into the larger context of God's story. This suggests that the process of living into our baptism means learning to renarrate the stories of our lives truthfully, in all their particularity and in the context of God's forgiving and reconciling love.

As we learn so to renarrate our lives and to listen so that we can help others narrate theirs, we are unlearning the destructiveness, violence, and depression — indeed, any and all ways in which we diminish and destroy one another and ourselves — so that we can learn the forgiving and reconciling love characteristic of mutual edification. But we cannot do so unless we take the time to hear each other's stories, to know the particular pasts of people's joys and griefs, hopes and fears, sin for which they need to repent and grace that they need to claim and celebrate. And that time is not a competition of each person seeking their own "airtime," their own fifteen minutes of celebrity status; rather, it is the time necessary as we learn — slowly, laboriously, and often painfully — to locate and live our lives as truthfully as possible in relation to God's perspective. It is the time necessary for us to offer support to one another *and* to call each other to accountability as we seek so to locate our lives.

The early Methodists in eighteenth-century England did this by gathering together in "class meetings." They would gather each week, under the leadership of a lay person, to offer one another support and challenge in their lives of discipleship. But the focus was not on a narcissistic attempt to focus only on one's "self," either in self-praise or self-humiliation; nor was it based on a theory of "small groups." Rather, the focus was on living faithfully in relation to God, seeking the Spirit's discernment both for the common life of the community and in relation to the particularities of each person's own life.

Such communities recognize that to know oneself is to be known by God. But our self-knowledge is never complete, for we are neither completely free from patterns of sin and self-deception nor in possession of full access to God's knowledge. Therefore, it is central to our activity of appropriating God's forgiveness through baptism *both* to recognize and claim the new self that we are given by God *and* to recognize that this new self is in need of continual transformation. It is in this sense that the forgiveness we receive from God, the forgiveness that provides us with new selves, induces an ongoing repentance as the Spirit of God forms and transforms us to be holy people. As Luther rightly insisted in one of his Ninety-five Theses, "When our Lord said, 'repent,' he meant the whole life of the Christian to be repentance." Baptism ought to create repentant people and a penitent Church.

The pattern of baptism, of our forgiveness as it gives us a new self and initiates a new life, is found in Christ's death and resurrection. Further, because our forgiveness engages with our particular pasts, and with the variety of ways in which sin and evil diminish and destroy us and others, that pattern must be quilted in irreducibly diverse ways. We tend to be more familiar with descriptions of forgiveness of sin that assume that the problem is primarily inherited or deserved guilt and that the new life is a release from that guilt. Those are often important descriptions, embodied particularly in the narratives of such people as the Apostle Peter, St. Augustine, and the not infrequent testimonies of conversions found particularly in pietist and evangelical traditions as well as in other literature.

But if, as I have been insisting, we need to see sin and evil fundamentally in relation to ruptures of communion (with God, with one another, and with the whole Creation) rather than to merely individual guilt, then we also need to claim forgiveness, at least in many cases, as the call to repent of having a diminished self. God's forgiveness, signified particularly in baptism, may be the conferral of an identity where one was lost. Or, even more, it may be the conferral of an identity where the prior identity was primarily a dehumanized and dehumanizing burden. This is especially urgent for those people who have been more the victims than the perpetrators of personal or systemic violence and oppression. For example, as James Cone has put it, "Sin for blacks is loss of identity."[7]

This theme can be seen not only in contemporary African American literature but also in the autobiographical narratives of ex-slaves and in spirituals. The forgiveness that the nineteenth-century slave "Old Elizabeth" receives from her encounter with Jesus bestows not a sense of unworthiness but rather "somebodiness."[8] Elizabeth's memoir, narrated orally in her ninety-seventh year, includes on its title page the baptismal affirmation of Galatians ("There is neither Jew nor Greek, there is neither bond nor free, there is neither male nor female, for ye are all one in Christ Jesus"). Elizabeth was born in Maryland in 1766 to slave parents. She was separated from her parents at age ten and became so lonely that she escaped from her new master to find her mother. When she was discovered and was about to be separated once again from her family, her mother indicated that she had "nobody in the wide world to look to but God." This did not console

7. James H. Cone, *A Black Theology of Liberation* (twentieth anniversary ed., Maryknoll: Orbis, 1990) p. 108.

8. See Delores S. Williams, "A Womanist Perspective on Sin," in Emelie M. Townes (ed.), *A Troubling in My Soul* (Maryknoll: Orbis, 1993) pp. 140-141.

Elizabeth; indeed, she notes that "these words fell upon my heart with pondrous weight, and seemed to add to my grief."[9]

The theme of heaviness, of a burden too great to bear, is found in many narratives of people who have suffered. Elizabeth's burden is a lost identity, a dehumanized and dehumanizing condition. But Elizabeth, whose parents were religious and belonged to the Methodist Society, does not allow this burden to overwhelm her. Indeed, "I betook myself to prayer, and in every lonely place I found an altar. I mourned sore like a dove and chattered forth my sorrow, moaning in the corners of the field, and under the fences" (p. 4). She weeps like this for six months and eventually finds herself in despair. She identifies herself as a sinner, unfit to be in the presence of God. But then she hears a voice telling her to "rise up and pray"; that voice gives her strength.

She says, "I fell on my knees and prayed the best I could the Lord's prayer. Knowing no more to say, I halted, but continued on my knees. My spirit was then *taught* to pray, 'Lord, have mercy on me — Christ save me.' Immediately there appeared a director, clothed in white raiment. I thought he took me by the hand and said, 'come with me.'" She embarks on a long journey that ends up at a fiery gulf, and she assumes that her hope in being saved was "no more than a hair; still, pray, and it will be sufficient." She renews her struggle, and finds that every cry for mercy and salvation raises her higher and higher. She then sees "the Saviour standing with His hand stretched out to receive me. An indescribably glorious light was *in* Him, and He said, 'peace, peace, come unto me.' At this moment I felt that my sins were forgiven me, and the time of my deliverance was at hand" (pp. 5-6).

Elizabeth describes this forgiveness in terms of being filled with "light and love." Immediately thereafter, however, she is also given a mission — even though she is not yet thirteen years old. As she narrates it,

> Immediately a light fell upon my head, and I was filled with light, and I was shown the world lying in wickedness, and was told I must go there, and call the people to repentance, for the day of the Lord was at hand; and this message was as a heavy yoke upon me, so that I wept bitterly at the thought of what I should have to pass through. While I wept, I heard

9. "Memoir of Old Elizabeth, a Coloured Woman," in Henry Louis Gates, Jr. (ed.), *Six Women's Slave Narratives* (New York: Oxford University, 1988) p. 4. The quotations from Elizabeth's memoir will be to this edition and will be cited parenthetically in the text.

> a voice say, "weep not, some will laugh at thee, some will scoff at thee, and the dogs will bark at thee, but while thou doest my will, I will be with thee to the ends of the earth."

The next day, Elizabeth says that when "I had come to myself, I felt like a new creature in Christ, and all my desire was to see the Saviour" (p. 7).

Elizabeth receives a transformative forgiveness in her encounter with Jesus. Not only is she given a sense of identity, of "somebodiness," but she also receives a mission to call people to repentance. She will continue to struggle to appropriate that forgiveness, both because of the appallingly dehumanizing conditions of slavery (she was not freed until she was thirty, and the effects would linger throughout her life) and because of the resistance she encounters as a woman, particularly as a black woman, proclaiming and embodying the gospel in prophetic terms. But she receives aid in that struggle from the Holy Spirit, whom she frequently invokes in her memoir, the Spirit who guides, judges, and consoles her as she perseveres as a forgiven and forgiving messenger of the gospel.

Elizabeth's struggle was to claim her lost self through a newfound identity, her status as a "new creature in Christ." She also had to struggle with the realization that people in the actually existing Church, including the clergy, often failed to exhibit that forgiveness that enables holiness. Indeed, such people did recognize the implications of baptism as conferring a sense of "somebodiness," for there was a widespread fear that baptism would necessarily emancipate the slaves. But rather than allowing baptism to challenge the institution of slavery, they passed laws that stated that baptism need not alter the condition of the slave.[10] Unfortunately, though the church people recognized the sacrament's practical effects, they failed to allow it to change their ecclesial and social practices.

Thus they resisted Elizabeth and set obstacles in her path. But their judgment was not definitive, for she also received support through other communities that testified to God's inbreaking Kingdom. Even so, as she narrates her life, she concludes by locating her life in God:

> When I went forth, it was without purse or scrip, — and I have come through great tribulation and temptation — not by any might of my own, for I feel that I am but as dust and ashes before my almighty Helper,

---

10. See the discussion in Albert J. Raboteau, *Slave Religion* (New York: Oxford University, 1978) pp. 98-99. I am indebted to Michael Cartwright for this reference.

who has, according to His promise, been with me and sustained me through all, and gives me now firm faith that he will be with me to the end, and, in his own good time, receive me into His everlasting rest. (p. 19)

It is regrettable, however, that neither the Church in her time nor in our own has been able to take the time not only to listen to Elizabeth's testimony but to hear it as a prophetic judgment.

The rhythms of Elizabeth's memoir are found also in African American spirituals. The spirituals are filled with laments concerning the people's suffering, but ultimately they affirm the people's hope that God is enabling a better future. That hope is both personal, as in the affirmation that there is a "balm in Gilead" that can heal the "sin-sick soul," and social, as in "Go Down, Moses" and the call to "Steal Away to Jesus." Or, more sharply put, the spirituals as a whole embrace both personal and social hope for a future not determined by the past, a hope that requires prophetic denunciation of the suffering and oppression found in the present. Further, the spirituals also recognize the importance of personal accountability and the priority of forgiven-ness to forgiving, seen in such spirituals as "Standing in the Need of Prayer."[11]

Elizabeth's story, as well as those found in the spirituals, focus in diverse ways on the struggle for people to embody a sense of "somebodi-ness" conferred by God in the face of a world that persistently tries to deny them that identity and, all too frequently, of Christians who do the same. By contrast, Dietrich Bonhoeffer's struggle was to discern some sense of who he was in the face of affirmation from the outside and despair in his interior life. In a poem entitled "Who Am I?" which he wrote in prison shortly before his death, Bonhoeffer reflects on his uncertainty about his identity. He contrasts the calm and cheerful disposition he would present to his jailers with an angry and impotent feeling within. He asks himself "Who am I? This or the other?" He asks this question, however, as a way of indicating that none of us can be sure that the way we tell our own stories is the most truthful narrative. We may remain caught in traps of self-deception, and others may have a perspective on our lives that we lack.

11. For instructive discussions of the power of the spirituals in African American culture and important reflections on sin and forgiveness in the context of black theology and the spirituals, see James H. Cone, *The Spirituals and the Blues* (Maryknoll: Orbis, 1972); Arthur C. Jones, *Wade in the Water: The Wisdom of the Spirituals* (Maryknoll: Orbis, 1993). See also J. Deotis Roberts, *Liberation and Reconciliation* (rev. ed., Maryknoll: Orbis, 1994).

So, Bonhoeffer concludes, "Whoever I am, thou knowest, O God, I am thine."[12]

Both Old Elizabeth and Dietrich Bonhoeffer situate the stories of their lives in relation to God and God's forgiveness. It is God who has the only true perspective on our lives; unfortunately, we do not and cannot have that perspective. Even so, we seek to be increasingly faithful to the divine perspective through the forgiveness we receive in baptism and through the Christian vocation of discipleship, of living into our baptism in pursuit of holiness. In so doing, we seek to unlearn the destructiveness of the world and of our own lives as we learn the ways of God. As Bonhoeffer's story illustrates, we need each other as we seek to understand and embody the gospel truthfully, for even after baptism we may remain caught in patterns of self-deception. And, as Elizabeth's story illustrates, it is a tragedy when we are unable to hear each other in ways that truly discern the work of God's Spirit in our midst, seeking to transform us and to restore us to communion with God, one another, and with the whole Creation.

I have highlighted these themes in relation to baptism in order to underscore several interrelated issues involved in practicing forgiveness. First, while baptism is the sacrament that signifies our initiation into God's Kingdom and our forgiveness from sin, it must also be appropriated continually throughout our lives as we seek to become holy people.

Second, our forgiveness is not a gift that we receive as isolated individuals; it is a gift from the Spirit that is irreducibly particular in terms of the narratives of our pasts, yet that gift calls us into communion. In such communion, we are invited and required to learn to tell the story of each of our pasts, not ultimately in terms of diminutions, of betrayals and being betrayed, of violence committed or suffered, but in terms of the new life that induces us to repent and invites us to become holy in the future. The Spirit guides Christian communities as we puzzle about how to appropriate most faithfully the decisive significance of Christ's forgiveness in our personal lives, in our corporate life together, and in the dynamics of the world.

Third, baptism emphasizes both the centrality of receiving a new self *and* the need for other people to help us understand the dynamics of unlearning the old self and learning to appropriate the new one. Recent writing in feminist, womanist, and other liberation theologies has sometimes criticized languages of selflessness, forgiveness, humility, and suffering

12. See Bonhoeffer, *Letters and Papers from Prison,* ed. E. Bethge, tr. R. Fuller, F. Clark, et al. (New York: Macmillan, 1971) pp. 347-348.

as ideologically driven masks that instill passivity on the part of the powerful in relation to the intolerable suffering of the powerless. This critique is significant, particularly given the ways those languages have too often been deployed. We need a sense of self in order to be appropriately a friend of God. Where there is no self, there can be no communion. This is part of what was behind the ancient monastic insistence that "In the world there is only myself and God." Yet, as Roberta Bondi notes, the paradox is that what follows from learning to say that is "the deep knowledge that the self does not exist for itself alone."[13] Indeed, this ancient monastic saying needs to be put alongside another one, namely Abba Anthony's point that "Our life and our death is with our neighbour."[14] This is so *both* in terms of the centrality of communities of the Spirit that exist and thrive on the exchange of our stories, thereby helping us learn to appropriate our forgiveness in new life, *and* in its insistence that we must prophetically protest and struggle against any situation in which any of our neighbors are diminished, destroyed, or made to suffer.

Fourth, baptism stresses the priority of forgiveness to our forgivingness. Contemporary discussions often stress the importance, and the difficulty, of forgiving others; this is particularly the case in situations of needing to forgive abusers, oppressors, and others who have perpetrated great destructiveness. But without denying the immense difficulty of such activity, we need also to insist that it matters *how* we tell the stories of trauma and oppression. The stories must be told, particularly if our self-knowledge is to become truthful and to be offered as a gift to others so that the cycles need not be repeated or exacerbated. But if we tell those stories in ways that invite descriptions of a primordial, and perhaps even essential, innocence that is violated only by evil others, then the cycles of victimizers and victims will continue to persist and intensify. For there is little hope among those who remain immersed in the turgid waters of victimization.

Elizabeth's story shows how her own need of forgiveness could be linked both to new life and to prophetic protest at *any* situations where people were being made victims. Similarly, Gustavo Gutiérrez, a Peruvian priest whose witness to the suffering of the poor in Latin America has had profound effects, nonetheless notes that "to acknowledge one's sins implies the will to restore broken amity, to which we are called by petition for

13. See Roberta C. Bondi, *To Pray and to Love* (Minneapolis: Augsburg Fortress, 1991) p. 94.

14. See Bondi, *To Pray and to Love*, esp. pp. 96ff., and the discussion of this passage above, pp. 127-128.

pardon and reconciliation."[15] And Elsa Tamez notes, also in the context of Latin American suffering, that "two truths run parallel in the human being: He or she is a son or daughter of God, created in God's image, and he or she is at the same time a being capable of killing a brother or sister. Both truths must be taken with the same seriousness as is faith in the one who raises the dead."[16]

The forgiveness signified by baptism thus creates a new context and capacity for community. It initiates people on a journey of living in communion with God, in friendship with God, that calls us to unlearn patterns of destructiveness and to learn to become holy people. We can be sustained in that journey in a variety of ways, and not least through liturgies of baptismal remembrance and renewal. But we are also sustained in our journeys by the eucharist, the meal that provides us with nourishment for our lives as we anticipate the messianic banquet in God's Kingdom. The eucharist enables us and teaches us to appropriate our forgivenness by remembering the past in hope rather than in despair.

Eucharist: Remembering the Past in Hope for the Future

The eucharist is an eschatological meal that recalls the past, anticipates the future, and sustains us in the present.[17] It recalls the past of Jesus' table fellowship with tax collectors and sinners, enacting the forgiveness of communion in concrete situations and lives, even as it also anticipates the messianic banquet in God's Kingdom, to which all are invited and in which no one will be hungry. It recalls the past of our desertions and betrayals of Jesus on Maundy Thursday and Good Friday, even as it also points us forward to the celebration of the Easter feast. It recalls the saving sacrifice of Christ's death and resurrection, even as it patterns our futures — and our collective future — in the light of that sacrifice. And, in so doing, the eucharist recalls the particularities of our pasts even as it enables and teaches

15. Gustavo Gutiérrez, *We Drink from Our Own Wells*, tr. Matthew J. O'Connell (Maryknoll: Orbis, 1984) pp. 99-100.

16. Elsa Tamez, *The Amnesty of Grace*, tr. Sharon H. Ringe (Nashville: Abingdon, 1993) p. 163.

17. For a sustained and powerful discussion of the eschatological significance of the eucharist, see Geoffrey Wainwright, *Eucharist and Eschatology* (New York: Oxford University, 1971).

us to remember them in hope for the future of new and renewed friendship with God in God's Kingdom.

The rhythms of the eucharist thus compel us to recognize our present, whatever it may be, as a context that can be sustained in hope only through an acknowledgment of our tendencies toward brokenness and an appreciation of the fragility of our communion. Hence, like baptism, the eucharist is both a sacramental activity of the Church and an ongoing practice of "eucharistic living." We are called to pattern our lives in the context of Christ's sacrifice both in preparation for and as a consequence of our celebrations of the eucharist. To be sure, there are destructive ways of understanding the language of "sacrifice" that can all too easily be used as a weapon of abuse and oppression of others. But this emerges only because of our failure to understand and appropriate properly the significance of Christ's sacrifice, which permits neither our scapegoating of others nor our desire to require others to sacrifice for our pleasures.

Rather, Christ's sacrifice relocates our lives as forgiven betrayers, as reconciled sinners, in communities of broken yet restored communion. In the eucharistic meal, Christ grants communion with himself through his presence and, in so doing, transforms our communion with one another. That is, the Triune God acts through the real presence of Christ in the eucharist, by the power of the Spirit, to give life to the Body of Christ and to renew the life of each member.

Further, the eucharist calls for our sacrifice as we learn to live in such communion (see Romans 12:1), as we learn to narrate and live with our pasts in ways that can envision and embody a hope not only for ourselves but for the new creation of all humanity. In this sense, the eucharist constitutes the Church. As Rowan Williams has argued, "when the Church performs the eucharistic action it *is* what it is called to be: the Easter community, guilty and restored, the gathering of those whose identity is defined by their new relation to Jesus crucified and raised, who identify themselves as forgiven."[18] By the power of the Holy Spirit, the eucharist constitutes the Church by transfiguring our past into a hopeful future — not only for ourselves, but for all.

Nonetheless, it is difficult to learn to live with the past. For the past includes not only joys but also griefs, not only hopes but also fears, not only loves sustained but also friendships betrayed, not only times of reconciliation but also desires for vengeance, not only a sense of communion but also the recognition of horrifying destructiveness. In response, we are

---

18. Williams, *Resurrection* (New York: Pilgrim, 1982) p. 58.

tempted by amnesia, by nostalgia, or by repression. We either want to pretend that the past is irrelevant, that we can re-create it (both in its retelling and as a place to inhabit) to suit our own fantasies and wishes, or that we can submerge it so deeply that it can be forgotten. If we grant that the past *is* relevant and that amnesia is not really an option, then we seem caught in a trap of either triumphalist nostalgia or despairing repression. The former thinks that Easter is ultimately about celebrating the newness of Spring, whereas the latter thinks that Judas had and has no alternatives. Much of all our lives remains caught in elaborately conceived and intricately woven webs of self-deception and fantasy.

Even so, eucharistic practice suggests that, by encountering the real presence of the crucified and risen Christ in his forgiving love, we can bear the past truthfully. We can do so in hope. We can do so, recognizing that the eucharist is an Easter feast — a feast that does not occur without Maundy Thursday and Good Friday, but one that is ultimately defined by the hopeful future rather than the sinful past. That is, the truth of Christ's loving forgiveness compels us to see the entirety of our past, but it does so for the healing of our memories and the restoration of our hope in the future of God's Kingdom. So Rowan Williams rightly notes that "if forgiveness is liberation, it is also a recovery of the past in hope, a return of memory, in which what is potentially threatening, destructive, despair-inducing, in the past is transfigured into the ground of hope."[19]

For some people like the Apostle Peter, this transformative forgiveness involves the recognition that our past reveals complicity in denial and betrayal; similarly for white Americans, it includes coming to terms with our own racism. For others like Mary at the tomb, it involves the recognition of despair and the sense of a lost self; similarly for Old Elizabeth, it means throwing off the dehumanized and dehumanizing identity given by her slave masters. But for all of us, our encounters with the crucified and risen Christ in the eucharist means that we are freed by the Holy Spirit to claim the past by *re*claiming our identity as children of a giving and forgiving, creating and re-creating God. For this, we give thanks and praise for the extraordinary self-gift of God in Jesus Christ and the continuing re-representation of that gift in the eucharist by the power of the Holy Spirit.

As Christians come to the eucharist, we are reminded in our encounter with the risen Christ that the healing of the past will not occur if we see ourselves solely as either victims or victimizers. To be sure, the patterns of our encounters with Christ are conditioned by the ways in which

19. Williams, *Resurrection*, p. 32.

we have been primarily either perpetrators or recipients of violence, destruction, and abuse. But if Christ is the pure Victim whose sacrifice transfigures our lives and sets us free from the cycles of violence and vengeance, then we need to encounter Christ in the eucharist as the One who enables us to claim our identities, shaped inevitably by our pasts, as people capable (to greater and lesser degrees) of great goodness and horrifying evil as well as both afflicting others and being afflicted by others.

For each of us in our particularities, the healing of remembrances, the ability to claim our past truthfully, involves a difficult struggle. It is not easy to renounce amnesia, to refuse nostalgia, and to resist repression. Those struggles require us to take the time to learn to identify and name those features of our past that most haunt us in the present. And, typically, we cannot do it alone. We need each other as we learn how to take the time to narrate our own and one another's stories, how to identify the bearing of our pasts on the present, in the context of the practices and friendships of Christian community. This is the time of practicing forgiveness, sustained by such practices as baptism and eucharist as well as (so I will suggest below) confession, prayer, and healing. To be sure, there are some circumstances that involve psycho-physiological issues requiring professional intervention. Yet we also need to confront the painful truth that much of the fascination with counseling in our culture is the direct result of failures to embody such Christian community, people marked by forgiving love for one another.

Indeed, one of the central problems for much of contemporary eucharistic practice is our failure to "discern the body." Too many Christian people have abandoned one another to be strangers to one another and estranged from one another. We have failed to remember that the eucharist recapitulates God's *judgment* of grace in Jesus Christ. That is, when Christ becomes present in the eucharist, he comes as Savior and as Judge. How can we celebrate the eucharist as an Easter feast if we fail to live as forgiven and forgiving people? So we are enjoined to be reconciled with our brothers and sisters before we come to the eucharist (see, for example, Matthew 5:23-24).

The practice of exchanging a kiss of peace in the context of the eucharistic celebration emerged as a sign of that forgiveness and reconciliation. It would be a sign that Christians had ongoing practices of discerning the body so that they could genuinely celebrate the eucharistic feast as forgiven and forgiving people. This discernment is an ongoing requirement of the Church's life.

Similarly, Vincent Donovan has described how the Masai in Africa deployed their long-standing cultural practice of "passing grass" around a village in preparation for the eucharist. Passing the grass was a sign of peace and happiness and well-being. If there were unresolved conflicts or other problems in the community, then the grass could not be passed. And so, on those occasions when the grass did not make it around the village, the people would not celebrate the eucharist.[20]

By contrast to these examples, if our practices of Christian community involve some overindulging while others go hungry, or if we think we can have our memories restored in hope while continuing to harbor bitterness toward one another, then we are living a lie. Paul reminds the Corinthian Church of this fact (1 Corinthians 11:27-34), insisting that those who come to the eucharist need to "discern the body." Otherwise, eucharistic practice is an occasion of judgment without grace.

This is so because of the ways in which we need to continue to unlearn the patterns of our past as well as our present tendencies toward sin. Hence, we have reminders from 1 John that anyone who claims to be without sin is a liar. The eucharist is thus inevitably an occasion of judgment: If we discern the body, it is an occasion of the judgment of grace that signifies our forgiveness of sin and the transformation of our pasts into the ground of our hope; but if we, or anyone else, partake of the eucharist *im*penitently, then we bring judgment on ourselves because we fail to recognize how God's forgiveness necessarily induces our lives of repentance.[21]

How do we know when we may be partaking "impenitently"? Paul would say we do so when we *fail* to "discern the body." By that, he almost certainly does not mean that we eat impenitently only if we have sinned or only if we have failed to say "I'm sorry." As I have been insisting all along, forgiveness and repentance are lifelong projects. It is a sign of our failure to understand either the eucharist or repentance or both if people stay away from the eucharist simply because they do not feel that they could ever be "worthy" to come to the table — as if we can earn our "worth" through repentance or any other works. By contrast, Paul seems to be suggesting that we eat impenitently if we fail to engage in penitential judgment about the state of our common life. That is, we must recognize and transform the

20. See Vincent Donovan, *Christianity Rediscovered* (Maryknoll: Orbis, 1978) pp. 124-128. I am grateful to Michael Baxter for this reference.

21. For further discussion of this issue in relation to both baptism and eucharist, see C. F. D. Moule, "The Judgment Theme in the Sacraments," in W. D. Davies and D. Daube (eds.), *The Background of the New Testament and Its Eschatology* (Cambridge: Cambridge University, 1956) pp. 464-481.

state of our lives in and through the community — repenting of the divisions and the material practices that lead to those divisions — if we are to appropriate the eucharist as an Easter feast of forgiveness and reconciliation rather than as an occasion of graceless judgment, destruction, and possibly even death (1 Corinthians 11:30-32).

Such discernment is necessary wherever two or three are gathered in Jesus' name. The Palestinian priest Elias Chacour recounts a powerful incident in his congregation in Ibillin, Israel, in 1966 that testifies to precisely this point.[22] The fact that he and his people have suffered greatly in the midst of intractable conflict is undeniable and hardly needs further explanation.[23] Further, Chacour notes that the village of Ibillin was also bitterly divided in diverse yet overlapping ways. Having recently arrived there, Chacour began preaching about the importance of ecumenism throughout the village, though without success. The only good result was a note from one of his parishioners enjoining him to "Begin first to reconcile brothers, sisters, families together" (p. 27).

Chacour was stung by the "absolute truth" of those words. So, on Palm Sunday 1966, in the midst of an overflowing congregation, he decided to do something. As he celebrated the eucharist, he felt burdened because he "could see so many people who were at odds with each other" (p. 29). In fact, he realized that "every time I turned around to bless the congregation, to give them Christ's peace, I was reminded all over again that there was in reality no peace among these people. Such peace had always been refused" (p. 30).

At the conclusion of the liturgy, Chacour made a startling decision. Before anyone could move, he defied the normal practice of remaining behind the iconostasis. He walked down the center aisle and at the back of the church locked the only two doors to the church and took the key. He then marched back up the aisle, turned around and told the people both that he loved them and that he was saddened to find them so filled with hate and bitterness for one another. In the midst of stunned silence, he went on to say:

22. The full story is told in Elias Chacour, *We Belong to the Land* (New York: HarperCollins, 1990) pp. 26-33. Further citations will be given parenthetically in the text.

23. Indeed, I write this sentence in the immediate wake of Baruch Goldstein's massacre of dozens of Palestinian Muslims in Hebron — simply the latest in a long series of blows to the possibility of some sense of peace, justice, and reconciliation in the region.

This morning while I celebrated the liturgy, I found someone who is able to help you. In fact, he is the only one who can work the miracle of reconciliation in this village. This person who can reconcile you is Jesus Christ, and he is here with us. We are gathered in his name, this man who rode in triumph into Jerusalem with hosannas ringing in his ears.

So on Christ's behalf, I say this to you: The doors of the church are locked. Either you kill each other right here in your hatred and then I will celebrate your funerals gratis, or you use this opportunity to be reconciled together before I open the doors of the church. If that reconciliation happens, Christ will truly become your Lord, and I will know I am becoming your pastor and your priest. That decision is now yours. (pp. 30-31)

Ten minutes passed, and no one said a word. The people sat in silence, locked inside their church.

Finally, one man stood up. It was Abu Muhib, a villager serving as an Israeli policeman, who was in his uniform. He stretched out his arms and said, "I ask forgiveness of everybody here and I forgive everybody. And I ask God to forgive me my sins." He and Chacour then embraced, with tears streaming down Abu Muhib's cheeks. Chacour then called for everybody in the church to embrace one another, and "tears and laughter mingled as people who had said such ugly words to each other or who had not spoken to each other in many years now were sharing Christ's love and peace" (p. 32).

Chacour told the congregation that they were now one community and forbade them from becoming divided from one another again. He then noted that "this is not Palm Sunday any longer. This is our resurrection! We are a community that has risen from the dead, and we have new life. I propose that we don't wait until next Sunday, until Easter, to celebrate the resurrection. I will unlock the doors and then let us go from home to home all over the village and sing the resurrection hymn to everyone!" (p. 32). After the people had left, Chacour removed the locks from the church doors and threw them away, along with the key. The unlocked church doors were to be a symbol of their new trust and openness. Chacour concludes his story by reflecting, "I had addressed my community and led them to a time of reconciliation. I had encouraged them to reach out to everyone in the village with their forgiveness and love. Now what? How could we build on the foundation established today?" (p. 33). Perhaps in that time of discerning the body, of practicing eucharistic reconciliation, the people were enabled to begin both the process of healing their past of hatred and bitterness within the congregation *and* the activity of embodying the struggle for forgiveness and reconciliation — including its dimensions of prophetic protest — in the village of Ibillin and beyond.

This story has a happy ending. But how do occasions of such reconciliation become regular practice, so that old wounds, bitterness and anger, and other effects of sinful patterns are not allowed to fester? If baptism and eucharist are concerned with embodying the truth of our lives in relation to the God of Jesus Christ by the power of the Spirit, how do we deal with those people in our midst who do not care about the truth — who seem unwilling to participate in practices of reconciliation? Does the practice of sustaining truthful community not require the exclusion of people who are unwilling to participate in discernment, to be exposed to the truth? Do we need boundaries that exclude people who are persistently impenitent? After all, Paul also instructed the Corinthian Church to exclude an impenitent man from their fellowship (1 Corinthians 5:1-5). On the other hand, does not such exclusion invite the return of self-righteous judgment and scapegoating, which undermine the very practices of forgiveness and reconciliation? Can we avoid letting boundaries become barriers?

Reconciling Forgiveness: Sustaining Permeable Boundaries[24]

There are four features that combine to make reconciling forgiveness both a centrally significant practice of Christian life *and* one that has great potential

---

24. It is difficult to know how to name this practice because the issues that it raises have historically divided Christian groups from one another. It has been described variously as penance, as reconciliation, as confession, or as binding and loosing. Components of the practice have been called exercising discipline, excommunication, or shunning. Further, is this practice a sacrament? Roman Catholics and Eastern Orthodox Christians have consistently identified it as such, while mainline Protestants have not (though it has an ambiguous status within the Anglican communion), and Anabaptists have described it in various terms. Closely related to the issue of its "sacramental" character is whether the person who hears the confession (and, if part of the practice, prescribes a penance) needs to be ordained. In part, these divergences involve different renderings of two passages concerning the injunctions about "binding and loosing" in Matthew: the giving of "the keys" to Peter in Matthew 16:18-19 and the description of discipline among followers in Matthew 18:15-20.

The various disputes, particularly in their historical contexts, are too complex to

for exacerbating conflicts rather than producing reconciliation or even miti-gating conflicts. First, as I have already suggested, the persistence of post-baptismal sin threatens the fragile communion we have with God, with one another, and with the whole Creation. As a result, the pursuit of holiness requires our ability to confess — to confess the praise of God, the truthful acknowledgment of our sin, and the proclamation of our faith. We need to do this both in relation to God and in our relations with others. Second, we typically need one another to help us narrate the truth of our lives, both in praise and penitence; further, we must recognize the authority that others, and most determinatively the Church, must have if we are *all* mutually to engage in this practice of reconciling forgiveness. Yet, third, because the dynamics of our relationships and of our communities involve issues of power, we must recognize how much easier it is to rupture trust through abuse of power or lack of commitment than it is to rebuild that trust necessary for sustaining the practice. Hence we must cultivate a "redemptive speech and silence" that can serve to (re-)shape and (re-)narrate the dynamics of our lives and our communities. Fourth and finally, we must acknowledge that those unwilling to engage truthfully in this practice exclude themselves from the communal life of those seeking to live "in truth." Such exclusion, however, ought to be seen only as temporary and always in the context of the hope that those subject to it will return to the fellowship.

---

enter into here. For discussions of the historical developments of the issues, see Bernhard Poschmann, *Penance and the Anointing of the Sick,* tr. Francis Courtney (New York: Herder and Herder, 1964), and G. R. Evans, *Problems of Authority in the Reformation Debates* (Cambridge: Cambridge University, 1992).

For a sampling of analyses from different traditions of the contemporary signif-icance of the issues, see (Roman Catholic) James Dallen, *The Reconciling Community* (New York: Pueblo, 1986); (United Methodist) Theodore W. Jennings, *The Liturgy of Liberation* (Nashville: Abingdon, 1988); (Lutheran) Robert W. Jenson, *Visible Words,* pp. 176-187; (Mennonite) Marlin Jeschke, *Disciplining in the Church* (Scottdale: Herald, 1988); and (Roman Catholic) Adrienne von Speyr, *Confession,* tr. Douglas W. Stott (San Francisco: Ignatius, 1985); and Max Thurian, *Confession,* tr. Edwin Hudson (2nd ed., Oxford: Mowbray, 1985).

My own term, "Reconciling Forgiveness," seeks to avoid some of the more polemi-cal contexts associated with other terms. Further, my analysis in this section seeks to draw on the strengths of several traditions, identifying the conceptual issues that ought to be at the heart of a theological understanding of the practice. I cannot deny that my own Wesleyan tradition significantly shapes my exposition, but I hope that it will be of broad ecumenical interest as well — particularly since the Wesleyan tradition, at its best, itself has significant ties to most of the relevant traditions (Eastern Orthodox, Roman Catholic, Anglican, Protestant, and Anabaptist).

As with all Christian practices, we need to recognize the crucial significance of the Holy Spirit's work in the practice of reconciling forgiveness. If we understand this practice in the context of seeking to discern the Spirit's judging, consoling, reconciling guidance, then we will be better able to avoid the ways in which we can and typically do exacerbate conflict rather than foster reconciliation. In order to see how this is the case, more needs to be said about each of the four features identified above.

The grace of God's forgiveness makes possible new and renewed lives of holiness. Such is the process of living into our baptism, of living into our vocation as eucharistic people. God's forgiveness transforms us so that we are no longer bound by or condemned to repeat the destructive patterns of the past; rather, we are enabled by God to remember the past so that we can be freed for new life in faithful witness to God's inbreaking Kingdom. This takes time and involves struggle, however; the persistence of the effects of sin and our continuing tendency to lapse back into sinful patterns and habits require that we make our patterns of forgiveness and repentance a lifelong process in the pursuit of holiness.

We are called to be holy not as some form of superhuman exercise of moral strength nor as an exercise of sanctimoniousness; rather, our holiness is to be a reflection of our gratitude for God's forgiving love for us and friendship with us. We are not required to change *in order to be forgiven* by God; as I have repeatedly insisted, there is nothing we can do to earn that forgiveness. Instead, we are enabled by God to become holy *because we have been forgiven.*

This is why confession is so important for Christians, and so easily misunderstood. We are called to confess our praise, our sin, and our faith — not in some vain attempt to make us worthy before God nor in the hope of earning forgiveness from God. Nor do we confess simply to weigh ourselves down with the burden of sin and a self-denying humiliation. As Augustine's *Confessions* show quite powerfully, the confession of sin must be contextualized within the larger significance of confessing our great joy in the God who loves us, gives us a self, and enables us to praise God in the disciplines of Christian community.

That is, we are enabled to confess in order to renarrate our lives (often by having it renarrated to us by others) so that we are capable of appropriating God's forgiveness into our lives as forgiven and forgiving people in community. We do so in the Spirit of praise and of penitence. Confession is a discipline of community that, through the guidance of the Holy Spirit, makes possible and contributes to our transformation into holy people. It does so as we learn to accept responsibility (a first person activity) for our own lives, pasts, and actions rather than always holding others responsible (a third person activity). Even more strongly, confession includes not only accepting responsibility for affirming our created goodness and receiving the forgiveness of sin, but also accepting responsibility for our part in the judgment under which the world stands and for the call to holy living in response.

In this sense, confession involves the continual remaking of our selves so that we are capable of engaging in practices of forgiveness that foster holiness and re-create relationships — with God (in response to God's prior forgiveness of us), with one another, and with the whole Creation.[25] But, the question might be asked, to whom do we confess? Is ordination necessary? This is, after all, one of the features of confession about which Christians have had radical disagreements and continue to disagree. Bonhoeffer's own practice and insights on this matter are instructive (see above, chapter 1, pp. 16-21, 30-32), yet occasionally ambiguous. Building on Bonhoeffer's insights, we need to distinguish different though interrelated issues.

We need to practice reconciling forgiveness with others. On the one hand, we need to confess our faith and our sin with one another in Christian community.[26] That is, we need the support and challenge from others within Christian community, including those who may know the particularities of our lives — including our tendencies toward self-deception and toward either prideful self-righteousness or shameful self-abasement (or

25. For further reflection on this point, see Terry Tilley's instructive chapter on confession and forgiveness in George Eliot's *Adam Bede*. For example, "declarations of confession (which ipso facto remake the self) and forgiveness (which ipso facto restore relationships) are counteractions to evil" (Terrence W. Tilley, *The Evils of Theodicy* [Washington: Georgetown University, 1991] p. 209). More generally, I am indebted to Tilley's arguments for helping me think through some of the dynamics of both confession and forgiveness.

26. For one example of this need, see the extraordinary reflection of Madelein Gray in "Giving Up the Gift: One Woman's Abortion Decision," *Commonweal* 121/4 (February 25, 1994) pp. 13-15. A Roman Catholic, Gray indicates that, while she recognized her action as sinful and in need of reconciliation, she was far more able to be reconciled to God than she could be to other Christians. She had been an active parishioner and a eucharistic minister, but she felt that to confess her action to others in the Christian community would be to encounter judgment without grace. The story points to the centrality of communities of disciples capable of providing discerning judgments of grace through support and accountability (as well as, I will suggest, confession to those who are ordained). For a scholarly discussion of these sorts of issues within Roman Catholicism, see Karl Rahner, "Forgotten Truths Concerning the Sacrament of Penance," in *Theological Investigations* II, tr. Karl-H. Kruger (New York: Seabury, 1963) pp. 135-174.

both) — better than any ordained person does. The authority given by Jesus to bind and loose, ritually focused in the ordained clergy, is given to all disciples. This points also to the importance of these disciples seeking to develop that scripturally and doctrinally informed imagination reflected in practical wisdom. It cannot be left to the clergy alone. Hence, we need to cultivate patterns of discipleship that enable mutual confession — understood as support and challenge — among particular people within the Church.[27]

But, on the other hand, it is also the case that whether the clarity about our lives comes through the confessional or in the disciplined conversations with fellow Christians, we need to seek out those against whom we have sinned and be willing to be sought out by those who have sinned against us. This is, in many situations, extraordinarily difficult — and I will return below, as well as in chapters 8 and 9, to this difficulty in situations of extreme abuse and brokenness. Further, different issues are raised when the other party or parties are fellow Christians than when they are not. In either case, however, forgiveness and the call to confession are either meaningless or distorting unless they occasion a turning — and re-turning — to those against whom we have sinned and who have sinned against us.

At the same time, however, it is important also to stress the significance for confession of ordination. The *Baptism, Eucharist, and Ministry* agreement of the World Council of Churches articulates an emerging consensus about the importance of the office of ordination.[28] The ordained ministry is a central office to represent and speak for Christ to, with, and against the Church. As such, a crucial component of that office ought to be the practice of reconciling forgiveness, regardless of whether it is understood as an official sacrament or not.[29] This is important, among other reasons, to preserve the confessional seal, to focus the centrality of forgiveness and reconciliation in the Church's life, to articulate the Church's doc-

---

27. This was, of course, one of the influential means by which the Wesleyan movement spread throughout England in the eighteenth century. People were gathered into "class meetings" and, for more concentrated focus, into "bands." Such communities were typically led by laity and were designed to produce "accountable discipleship." For further description, see David Lowes Watson, *The Early Methodist Class Meeting* (Nashville: Discipleship Resources, 1985).

28. See *Baptism, Eucharist, and Ministry* (Geneva: World Council of Churches, 1982).

29. I would argue for the importance of understanding this practice in sacramental terms, though defending that judgment would take me too far afield at this point.

trinal standards and teachings in relation to these issues, and to promote more effective understandings and embodiments of Christian forgiveness.

Unfortunately, too many contemporary Christians are unwilling to practice communal confession in any sense with one another, even as we seem to revel in the autobiographical exhibitionism and gossip of American society's culture of exposure. Bonhoeffer rightly worried about communal confession creating a climate of autobiographical exhibitionism on the one hand and gossip on the other, both of which undermine Christian community. But we need to worry equally about a privatized Christianity that presumes that forgiveness can be had apart from the disciplines of Christian community and the need to turn to those we victimize and those who have victimized us.

This brings us to the second feature of the practice of reconciling forgiveness. We typically need one another to help us narrate the truth of our lives, both in praise and penitence; further, we must recognize the authority that others, and most determinatively the Church, must have if we are *all* mutually to engage in this practice. The practice of reconciling forgiveness presumes our acknowledgment that any of us may *not* have the best or most truthful perspective on our own life or on the issues we face. We often find it difficult to know even where to begin in gaining such a truthful perspective. Yet those involved in the practices of Christian community often find this in surprising ways and places.

For example, in one small Catholic parish, a couple in their mid-50s had been admirably serving as foster parents for children born to mothers with AIDS. They would take care of these children while they lived and typically cared for them in their dying. In one particular case, however, one of their foster children was tested at age two and was found not to have the HIV virus. The mother of the child had recently died. The couple determined that they ought to give this child up for adoption. However, when the wife told a gathering of the Altar and Rosary Society, she was met with a surprising response. They told her that she and her husband needed to adopt the child. After all, they said, the child had been baptized in their parish; so the responsibility for raising that child belonged to the whole Church, and more specifically to that parish. When the foster mother protested that she and her husband were too old, the people responded that they would help raise the child in very tangible ways. When she further protested that they would be too old, if even alive, to be able to support the child through college, the people responded that the Church would help support — including financially — the child throughout her life, including college. The couple adopted this child who was already the responsibility not only of the couple but of the whole community. They had their lives, and their commitments, narrated to them in surprising ways — and in the midst of an ordinary meeting of the Altar and Rosary Society.

The Spirit often speaks to us precisely through the Church's teachings and through the gift of others in the community. The Spirit guides us in our puzzlement about how best to appropriate Christ's forgiveness through a confession that recognizes both the appropriateness of the Church's authority and the ways in which others' perspectives on our lives can enrich, support, and challenge our own.[30]

This, of course, raises several problems. There is the characteristically modern problem of authority. Modern people, particularly (though not exclusively) in developed Western societies, are notoriously suspicious of authority of all kinds. This is partly because of a healthy wariness of the ways in which authority can become, and has too often become, authoritarian and oppressive. But it is also partly because of an unhealthy infatuation with the authority of personal experience and of an untutored individual conscience.[31] That is, our wariness of oppressive authoritarianism has not resulted in an adequate rethinking, much less an acceptance, of the importance of the authority needed to sustain practices and institutions. We have simply substituted one bad conception of authority for another.

This is compounded by another, closely related problem: What do I mean by "the Church"? Different church traditions have different standards for what constitute the sins that need the practice of reconciling forgiveness. As John Howard Yoder has suggested, "the criteria, whereby people will state their belief that 'your brother or sister has sinned,' are often matters on which sincere believers differ. Killing in war is a sin for a Mennonite congregation and not for a Lutheran one. Knowing of the presence of other churches with different standards may well undercut the readiness of the person being admonished to grant the nature of the offense."[32]

The problem is compounded further by the recognition that even congregations within the same tradition may diverge substantially on these issues. Here we also see recurring the general suspicion of authority, and the largely disabled character of the practice of reconciling forgiveness

---

30. For further reflection on the Spirit's guidance of Christian communities in the context of "ongoing puzzlement" about how most faithfully to re-present Christ, see my *Transformed Judgment*, chapter 3.

31. See the instructive insights in Pope John Paul II's 1993 encyclical *Veritatis Splendor*, part II.

32. John Howard Yoder, "Binding and Loosing," in his *The Royal Priesthood*, ed. Michael G. Cartwright (Grand Rapids: Eerdmans, 1994) p. 355.

across the traditions, now conjoined to ecclesial fragmentation and "consumer choice" visions of church "shopping."[33] There are no easy answers to these difficulties; even diagnosing the range of problems exceeds the scope of my argument here.

Even so, the Church's practice of reconciling forgiveness requires the authority that establishes boundaries — even if, in practice, we need to begin reclaiming that on a very local level. On the one hand, we need to remember that Christians are made, not born. No one is compelled to be a part of the Church, to identify oneself as a Christian. So the Church needs to become clearer about the nature of its confession and of its disciplined practices in the very process by which people are invited to participate, much less by which they are inducted and formed. On the other hand, we need to acknowledge and foster mutual conversation and criticism — including prophetic judgment — about the quality of our confession and our disciplined practices. This is so within the covenants of particular communities as well as in the larger contexts of church traditions and ecumenical relations.

Yet we need to be aware of the temptation to turn legitimate boundaries into human barriers, to quench the Spirit by reifying our confessional practices. We must remember that, though we are in search of the Truth and claim to have seen it definitively revealed in Jesus Christ, we still see as through a glass darkly (1 Corinthians 13:12). Our confession and our practice of reconciling forgiveness must be eschatologically focused. Further, we need to be constantly vigilant to ensure that the authority by which we engage in practices of reconciling forgiveness is the authority of the Spirit revealed in the crucified and risen Christ.

This vigilance is all the more important because we can recall situations like one narrated by Albert Raboteau in *Slave Religion*.[34] Nancy, a slave who was also a Christian, sought to bring a complaint before her Baptist Church about the treatment she was receiving from her master and his wife. But not only did she have to voice the complaint through a white spokesman and not only were the charges dismissed; Nancy was in turn found guilty of a countercharge and excluded from the fellowship. Raboteau notes the significant point that Nancy thought she had some recourse through practices of church discipline (hence a positive sign often lacking

33. For an instructive analysis of this commodification of church membership, see Philip D. Kenneson, "Selling [Out] the Church in the Marketplace of Desire," *Modern Theology* 9/4 (October 1993) pp. 319-348.

34. Raboteau, *Slave Religion*, pp. 182-183.

in contemporary churches), though regrettably the power of that discipline was the unjust patterns of white slaveholders rather than that of the Spirit of the crucified and risen Christ.

The dangers of our "normal" patterns of speech ought to be obvious: They include the manipulation of language by the powerful to keep the powerless silent, self-righteous (or self-abasing) judgmentalism, casual indictments designed to bolster one person's fragile ego by denigrating other persons, by perpetuating gossip, and by creating scapegoats. The book of James devotes an entire chapter (James 3) to identifying the destructive capacity of the tongue. It identifies the tongue as "a restless evil, one that is full of fatal poison" (3:8). Nicholas Lash has suggested that carefulness with language, "meticulous and conscientious concern for the quality of conversation and the truthfulness of memory" is "the first casualty of sin."[35] As sin undermines community, language becomes an instrument of confusion, control, and domination rather than a means of sustenance and faithfulness for God's people.

The third feature of the practice of reconciling forgiveness follows immediately on this claim: Because the dynamics of our relationships and our communities involve issues of power, we must recognize how much easier it is to rupture trust through the abuse of power or through lack of commitment than it is to rebuild that trust necessary for sustaining the practice. Hence we must cultivate a "redemptive speech and silence" that can serve to (re-)shape and (re-)narrate the dynamics of our lives and our communities, particularly in relation to power and commitment.

By contrast, the practice of reconciling forgiveness calls us to unlearn the language that confuses, dominates, and controls and learn the "redemptive language" that enables us to sustain community. Issues of forgiveness and reconciliation invariably involve issues of power; but if we approach them in the context of forgiven lives and redemptive speech, we can struggle toward deploying the power of Christ's cross and resurrection rather than powers of domination. Cruciform power does not destroy, but seeks to reconcile and make new. Nicholas Lash rightly suggests that we need an "appropriate engagement with destructive violence, the strenuous exercise of a kind of power set to the service of a kind of politics, construction of the kind of culture of reconciliation and the binding up of wounds which might embody, sustain, and publicly communicate the announcement of

---

35. Nicholas Lash, "Ministry of the Word or Comedy and Philology," *New Blackfriars* 68 (1987) p. 477.

God's peace."[36] That is, how people deploy power in the process of identifying sin and in talking and listening and acting with one another in the pursuit of personal and social holiness not only makes a difference; it makes all the difference in whether communities are sustained or destroyed and whether selves are remade or fail to be remade as forgiven and forgiving people. And redemptive language is necessary for that power.

Indeed, central practices of Christian worship are designed to form and sustain people in their capacity for utilizing redemptive language for the sake of the gospel's power. Such practices as prayer, preaching, Scripture reading, hymn singing, and discerning the Spirit (e.g., Acts 15) cultivate this alternative power and (re-)shape our capacity for redemptive language.[37]

Further, we need not only redemptive speech but also redemptive silence. Ingredient in the practice of reconciling forgiveness is knowing when to speak, when to listen, *and* when to be silent. We should not point out every fault we see in ourselves or in others, nor should we confuse telling everything we think with being truthful in confession and community. Job's friends truly were friends when they sat with him silently for seven days. It is when they spoke, using pious-sounding but unredemptive speech, that they exacerbated the situation he faced. And so they were judged by God (Job 42:7-9). Our confession is most clearly a part of the practice of reconciling forgiveness when we are able to sustain redemptive silence and speech, when we recognize that our speech is most appropriate when it arises out of the sometimes beautiful, sometimes terrifying silences. We need the practice of contemplative silence whereby we learn those patterns of dispossession — understood not as self*less*ness but as selves who find inestimable worth in prayer to, praise of, and even lamentations to

36. Lash, "Not Quite Politics or Power?" *Modern Theology* 8/4 (October 1992) pp. 353-364, here p. 363.

37. See, for example, Talal Asad's comment on the role of preaching in medieval monasticism (*Genealogies of Religion*, p. 144):

> The sermons that give authoritative exegesis of biblical texts provide a new vocabulary by which the monks themselves can redescribe, and therefore in effect construct, their memories in relation to the demands of a new way of life. This redescription of memories depends on a long and complex process. In it, (1) the authoritative preacher and the monk addressed, (2) the monk interacting with fellow monks, (3) the confessor and the monk in confession, and (4) the remembering religious self and the secular self remembered, all contribute in the production of a moral description by which the monk's desires and feelings are reconstructed.

God — that can help to reshape our memories and desires, and thereby also our language.

In a world — and, unfortunately, even in churches — where language is more often used carelessly than carefully, such redemptive speech and silence may need to be learned once again in communities of the "arcane discipline" (to use Bonhoeffer's phrase). We have allowed central Christian notions and practices to become trivialized through careless uses of language; we need the rhythms of silence and speech, allowing our silence to correct and enrich our speech, even as our speech needs to resist the temptation to remain quiet.

If we are able to cultivate a practice of reconciling forgiveness where confession and repentance emerge out of the patterns of redemptive language and silence, then we will have moved a long way toward the sustenance of communities in which people learn to live in communion rather than always blaming others. Indeed, in such a case the passage about confronting sin in Matthew 18:15-20 becomes much less daunting (even if still difficult to practice well). We often shy away from confronting our brother or our sister because of our fears, and perhaps even our experience, of how such confrontation exacerbates rather than resolves conflicted situations. We sometimes refer to avoiding such confrontations as a form of "keeping the peace." But the logic of the passage, and of the gospel, suggests that we will be able to "keep the peace" only insofar as we foster practices of forgiveness and reconciliation in which sin is acknowledged and confronted.

This process of confronting sin is defined in Matthew, and in a correlative passage in John (20:22-23), as "binding and loosing." These terms are derived from rabbinic usage (in turn based on Leviticus 19:17), and they have two interrelated meanings.[38] In relation to moral discernment, to "bind" is to enjoin, to forbid, or to make obligatory; to "loose" is to leave free, to permit. In relation to forgiveness, to "bind" is to withhold fellowship, to "loose" is to forgive. John Howard Yoder aptly describes their interrelation:

> Moral discernment and forgiveness condition and enable one another in complex ways. Admonition presupposes prior discernment; otherwise the criteria for admonition would not be common to both parties. Con-

---

38. In what follows I am indebted to John Howard Yoder's analysis in "Binding and Loosing," pp. 328-329. See also his discussion in *Body Politics* (Nashville: Discipleship Resources, 1992) pp. 1-13.

versation with reconciling intent is the most powerful way for a community to discover when the rules they have been applying are inadequate, so that they may be modified. Asking whether there has really been an offense helps determine which differences need to be resolved by coming to unanimity by means of dialogue and forgiveness and which call for an agreement to differ. Having experienced forgiveness together enables a community to deliberate in an otherwise inaccessible mode of mutual trust.[39]

The use of redemptive language and silence can enable us to confront sin, and even to engage in discernment and debate about whether something is sin, in ways that further reconciliation rather than promote conflict and distrust.

This pattern of binding and loosing describes communities where practices of discernment and forgiveness are central to their ongoing life, where the gospel of God's reconciliation shapes their struggle to live with one another as reconciled and reconciling people. This requires trust as well as redemptive speech and silence, the capacity to discern wisely each life and situation in their particularity as well as to cultivate authoritative assumptions about the shaping of the common life together. And this pattern is seen in communities of the Holy Spirit engaged in ongoing puzzlement and discernment of how to embody Christ's forgiveness in the present. As they do so, the practice of Christian community becomes a sign of God's redemption in the world. James McClendon offers some instructive comments on the significance of binding and loosing, particularly as described in Matthew 18:

> It is exactly this skill of forgiveness that is the divine gift enabling disciple communities to cope with the looming power of their own practice of community, otherwise so oppressive, so centripetally destructive. Without forgiveness, the social power of a closed circle may crush its members, soil itself, and sour its social world. Examples of such soured communitarianism litter the pages of every honest church history. But with forgiveness controlling everything, the closed circle is opened, the forgiven forgivers' practice of community is redeemed and becomes positively redemptive; thus this powerful practice renders obedience to the law of the Lord Jesus.[40]

39. Yoder, *Body Politics*, p. 6; cf. "Binding and Loosing," p. 328.

40. James William McClendon, *Ethics: Systematic Theology, Volume I* (Nashville: Abingdon, 1986) pp. 229-230.

The passage in Matthew's Gospel envisions practices of binding and loosing where forgiveness and reconciliation are both the process and the goal. But it also recognizes that there will be circumstances in which, and people for whom, forgiveness and reconciliation will not be, at least contingently, fully possible. This brings us to the fourth feature of the practice of reconciling forgiveness: We must acknowledge that those unwilling to engage truthfully in this practice exclude themselves from the communal life of those seeking to live in truth. They refuse to accept responsibility for learning to live in communion, preferring always to blame others. Such exclusion, however, ought to be seen only as temporary and always in the hope that they will return to the fellowship.

That is, according to Matthew 18:15-20, the primary reason that forgiveness may not be fully accomplished is that the offenders may not acknowledge their need for forgiveness.[41] In such situations, the way of forgiveness is truncated and the prospects for reconciliation are, if not temporarily eclipsed, at least not fully possible. If offenders persistently refuse to acknowledge their need for forgiveness as the extensive process of people talking with them described in the passage goes on (and assuming that the people come as those who have been forgiven and are deploying redemptive language and silence), then they ought to be treated as "Gentiles and tax collectors." There would be no doubt for the Jewish Christian community of Matthew's Gospel what such a designation referred to: people who by their behavior had excluded themselves from the community. As Stanley Hauerwas has contended, such people "are acting like those who have not learned that they have been forgiven. To act like one not needing forgiveness is to act against the very basis of this community as a community of peacemaking."[42] These people are Christians who live as if there is no God. This description makes sense of Matthew's description of the "unforgivable sin" in 12:31-32: The sin is unforgivable not because of the action done (be it murder, adultery, or apostasy), since such actions are not outside the realm of forgiveness. Rather, what makes the sin unforgivable is people living in a way that persistently denies any *need* for forgiveness.

41. This is a different case than those difficult situations where forgiveness involves people who cannot repent (e.g., because they are dead). There full reconciliation may not be contingently possible — in that sense, it can only await the Kingdom — but there is not the risk of continuing ruptures of communion being perpetrated by impenitent "members" of the community.

42. Stanley Hauerwas, *Christian Existence Today* (Durham: Labyrinth, 1988) p. 94.

Further, such a description is consistent with the parable of the Un-forgiving Servant, which concludes Matthew 18 (vv. 23-35). The servant is punished because of his failure to manifest forgiven-ness in his relations with those who are indebted to him. The implication of both texts seems to be that, while repentance and confession are not *conditions* of receiving God's forgiveness, they are indispensable means of acknowledging our *need* for forgiveness and hence embodying that forgivenness in our relations with others.

But what should we say about, and how should we act toward, these people who refuse to engage in the practice of reconciling forgiveness, even if — or perhaps especially if — there are differences in perception about the wrongdoing? How should we respond to an unrepentant racist, an impenitent liar, or a chronic abuser? By their refusal to engage in the practice of reconciling forgiveness, including its assumption of lifelong forgiveness and repentance, they have excluded themselves from the realm of the Body of Christ, understood as the community of the forgiven, and so ought to be treated as such. The truthfulness of Christian community demands such judgment. As people who have excluded themselves from the fellowship of the Body, they may even be termed "enemies" of the cross of Christ.

Before we move too quickly, however, we need to remember how Jesus treats such "enemies" as Gentiles and tax collectors. He continues to reach out to them, to bring them (back) into the fold of God's covenant of grace. We should not coerce them into the fold, nor should we pretend that the conflict and division do not exist. But neither should we "demonize" them, as we so often want to do with enemies, or turn them into "scapegoats."[43]

Earlier in Matthew's Gospel, in the Sermon on the Mount, Jesus enjoins his disciples to "love your enemies and pray for those who persecute you" (Matthew 5:44). Such a call to love one's enemies is startling in its frank acknowledgment that faithful Christians will have enemies. While Christ decisively defeated sin and evil through his cross and resurrection, the influence of sin and evil have not fully come to an end. So in at least one sense, we still live on *this* side of the fullness of Easter.

But, even if we do and probably always will have enemies — if we are faithfully following Jesus — we are nonetheless called to *love* them. That is a reminder that, in the absence of the fullness of forgiveness and reconciliation,

---

43. In a number of important works, René Girard has insightfully discussed the significance of "scapegoats" and the ways in which Christian convictions about Jesus Christ challenge the necessity of scapegoating. See particularly *The Scapegoat*, tr. Yvonne Freccero (Baltimore: Johns Hopkins University, 1986).

the craft of forgiveness nonetheless requires the difficult step of loving enemies, a step whose *telos* must always be the hope — even if it is at best an eschatological hope — for reconciliation, the transformation of enemies into friends. This may require that we be separate from the enemies, since their presence may threaten our very identities in relation to God.[44] At a minimum, it requires of us the struggle to learn to wish them well even when we cannot be present to them. We cannot allow legitimate and fundamentally important (even if typically fuzzy) boundaries to become barriers.

Such love of enemies has been embodied in many of the holy lives of those we call "saints," who are often unknown to many others, but their faithfulness bears witness to the forgiving and sanctifying grace of God revealed in Jesus Christ. Yet there are also examples of people better known to us, whose fidelity to the gospel became most clear in their refusal to demonize others, in their commitment to love even — and perhaps especially — their enemies.

To be sure, this section of this chapter, and particularly these last comments on loving enemies, requires more extensive exploration and elaboration. It has touched on some of the most fundamental features of our brokenness and the cycles of sin and evil that continue to beset our world and our lives. I will return to them again in chapter 8. But we also need to recognize that one of the central reasons that these issues are in such need of further elaboration is the contemporary Church's disastrous failure to embody the practice of reconciling forgiveness, to cultivate the alternative power of Christ's cross and resurrection. There are pockets where it is being done better rather than worse, or where it is at least being tried. But perhaps one of the first things the contemporary Church — across the traditions — needs to do is to confess to God our failures to be genuinely a confessing Church, to sustain communities of reconciling forgiveness.

To be sure, the Church is also afflicted with controversies and divisions about precisely what constitutes sound doctrine and teaching about sin and thus about what needs forgiveness, about Christ and how to narrate Christ's redeeming work, and even about the character and identity of God. In the midst of such conflicts, we need that charity that recognizes that we must struggle fully to understand the other's speech and silence so that we do not dismiss fellow brothers and sisters in Christ, *along with* that firm centeredness in sound doctrine that orients all our feeling and acting, all

44. For insightful reflection on this important point, see Roberta C. Bondi, "Becoming Bearers of Reconciliation," *Weavings* 5/1 (January/February 1990) pp. 6-17.

our silence and speech, and all our suffering and living in relation to the creative and re-creative work of the God of Jesus Christ. This takes time, and it involves the ongoing struggle to discern the work of the Spirit *of Jesus Christ* (as distinguished from other "spirits"); but as the Council of Jerusalem discovered (Acts 15), such discernment is possible if we are willing patiently to seek what seems good to the Spirit *before* we decide what seems good to any particular person or interest group. This is one of the central features of a Church that knows how to confess and how to engage in the Christian practice of reconciling forgiveness.

At the same time, we need to acknowledge the intense pain, anger, and bitterness that exist for people who have suffered and continue to suffer the effects of sin and evil in our world. Cultivating a practice of reconciling forgiveness takes time, a creative reclamation of understandings of sin and forgiveness in relation to the doctrine of God, and the re-membering of our identities through the sustenance of a number of other practices of Christian community. Reconciling forgiveness is not easy; it is costly. It is not quick; it is a lifelong struggle. It is not a commodity; it is the investment of the entirety of our lives.

As such, I have already alluded to the ways in which reconciling forgiveness also involves prayer and healing. It does so precisely because of the recurring and lingering effects of our memories of sin and evil, both committed and suffered, on both our souls and our bodies. Hence, I conclude this chapter with some gestures toward the significance of reclaiming these practices in the Christian life of forgiveness.

Prayer and Healing: Living in the Power of God

Situations of extreme brokenness, times and circumstances in which reconciliation seems virtually impossible, are reminders of the difficult movements of silence and speech — of knowing what to say and when nothing can or should be said. But at the very least, such situations can be lifted up in the context of prayer and of the hope for God's healing.[45] An important passage in the book of James (5:13-16) reflects this conjunction of prayer, healing, and forgiveness:

45. I am indebted to John Koenig for helping me think through the connections and issues involved in the conjunction of prayer, healing, and forgiveness. See the chapter on "Prayers of Forgiveness and Healing," in his *Rediscovering New Testament Prayer* (New York: HarperCollins, 1992) pp. 95-113.

Are any of you suffering? They should pray. Are any of you cheerful? They should sing songs of praise. Are any of you sick? They should call the elders of the church to pray over them, anointing them with oil in the name of the Lord. The believing prayer will save the sick, and the Lord will raise them up, and anyone who has committed sins will be forgiven. Therefore, confess your sins to each other and pray for each other so that you can be healed. The prayer of the righteous is powerful and effective.

This passage raises a number of significant issues; of these, perhaps the most difficult, and also one of the most awkward, is the seeming connection between sickness and sin.

To be sure, this is a theme found throughout the Bible, addressed in diverse ways in such texts as Deuteronomy and Job, Mark 2 and John 9. Unfortunately, the linkage of sickness and sin is also a cause of considerable consternation for people who find themselves with particular illnesses or with seemingly inexplicable suffering. It would be inaccurate and callous, indeed sinful, to claim a simple causal connection between sin and sickness or between sin and suffering, as did Job's friends, and there is no indication that James does so. Indeed, Jesus in his healing ministry does not accuse people of having caused their sickness because of sinning; he focuses instead on the task of healing. In the New Testament, it is demonic forces who use illness as an occasion for oppression (see Acts 10:38).

On the other hand, it should also be acknowledged that the New Testament does at times suggest that illness may be a warning from God intended to produce repentance on the part of those who arrogantly think they are beyond God's reach: so Paul's denunciation of Elymas (Acts 13:10-11), his warning to the Corinthian Church about eating unworthily at the Lord's table (1 Corinthians 11:30), and the risen Christ's stern judgment on a false prophetess (Revelation 2:21-22). John Koenig's comments on these passages are instructive: "In each of these cases it is important to notice that the individuals afflicted are explicitly faulted for thinking of themselves as beyond reproach in God's eyes. They are the very opposite of those who declare their humility and need by calling on God for help."[46]

James does not articulate any clear relationship between sin and sickness or suffering. That there may be some connection would seem to be undeniable, given the ways in which our bodies and our souls are bound up together. But it is dangerous and offensive to assume any causal con-

46. Koenig, *Rediscovering New Testament Prayer*, p. 98.

nections, because illness and suffering strike the just and the unjust, the most miserable sinners and the most holy saints.

James's focus is on healing; and here he seems to be suggesting that prayers for healing may induce desires to confess and be forgiven of particular sins. Pain, whether physical or psychic (and the two are often difficult to distinguish), often causes our worlds to contract, so that we are increasingly focused on (and perhaps obsessed with) introspection. In such situations, the pain may also induce a desire to unburden whatever struggles we might be feeling in our souls.[47] In this context, we should not be surprised if prayers for healing, and indeed the act of anointing with oil, foster the desire to confess.

That confession, however, need not be only of sins that we have committed against others. It may also need to be confession of one's sense of anger over what has been suffered from others, or — even more poignantly — of one's sense of despair in the face of either explicable or inexplicable suffering. This is particularly the case once we recognize the ways in which the effects of recurring violence and abuse perdure in our bodies and our souls long after the violence and abuse have stopped. Hence the importance of confession and forgiveness becoming a habit that we embody so as to heal the effects of sin in our bodies and in our souls.

But even in these contexts, we need to remember the communal nature of confession. We still need to help one another recognize and narrate our confession in ways that are genuinely oriented toward the reestablishment of communion; it is, after all, too easy to trivialize the issues by developing a "victim complex" in which I either arrogantly or despairingly am self-deceived into assuming that the suffering I have inflicted on others or that has been inflicted on me is always everyone else's fault. Confession, even in the midst of prayers of forgiveness and healing and of the practice of anointing (and perhaps especially there), needs to focus on eliciting the truth with one another so that communion can be reestablished.

The conjunction of prayer and healing with forgiveness reminds us both of the "timeful" (time-filling) character of forgiveness and reconciliation and that forgiveness and healing are less things we can will than

47. See Elaine Scarry, *The Body in Pain* (New York: Oxford University, 1985), for further reflections about how pain in the body serves to contract and "unmake" the world.

48. Seeing forgiveness as something to be discovered rather than "done" is one of the central themes of John Patton's *Is Human Forgiveness Possible?* (Nashville: Abingdon, 1985).

achievements that come as the gift of God's grace.[48] Even when we find a particular situation so intransigent that we cannot imagine forgiveness, much less reconciliation, we can nonetheless engage in prayers of forgiveness and healing. Such prayers are enjoined on Christians in the Lord's Prayer and in several other New Testament passages (e.g., Matthew 5:44; James 5:16; Colossians 3:13-17). It is in this context that a person harboring bitterness against another might be asked, "Can you pray for that person?" Doing so might begin to create a thaw not only in the interactions (if there still are such), but also in our own hearts.

Further, we need also to recognize the centrality of prayers of intercession offered by others in the community, even when I feel unable to proceed further along the path of forgiveness and reconciliation. Simon Tugwell puts the matter well: "There is a great ministry here which we can perform for one another. Often it is morally impossible for me to forgive someone who has harmed me; I may want to forgive, but somehow find it beyond my powers. The support of my brothers and sisters in Christ, forgiving for me, may well be the means by which eventually I too can learn to forgive."[49] The converse is equally true; perhaps when we feel so guilty or so ashamed that we cannot claim our own forgiven-ness, the prayerful support of brothers and sisters in Christ, accepting forgiveness for us, may well be means by which eventually we, too, can learn to be forgiven.

In either case, the focus is on the intercessory prayer of the larger community of Christians. Paul urges Christians to be people of reconciling forgiveness, urging "those who have received the Spirit" to restore transgressors "in a spirit of gentleness" and with due self-examination to avoid temptation. More generally, Christians are called to "bear one another's burdens" (Galatians 6:2) along the path of forgiveness and reconciliation. We do so as those created for friendship with the Triune God, restored to friendship by Christ's gracious forgiveness, and sustained in our appropriation of that forgiving friendship by the judging, consoling, and guiding work of the Spirit. In that process, we need the strength and transforming power of personal and intercessory prayers of forgiveness and healing.

This is also true of the practice of anointing the sick.[50] As I have

49. Simon Tugwell, *Prayer* (Springfield: Templegate, 1975) p. 90, cited in Koenig, *Rediscovering New Testament Prayer*, p. 103.

50. As with the practice of reconciling forgiveness, there are disputes among Christians about the status of this practice. Should it be considered a sacrament? Roman Catholics and Eastern Orthodox Christians think so, but Protestants have tended to think not. Unfortunately, unlike the practice of reconciling forgiveness, which Protes-

already suggested, James does not draw any precise boundaries between the healing of the body and the healing of the soul, and neither should we. Anointing the body is a central sign of the healing power of Christ, now effected by the gracious power of the Holy Spirit. That healing power is found throughout Jesus' ministry, and is explicitly linked to forgiveness in the story of the paralytic in Mark 2:1-12 and in James 5:13-16. Jesus recognizes our need of healing in diverse circumstances and diverse ways, and he frequently heals through the power of physical touch.

In general, people who are wounded — whether through physical or psychological violence, or simply through inexplicable suffering or sickness — often need to have those wounds salved through the healing power of touch. This is often difficult since those who have withdrawn or been forced to withdraw into their wounds may find it painful to be touched. Further, those who self-righteously feel free of woundedness often have great difficulty in being willing to touch the wounds of others and being touched themselves. But the sacramental character of anointing, the care with which it ought to be done, and more centrally its gracious action by the Holy Spirit ritually focus the significance of our need for the healing of our bodies and our souls. Indeed, a recent Eastern Orthodox catechism treats issues of forgiveness and repentance within the larger context of the sacrament of anointing.[51]

The practice of anointing is a ministry that may or may not result in or contribute to physical healing, though it always can affect and enhance our spirits. Christians are called to anoint the sick; whether the sick are healed is another matter. In any event, the processes of healing, as also of forgiveness, typically take time. We should not become too impatient as we seek to bear witness to God's re-creating work in our lives and in the world.

---

tants have tended to practice (to be sure, to better and worse degrees!), the rejection of the sacramental status of anointing has tended to result in its virtual disappearance. I would be in favor of restoring its practice to sacramental status within those Christian traditions that have abandoned it. But, without arguing that point, I would affirm most strongly in this context its importance as a practice that sustains the larger doctrinal claims about Christian forgiveness. And examples of rites for this practice can be found within the liturgical resources of diverse traditions.

51. See *The Living God*, vol. II (Crestwood: St. Vladimir's Seminary, 1989) chapter 29. Unfortunately, despite this insight the catechism adopts a curious "stage" theory of forgiveness and repentance, in which both conversion and confession are understood to precede the granting of forgiveness. As I have suggested throughout Part II of this book, such a claim conflates important distinctions.

We need to remember that God does not always provide physical recovery to people, even in response to prayer and anointing. Sometimes God does answer prayer and work through anointing. Still, even in the absence of bodily healing in particular circumstances, the practice witnesses to the power of God's Spirit to restore and make new.[52]

This is particularly the case in regard to the relationship between healing and forgiveness. We are never sure of the dynamic interactions of our bodies and our souls; hence, the practices of Christian healing in general, and of anointing in particular, ought to be understood in relation to the forgiveness of sins.[53] Further, this is an indication that physicians and clergy should understand their vocations in much more interactive ways than presently tends to be the case. Indeed, John Koenig notes that many non-Western cultures have done a better job of combining intercessory prayer with conventional medicine, citing in particular the special institutions developed by the Lutheran Church of Madagascar.[54] Such an example is a reminder of the manifold ways in which we need to reclaim and enhance practices of Christian community that sustain and enable a more adequate appropriation, by the power of the Spirit, of Christ's forgiveness and healing.[55]

To understand and practice forgiveness in relation to healing is also to begin to see more clearly the "timeful" character of both, the process by

52. See Koenig, *Rediscovering New Testament Prayer*, pp. 106-113, for some insightful reflections on the importance of prayers for healing and anointing even when they are not "answered" by physical recovery. After all, every person who has ever prayed for healing, or been prayed for, has ended up dying. But that does not lessen the importance, both for the person and for the larger community, of continuing the practice.

53. This can be seen, for example, in the recent recovery of services of healing by United Methodists. In their new *Book of Worship* there are two services of healing, and both of them include frequent references to God's character as a forgiving God, the citation of the passage in James, prayers for forgiveness and a declaration of pardon, and the celebration of the eucharist (preceded by the passing of the peace). See *The United Methodist Book of Worship* (Nashville: United Methodist Publishing House, 1992) pp. 615-623. See also the section on "Ministry with the Dying," pp. 166-167.

54. Koenig, *Rediscovering New Testament Prayer*, pp. 109-110.

55. A similar point could also be made about the practice of footwashing and its symbolic significance in cleansing post-baptismal sin. See, for example, the argument of John Christopher Thomas in *Footwashing in John 13 and the Johannine Community* (Sheffield: JSOT, 1991). The practice is most frequently found in Anabaptist and Disciples of Christ communities, but the whole Church would do well to foster and reclaim its significance.

which God is patiently re-creating us and the world and restoring us to communion with God, with one another, and with the whole Creation. It is to recognize that, just as we need to develop good habits of health so as to counteract and challenge the forces of disease, so we need good habits of forgiveness so as to counteract and challenge the forces of sin and evil in our midst. What God is in God's very being — namely, the communion of self-giving love — we are called to grow into through the practices of Christian communion. Just as God creates an original and eschatological peace that precedes conflict and produces reconciliation, so we are called to be and to become the Church of peaceful reconciliation.

In so doing, we need to focus on the rhythms of forgiveness and repentance, of selves being discovered and communities being poured out for others, of identities being forged and horizons being extended, of memories being healed and hopes being created anew, of silence being heard and language being transformed. We come to be the Church through such rhythms of practicing forgiveness, understood as embracing — and being embraced by — the sacraments through which God becomes present to us. Learning so to practice forgiveness, and to understand what is entailed thereby, is a difficult matter; it involves us in ongoing puzzlements by which the Spirit of Jesus Christ guides our discernment and our developments of doctrines and rules, our binding as well as our loosing. In so doing, the Spirit is conforming us to the form of Jesus Christ, the icon of the Father. As such, we are constituted by God in the shape and pattern of trinitarian community.

Through our practices of trinitarian community, we attempt to grasp how, in diverse ways, we have become complicit in breaking apart and further dividing God's harmonious Creation. In so doing, we begin to unlearn those patterns of destructiveness as we also begin to learn — slowly, fitfully, and painfully — the patterns and habits of God's forgiveness through holy living. This is part of what it means to practice the craft of forgiveness.

Even so, Christian practices of forgiveness and reconciliation also regrettably produce new divisions — now between those who practice forgiveness and those who do not, those who confess and those who do not, and those who repent and those who remain impenitent. Even in the midst of such divisions, however, we cannot allow the legitimate boundaries necessary for truthful community to become barriers. We are called to love our enemies, seeking to make them friends. Hence the Church must maintain its distinctive practices of forgiveness, showing through its holiness the truth of the gospel and its separation from all that diminishes and destroys human life. In so doing, the Church witnesses through its practices to the truth of the Spirit who is making all things new. As such, Christians bear witness to our hope for a new humanity, to the eschatological hope that one day all people will be able to enjoy fellowship and communion with God and with one another. After all, it is to that hope, as the Letter to the Ephesians indicates, that we have been called.

PART III

PART III

7 The Craft of Forgiveness

Traditions, Parables, and Making and Remaking Responsible Human Life

I HAVE BEEN advancing the argument throughout Part II that forgiveness ought to be understood paradigmatically in the context of the Triune God's work. That is, I have been developing an account predicated on two methodological claims: first, that it is God's forgiveness, not interhuman forgiveness, that ought to provide the contours for our understanding of forgiveness; and, second, that a specifically Christian theological account of God's forgiveness, centered in Jesus Christ, ought to be the means of articulating that understanding. Further, in the process of developing that account I have argued that God's forgiveness initiates and sustains, by the power of the Holy Spirit, specific friendships and practices of Christian community and Christian life. It is in and through such friendships and practices of the Body of Christ that we learn to embody forgiveness.

Such an approach has some obvious advantages. For example, it situates human forgiveness analogically in relation to God, reminding Christians that both our understanding of forgiveness and our call to live as forgiven and forgiving people must be set in the context of the work of the Triune God. Further, such an approach provides specificity to the Christian doctrine of God and thereby links that doctrine to particular friendships and practices of Christian community and Christian life. Perhaps most importantly, however, it provides a paradigmatic account within the contours of which we can discern better and worse ideas about and practices of forgiveness as we seek to become holy people according to the pattern of the crucified and risen Christ.

207

But this approach also gives rise to some obvious objections. For example, is such an account "sectarian"? In other words, is it focused exclusively on Christian forgiveness yet unable to account for and appreciate the presence and reality of forgiveness — both as practiced and as understood — among adherents of other (religious and nonreligious) traditions? Or, perhaps less sharply, can such a Christian account of forgiveness contribute to our understanding of difficult issues between Christians and non-Christians in social and political spheres where issues must be faced, decisions made, and human brokenness engaged without (at least in many cases) the possibility of specific, persuasive recourse to the Christian doctrine of the Triune God? Is my account a matter of "preaching to the choir" while avoiding responsibility for addressing "the world" and other religious traditions beyond or outside the Church? Further, once we raise this set of concerns, are there some people who simply are unforgivable?

These are serious issues. And if the objections reflected in them are compelling, they substantially weaken, if not undermine, the force of my argument. Needless to say, I do not think they are compelling. Even so, the issues must be addressed. And it is the task of the three chapters in Part III to do so.

In this chapter, I begin that task by analyzing how and why my account not only makes attention to issues of forgiveness beyond and outside of explicitly Christian contexts possible, but indeed necessary. It is necessary as an implication of the Christian doctrine of the Triune God. Christians believe that all people are creatures of a gracious God, created by the Triune God for communion. We are also destined for such communion in God's Kingdom. So it should not surprise Christians that even those who do not profess belief in the Christian God (or perhaps in any god) might nonetheless recognize — by virtue of having been created in God's image and destined for communion with God — the importance of forgiveness and reconciliation as a means of responding to sin and evil, and more specifically to the brokenness that pervades so much of our lives.

Even more, if this is the case for specific people, we should not be surprised to find that adherents of other traditions, religious and nonreligious, might also have practices that are analogous to Christian practices of forgiveness. After all, as there are diverse but overlapping accounts and practices of love, so there are also diverse but overlapping accounts and practices of forgiveness. In addition, it is the case that these other accounts might offer important correctives, challenges, and enrichments to a Christian account of forgiveness (though not, according to my exposition, correctives to the definitiveness of the revelation of God in Jesus Christ). Indeed, my exposition in this book has been particularly influenced (albeit in diverse ways) by Jewish theology, by Aristotelian moral philosophy, and by contemporary social and political theories. The crucial issue involves *how* we go about attending to these diverse but overlapping accounts of forgiveness.

I suggest that we do so within the context of understanding forgiveness as a craft. Christians practice forgiveness as a craft in a number of different contexts: in making and remaking the various dimensions of our own lives, in our engagements with others as we seek to discern in very specific contexts what forgiveness does or does not entail, and as we seek to find analogues to Christian forgiveness in the world of God's good Creation and, more specifically, in other traditions.

However, I only turn to an exposition of the craft of forgiveness in the third section of this chapter. In the first two sections I do some methodological "brush-clearing" in order to suggest why, for example, the (by now) conventional options of either particularity *or* universality (or, more negatively put, "sectarian relativism" or "abstract dogmatism") represent a misdiagnosis of the issues that we face. This point has been made with considerable power (albeit in diverse yet overlapping ways) by philosophers such as Donald Davidson and Alasdair MacIntyre; but the Christian doctrine of the Triune God reveals an even more significant and crucial means of specifying why we are not compelled to choose one or the other — and indeed why choosing one or the other ends up in distorting or leaving incomplete an adequate account of forgiveness.

In the first section of this chapter, I argue that discussions of forgiveness in modernity have tended either to fail or be weakened by their reliance on problematic methodological assumptions and claims. I then sketch, in the second section, an alternative methodological argument for dealing with diverse but overlapping accounts of forgiveness, an account that attends to both the particularity of arguments and claims for their universal significance. More specifically, I develop an account that draws on Karl Barth's notion of "secular parables." My alternative presumes the necessity of ongoing discernment of what constitutes authentic forgiveness in the irreducibly diverse traditions and situations in which people find themselves. Finally, in the third section I turn to an explicit discussion of forgiveness as a craft. This section focuses on how the notion of craft can illumine our understanding of what is involved in the making and remaking of responsible human life (ours and those of others).

Methodologically, my argument joins a Barthian insistence on the priority of theology with an Aristotelian-Thomist emphasis on the continuities of habits, crafts, and traditions. That is, Barth's emphasis on "secular parables" provides a *theological* context for understanding and evaluating forgiveness. But such parables are insufficient to generate the continuities of a craft, the accumulated wisdom over time of a tradition. By contrast, an Aristotelian-Thomist emphasis ensures that forgiveness is understood as a human practice, one that is best understood as a craft within an ongoing tradition. On the other hand, some Aristotelian-Thomists (e.g., Alasdair MacIntyre) have not adequately recognized the importance of how a theological account of forgiveness qualifies their understanding. Hence, by the end of this chapter I will have argued that, while the craft of forgiveness is embodied most specifically in the friendships and practices of Christian communities, it also finds analogues in the world of God's good Creation and specifically in many other (religious and nonreligious) traditions.[1]

Whose Forgiveness Is It Anyway?

People attending to forgiveness in modernity have tended to make one (or more) of three mistakes in their accounts: (1) They have tended to assume that a philosophical account of forgiveness can be offered independently of any theological convictions. They have often assumed that their analysis is congruent with, or at least could be applied without recourse to, Christian understandings; unfortunately, because of their refusal to engage theological arguments, their proposals typically diverge in significant ways from an appropriately Christian account of these issues. (2) Those accounts that have attended to the theological issues have tended to do so by engaging a "theistic" perspective rather than a trinitarian doctrine of God. As a result, their accounts of what it means for "God" to forgive has tended to be truncated rather than fully developed, and the links between the work of

1. This way of formulating the issues raises obvious questions about "natural theology" as well as "natural law," particularly as those notions have been the focus of comparisons and contrasts between Barth's theology and Thomas's. Though I cannot attend to those issues in any detail in this context, my argument in this chapter (and more broadly, in this book) should suggest to attentive readers the ways in which I would go about doing so; clearly, there are some formulations of "natural law" to which Christians ought to be far more sympathetic and committed than others. But explicating how and why that is the case would take me too far afield here.

the Father, Son, and Holy Spirit in forgiveness have not been sufficiently explicated. (3) Philosophical accounts of forgiveness have tended to be indebted to theories of morality that are, at least from the Christian perspective I have been developing, fundamentally misleading. Insofar as philosophical accounts attend to forgiveness, my Christian account will contend that they ought to do so within a qualified, broadly Aristotelian-Thomist perspective, one that emphasizes forgiveness as a craft in the context of learning virtue.[2]

Each of these mistakes reflects the temptation to try to provide "universal" perspectives that avoid recourse to arguments grounded in particular traditions. In such cases, the operating presumption has been that such recourse to particular traditions (particularly theological traditions) or specific contexts is either illegitimate or, less strongly, significantly weakens the argument. It is important to analyze these arguments and the mistakes they make in order to grapple more directly with possible objections to both the method and the content developed in Parts I and II of my argument.

The first mistake identified above is symptomatic of modernity's marginalization of theology. The emergence of the Enlightenment in the eighteenth century created the dominant conviction that untutored reason is the necessary and sufficient condition for philosophy in general and ethics in particular. As modernity has progressed, this has increasingly meant not so much that theology is attacked as that it is ignored.[3] Further, despite the "postmodern" critiques of Enlightenment epistemologies, people have continued to refer to theological issues and practices without seriously engaging them theologically.[4]

---

2. It is important to indicate that this is an Aristotelian-*Thomist* perspective. Aristotle marginalized forgiveness, thinking that it is acceptable for a virtuous person to forgive others, though that person should never want to need to be forgiven. By contrast, St. Thomas's account, which makes charity (understood as friendship with God) the center of his moral reflection, transforms Aristotle's understanding and relocates forgiveness at the heart of the moral life. For a discussion of how Aquinas transforms Aristotle's moral perspective, see my *Transformed Judgment: Toward a Trinitarian Account of the Moral Life* (Notre Dame: University of Notre Dame, 1989), chapter 2.

3. For a significant diagnosis of the historical issues leading to theology's marginalization, see Jeffrey Stout, *The Flight from Authority* (Notre Dame: University of Notre Dame, 1981). But I am far less persuaded by Stout's understanding of what is required if theology is to rehabilitate its place in intellectual discourses. See also his *Ethics after Babel* (Boston: Beacon, 1988).

4. I use the term "postmodern" quite loosely here. I include not only the critiques

This problem is reflected in several recent philosophical discussions of forgiveness. For example, Joram Graf Haber indicates in the Introduction to his book *Forgiveness* that his philosophical argument is independent of any theological considerations. He writes, "Throughout this essay, I operate on the assumption that we can analyze forgiveness irrespective of its characterization as a religious virtue." He notes that there is "a great deal of literature (which I largely ignore) that raises interesting questions of theological importance." But they do not affect the substance of his argument. Haber concludes his argument by suggesting that he sees "no problem extending what I have to say about forgiveness to theological discussions of the subject." But for Haber the justification of divine forgiveness would have to be "analogous" to the justification of human forgiveness, which is the focus of his argument.[5]

It is worth noting that Haber's own method (of assuming that our thinking about divine forgiveness should be analogically derived from our philosophical judgments about human forgiveness) is a controverted position within theology. However, it is more directly relevant to note how Haber handles the one New Testament passage that he discusses (albeit for only two paragraphs on the penultimate page of the book!). He mentions the parable of the Unforgiving Servant (Matthew 18:23-35) in the context of identifying "another reason we sometimes consider in tendering forgiveness — namely, that we ourselves are in need of forgiveness." Haber indicates that such a view would place forgiveness in close proximity to the virtue of humility. Even so, he concludes that "I do not think this is a good reason to forgive, if only because, in the forgiveness situation, our own moral history is not at issue. Therefore, regardless of whether we ourselves stand in need of forgiveness, such a reason cannot be countenanced."[6]

---

made by such "neo-Nietzscheans" as Derrida and Foucault but also the recent work of scholars such as Alasdair MacIntyre and Charles Taylor. These latter scholars not only criticize Enlightenment epistemologies; they also explicitly indicate the central significance of theology for intellectual discourse in general and moral inquiry in particular. See, for example, MacIntyre's *Three Rival Versions of Moral Enquiry* (Notre Dame: University of Notre Dame, 1990) and Taylor's *Sources of the Self* (Cambridge: Harvard University, 1989).

5. Haber, *Forgiveness* (Savage: Rowman and Littlefield, 1991) pp. 7-8. Aurel Kolnai also argues for the significance of forgiveness as an "ethical" notion that is independent of any theological convictions. See his "Forgiveness," *Proceedings of the Aristotelian Society* 75 (1974) p. 91.

6. Haber, *Forgiveness*, p. 109. Haber's indication of the connection between forgiveness and humility in the parable of the Unforgiving Servant is drawn from the arguments of Jeffrie Murphy, whose perspective I treat briefly below.

Question: Why not? Haber does not extensively engage the theological perspective that provides the underpinning for the parable, nor does he adequately provide a counterargument against the account of forgiveness implied in the parable. His conclusion seems driven by two convictions. First, he thinks that theology is irrelevant to his discussion, so he treats the parable as a piece of moral philosophy abstracted from the shaping contexts of Scripture and theology. Secondly, he assumes (along with much modern moral philosophy) that insofar as the subject matter of ethics focuses on agents rather than actions, it is dealing with moral agents who are autonomous. As such, the focus of forgiveness is on isolated situations of wrongdoing and guilt; hence, he makes the implausible assumption that "our own moral history is not at issue."

By contrast, the Christian account I have been developing insists that our own moral histories *are* precisely what are at issue, because forgiveness is focused on the reconciliation and healing of our broken pasts, not simply the absolution of guilt. The parable fits well within this context, even if (perhaps particularly if!) it seems offensive to non-Christian ears. This is not to say that arguments cannot be offered against the perspective I am defending and the parable's place within it; rather, it is to say that the arguments that are offered must not stipulate definitions that exclude "theological" perspectives while simultaneously masking their own alternative theological or anti-theological arguments.

This same problem also besets Jeffrie G. Murphy's somewhat more extensive and sophisticated arguments in his chapters of *Forgiveness and Mercy,* a book coauthored with Jean Hampton. Murphy's arguments are richer than Haber's, at least in part because his account is constructed in conversation with Hampton's account, and Hampton explicitly indicates that her concern with forgiveness arises out of her Christian convictions.[7] Hence, Murphy engages more explicitly with some Christian texts and perspectives.

---

7. Jeffrie G. Murphy and Jean Hampton, *Forgiveness and Mercy* (Cambridge: Cambridge University, 1988). Hampton's essays in this book are highly interesting, because she writes both as a philosopher and as an avowed Christian. She offers some rich and significant reflection on forgiveness that bears on my own analysis; however, her own argument is weakened by a lack of adequate attention to the ways in which the Christian doctrine of the Triune God ought to shape even philosophical reflection on issues such as forgiveness, repentance, and "moral hatred." Even so, the force of this latter observation is mitigated by the fact that modern Christian theologians and churches have not done an adequate job of explicating or embodying forgiveness's theological significance and so have failed to provide Hampton with better resources and examples from which to draw.

But, like Haber, Murphy treats them as if they are pieces of secular moral philosophy abstracted from their shaping contexts of Scripture and theology. This is the case in his more extensive discussion of the same parable, the parable of the Unforgiving Servant. But it is even clearer in his parenthetical comment earlier in his analysis that " 'Father forgive them for they know not what they do' would go better as 'Father *excuse* them for they know not what they do.' "[8] Not only does such a comment fail to recognize that Jesus' cry receives its full intelligibility from the Jewish practice of sacrifice for unintentional sins (see, for example, Numbers 15:27-31), it also fails to examine how such a plea fits within the larger understanding of the nature of God's forgiveness. Examining such issues might still fail to persuade Murphy of the relevance of Jesus' cry to his own account of forgiveness; but then there would be a clear context for an argument, rather than his rather pathetic attempt to correct what he takes to be Jesus' philosophical sloppiness.

Other philosophers have engaged theological issues, but have made the second mistake of engaging only with a "theistic" perspective rather than the trinitarian doctrine of God. These engagements have resulted in both attacks on Christian forgiveness and defenses of it. For example, Anne C. Minas has objected that the very notion of "God" (or any divine being) forgiving is incoherent: "Far from its being the case that divine nature makes its possessor especially prone to forgive, such a nature makes forgiveness impossible. Such a being logically cannot forgive, since possession of divine attributes logically precludes conditions that are necessary for forgiveness." So, she claims, "far from its being the case that human frailty makes forgiveness difficult or impossible, it is the possession of distinctly human, non-divine characteristics that makes forgiveness appropriate for human beings. Only a human being can forgive — a divine being cannot."[9]

However, Minas's analysis is determined more by the requirements of one kind of philosophical metaphysics than by the specific character

8. Murphy, "Forgiveness and Resentment," in Murphy and Hampton, *Forgiveness and Mercy*, p. 20, referring to Luke 23:34. I am tempted simply to assume that "those with ears to hear" will recognize the theological absurdity of this perspective. However, given that Haber quotes Murphy's comment with approval (see Haber, *Forgiveness*, p. 109), and that many Christians do not understand the Jewish context of sacrifices for unintentional sin (see the discussion in chapter 4 above), the comment is, unfortunately, likely to receive a favorable hearing unless challenged.

9. Anne C. Minas, "God and Forgiveness," *The Philosophical Quarterly* 25 (1975) p. 138.

(and thus theological metaphysics) of the God whom either Jews or Christians worship. Margaret Paton's comments in response to Minas are apposite:

> Part of the difficulty that philosophers have with the notion of a forgiving deity and the presupposition of a divine-human relationship, is that they are primarily interested in the concept of God from a purely theoretical standpoint. Consequently, they tend to conceive of God formally or systematically as the unifying concept of a metaphysical system, as the First Cause and ultimate ground of all existence. The deity is thought of as the supreme, transcendent being the sum total of whose perfections includes omniscience, omnipotence, eternity, immutability and justice. This largely depersonalised concept of the deity takes God to be a self-sufficient being, akin to the Platonic Form of the Good. Philosophers tend to be pre-occupied with the logic of concepts such as omnipotence and eternity, rather than with the personhood of God. What is likely to happen, however, is that philosophers run the risk of talking about the conception of God that is theologically perilously empty.[10]

This is not to deny the legitimacy and importance of philosophical and, more specifically, metaphysical questions about the coherence and consistency of claims that God forgives. But those philosophical and metaphysical issues need to be addressed in relation to the Christian doctrine of the Triune God.[11]

By contrast to Minas, Carl Reinhold Brakenhielm's book *Forgiveness* is designed to engage both the philosophical and theological issues surrounding forgiveness from within a Christian perspective. Brakenhielm identifies himself clearly as a theologian. And yet, when he attends to theological issues (and then only in the last two of six chapters!), he does so only within a "theistic" perspective rather than a trinitarian doctrine of God. Indeed, it is somewhat surprising that Brakenhielm devotes very little space to a discussion of Jesus' sayings and practices concerning forgiveness.

---

10. Margaret Paton, "Can God Forgive?" *Modern Theology* 4/3 (April 1988) p. 230.

11. My analysis in this book presumes some judgments about ways to respond to these issues, but an explicit discussion of them would take me too far afield. For an impressive account of how the theologian Hans Urs von Balthasar does this within his theological project, see G. F. O'Hanlon, *The Immutability of God in the Theology of Hans Urs von Balthasar* (Cambridge: Cambridge University, 1990); for a constructive account that significantly advances the discussion, see Bruce Marshall, *Trinity and Truth* (Cambridge: Cambridge University, forthcoming in 1996).

The section on "God's forgiveness in the Old and New Testaments" contains barely two pages of discussion, and the main conclusion — if one can call it that — that Brakenhielm draws about Jesus' ministry is: "It is not altogether clear, however, where Jesus stands on the central question concerning conditional or unconditional forgiveness."[12]

Brakenhielm does not explicitly reflect on the character of the God who forgives, nor does he adequately situate Jesus' forgiveness in relation to his identification of God. Even more, his almost complete neglect of a doctrine of the Holy Spirit results in his failure to devote any systematic treatment to the Church as the primary context, or even as a context, in which forgiveness is practiced, learned, and embodied. Throughout the book, Brakenhielm refers to God largely in "theistic" terms. As a result, we are left with a book that in places offers (at its best) a truncated account of Christian forgiveness and in other places offers (at its worst) highly misleading conceptual distinctions about the nature and practice of Christian forgiveness.

A far more adequate account of Christian forgiveness has been suggested in a recent essay by the philosopher Marilyn McCord Adams. Yet even here, in the midst of many insightful and illuminating distinctions and arguments, Adams's perspective remains somewhat truncated and in that sense fails adequately to articulate the nature of God's forgiveness. To her credit, Adams aims to situate forgiveness explicitly within a "Christian framework." Indeed, she notes that there are "dangers" for Christian philosophers who do not integrate their "ethical reflections with theological commitments."[13] She develops her argument by engaging several recent writers, including Murphy, who attempt to articulate a "secular" account of forgiveness. She then provides a brief sketch of "A Christian Model of Forgiveness."[14]

12. Carl Reinhold Brakenhielm, *Forgiveness,* tr. Thor Hall (Philadelphia: Fortress, 1993) p. 60.

13. Marilyn McCord Adams, "Forgiveness: A Christian Model," *Faith and Philosophy* 8 (July 1991) p. 278.

14. The use of the term "sketch" is intentional. Adams notes that her attempts to characterize Christian forgiveness "may contain the makings of but do not (as they stand) constitute an *analysis* of forgiveness" (p. 292). In this sense, it is perhaps a bit unfair to accuse her of having a truncated perspective. Yet I would suggest that the problem is not with the space allotted a single essay or the need for further development but with the outline itself. Even as she begins to develop her "model," there should be more explicit attention to the work of Christ and of the Spirit in showing the Christian way of forgiveness.

There is much to commend that sketch. For example, Adams rightly notes that the Christian commitment is to God as a "Trinity of persons," that for Christians "it may be morally legitimate to forgive not only harms or wrongs to oneself, but also offences against those with whom one identifies," that Christian forgiveness "will be imbedded in prayer, because it involves a *process* of letting go of one's own point of view (regarding the situation, one's self and/or the victim, and the offender) and entering into God's point of view," and that God is ultimately concerned with "the *growth and reform of the offender* into a person who shares in His projects."[15] Adams's analysis here is extremely significant and suggestive, particularly her emphasis on the lifelong commitment to practices of forgiveness that enable our transformation into people who *share* in God's projects.

However, Adams somewhat inexplicably concludes her analysis by suggesting that "my model makes forgiveness a process within the context of a triangular relationship, among the victim, the offender, and God."[16] There is no discussion of the Church, nor any explicit identification of the ways in which God in Word and Spirit is making all things new through the eschatological forgiveness that orients us toward holiness and participation in the divine life of the Trinity. Hence, Adams's analysis ultimately produces a truncated account whose insights are left dangling, shorn from their proper trinitarian context.

The third mistake typical of many modern discussions of forgiveness is the accounts of morality to which they are indebted. But the mistake needs to be described even more strongly. For the dominant accounts of morality in modernity, namely Kantian deontology and Benthamite/Millian utilitarianism, have conspired to marginalize forgiveness as a significant moral issue or practice. So part of the problem is that there have been few discussions of forgiveness *at all* in modernity. Indeed, in 1962 Peter Strawson remarked that forgiveness "is a rather unfashionable subject in moral philosophy."[17] This is the case because theories of morality since the Enlightenment have tended to focus either on metaethical inquiries (e.g., what is the logical status of the claim "x is good"?) or on the moral status of particular actions.

Indeed, it would appear that the recent resurgence of interest in

15. Adams, "Forgiveness: A Christian Model," pp. 291, 292-293, 293, 297. Emphasis in original.

16. Adams, "Forgiveness: A Christian Model," p. 299.

17. P. F. Strawson, *Freedom and Resentment and Other Essays* (Oxford: Methuen, 1974) p. 6.

Aristotelian moral philosophy, and more specifically in such Aristotelian themes as virtue, character, and the emotions, has brought with it a renewed interest in the philosophical significance of forgiveness.[18] However, people have typically grafted their discussions of forgiveness onto the mistaken assumptions and methods of the modern moral philosophy in which they have been trained. Hence, most of the discussions continue to focus primarily on the *act* of forgiveness, while giving only minimal attention to notions of forgiveness as a specific practice or trait of character — much less as an embodied way of life. As such, they fail to see that forgiveness should not be confined to an analysis of specific, isolated acts, or even to the process of dealing with specific, isolated acts.[19]

From the Christian perspective I have been developing, forgiveness is not primarily a word that is spoken or an action that is performed or a feeling that is felt. It is a way of life appropriate to friendship with the Triune God. As such, it includes within it appropriate words, actions, and feelings. But it cannot be confined to any one of them. In this light, it would seem that insofar as philosophical accounts attend to forgiveness, they might more fruitfully do so within a broadly Aristotelian-Thomist perspective that emphasizes forgiveness as a craft in the context of learning virtue.[20] I characterize it as a "broadly" Aristotelian perspective, since the substance of my Christian account diverges in some significant ways from Aristotle's own perspective (including the moral status of forgiveness itself!). Even so, the Thomist tradition within Christian theology and in moral philosophy has charted a way for appropriating such Aristotelian themes within an explicitly Christian perspective.

I shall return, in the third and last section of this chapter, to a con-

18. The turn to Aristotelian moral philosophy is often traced to G. E. M. Anscombe's 1949 essay "Modern Moral Philosophy." Its recent popularity is significantly indebted to Alasdair MacIntyre's *After Virtue* (second ed., Notre Dame: University of Notre Dame; the first edition was published in 1981). Strikingly, most of this century's philosophical discussion of forgiveness has occurred in the last twenty years.

19. This is part of why Haber fails so miserably to see the significance of the parable of the Unforgiving Servant. The issue of forgiveness there is not primarily about a specific isolated act (though it involves the servant's failure to act forgivingly with the one indebted to him) but rather about the servant's failure to embody the forgiveness that he has received in his relations with others.

20. In a currently unpublished paper entitled "Forgiveness as a Virtue," Robert C. Roberts has developed a rich account of forgiveness understood in relation to broadly Aristotelian concerns with virtue and the emotions. I am grateful for his willingness to share a copy of his typescript with me.

sideration of forgiveness as a craft. Before doing so, however, I need to develop a constructive account that both avoids the three mistakes identified above and can account for the possibility of practices of forgiveness and reconciliation in many (religious and nonreligious) traditions and settings beyond and outside explicitly Christian contexts. As my analysis has suggested, it will need to be an account situated, at least implicitly, within the Christian doctrine of the Triune God, yet also able to deal with accounts, moral and political situations, and people's lives that are not, at least explicitly, specifically Christian.

Parables of Christian Forgiveness

It is hardly a disputable point, nor should it be a surprising one, *that* authentically Christian forgiveness occurs beyond or outside explicitly Christian contexts. The Holy Spirit is at work both in the Church and in the world, engaging in the work of re-creation. More specifically, given that Christians claim that we are creatures who were created for communion with God, the Spirit is at work throughout the world seeking to restore people to communion with God, with one another, and with the whole Creation. Thus, even the effects of sinful distortions do not inevitably or even typically erase the human capacity to recognize and embody the centrality of forgiveness for that communion or reconciliation. Indeed, the crucified and risen Christ is none other than the Word by and in whom the world was created through the power of the Spirit. As St. Augustine put our often inchoate but nonetheless persistent desire for communion, "Our hearts are restless until they rest in Thee."

What is disputable, however, is *how* we discern authentically Christian forgiveness from its simulacra and *how* it is to be understood in relation to alternative accounts of what constitutes authentic forgiveness (where an intervening adjective such as Jewish, Muslim, or Marxist, etc., might also be supplied). If there is no such thing as "forgiveness" *per se,* then how do we learn to describe and analyze the competing notions that often go by that name while recognizing that a proper understanding and embodiment of forgiveness is no one's possession in particular?

An important initial step is to recognize that notions such as forgiveness are inextricably imbedded in larger narratives — Christian forgiveness in the narrative of the Triune God. More specifically, Christians claim that forgiveness has been decisively enacted and embodied in the life, death, and resurrection of Jesus of Nazareth and that this is of universal, unsurpassable significance. We discover the truth of our brokenness, and also our origin in and destiny for communion with God, in and through Jesus Christ.

Further, the significance of Jesus Christ's forgiveness is being continually re-presented in irreducibly diverse settings and lives by the power of the Holy Spirit. Hence, from within the particular yet universally significant narrative of the Triune God, we also find the resources to explain both how and why people who are not Christians can understand and embody the truth of Christian forgiveness and how we can and should deal with other religious traditions' diverse yet (likely) overlapping understandings and practices of forgiveness.

Karl Barth proposes the notion of "secular parables" as a way of dealing with these issues.[21] Barth seeks to explain how the "world" sometimes seems to shine forth the light of God's forgiveness, putatively without any reference to the one true Light of Jesus Christ, and perhaps even better than the "church" does. In the first place, Barth insists that the truth of any human words "must be in the closest material and substantial conformity and agreement with the one Word of God Himself and therefore with that of His one Prophet Jesus Christ" (p. 111). Hence, Barth insists on the methodological priority of Jesus Christ; we must move from the one true Word to human words, not the other way around (as, for example, many modern philosophical discussions of forgiveness tend to do).

Even so, Barth turns to the parables of the New Testament to suggest how these human words can nonetheless be true. They are "secondary forms" of the Word of God. In the hands of Jesus and as recounted by Jesus, the ordinary, everyday happenings of the parables "become what they were not before, and what they cannot be in and of themselves." In this sense, therefore, "the New Testament parables are as it were the prototype of the order in which there can be other true words alongside the one Word of God, created and determined by it, exactly corresponding to it, fully serving it and therefore enjoying its power and authority" (p. 113).

Barth construes the relationship between Jesus Christ, the One True Word, and other human words through an image of three concentric spheres. As George Hunsinger describes them, they are "an inner sphere (that of Bible and church) surrounded by two distinct outer spheres (those

---

21. Barth's discussion of "secular parables" is found in *Church Dogmatics* IV/3/1, tr. G. W. Bromiley (Edinburgh: Clark, 1961) pp. 38-165, esp. pp. 110-135. Further references to this volume will be given parenthetically in the text. George Hunsinger provides an extensive description of Barth's account in *How to Read Karl Barth* (Oxford: Oxford University, 1991), pp. 234-280.

of mixed and, farther out, of pure secularism). All three are envisioned as having Jesus Christ as their center (at least insofar as true words arise from within them)."[22] The mixed sphere signifies those cultures and people that have been influenced by the gospel and do not deny it, but whose lives are determined primarily by standards and practices alien to it. The outer sphere of "pure secularism" consists of those people who live in virtual isolation from the gospel.

Even so, all three spheres are given their shape and defining understanding of notions and practices of forgiveness from Jesus Christ. Even the most secular of people may, in their contexts, recognize, understand, and practice Christian forgiveness. This is because the whole world is the theater of the Triune God's work. As Barth describes it,

> If with the prophets and apostles we have our starting-point at His resurrection and therefore at His revelation as the One who was and is and will be; if we recognise and confess Him as the One who was and is and will be, then we recognise and confess that not we alone, nor the community which, following the prophets and apostles, believes in Him and loves Him and hopes in Him, but *de iure* all men and all creation derive from His cross, from the reconciliation accomplished in Him, and are ordained to be the theatre of His glory and therefore the recipients and bearers of His Word. (pp. 116-117)

In the theater of Creation that is Christ's glory, Christians cannot but search for signs of forgiveness wherever they may be found. We must place ourselves deeply within the world, "eavesdropping" on the world's patterns and practices as we seek to "hear the voice of the Good Shepherd even there too" (p. 117).

We must do so, remembering that even if human beings deny God, God does not deny us. In Barth's terms, "in the world reconciled by God in Jesus Christ there is no secular sphere abandoned by Him or withdrawn from His control, even where from the human standpoint it seems to approximate most dangerously to the pure and absolute form of utter godlessness" (p. 119). We ought to be wary of descriptions and practices that emerge from the world, for it is all too easy to substitute the simulacra of forgiveness (which masks continuing violence or perhaps exacerbates it) for the authentic judgment of grace, which reconciles and makes new. Even so, we ought to be on the lookout for signs of Easter, celebrating authentic

22. Hunsinger, *How to Read Karl Barth*, p. 257.

forgiveness and reconciliation wherever it is found and practiced, even as we recognize that the source and sustaining power of that authenticity is the Spirit of the crucified and risen Jesus.

Barth strengthens his claim by suggesting that Christians are more likely to find signs of authentic forgiveness and reconciliation in the world precisely to the extent that we embody it ourselves. Barth turns skepticism about the dangers of the "world" and hostility toward the failings of Christendom on their heads by focusing on the gracious vitality of Christ's presence throughout the theater of Creation. He writes, "The more seriously and joyfully we believe in Him, the more we shall see such signs in the worldly sphere, and the more we shall be able to receive true words from it" (p. 122).

Unfortunately, the converse would seem to be equally true. Could it be that one of the reasons Christians see so little authentic forgiveness in the world is that, because our own lives are too marked by either cheap grace or bitterness and violence (or both), we have had our vision eclipsed by our own failures? Barth insists that Christians may be forced to recognize "with shame" that the secular realm has often attested certain aspects of the truth "far better, more quickly and more consistently" than the Church seems to have done (p. 124). Indeed, Barth identifies "the warm readiness to understand and forgive" as well as "a humanity which does not ask or weigh too long with whom we are dealing in others, but in which we find a simple solidarity with them and unreservedly take up their case" as two aspects of the truth that the Church ought to (re-?)learn from the secular spheres (p. 125).

Barth's analysis focuses on the distinction between the Church and secular spheres, but the structures of his analysis can easily be transposed into discussions among different religious traditions. The definitive centrality of Jesus Christ rules out "pluralist" and "inclusivist" options (at least as those are typically described), but the logic of "secular parables" and the claim that the entire world is the theater of the Triune God's glory argue against an "exclusivist" option. Rather, recognizing that there are likely to be overlapping but diverse practices and understandings, Christians ought to engage in ongoing conversation and argument with others about how particular practices and understandings fit into the overall pattern of life normatively commended by each other's traditions.[23] With respect to forgiveness, this means that we should not be surprised to find analogues to

---

23. A version of this proposal has been advanced in rich ways by J. A. DiNoia. See *The Diversity of Religions* (Washington: Catholic University of America, 1992).

Christian forgiveness in other religious traditions, but neither should we assume that all other traditions have the same understanding. We are looking for parables of Christ's forgiveness at the same time that other traditions are looking for analogues to their own understandings and practices. As in our discovery of "secular parables," our own understandings and practices of the definitive uniqueness of Christ's forgiveness may be challenged, corrected, or enriched by the understandings and practices of other traditions (and presumably their understandings of their aims by ours), though we also operate from a particular vantage point that claims to be true.[24]

Whether dealing with "secular parables" or the understandings and practices of other religious traditions, we need the practice of discernment to separate authentic forgiveness from its simulacra. George Hunsinger's characterization of this practice is instructive: "In considering any secular word as a possible expression of truth, the Christian community will need to strike a delicate balance between faithfulness and perplexity, suspicion and openness, and self-affirmation and self-criticism. It will need to remain faithful above all to its own special task of speaking true theological words in the freedom and power promised to it."[25]

Such fidelity is exercised in the recognition that, from a Christian perspective, the truth in either secular or religious traditions and practices of forgiveness will find their true home not only in their original context but, more determinatively, by being set in the context of the Triune God. Further, Barth rightly insists that true human words, whatever their original context, are "not exhausted by what they are in themselves," and indeed "may even speak against themselves" (p. 125). Yet, he goes on to note, this is not materially different from what goes on even in Christian contexts. He writes, "Even in Christian circles is it not grace and miracle, and the continual transcending of a whole mass of subjective ineptitude and distortion, if true words are spoken and heard? Should we not always ask with great attention and the greatest openness whether on the basis of the same miracle true words may not also be spoken without, and seriously recognised as such?" (p. 126).

However, in our discernment we need criteria so that we can properly distinguish those words linked to the "light that lightens the darkness" from

---

24. Obviously I cannot fully defend here the epistemological arguments underlying my claims about traditions in this section. For perspectives on this issue with which I am in broad sympathy, see Alasdair MacIntyre, *Whose Justice? Which Rationality?* (Notre Dame: University of Notre Dame, 1988); Marshall, *Trinity and Truth*.

25. Hunsinger, *How to Read Karl Barth*, p. 265.

those linked to the darkness itself. As Barth goes on to say, criteria are needed "to distinguish the truth of true words themselves from the untruth which will also cling to them" (p. 126). Barth identifies three such criteria: Scripture, the dogmas and confessions of the Church, and the fruits that true words bear in the world. In each case, the true words will not lead us away from Scripture, the Church's dogmas and confessions, or bearing fruits in the world; they will, rather, illumine these criteria and lead us more deeply into them.

We may test these words and the practices that they signify by how they affect our origin and destiny for communion. True words from whatever source will have, so Barth suggests, in indissoluble unity "the character of affirmation and criticism, of address and claim, of a summons to faith and a call to repentance" (p. 128). Hence the Church should not receive such words in either pride or sloth, but in the discerning openness of the Spirit who is judging, guiding, and consoling the Church in its ongoing puzzlement about how, most faithfully, to embody practices of redemptive speech and silence characteristic of Christ's forgiveness and call to holiness.

The practice of such discernment constitutes one dimension of the craft of forgiveness. For throughout our lives, and in whatever contexts and situations we find ourselves, Christians are called to learn and to discern more deeply and more richly what is the precise nature, purpose, and scope of Christian forgiveness. We can never stop and say, "Now I know fully and wholly what Christian forgiveness is." Our discernment of Christian forgiveness by the power of God's Spirit is a never ending process, though it is a process that certainly can deepen and become enriched as we seek to become holy people, people of the Truth.

Before turning to a more extensive exploration of the craft of forgiveness, however, it is important to return briefly to the issues identified in the first section of this chapter and to ask what place, if any, there is in my account for philosophical analyses of forgiveness (as well as analyses from other disciplines). To put my response oversimply, such analyses *can* and sometimes *do* exercise a fundamentally important role in clarifying, testing, enriching, and deepening our understandings of the grammar, logic, and scope of forgiveness. But we need to recognize that such philosophical investigations are also embedded in larger traditions. Hence there *ought* to be a difference between how Christian philosophers investigate the issues, from within a doctrine of the Triune God, and how philosophers who inhabit other (religious or nonreligious) traditions do so. We ought to test the latter investigations by the criteria for secular parables described above.

Philosophical investigations, as well as psychological, social, political, and other forms of inquiry, are crucial to our craft of continually clarifying and deepening our understandings and practices of forgiveness. For example, such investigations are important when philosophers carefully distinguish between, say, forgiveness and condoning, when psychologists investigate patterns of individuation and connection and the diverse problems that often diminish and destroy people's abilities to foster and sustain relationships, and when social and political theorists analyze the ways in which economies and structural systems produce and replicate patterns and practices that undermine people's capacity for communion with one another. And the list could go on.[26]

Even so, in order for these investigations to be integral to the craft of Christian forgiveness, Christians need to recognize and critically assess the ways in which nontheological inquiries are already embedded in traditions that may or may not cohere or overlap with a theological context shaped by and focused on the Triune God. The problem with too many modern discussions, as I suggested in the first section, is that they have increasingly diverged from such a theological context. But that divergence is a critique of their practices, not of the importance of the enterprise itself.

Crafting Human Forgiveness

Throughout this book I have been arguing that forgiveness ought to be understood as a way of life that requires the cultivation of specific habits and practices. More specifically, I suggested in chapter 6 that Christian forgiveness is, paradigmatically, learned and embodied in the friendships and practices of Christian communities. But most of us, it might be objected, do not live our lives wholly within Christian communities. How does forgiveness become a way of life encompassing the entirety of our lives? And how do we distinguish the habit of embodying forgiveness from specific occasions and situations when we have to discern whether or not to forgive, or whether forgiveness is even the appropriate response?

---

26. Examples of these sorts of investigations would include Adams, "Forgiveness: A Christian Model"; Hampton's contributions in *Forgiveness and Mercy*; Jonathan Lear's *Love and Its Place in Nature: A Philosophical Interpretation of Freudian Psychoanalysis* (New York: Farrar, Straus, and Giroux, 1990); and Michel Foucault's *Discipline and Punish,* tr. Alan Sheridan (New York: Vintage, 1977).

We should begin doing so by identifying forgiveness as a craft.[27] The craft of forgiveness is a lifelong learning process that people are initiated into as apprentices to those who excel at the craft. Those who excel have a moral authority as teachers, and apprentices must recognize a gap between their present competencies and genuine excellence. As Alasdair MacIntyre has argued, there are two key distinctions that apprentices in any craft must learn to apply. "The first is the distinction between what in particular situations it really is good to do and what only seems good to do to this particular apprentice but is not in fact so." And "a second key distinction is that between what is good and best for me with my particular level of training and learning in my particular circumstances to do and what is good and best unqualifiedly."[28] Failure to make the first distinction in the craft of forgiveness often results in problems of either "cheap grace" or harboring unjustified anger or desires for vengeance. Failure to make the second distinction results in thinking that perhaps what one is able to discern or embody *here and now* is necessarily the best that one can do *at any point in the future.*

Further, learning a craft is accomplished more by participating in particular activities under the guidance of those who excel than by studying texts (unless that study is conceived of precisely as a practice in which the apprentices and the exemplars are engaged together). To be sure, there is an important place for reading books; even so, they ought to be seen as aids to a much larger and more comprehensive craft rather than as the primary means by which someone comes to understand a craft such as forgiveness.

A comparison might be offered to the craft of medicine. Reading anatomy textbooks is important, and people want to be sure that their doctors understand the conceptual differences between various chemical compounds as well as the differences among diverse diseases. Even so, a doctor's education is not only a matter of studying texts (and particularly not only in classrooms); it also is a matter of learning to diagnose situations and cases as wiser and more senior doctors do. So, for example, patients in a teaching hospital are asked to bear with their attending physician while the doctors-in-training learn to attend to and diagnose specific cases.

---

27. Interestingly, two novels, George Eliot's *Adam Bede* and Anne Tyler's *Saint Maybe*, both suggest the analogies between learning the practice of forgiveness and the specific craft of woodworking. I provide a reading and analysis of Tyler's novel in "The Craft of Forgiveness," *Theology Today* 50 (October 1993) pp. 345-357.

28. MacIntyre, *Three Rival Versions of Moral Enquiry*, pp. 61-62.

Through such a process, medical students are developing specific habits and patterns of acting, feeling, and thinking that will guide them throughout their medical practice.

Indeed, we need to emphasize that such learning never ends. Even senior attending physicians need each other as they continue to learn to practice their craft better and to approximate more closely the *telos* of the craft by extending its range of excellences. For surgeons, this has become institutionalized through both informal everyday practices such as second opinions and formal processes of coping with medical failures. They learn how to differentiate unavoidable failures from human error and thus also to differentiate tragedies that cannot be avoided from mistakes that need forgiveness and penance.[29]

Such learning never stops because the presentation of ever-new situations, circumstances, and lives never ends. Similarly, learning the craft of forgiveness never stops. As people excel in the craft, they develop a deeper and wider range of discernment about what the appropriate response ought to be to this or that situation or circumstance and what is needed in relation to the particularities of this or that person's life. Just as a doctor's diagnosis cannot be general or abstract, so also with forgiveness; wise and appropriate discernment is to be found in the process of attending to the particular.[30]

This attention, however, does not occur in isolated segments. We learn to attend to the particular as we learn to become people of character, or, more precisely, as we learn to become holy. In the craft of forgiveness, this involves attending to the work of the Spirit as we seek — paradigmatically, in the context of Christian community — to discern what forgiveness entails in specific contexts and specific lives. Being initiated into the craft of forgiveness involves us in a twofold process: On the one hand, we are learning what it is about ourselves that needs to be transformed if we are to become holy people; on the other hand, we are learning how to diagnose and discern the craft of forgiveness in the situations and contexts that we and others face in the world around us. These two dimensions of our learning are distinct though inextricably interrelated.

Further, learning the craft of forgiveness has both diachronic and

29. These issues have been described with great power and insight in Charles L. Bosk, *Forgive and Remember: Managing Medical Failure* (Chicago: University of Chicago, 1979).

30. Readers familiar with Aristotle's *Nicomachean Ethics* will note the resonances of that text with the claim made here. See also my discussion in *Transformed Judgment*, chapter 2.

synchronic components. Diachronically, we need to learn the traditions of those who have come before us. Indeed, in the very process of being initiated into the Christian life, and more specifically into the craft of forgiveness, we are initiated into the traditions of Christian life and thought. As we learn these traditions, we are seeking to understand how our forebears succeeded and failed in the task of embodying forgiveness (as well as in reflecting theologically on the issues entailed therein).

We should learn these traditions neither to glorify (and hence reify) the past, as if the issues were and are settled, nor to caricature (and hence dismiss) the past, as though our forebears have nothing to teach us. Rather we ought to do so in order to discern in the power of the Spirit, throughout the successes and failures of our histories, the ongoing genesis of the Church through Christ's forgiveness, and to draw appropriate analogies from that discernment for our own situations, contexts, and lives. More particularly, we ought to count first and foremost among those from whom we can learn those saints who have gone before us and who, as such, have shown themselves to be exemplars of the craft of forgiveness.

Synchronically, Christians must be attentive to those among us who excel at the craft, and more specifically we must be attentive to the ways in which they practice their craft. Exemplars of the craft of forgiveness focus on the particular circumstances of the situations and lives with which and with whom they are involved; further, they attend to those particularities in all of their complexity. They recognize the power of redemptive speech and silence, and they also know both the power of forgiveness and its possibility for abuse. They recognize the lurking dangers of self-deception, and they have developed patterns and practices of life that cultivate truthful holiness in friendship with God.

So, for example, Bonhoeffer became an exemplar of the craft of forgiveness because he was attentive to both the diachronic and synchronic components of forgiveness. He learned from, and critically appropriated, practices of forgiveness embodied by Christian forbears in the tradition, and he sought to draw appropriate analogies for discernment in his own time and situation (e.g., the arcane discipline). At the same time, however, he sought to cultivate an acute sensitivity to the particular needs of the people and situations around him. Even in prison, he continued to struggle against the dangers of self-deception as he also sought to articulate truthfully the conditions for the call to saintly living before God and to embody that call himself.

By contrast, one of the most offensive things Christians all too often do is to proclaim a general and abstract forgiveness without any regard for the complexities of a specific situation or a particular person's life. Such proclamations often misfire because they have failed even to diagnose the relevant issues; even worse, however, is their tendency to trivialize the suffering endured (and, worse, to trivialize the suffer*er*). God's forgiveness is universal in scope; but it cannot be abstract. Knowing how to practice the craft of forgiveness involves an ever-deepening and ever-expanding ability to provide accurate discernment of the particular.

It might be objected, however, that my description simply substitutes vague exhortation for rigorous conceptual analysis. The objection is relevant, though its force is misplaced. To be sure, we certainly do not want to substitute conceptual vagueness for appropriate rigor; neither do we want simply to exhort people to forgive where analytical clarity is needed. However, we need to appreciate the significance of having *appropriate* conceptual rigor.[31] Aristotle rightly emphasized that a "well-schooled" person "is one who searches for that degree of precision in each kind of study that the nature of the subject at hand admits: it is obviously just as foolish to accept arguments of probability from a mathematician as to demand strict demonstrations from an orator."[32]

Christian forgiveness admits of considerable conceptual clarity, but that clarity is no substitute for the need for ongoing discernment. Christians can certainly learn from the careful analyses of analytic philosophers who discuss the ways in which diverse accounts of forgiveness are similar to, and different from, related notions such as understanding, condoning, excuse, pardon, or mercy. But at a more fundamental level such distinctions are most appropriately learned as people engage in the ongoing craft of forgiveness; in developing the habits of thinking, feeling, and acting well that are aspects of learning the craft, people will also develop ever more careful distinctions as to how and why forgiveness entails different judgments in different situations. For example, forgiveness might entail something much closer to "excuse" in one situation or at one point in the overall context of a relationship, whereas it might look much closer to "retributive punishment" in another situation or at another point in that relationship. If a

---

31. One might note the similarity of my point here with MacIntyre's critique of the standards of "genealogists" and "encyclopediasts" in *Three Rival Versions of Moral Enquiry*. Indeed, in MacIntyre's categories the modern philosophical expositors of forgiveness have typically been "encyclopediasts," and opponents of forgiveness "genealogists." As MacIntyre suggests, both types of enquiry share a methodological and substantive hostility to theology.

32. Aristotle, *Nicomachean Ethics*, tr. Martin Ostwald (Indianapolis: Bobbs-Merrill, 1962) 1094b 24-27.

person hits another person once in a fit of anger, forgiveness may require that the person not be held particularly accountable; but if such hitting becomes habitual, then the only means of expressing the aims of forgiveness and reconciliation may be something much closer to retributive punishment.

We can understand more clearly why this is the case by recalling the twofold nature of Christian forgiveness. Christian forgiveness is at once an expression of a commitment to a way of life, the cruciform life of holiness in which we seek to "unlearn" sin and learn the ways of God, and a means of seeking reconciliation in the midst of particular sins, specific instances of brokenness. In its broadest context, forgiveness is the means by which God's love moves to reconciliation in the face of sin. Hence the craft of forgiveness involves the ongoing and ever-deepening process of unlearning sin through forgiveness and learning to live in communion with the Triune God, with one another, and with the whole Creation. This priority of forgiveness is a sign of the peace of God's original Creation as well as the promised eschatological consummation of that Creation in the Kingdom, and also a sign of the costliness by which such forgiveness is achieved. In this sense, then, forgiveness indicates the ongoing priority of the Church's task to offer the endlessly creative and gratuitous gift of new life in the face of sin and evil.

Within that horizon, however, there are the difficult tasks of discerning whether forgiveness is relevant to this or that situation, whether or not specific words of forgiveness are appropriate in a specific moment (and if so, who is authorized to speak them), and what it would mean to suggest that authentic forgiveness has occurred. For example, not all situations of brokenness call for specific words of forgiveness or requests for forgiveness. In the face of inexplicable tragedy, Christians might be called on to *endure* (as did Job), we might well *lament* the destructive consequences of an unfortunate accident (as does Nicholas Wolterstorff),[33] or we might issue a *plaintive cry* for deliverance from specific oppressive circumstances (as do a number of the Psalms).[34] In any of these situations, anger and frustration are certainly understandable and can indeed be signs of the depth of our

---

33. Wolterstorff, *Lament for a Son* (Grand Rapids: Eerdmans, 1987).

34. To be sure, the laments of the Old Testament are also appropriate in situations where forgiveness is more directly relevant. That is, one might lament when in exile because of a longing for deliverance and the possibility of new life, even while recognizing that the exile was brought about by one's own (or one's people's own) actions. See chapter 8 below for further reflections on this in the context of the call to "love our enemies."

longing for the consummation of God's Kingdom. That is, in the face of inexplicable tragedy, such judgments ought to be situated in the overall context of God's forgiveness, God's work, which is making all things new; but they are not in themselves instances that call for specific words of or requests for forgiveness. They are not so because there is no person who is clearly responsible for the situation.[35]

Similarly, in situations where there are persons or groups of people who are clearly responsible, Christians must discern how to embody the craft of forgiveness in diverse ways. Again, we might *lament* our situation, whether it is an exile produced by our own sinfulness or the suffering produced by unjust oppressors (on both, see various Psalms as well as Lamentations); we might issue a *prophetic indictment* and call to repentance (as do Old Testament prophets and Jesus); or we might be called to *rejoice* in the face of sufferings brought on by fidelity to Christ (as does Paul in his letter to the Philippians). In any of these situations, our judgments and actions are contributions to the craft of forgiveness, expressions of our commitment to forgiveness as a way of life in friendship with the Triune God. Further, whether words of forgiveness or explicit requests for forgiveness should be offered in such situations depends on a variety of contextual factors that cannot be determined in advance — including the relative disparities of power (and who has the power), the likelihood of those words or requests producing repentance and greater accountability so that new life can be achieved, and the relative readiness (in patterns of feeling, thinking, and acting) of those who have been afflicted to speak the words or to have them spoken on their behalf.[36]

In this context, then, we can indicate several features that are conjoined in the craft of forgiveness: truthful judgment about what has happened or is happening, a willingness to acknowledge both the propriety of anger, resentment, or bitterness and a desire to overcome and be freed from it, a concern for the well-being of the other(s) as children of God, recognition of the ways

---

35. That is, there is no one responsible other than, perhaps, God. Even so, Christians have traditionally held that though we may not understand specific instances of "natural" evils or the circumstances that produce "bad luck," it is inappropriate to hold God "responsible" as the author of particular evils. Hence, though it might be psychologically comforting to "forgive God," as Lewis Smedes proposes in *Forgive and Forget: Healing the Hurts We Don't Deserve* (New York: Harper and Row, 1984), that is a theological and ethical mistake (see chapter 2 above). There are other ways to deal with such situations than to engage in the mistake of thinking that we can or should "forgive" God.

36. I return to these factors in the next two chapters.

in which we have all needed to be forgiven (thus suggesting the close links between forgiveness and other virtues such as humility, generosity, and compassion),[37] an acknowledgment that the truthful judgment requires accountability directed toward the grace of new life (which thus may require occasions where the fullness of forgiveness is "withheld"), and the hope for eventual reconciliation (though in extreme cases this may be a matter of "hoping against hope"). These are not inevitable "stages" of forgiveness; they are diverse though interrelated themes that interact in different ways in the craft of forgiveness. How they are conjoined in particular circumstances, situations, and lives cannot be determined in advance; they are the focus of ongoing discernment within the craft, led by the exemplars who excel in the craft (and hence are gifted at wise discernment), and preeminently guided and judged by the work of the Holy Spirit.

So, for example, people who have suffered or continue to suffer severe injustice may have to struggle throughout their lives to give expression to anger or bitterness but not be overcome by it; but even within such groups, there are differences between, say, Martin Luther King's sermons and exhortations and those of Malcolm X. And there are also differences in their struggles in different periods of their lives.[38] Further, in some situations a person's ability to recognize a truthful judgment comes quickly, as with Ruby Turpin; for others, the discovery of one's sinful practices of racism may come only gradually. In yet other situations, it is much easier to accept a truthful judgment than it is to become accountable through repentance; so a person might earnestly acknowledge his patterns of lying, but find it difficult to begin the time-consuming, arduous task of repairing the damage his lies have created and cultivating virtues that sustain the habit of truthfulness.

In some situations, these features are conjoined in particularly complex ways. For example, when the offender(s) are dead, say in the case of abusive parents or Nazi soldiers, the desire to be freed from anger and bitterness cannot be linked — at least in any obvious ways — to a mutuality of reconciliation. At most, one can learn to hope for the possibility of reconciliation in the Kingdom (and even learning to envision that hope may take a lifetime of struggle!); in such circumstances, the craft of forgiveness must be envisioned and embodied in ways that take into account the *im*possibility, at least contingently, of being able to achieve reconciliation in this life.

37. For the significance of these links, see Roberts, "Forgiveness as a Virtue."
38. On this point, see James H. Cone, *Martin and Malcolm and America* (Maryknoll: Orbis, 1991).

These features of forgiveness, conjoined in different ways in diverse situations and lives, help us to locate properly the place of resentment and anger within the overall craft of forgiveness. Most contemporary discussions of resentment refer to Bishop Joseph Butler's famous sermons "Upon Resentment" and "Upon Forgiveness of Injuries."[39] Butler indicates that resentment is important because this "natural passion" might enable us to be "better qualified to prevent, and likewise (or perhaps chiefly) to resist and defeat, sudden force, violence, and opposition, considered merely as such, and without regard to the fault or demerit of him who is the author of them."[40] However, if resentment is not to ossify into hatred and desires for revenge, it must be contextualized within the larger horizon of (God's) forgiving, reconciling love. In this light, forgiveness involves (but is not defined by) the struggle to overcome the ossifying effects of resentment while nonetheless recognizing its validity, within acceptable bounds, and perhaps even in appropriate circumstances its central importance in resisting evil.[41] But we can only adequately understand how people are dealing with anger or resentment by examining their progress (or lack thereof) over an extended period of time.

This suggests one reason why narratives are so important to understanding and embodying the craft of forgiveness. We learn to judge our progress in the craft of forgiveness not by examining isolated actions, feelings, or thoughts; we must see how they are contextualized in broader patterns of life.[42] What may initially seem to be unjustified anger may

39. *Sermons by Joseph Butler*, ed. W. E. Gladstone (Oxford: Clarendon, 1896) pp. 136-167.

40. Butler, *Sermons*, p. 140.

41. While I agree with Haber's criticism of Jeffrie Murphy that forgiveness should not be *defined* as the overcoming of resentment, I think Haber's larger analysis of the issues surrounding resentment is mistaken. To be sure, Haber's emphasis on the importance of resentment (he even indicates that it may be called a "virtue" if it means having the proper resentment at the proper time) is significant. However, his analysis of its relation to forgiveness is mistaken because, among other problems with his overall perspective, he collapses his discussion into an analysis of when forgiveness can be said to have occurred, and hence is worried about whether resentment would have been fully overcome. By contrast, seeing forgiveness as a craft relativizes the question of when it has been accomplished and situates issues of resentment (and indeed its importance within the craft of forgiveness) in relation to other concerns. See Haber, *Forgiveness*, especially chapters 1 and 4.

42. So, for example, in Anne Tyler's novel *Saint Maybe*, Ian Bedloe, the main character, engages in many isolated actions of forgiveness and repentance, at times feels forgiveness, and spends a great deal of time thinking about forgiveness. But when the

appear justified once we know more details about the circumstances of the past, both in terms of what happened to the person and what progress the person has made in situating that anger in relation to forgiveness. Similarly, what may initially seem to be an instance of gracious forgiveness may, once we learn more, begin to appear as a well-masked repression of anger that festers into bitter desires for vengeance.

More generally, then, narratives are important because we can most adequately learn from others' understandings and embodiments by attending to the contexts in which they live, the situations and issues they face, the arguments they offer, and the arguments to which they respond. This is as true of the narratives of historical communities and specific persons' biographies as it is for accounts offered in modern literature.[43]

There is also a close connection between narratives and the craft of forgiveness because of the "timeful" character both of learning a craft and of practicing forgiveness. In terms of the former: Some accounts of forgiveness seem to suggest that we all at some level "know" what forgiveness is and just want to figure out whether it is a good or a bad thing to do in this or that situation. However, beginning to think about forgiveness by focusing on a specifically horrifying "crisis" is a bit like beginning to think about sexual ethics in the back seat of an automobile; we do not want to denigrate the significance of thinking about important issues, but the context is hardly likely to produce clarity either about the issues or about the people involved.

That is, how we handle a particularly difficult "crisis" concerning forgiveness is likely to have already been heavily determined by the habits and practices we have developed leading up to that crisis. So, for example, people just beginning to learn the craft of forgiveness might have a much greater difficulty in avoiding either "cheap grace" or "vengeance" in a particular situation, whereas those who are more skilled at the craft will likely find it much easier to discern and embody appropriate forgiveness. It will have become much more like "second nature" to them. Learning a craft,

---

reader sees the pattern of his life and how he is increasingly beset by despair, we learn to look at those actions, feelings, and thoughts in a different light. See also my discussion in "The Craft of Forgiveness."

43. Numerous examples could be offered; for samples, see Peter Brown's extraordinary biography *Augustine of Hippo* (Berkeley: University of California, 1967), and Fyodor Dostoevsky, *The Brothers Karamazov*, tr. Richard Pevear and Larissa Volokhonsky (San Francisco: North Point, 1990). Alas, there is a relative paucity of thick descriptions of forgiveness as practiced in specific historical communities over time.

particularly a craft as complex, difficult, and (at times) comprehensive as is forgiveness takes (and also makes) time.

Narratives are also important because of the timeful character of forgiveness itself. Forgiveness does not typically happen overnight; nor is it something that is easily willed. Rather, it is characteristically a *retrospective* judgment made from the standpoint of the new life (and in many cases the reconciliation) whose achievement comes to us as a gift.[44] If we want to know whether a person forgives another person (or people forgive other people) in a particular situation or circumstance, we are more likely to discern a wise answer by attending to the larger, timeful character of what preceded that situation and what followed it. It is in attending to such larger narratives that we can begin to discern how forgiveness is crafted (or fails to be crafted) throughout people's lives.

To be sure, how long forgiveness takes depends on a variety of factors pertaining to the relevant situation. For example, Joram Graf Haber suggests that "much depends on the relationship of the parties (e.g., whether it is intimate and continuous or distant and temporary); on the culpability of the wrongdoer (e.g., whether the injury was deliberate or negligent); and on the magnitude of the injury."[45] That is, the time involved in forgiveness (even whether forgiveness can be envisioned, much less embodied) is typically much greater in, for example, an intentional betrayal by a close friend or by a spouse, parent, or child, particularly if the injuries involved are physical as well as emotional, than in an act of negligence by a stranger or acquaintance, particularly if the injuries involved are relatively inconsequential. And one can imagine how various other configurations would also affect the time one might expect it to take to discover that forgiveness has occurred.

Often, much also depends on whether that which needs forgiveness is a new, isolated situation or a recurring phenomenon for which there has already been an ongoing struggle to embody forgiveness and reconciliation. This bears on each of the themes identified by Haber, but it has its own significance; for the process of forgiveness typically takes more time when it involves a struggle to bear with a recurring phenomenon (even if there is sincere repentance, the growth that occurs in "unlearning" deeply en-

---

44. More precisely, Christian forgiveness is characteristically *prospective*, because it is eschatologically shaped; it is from that prospective commitment that it is therefore *retro*spectively known and evaluated. I am grateful to Jim Buckley for pressing this question.

45. Haber, *Forgiveness*, p. 19. See also Martin Golding's discussion in "Forgiveness and Regret," *Philosophical Forum* 16/1-2 (1984-85) pp. 121-137.

trenched habits is likely to be much slower than the forgiver would desire) than if it is an isolated occurrence.[46]

Indeed, while our attention is often (and understandably) focused on difficult situations of horrifying sin and evil, it may be the case that some difficult situations — particularly one-time occurrences — may be less difficult to forgive than the daily offenses and aggravations with which we must learn to bear (even if the offender is struggling mightily to minimize such offenses). To be sure, it *might* be extraordinarily difficult to forgive a single great injury — particularly if that injury is a rape, a betrayal, or the murder of a loved one. But the crucial point is that those activities that become habits that we do *or that we suffer,* including what C.S. Lewis called "the incessant provocations of daily life,"[47] are often difficult to accept forgiveness for or to forgive precisely because they become embedded throughout our lives.

That is why practices of forgiveness are so important in nurturing the craft. For in the disciplines of such practices Christians are enabled to mark time through the cultivation of specific habits of thinking, feeling, and acting. But even with such practices, the time needed to find the appropriate convergence of our language, feelings, and actions may be agonizingly long. In one of his letters to Malcolm, C.S. Lewis reflects on his practice of prayer in relation to the lengthy time it has taken for him to discover forgiveness. "Last week," he notes, "while at prayer, I suddenly discovered — or felt as if I did — that I had really forgiven someone I had been trying to forgive for over 30 years. Trying, and praying that I might."[48] Thirty years might seem an extraordinarily long time to some, realistic to others, and to yet others — particularly those who have unjustly suffered something, or some things, of great magnitude — it might seem unexpectedly brief.

This timefulness indicates the significant yet limited relevance of performative declarations such as "I forgive you."[49] They may be significant

46. There are rich traditions within Christianity (e.g., in monastic communities) that bear on these questions and that could help restore the ecclesial and theological contexts for these distinctions. That Christians in modernity have often lost sight of these traditions remains one of the troubling indications of the ways we have failed to embody our own best sources for insight.

47. C. S. Lewis, "On Forgiveness," in W. Hooper (ed.), *Fern-Seeds and Elephants* (London: Collins, 1975) p. 43.

48. C. S. Lewis, *Letters to Malcolm: Chiefly on Prayer* (New York: Harcourt, Brace and World, 1964) p. 106. I am indebted to John Koenig, *Rediscovering New Testament Prayer* (New York: HarperCollins, 1992) p. 104, for directing me to this passage.

49. For the notion of forgiveness as a "performative utterance," see Haber, *Forgiveness,* chapter 2.

at the outset of the process, indicating the forgiver's intentions to cultivate those habits necessary for reconciliation. By contrast, such a declaration might be withheld until the forgiver has already moved significantly along the path of forgiveness, having become a sign of changes that already have occurred and are occurring in the relationship. Or the declaration might never be actually uttered, but nonetheless be presupposed in the overall patterns of a particular relationship. In any case, such declarations are an indication to those needing forgiveness of the horizon in which the situation will be approached — namely, a craft in which reconciliation rather than vengeance is the aim. Even so, we should not assume that such declarations are either necessary or sufficient means for identifying when forgiveness has occurred. The discovery of forgiveness requires the convergence of our language with our feelings and our actions.

Further, even once a specific instance of forgiveness has been discovered and enacted, the craft of forgiveness must continue. For though I may be able to make a retrospective judgment that "I have forgiven" the other(s), forgiveness cannot be confined to a moment — even a moment at the conclusion of a long, timeful process. For we must continue to embody that forgiveness into the future. "To forgive for the moment is not difficult," Lewis writes to Malcolm, "but to go on forgiving, to forgive the same offence again every time it recurs to the memory — there's the real tussle."[50] It is indeed a tussle, but a tussle that is significantly ameliorated if we are involved in ongoing practices of forgiveness that enable us continually to locate our lives in the craft of forgiveness. Hence, the craft of forgiveness requires an ongoing process of renarrating the past so that we can remember it truthfully *and well;* and as such, we need not to "forget" but to cultivate a timeful embodiment that enables us to remember the past in the context of a liberating new life oriented to God's eschatological future.

There is one final reason why narratives are important to the craft of forgiveness. Implicit throughout my account has been the presumption that forgiveness is not only an action or a feeling or a judgment, but also — and more determinatively — a trait of character that must be embodied throughout our lives. It is a specifically Christian virtue (and inextricably interrelated with other virtues), a virtue accomplished by way of the gift of God's gracious Spirit. That is, forgiveness is a way of life in the pursuit of holiness cultivated through — though not confined to — specific practices under the guidance of the Holy Spirit. Through those practices, people

50. Lewis, *Letters to Malcolm,* pp. 29-30.

learn to embody particular dispositions and habits of thinking, feeling, and acting. And we can map the ways in which people embody forgiveness, or fail to embody forgiveness, by telling the narratives of their lives.[51]

Further, the narratives of this embodiment cannot be confined to Christian practices or even Christian contexts. For though the craft of forgiveness is paradigmatically learned and named in specific Christian practices, it must be lived in all of the diverse settings, contexts, and circumstances of our lives. And it should not surprise us to find that people throughout God's Creation might be embodying forgiveness themselves in profound ways. Hence, forgiveness ought to be celebrated wherever it is found to be authentic. This is a reminder that while forgiveness has a very specific focus in the work of the Triune God, it is universal in scope; it is in the service of our reconciliation (with God, with one another, and with the whole Creation) and of the making and remaking of responsible human life.

This final point occasions a return to the larger perspective of this chapter. As we engage in specific practices of Christian forgiveness, we ought to be simultaneously involved in learning to see forgiveness as a craft. In so doing, we will be enabled to discern more clearly the connections between our specific practices and the understandings and convictions that arise from them, on the one hand, and the different yet overlapping issues and understandings that arise in the world of God's good Creation and in other traditions, on the other.

That is to say, the craft of forgiveness embraces the entirety of our lives. As such, it calls us to an ongoing (and, hopefully, ever-deepening) discernment in diverse contexts: (1) In our own lives, Christians are called to engage in the craft as we seek in all that we are and do to "unlearn" the ways of sin and to learn the ways of God's gracious, forgiving and reconciling love; (2) in our engagements with others, we are called to engage in the craft as we seek to embody forgiveness while recognizing the complex issues that are entailed therein; and (3) in our engagements with divergent yet (likely) overlapping views of forgiveness, we are called to seek analogues to a Christian understanding of forgiveness wherever they can be found.

51. More specifically, I would say that Christians do so by mapping how the narratives of people's lives are located in the narrative of the Triune God. For reflections on the centrality of God to issues of autobiography, see my "For All the Saints: Autobiography in Christian Theology," *Asbury Theological Journal* 47/1 (Spring 1992), pp. 27-42.

In all of these contexts, we seek faithfully to discern the working of God's Spirit in the Church and in the world.

Indeed, in this process we might discover that, by learning more clearly what *Christian* forgiveness entails and embodying it more faithfully, we will be able to recognize and to articulate the working of God's Spirit in the world beyond the Church, and even to hear in that articulation a judgment against the corruptions of the Church's own practices; yet the Church might also be enabled more clearly to articulate a prophetic witness to the world of the power of God's forgiveness. Conversely, through a more coherent account of Christian forgiveness, non-Christians might learn to articulate judgments and practices that they have inchoately already been embodying and believing, even as they perhaps correct, challenge, and enrich Christian accounts from the perspective of their own practices and understandings; yet they might also be compelled to repent of particular judgments and engage in far more comprehensive reconstructions of their practices and understandings. But we cannot know the results apart from the patient, timeful craft of seeking to discern the most truthful account of God and how God is related to the world and, more specifically, to human life.

Yet we are still left with unresolved questions. Despite Jesus' announcement and enactment of the Kingdom's inauguration and despite the promise that this Kingdom will one day be consummated in its fullness (so that there will be a time when God's Creation will be "finished"), sin and evil continue to persist. Indeed, their persistence often results in situations of such extreme brokenness that it is difficult even to envision or desire, much less embody, the craft of forgiveness. And so we are compelled to ask: Is hatred or a desire for vengeance ever justified, particularly in the absence of repentance (or of the redistribution of power)? Or, put more in social and political terms, is "retributive punishment" ever appropriate? How are such themes as punishment and accountability related to forgiveness, particularly when there is a refusal to acknowledge the horizons of forgiveness? Are there some people who are simply unforgivable?

Such questions cannot be avoided. For if a Christian account of forgiveness is to be defended as true, we cannot be content with an admission that Christian forgiveness must be of limited scope because the only effective way to deal with unrepentant wrongdoing is through retributive punishment. Nor can we be content with suggestions that forgiveness is personally "helpful" but socially and politically irrelevant or, worse, genuinely dangerous. It is to an examination of these and related questions that I now turn.

8 Loving Enemies

Living with Others in the Absence of Reconciliation

W E LIVE in a world marked not only by created goodness and reconciling forgiveness but also by the persistence of sin and evil. Indeed,
the persistence of that sin and evil, the patterns of diminution and destruction that are deeply embedded in our lives and in our structures, make the
craft of forgiveness difficult if not — at least in some circumstances, in
some lives — either impossible or morally unjustified. This is even more
the case when those who are powerful use forgiveness as a weapon to keep
their subjects powerless or when the lack of repentance by the offender(s)
suggests that the offense(s) will persist or perhaps even become exacerbated.
In such cases, it is difficult to imagine how, if at all, the craft of forgiveness
has any significant role to play in our lives or in our world. This is so even
for Christians who are otherwise committed to the central significance of
forgiveness in relation to God, the world, and specific human lives.

For example, the Palestinian priest Elias Chacour, whose eloquent
embodiment of the craft of forgiveness bears poignant witness, recently
told me of the struggles he has had to convince young Palestinian children
in the occupied territories not to be consumed by hate. He added, "In your
book, please don't make forgiveness seem too easy." Again: a young rape
victim, who took my class on "Forgiveness and Reconciliation" in the midst
of the trial of the man who raped her, wanted to know if there was any way
to hold together her belief in a forgiving God and her anger and sense of
betrayal at a world in which men rape women and at a particular man who

241

seemed to be sorry only that he had been caught. Again: a friend of mine, who had been betrayed by one of his coworkers, was filled with venom for his unrepentant coworker. This betrayal had not only ruined their relationship but had made him find it increasingly difficult to trust anyone because the coworker continued to try to undermine him. Consequently, he did not think it possible to envision them being reconciled.

In each of these examples, a Christian was struggling to imagine how to practice the craft of forgiveness in a situation, or in relation to people, where reconciliation seemed a dim prospect on a distant horizon. In each instance, the parties involved were not all Christian, so there was no prior communal commitment that could provide a context for the practice of reconciling forgiveness — including its focus on "loving enemies." But even more, the very notion of "loving enemies," tossed off lightly as an injunction, seems to ignore or trivialize the genuine significance of the anger and hostility felt by the people who had been victimized.

Indeed, it seems insufficient (at best) simply to suggest (as I have in chapter 7) that such responses as anger, lament, and prophetic indignation have an important role in the craft of forgiveness. The struggles that people feel in relation to their anger, hatred, and desires for revenge not only are real; they seem to reflect morally significant attitudes. In this sense, those who defend the significance of revenge and those who oppose Christian forgiveness are often tapping into legitimate concerns that sin and evil be taken with appropriate seriousness. Even more, these desires for revenge, or more specifically institutionalized as a desire for retributive punishment, seem to be important crucibles of our seriousness about justice and the defense of those who have been victimized. For retribution signifies a social commitment that order is better than disorder.

Hence, even if Christians reject an ontology of violence, and posit the central significance of forgiveness as the costly means by which God's love moves toward reconciliation in the face of sin and evil, we cannot ignore the importance of people's feelings of hostility and hatred and desires for vengeance or retributive punishment. Thus we are presented with the question of whether there are, or at least ought to be, some limits to the craft of forgiveness. That is, are there not some people whom it is better to hate and to desire vengeance against, particularly in the absence of repentance (or of the redistribution of power)? Or, put more in social and political terms, isn't "retributive punishment" appropriate as a society's way of expressing its revulsion against particular offenses? If not, how are such themes as punishment and accountability related to forgiveness, particularly when there is a refusal to acknowledge the horizons of forgiveness?

Are there some people who simply are unforgivable? What implications does the injunction to "love your enemies" have in relation to these issues?

Ironically, each of these questions can be posed of God as well as of ourselves. That is, are there not some people whom God will bring vengeance against, or at the very least will eternally punish? Does the understanding of the final judgment in Matthew 25:31-45 or the overall context of the book of Revelation suggest that some will be saved and some will be damned to eternal punishment? Does the doctrine of Hell, held by Christians throughout the centuries, suggest that some people make themselves unforgivable — precisely by God? Jeffrie Murphy contends that "if hatred and vengeance are permissible for God, then there must be a sense in which these responses are *in principle* permissible. Note also that the passage from Rom. 12:19, far from being an argument against the desire for vengeance, is a *promise* of vengeance."[1]

Hence an adequate discussion of these issues plunges us into questions of soteriology (i.e., the Christian doctrine of salvation) as well as of ethics and politics. While a full discussion of these issues transcends the scope of this chapter and this book, attending to their implications is necessary if we are to understand the place of, and learn to embody the vocation of, loving enemies in the craft of forgiveness. My argument in this chapter develops in the following four steps: (1) I analyze why anger, hatred, and desires for vengeance (or, less severely, for retributive punishment) have a powerful and morally significant hold on our imagination; (2) I discuss some pivotal New Testament texts that would seem to sanction desires for vengeance and punishment rather than forgiveness, both in relation to God's work of salvation and damnation and to our relations with one another; (3) I describe what the task of "loving enemies" ought to entail within the context of Christian forgiveness; and (4) I propose an understanding of punishment appropriate to the craft of forgiveness.

The Moral Significance of Anger, Hatred, and Retribution

It is not difficult for most of us to imagine people and circumstances where we unreflectively think that anger, hatred, and perhaps even vengeance are more desirable responses than forgiveness. The list of such people often

1. In Jeffrie G. Murphy and Jean Hampton, *Forgiveness and Mercy* (Cambridge: Cambridge University, 1988) p. 98, n. 13.

begins with Hitler, with serial killers such as Jeffrey Dahmer, or with the Oklahoma City bombers, but it could just as easily begin with specific impenitent people who have committed some serious offense against a particular individual, ranging from murder to rape to robbery to betrayals of trust. Or the list of such situations or circumstances would readily include mass genocide in Rwanda, the enslavement of Africans, or the persistence of child abuse. Our hatred and our desires for revenge are often reflected in the popular media; films such as "Rambo" and "Death Wish" (and, for those who saw them in theaters, the crowd's reactions) testify to a strong desire among people for others to "get theirs."[2]

Even so, it is also the case that many Christians have suggested that, on reflection, the appropriate response to such situations ought to be forgiveness. Yet in so doing they have often seemed to trivialize sufferers' feelings of anger, hatred, and (perhaps) legitimate desires for vengeance. So some Christians proclaimed shortly after World War II that the Nazis were (or already had been) forgiven, outraging Jews and others who had suffered at the Nazis' hands. And Christians sometimes tell women that they ought to forgive their abusers and go back to the same situation to have it repeated or even exacerbated. Or Christians sometimes suggest that we should *not* punish people for their offenses but instead should show them love and help rehabilitate them — failing to recognize the ways in which such "softness" both encourages crime and seems to trivialize the suffering of victims. Christians have too often supported forgiveness, love, and forbearance, while failing to acknowledge the moral force of anger, hatred, and vengeance.

It is precisely this latter claim that has opened the door to Nietzschean critiques. To oversimplify his complex views, Nietzsche charged that Christian teachings about love and forgiveness do not acknowledge people's desires for revenge and for a will to power; they mask and repress them. In Nietzsche's view, Christian virtue is "the vengeful cunning of impotence," in which weakness casts itself as strength and pretends to engage in forgiveness when it is really an inability to secure vengeance. Nietzsche argues that "weakness is being lied into something *meritorious*,"

> and impotence which does not requite into "goodness of heart"; anxious lowliness into "humility"; subjection to those one hates into "obedience"

---

2. Susan Jacoby has explored these impulses and their implications for our thinking about matters of justice in her *Wild Justice: The Evolution of Revenge* (New York: Harper and Row, 1983).

(that is, to one of whom they say he commands this subjection — they call him God). The inoffensiveness of the weak man, even the cowardice of which he has so much, his lingering at the door, his being ineluctably compelled to wait, here acquire flattering names, such as "patience," and are even called virtue itself; his inability for revenge is called unwillingness to revenge, perhaps even forgiveness ("for *they* know not what they do — we alone know what *they* do!"). They also speak of "loving one's enemies" — and sweat as they do so.[3]

To deny one's desire for vengeance out of weakness is to practice a "forgiveness" and a "love" whose effects are not reconciliation and new life but rather repressed bitterness and hatred. In such situations, our "love" of neighbors or of ourselves, much less of our enemies, is hardly a sign of authentic virtue.

Further, Nietzsche suggests that this weakness becomes even more pernicious through an internalization of those judgments concerning who ought to be punished for one's suffering. This is accomplished, Nietzsche suggests, through Christianity's deployment of the language of guilt and pastoral power (i.e., through the "ascetic priest"). Merold Westphal describes Nietzsche's strategy well:

> It is the guilt potential of the ascetic ideal that the priest is able to exploit, and one could say that his moral authority is simply his ability to do so. To heal he must first wound, since a religion of forgiveness makes sense only to sinners. The priest does this when he *"alters the direction of ressentiment."* We all seek an explanation for our suffering. Resentment seeks "a *guilty* agent," one who is evil and deserves to be punished (since even if I lack the power to punish, there is satisfaction in knowing that my enemy deserves it).[4]

By redirecting the guilt to the agent herself, the priest gains enormous power to create a passive subject whose guilt produces a passive acquiescence in forgiveness. Nietzsche writes: " 'I suffer: someone must be to blame for it' — thus thinks every sickly sheep. But his shepherd, the ascetic priest, tells him: 'Quite so, my sheep! someone must be to blame for it: but you yourself

---

3. Friedrich Nietzsche, *On the Genealogy of Morals*, tr. Walter Kaufman and R. J. Hollingdale, ed. Walter Kaufman (New York: Vintage, 1989) essay 1, section 14. The reference to the "vengeful cunning of impotence" is from essay 1, section 13.

4. Merold Westphal, *Suspicion and Faith: The Religious Uses of Modern Atheism* (Grand Rapids: Eerdmans, 1993), p. 242.

are this someone, you alone are to blame for it — *you alone are to blame for yourself!* — This is brazen and false enough: but one thing at least is achieved by it, the direction of *ressentiment* is *altered.*"[5] Regrettably, such redirection and internalization happen all too regularly when clergy (and laity, sometimes acting with "priestly power") blame the sufferers for suffering and do so in ways that perpetuate injustice and eclipse the possibility of authentic forgiveness.

Nietzsche's critique is not insurmountable, but its prophetic indictment is haunting.[6] Christian forgiveness should not be a refusal of strength, but rather ought to manifest an alternative power; Christian love, whether of neighbors or of enemies, should be a sign not of repressed anger and hatred but of anger and hatred confronted and, eventually, overcome and transcended; it should not be an internalized guilt that further diminishes and destroys but a truthful engagement with the causes and motivations underlying the situation of brokenness.

In confronting such misunderstandings and distortions, we need to recognize (to borrow a phrase from Beverly Harrison) "the power of anger in the work of love."[7] Most specifically, anger can express (or reclaim) a sense of one's self-worth and hence a refusal to be passive, or pacified, in the face of injustice and suffering — whether inflicted on oneself or on others. In this sense, anger is a moral protest against the diminution and destruction that has been effected by sin and evil, whether on oneself or on others.[8] Hence, we ought to be more terrified by the effects of a person whose emotions have been anesthetized (creating a "passive death") or

---

5. Nietzsche, *On the Genealogy of Morals,* essay 3, section 15.

6. For a suggestive reading of Nietzsche as a "prophetic critique" of Christianity, see Westphal's discussion in *Suspicion and Faith,* Part IV.

7. See Beverly Wildung Harrison, "The Power of Anger in the Work of Love," *Union Seminary Quarterly Review* supplementary volume 36 (1981) pp. 41-57. Harrison's essay was significant in focusing attention on the importance of anger, and at several points she articulates well the creative power of anger. My own analysis is in many ways indebted to her arguments. However, I am less persuaded by her claims on p. 49 that anger "always" is "a sign of some resistance in ourselves to the moral quality of the social relations in which we are immersed," or that "*all* serious human moral activity, especially action for social change, takes its bearings from the rising power of human anger" (emphasis added). Such sweeping judgments fail adequately to nuance issues surrounding anger, and particularly to differentiate "righteous anger" from other forms of anger.

8. For further discussion of the significance of this "moral protest," see Jean Hampton's discussion in chapter 3 of Murphy and Hampton, *Forgiveness and Mercy.*

whose anger has been turned inward into depression (often creating an "active" and very real death, either of another, of others, or of oneself through suicide).

Further, recall Bishop Butler's injunction, cited in the last chapter, that anger and resentment help us not only to preserve a sense of self-worth but also to resist and defeat violent attacks from others. "Righteous anger" is a crucial element in the craft of forgiveness, reminding us of the gaps between our commitment to the holiness of God's Kingdom and the often harsh realities that we and others have to struggle with each day. From this perspective, Christians ought to be filled with more, and more intense, righteous anger than those "realists" or "cynics" content to identify the way things are as the way things will likely continue to be.

The question, then, is not whether anger is legitimate or important; it certainly can be. Rather the question is what we become angry about and, more specifically, toward what ends our anger is directed. The letter to the Ephesians indicates the need for discriminating judgment: "Be angry, but do not sin. Do not let the sun go down on your anger" (4:26). Here there is an acknowledgment that people will be angry and presumably also an injunction that there are things about which people *should* be angry. The question is not whether or not we should have anger; it will be there. Hence, though we may try to repress or ignore it, we cannot evade its reality. But we are enjoined to ensure that our anger, whatever its cause, is transformed into the service of God's inbreaking Kingdom rather than as an occasion for sin (and hence the perpetuation of diminution and destruction).

That is, this injunction in Ephesians is set in the larger context of learning to be truthful. Further, the concluding part of the passage enjoins the community to "get rid of all bitterness, wrath, anger, fighting, and slander, together with all malice. Be kind to each other, tenderhearted, forgiving each other, as God has forgiven you in Christ. Imitate God in this way, as God's beloved children, and live in love, as Christ loved us and gave himself for us, a fragrant offering and sacrifice to God" (Ephesians 4:31–5:2).

Set in this context, the injunction would seem to suggest that anger can be legitimate if it is in the service of God's inbreaking Kingdom, in the sustenance and edification of those who are "members of each other" (4:25). But anger can also lead to sin, particularly if it is allowed to ossify into hatred and desires for revenge. So while it is clear that anger has a place in the craft of forgiveness, we have also to consider the sharper question: Why are hatred and a desire for revenge — or if not revenge, at least a desire for retributive punishment — linked to sin? Is not such a claim still susceptible to Nietzsche's critique? Is there not a case for the moral significance of hatred and revenge that are not a part of forgiveness?

Such a case has been suggested not only by Nietzsche but also by philosophers more favorably disposed to the moral significance of forgiveness. For example, toward the end of his analysis in his book *Forgiveness*, Joram Graf Haber notes that "there simply are people whom it is better to resent than it is to forgive."[9] For Haber, such resentment is crucial if the offender fails to repent; according to his analysis, we need this resentment in order to maintain standards of accountability in our moral and political lives.

A somewhat different and more sustained argument for the limits of forgiveness in relation to hatred and vengeance is offered by Jean Hampton. She proposes the term "moral hatred" to signify our sense that there are situations where people want to say that both the action *and the person who performed the action* ought to be despised and hated. Hampton distinguishes moral hatred from "malicious" and "spiteful" hatred, which are, she suggests, linked to desires for vengeance, are likely to intensify the cycles of violence and injury, and are self-defeating. They are so because at their best they bring the other down to the offended one's level and do not restore or elevate the offended person's self-worth. Hampton suggests that such forms of hatred are species of Nietzschean *ressentiment*.

By contrast, moral hatred is indignation directed at the insulter/offender. As Hampton describes it,

> the indignant person who opposes the message in the insulter's action is expressing an aversion for the immoral cause her [the insulter's] action promotes, and feels aversion to the insulter herself — her character, her habits, her disposition, or the whole of her — if he takes her, or at least certain components of her, to be thoroughly identified with that cause. Such aversion for her cause and to *her* is motivated by morality; for this reason I have named it "moral hatred." It involves believing, by virtue of the insulter's association with the evil cause, that she has "rotted" or "gone bad" so that she now lacks some measure of goodness or moral health.

Hampton adds that moral hatred can come in degrees, suggesting that the strongest degree would be reserved for mass murderers and Nazis such as Goebbels, who seem "irredeemably 'rotten' like a piece of meat that has been allowed to become full of maggots and decay."[10]

9. Joram Graf Haber, *Forgiveness* (Savage: Rowman and Littlefield, 1991) p. 107.
10. Hampton, in Murphy and Hampton, *Forgiveness and Mercy,* p. 80.

Hampton suggests that we want simply to repudiate such people, believing that they not only are "cloaked" in evil but are themselves a bad thing. It is this judgment that leads to moral hatred in the full sense. On the other end of the spectrum, there are people who are much less severely "rotted" and would be more amenable to "treatment" and reclamation of their moral identity. We would still oppose their wrongdoing, but in the spirit of wanting to correct it because of a conviction that they are still reclaimable. The degree to which we want to repudiate rather than correct a wrongdoer will also indicate the relative strength of our moral hatred.

On Hampton's analysis, no person ought to be pressured to give up moral hatred. For, she notes, "not to experience indignation at an immoral action, not to have moral hatred for the immoral cause upon which the wrongdoer acted, and not to feel this same aversion towards the wrongdoer himself if he thoroughly identifies himself with that cause, appear to involve giving up one's commitment to the cause of morality."[11] Further, she suggests that it is not clear that Jesus was categorically opposed to the emotion of moral hatred as she defines it. She suggests that, despite Jesus' opposition to malicious hatred (see Mattthew 5:23), he does "appear to encourage us to sustain opposition to our moral opponents, and not to reconcile ourselves with them for as long as they remain committed to their bad cause. ('I have not come to bring peace, but a sword. I have come to set a man against his father, and a daughter against her mother, a son's wife against her mother-in-law; and a man will find his enemies under his own roof')."[12]

To her credit, Hampton notes several dangers with moral hatred: It may lead us to believe unfairly that those who have committed wrongdoings are morally worse, it may blind us to the humane and decent elements within them, and it may lead us to morally hate ourselves.[13] Indeed, these are dangers that Hampton identifies in relation to both the parable of the Unforgiving Servant and the injunction in Matthew's Gospel that we will be judged according to the judgment we give out. Hence, Hampton insists that moral hatred ought to be resisted for as long as possible and that we ought to be both generous in our judgments and sensitive to the ways in which our love in the face of wrongdoing (and in spite of clear evidence

11. Hampton, in Murphy and Hampton, *Forgiveness and Mercy,* p. 148.

12. Hampton, in Murphy and Hampton, *Forgiveness and Mercy,* p. 149, quoting Matthew 10:34-36.

13. See Hampton, in Murphy and Hampton, *Forgiveness and Mercy,* pp. 149-157. It should be noted that the first two of these dangers are identified by Murphy in the preceding chapter. See especially pp. 98ff.

of "rottedness") may be able to prompt repentance. Even so, Hampton rightly does not want to suggest that we live in a world where all sins are gray. Moral hatred, she suggests, is an important expression of our aversion to the ways in which people can become morally sick and rotten.[14]

Hampton presents a powerful case for the moral and political significance of moral hatred. However, it would seem to conflict with some of the central themes I have been developing throughout this book, and par-

14. In his analysis of hatred, Jeffrie Murphy refers to the victims of a series of vicious rapes in Phoenix perpetrated by a man known as the "Camelback rapist" (Camelback is a neighborhood in Phoenix). When the victims testified, they indicated that they wanted the rapist, who had utterly destroyed the lives of some of them, to be sentenced to the maximum term that the law allowed, and many of them openly admitted that they were acting out of anger and hatred. Murphy adds, "I would have found it indecently insensitive and presumptuous had anyone charged them with the vice of failing to forgive and love their enemies . . . had, in short, anyone attempted to add to their already considerable burdens by making them feel guilty or ashamed over a reaction that was, given what was done to them, natural, fitting, and proper." He concludes by noting that "*this* is the kind of case that must be discussed and made central in any comprehensive attack on the nature and justification of hatred" (Hampton and Murphy, *Forgiveness and Mercy,* p. 92). For a further exploration of our responses to people who unabashedly indicate their anger and desire for vengeance or retribution (albeit one whose normative judgments diverge considerably from my own), see Jacoby, *Wild Justice.*

There is much to be said for Murphy's point, and I return to it below. However, at this point I would add two remarks by way of caution. The first draws on Hampton's response to the case, in which she says that while we can "sympathize" with the women, and "share their outrage at the rapist's deed," we do not typically see them as *noble* or as in any way "exceptionally meritorious" (specifically in contrast to Jesus' words from the cross). She concludes, "Perhaps the only reason we are reluctant to criticize these victims for their hatred is because we believe they are already experiencing too much pain to make it right to inflict any more" (p. 120).

Secondly, I would add that attending to issues of forgiveness as a way of life would suggest that the sorts of habits and virtues people have cultivated over time may affect the ways in which they respond to such an outrageous situation. That is, while we can all agree with the need for sympathy for the women and can be outraged at the action of the rapist, we should not presume that all people in similar situations would necessarily characterize the nature of that sympathy or that outrage in precisely the same way. This is another way of saying that the traditions that cultivate particular practices and, through them, specific habits of thinking, feeling, and acting make a crucial difference in how we describe and respond to such crisis circumstances. Murphy himself indicates the importance of virtues in a note on p. 106, but that acknowledgment does not seem to shape his analysis in any significant way.

ticularly in the three chapters of Part II. More specifically, it would seem to violate Jesus' injunction to "love your enemies." How could moral hatred be compatible with an injunction to love even one's enemies?

Hampton considers this issue, recognizing that Jesus' call to "love your enemies" may be an indication that "in spite of any evidence provided by overt actions or words" we are nonetheless required to believe that people can "never become so rotted as individuals that they lose all decency and goodness." Hampton admits to having trouble with this counsel and acknowledges that this may place her "outside the proper sphere of Christian faith and charity." If it does, however, she thinks she will be joined by many others who "*for moral reasons* cannot sustain the charity this religion would require of them."[15]

Further, Hampton wonders whether the injunction to "love your enemies" is all-embracing. After all, she suggests, Jesus himself seems prepared to have judged some people as "rotted" beyond hope and "fit only for the fires of hell," for example, the Pharisees in Matthew's Gospel. She adds that the idea that some people might be beyond redemption and consigned to Hell is at least a part of Christianity's tradition, even if it is not currently popular. She concludes, "Jesus' injunction to love one's enemies thus may be intended only to encourage generosity of judgement towards many, not to require it in every case. So, at any rate, I want to propose."[16]

Here Hampton's proposal for the significance of moral hatred merges Christian understandings of the doctrine of salvation with ethical and political concerns. And while it must be admitted that there is considerable force (and textual backing in the New Testament) behind her intuition, we need to disentangle soteriological concerns from ethical and political concerns before determining precisely how to respond to proposals for moral hatred in relation to the call to love one's enemies. So it is to such disentanglement, specifically through the analysis of some New Testament passages, that I now turn.

God's Forgiveness, God's Vengeance, and Ours

Although they do so in different ways, both Hampton and Murphy suggest that a defense of moral hatred (or what Murphy calls "retributive hatred")

15. Murphy and Hampton, *Forgiveness and Mercy*, pp. 152-153.
16. Murphy and Hampton, *Forgiveness and Mercy*, p. 153.

may not be incompatible with Christianity. They refer to notions of God's vengeance (specifically as found in Romans 12:19, citing Deuteronomy 32:35), to Jesus' judgment that some people may be irredeemably rotten (specifically to Jesus' woes against the Pharisees in Matthew 23), and more generally to traditional Christian understandings of hell. To these they certainly could have added other texts, perhaps most notably some of the "lament" Psalms and the Book of Revelation.

Here I will take up the issues raised by these texts, and more specifically the arguments of the texts themselves, in three steps. First, I will consider the question of salvation, namely whether God will eternally punish some people rather than forgive them and allow them to become reconciled to God. Second, I will turn to the passage at the end of Romans 12, where notions of God's vengeance and the call for us to love our enemies are conjoined. Then, third, I will explore the question of whether we might nonetheless be permitted morally to hate other people, focusing on the difficult test cases of a lament Psalm and the Book of Revelation. Analyzing these issues will not only advance our discussion of the merits of moral hatred but also help to clarify what the call to love one's enemies actually entails.

Hampton is right both to suggest that Christians have traditionally held to a doctrine of hell and to note that it is currently not very popular. However, its lack of popularity should not count as an argument against its importance, particularly since judgments about it are often made unreflectively. Further, the arguments that have been offered against the doctrine of hell are themselves capable of being refuted.[17] There are important reasons for holding to a doctrine of hell, not least of which is its prominence in the New Testament in general and in the teaching of Jesus in particular (see, e.g., Matthew 5:22, 29ff.; 10:28; 22:11ff.; 25:46; Mark 9:43; Philippians 3:19; 2 Thessalonians 1:6ff.; Revelation 19:20; 20:10; 21:8).

Even more, a doctrine of hell points both to the reality of God's judgment and the centrality of human accountability. If we do not respond

17. For a philosophical defense of the doctrine of hell that takes up the most cogent philosophical critiques of that doctrine, see Jerry L. Walls, *Hell: The Logic of Damnation* (Notre Dame: University of Notre Dame, 1992). Though there is much to be learned from this book, I disagree with its concluding chapter, most specifically from its too easy categorization of Hans Urs von Balthasar's book *Dare We Hope "That All Men Be Saved"?* as a "Roman Catholic defense of universalistic exegesis" (p. 176, n. 2). As I suggest below (indeed, following von Balthasar's subtle analysis), the options and issues (at least on this side of the final judgment and the Kingdom) are more supple than the stark alternatives of eternal punishment or universalism.

to God's judgment of grace through lives of forgiven-ness in the pursuit of holiness, then we become susceptible to a judgment without grace. "Judgment will be without mercy to anyone who has shown no mercy" (James 2:13a). We must be accountable for our choices and our actions; if we refuse God, if we are unable to come prepared for the messianic banquet (a preparation whose signal requirements are forgiveness and a desire to be clothed in God's righteousness), then we are cast — or better, we cast ourselves — into the "outer darkness" (see Matthew 18:23-35; 22:1-14).[18] God's grace is costly, not cheap; it requires from us an accountability for our lives through forgiveness, a forgiveness that sets us free from the past (by allowing us to "own" the past responsibly) to become holy people in the present and in the future. If we fail to accept that forgiveness through repentance and the pursuit of holiness, then we must confront the possibility that God will hold us accountable to judgment and consign us to eternal punishment.

On the other hand, there are also passages that would seem to hold out the prospect of ultimate universal redemption. Paul indicates at the conclusion of his meditation on the fate of Israel that "God has imprisoned all in disobedience so that he may be merciful to all" (Romans 11:32). Further, 1 Timothy indicates that the Church should pray for "everyone" because "God our Savior" "desires everyone to be saved and to come to knowledge of the truth" (2:1, 3-4). Other texts invoking the sense that God desires to save *all* people could easily be adduced (e.g., John 12:32; Colossians 1:20; Titus 2:11; Ephesians 1:10; 2 Peter 3:9). Even more, the passage from James cited above, indicating a "judgment without mercy" for those who show no mercy, nonetheless has these words immediately following: "Mercy triumphs over judgment" (James 2:13b).

There is no way to synthesize all these passages. Those that indicate

---

18. On the notion that we "cast ourselves" into the outer darkness, that the only real punishment in this sense is self-punishment, see John Milbank's comment on the ninth-century theologian John Scotus Eriugena (Milbank, *Theology and Social Theory* [Oxford: Blackwell, 1990] p. 420):

> Eriugena declares that God neither foresees nor forewills punishment, any more than he foresees or forewills human sin. God is not in time, and he only knows sin as it happens, in terms of its negative effects. He does not will to punish sin, because punishment is not an act of a real nature upon another nature, and God always remains within his nature. Punishment is ontologically "self-inflicted," the only punishment is the deleterious effect of sin itself upon nature, and the torment of knowing reality only in terms of one's estrangement from it.

the possibility of being lost for all eternity exist side-by-side with those that indicate God's will, and God's ability, to save all humanity.[19] The reality of hell must be acknowledged, as also must the possibility that ultimately hell will be empty.[20] However, it is not a matter of simply lining up passages on each side to see whether there are more of one than the other, or even of simply picking and choosing. Rather, I would suggest that passages about hell and doctrines of hell need to be placed in the context of the larger theological horizon of God's *intention* to restore friendship with the entirety of God's Creation. That intention is manifested in the costly, self-giving love of Jesus' crucifixion and resurrection, suggesting that we may not know the depths to which God's grace may go to reach anyone with even the slightest possibility of response.[21]

Even so, none of us can *presume* God's forgiveness regardless of the lives we lead. Rather, each and every one of us must show that we trust in God's forgiveness precisely by our pursuit of holiness in an ever-deepening friendship with God manifested in friendship with others. Christian understandings of hell are, at least in the first instance, a summons to each of us to accept God's judgment of grace. That is, it is a call for each of us to accept responsibility for our own lives rather than always blaming others so as to excuse ourselves. And that call always carries with it the recognition that God's gracious judgment can also take the character of wrath.

Further, we ought to recognize that teachings about eternal punishment, whether on the lips of Jesus or of others, are consistently cast as *warnings*, polemically urging people — whether individually or corporately — to repent. This is true also of apocalyptic literature, in which the warnings of judgment and punishment are calls to repentance more than anything else. Such warnings are important signs of the centrality of account-

19. For an instructive discussion of the various passages that does not seek to provide a synthesis of them, see Hans Urs von Balthasar, *Dare We Hope "That All Men Be Saved"?* tr. David Kipp and Lothar Krauth (San Francisco: Ignatius, 1988) pp. 29-46.

20. The statement that hell might be empty is crucially different from the claim that "there is no hell," first, because it acknowledges the reality of hell and, second, because it only asserts a possibility, not a certainty. For a discussion of the hope that ultimately hell will be empty, see Geoffrey Wainwright, *Doxology: The Praise of God in Worship, Doctrine, and Life* (New York: Oxford University, 1980) pp. 458-460.

21. This suggests the importance of the phrase in the Apostles' Creed that affirms Christ's descent into hell, which is unfortunately deleted from some contemporary versions of the Creed. For a significant meditation on Christ's descent on Holy Saturday, see Hans Urs von Balthasar, *Mysterium Paschale*, tr. Aidan Nichols (Edinburgh: Clark, 1990).

ability, and they provide a negative witness to what communion — with God, with one another, and with the whole Creation — ought to be. That some might persistently, and even eternally, refuse to repent is certainly a possibility; but we should not confuse polemical, prophetic warnings with certain knowledge of God's ways. For we cannot know with any certainty what anyone's fate is in the hands of God. While our choices and actions do matter and while God's judgment is real, we cannot know with certainty how God will respond to any of us, except that God's character is such that God's judgment and even God's wrath are oriented toward grace and reconciliation.

Oriented toward, some might object, but not guaranteed to produce reconciliation in the absence of any human response. Is it possible that, for enemies of the gospel, God's wrath will be determinative? Yes, but that is for God to determine. That possibility should not shape either our ethical and political relations with others, even our enemies, or our hope for their salvation. That is, regardless of whether God's judgment will ultimately repudiate some or, through some purgative fire, "correct" even the impenitent, we humans are forbidden to repudiate anyone ultimately and are enjoined to pray, love, and live for the "correction" and salvation of others — even, perhaps especially, our enemies.

This is clearly the case with those within the fellowship of Christians who nonetheless exclude themselves by their impenitence. As I suggested in chapter 6, Jesus' injunction to treat such people as "Gentiles and tax collectors" suggests both their self-exclusion from the community *and* the requirement to reach out continually to draw them back in — precisely for the sake of their salvation. Similarly, in 1 Corinthians 5:1-5, Paul enjoins the community to "hand over" an impenitent man "to Satan for the destruction of the flesh"; but, Paul adds, they are to do this so that the man's "spirit may be saved in the day of the Lord."

But is this also the case for those who are more determinatively enemies of the gospel? To be sure, Jesus tells his disciples in the Sermon on the Mount "Love your enemies and pray for those who persecute you, so that you may be children of your Father in heaven" (Matthew 5:44). But when Paul gives a similar injunction about doing good in relation to enemies in Romans 12:9-21, it is unclear whether the motivation for doing so is the correction or the eventual repudiation of those enemies. The crucial verses are:

> Bless those who persecute you. Bless them and do not curse them. . . .
> Do not repay anyone evil for evil, but consider what is honorable in the

sight of all people. If it is possible and so far as it depends on you, be at peace with all people. Beloved, do not ever avenge yourselves. Rather, leave room for God's wrath, for it is written, " 'Vengeance is mine; I will repay,' the Lord says." No, "if your enemies are hungry, feed them, and if they are thirsty, give them something to drink, for by so doing you will pile burning coals on their heads." Do not be overcome by evil, but overcome evil with good.[22]

On the one hand, it is clear that Christians are forbidden from taking vengeance into their own hands and are enjoined to try to "overcome" evil with good. But, on the other hand, they are to "leave room" for God's wrath, on the presumption that God will "repay" vengeance on God's enemies; even more, by feeding and providing drink to enemies, Christians will "pile burning coals on their heads."

Unsurprisingly, there are marked divergences among people about how best to interpret this passage.[23] For example, some interpret it wholly as referring to a "love" (a term not used in the passage) for enemies aimed at their conversion and reconciliation. That is, putting "burning coals on their heads" means either that loving enemies will shame them into repentance or simply that the Christian is resolved to pursue reconciliation with his or her enemy.[24] Unfortunately, such a view tends to downplay notions about leaving wrath and vengeance in God's hands, suggesting that, as Zerbe characterizes it, "the call is simply to trust in God's sovereignty or to hope that God's educative wrath will lead adversaries to repentance."[25]

By contrast, others have argued that this passage has an apocalyptic background, hence requiring that it must be interpreted in the context of

22. Romans 12:14, 17-21; the internal quotations are from Deuteronomy 32:35 and Proverbs 25:21-22.

23. For the delineation of these options within New Testament scholarship I am indebted to the discussion in Gordon Zerbe, "Paul's Ethic of Nonretaliation and Peace," in Willard Swartley (ed.), *The Love of Enemy and Nonretaliation in the New Testament* (Louisville: Westminster/John Knox, 1992) pp. 177-222, especially pp. 181-184.

24. The former is the position more frequently found in church fathers such as Origen and Augustine and contemporary scholars such as C. E. B. Cranfield in *A Critical and Exegetical Commentary on the Epistle to the Romans* II (Edinburgh: Clark, 1979) p. 649. The latter view is suggested by, among others, William Klassen in "Coals of Fire: Sign of Repentance or Revenge?" *New Testament Studies* 9 (1962/63) p. 349, and *Love of Enemies* (Philadelphia: Fortress, 1984) p. 120. Further references to both views can be found in Zerbe, "Paul's Ethic of Nonretaliation and Peace," p. 208, nn. 34 and 35.

25. Zerbe, "Paul's Ethic of Nonretaliation and Peace," p. 182.

persecution.[26] From this perspective, nonretaliation and good deeds are the best tactical response available to those who have enemies whom they cannot avoid and are unable to defeat. At the same time, however, believers are assured that God will bring about vengeance on their enemies through an eschatological judgment. Indeed, some suggest that believers are actually invited to desire that vengeance will be brought to their enemies. Zerbe's summary of this line of interpretation is instructive:

> "Heaping coals of fire" is understood as a reference to eschatological judgment, which the enemies of the church are storing up against themselves. Good deeds are not to be understood as a type of love and not intended necessarily to have any reconciling effect; rather, they actually contribute to the culpability of the enemies on the day of wrath. Nonretaliation, then, is essentially an apocalyptic restraint, motivated primarily out of deference to God's judgment.[27]

Unfortunately, such views tend to downplay the concluding injunction to "overcome evil with good," suggesting that this is primarily an assurance of God's eschatological triumph over evil rather than (as the text seems to imply) an exhortation for believers to engage evil through doing works of mercy.

Both views have something in their favor, but neither is wholly adequate. That is, it would appear *both* that God will provide an eschatological judgment, thus giving comfort to those who are suffering persecution (or who are victims of persistent abuse), *and* that nonetheless we are called to do good for enemies and those who persecute us, to bless them and to seek to be at peace with them.[28] In this context, there is no difficulty in claiming that the notion of "piling coals on their heads" could include *both* the belief that love of our enemies and doing good to them might shame them into repentance *and* the conviction that, if they still fail to repent, the compassion shown toward them actually increases their culpability on the day of judgment. But even such a reading is difficult, for it opens the doors to a Nietzschean charge that Christians are only deferring or masking their true hopes that their enemies will not repent.

---

26. See, for example, Krister Stendahl, "Hate, Non-Retaliation and Love: 1QS x, 17-20 and Romans 12:19-21," *Harvard Theological Review* 55 (1962) pp. 343-355.

27. Zerbe, "Paul's Ethic of Nonretaliation and Peace," p. 183.

28. This view is defended, with some minor variations, both by Zerbe, "Paul's Ethic of Nonretaliation and Peace," and by John Piper, *"Love Your Enemies": Jesus' Love Command in the Synoptic Gospels and in the Early Christian Paraenesis* (Cambridge: Cambridge University, 1979).

Indeed, neither of the views described above captures probably the most popular "Christian" reading of this passage in contemporary Western cultures. Here Christians are tempted to remember the "vengeance is mine" without "says the Lord." Or, more perniciously, they cite the whole passage as a justification for their own acts of revenge, as does Mr. Shortley in Flannery O'Connor's short story "The Displaced Person."[29] And, in cultural contexts (such as my own) where people are habituated into, and rewarded for, hating their enemies and bringing about vengeance, we need to be delivered from temptations to defer or mask our desires for vengeance — even if, indeed especially if, it is cloaked in pious-sounding rhetoric.

Christians should not use the possibility that God will eternally punish some as an excuse for our own cultivation of moral hatred.[30] We are called to love our enemies, hoping that this love *might* produce repentance, conversion, and eventually reconciliation and salvation; at the same time, however, we leave the final judgment concerning and realization of God's eschatological justice where it belongs, in the hands of God.

Hence, more generally, we are not only permitted, but obliged, to *hope* that all people will eventually be saved. This means that we ought to live and love in such a way that aims at not only our own salvation but the salvation of all. Such a stance neither affirms that all will be saved nor claims that some (usually others, but even myself) will *necessarily* be damned. Both

---

29. See *3 By Flannery O'Connor* (New York: Signet, 1962) p. 297. I am grateful to David Cunningham for directing me to this story as an example of the ways the passage about vengeance is often used.

30. Zerbe argues that it is not simply a "possibility" that God will eternally punish some, but is a more specific *promise* of retribution (see especially pp.196-202). However, his reasons for saying this are unpersuasive; while admittedly there are passages both in the background of Paul's usage of "coals of fire" and elsewhere in Paul's writings to support the notion of *promised* eschatological punishment (and, indeed, in some places in Paul, punishment that he seems to desire — e.g., Romans 3:8; Galatians 5:10; Philippians 3:19), there are also other passages that would suggest the prospect that God's wrath is ultimately in the service of God's universal reconciliation (e.g., Romans 11:32; 2 Corinthians 5:19; Colossians 1:20).

Even the passage earlier in Romans that deals with God's wrath and God's mercy (2:1-12), which promises that God "will recompense according to each person's deeds: To those who by patiently doing good seek glory, honor, and immortality, he will give eternal life; but for those who are self-seeking and who obey not truth but wickedness, there will be wrath and fury" (2:8-9), does not preclude the possibility that ultimately God's mercy will triumph over God's judgment and wrath. Zerbe's conclusion about the interpretation of "heaping coals of fire" is simply stronger than is warranted by the text and seems also to work against the larger horizons of his argument.

are possible; it is not up to humanity either to know or to decide. We are called, in imitation of the Triune God, whose defining character is love and whose intention is for all to be saved (so 1 Timothy 2:3-6, which explicitly invokes Christ's reconciling work), to *hope* that all will be saved, and to pray and love others accordingly.[31]

Even so, an objection arises almost immediately. What about those "lament" Psalms in which the psalmist is pleading not for the enemies' salvation, but for vengeance and the enemies' destruction? At the end of Psalm 137 we hear the psalmist say, "Happy will they be who pay you back what you have done to us! Happy will they be who take your little ones and dash them against the rock!" Or what about John of Patmos's vision in the Book of Revelation, in which those people lacking the seal of God on their foreheads are tortured by locusts so that they "seek death but do not find it" (Revelation 9:6a)? Or even more strongly, how do we deal with that part of the vision in which one-third of humankind is destroyed (9:18)? In each of these passages, as in others, the plea for or promise of retribution and vengeance looks far more like hatred, moral or otherwise, than love — even love of one's enemies.

There is considerable force to this objection, for these passages do seem to indicate hatred, and perhaps it is more vindictive (even sadistic?) than moral. But we also need to situate such passages in larger contexts of interpretation. For example, they ought to be interpreted in the larger story of God's creative and re-creative work. There is a long tradition in Christian exegesis that the lament Psalms need to be interpreted, first and foremost, as prayers of Jesus Christ.[32] In that context, the Psalmist's desires for vengeance are relocated in the judgment of grace wrought by Christ and thus are ultimately seen in the light of Christ's reconciling work in the power of the Spirit. Even more, in the Book of Revelation these passages are already contextualized by the vision of "the lamb who was slain" and the coming of "the new heaven and the new earth" (Revelation 5:6; 21:1). So the

31. This is the conclusion reached by von Balthasar in *Dare We Hope "That All Men Be Saved"?* It has stirred opposition from both those who are more certain that some (or many) will be damned and those who see no point to discussions of hell. Even so, I think von Balthasar is right that we not only may dare, but are *obliged*, to hope for the salvation of all precisely because of the character of God's costly forgiveness as revealed in the slaying and raising of Jesus and as manifested in the work of the Spirit who is making all things new.

32. See, e.g., Dietrich Bonhoeffer, *Life Together*, tr. John W. Doberstein (New York: Harper and Row, 1954) pp. 49ff., and more generally Bonhoeffer's *Psalms: Prayer Book of the Bible*, tr. James H. Burtness (Minneapolis: Augsburg, 1970).

passages about vengeance do not stand alone, nor are they self-interpreting; they reflect the understandable desire for God's justice to be carried out — and also the very particular, merciful character of God's justice as revealed in the work of the crucified and risen Christ and the Spirit who is making all things new.

We need also to differentiate an *understanding* of the situations, experiences, and lives that would produce such hatred from a normative judgment about its *goodness*. That is to say, we might acknowledge that such hatred is understandable in situations of oppression (or persistent abuse), as both of these sets of texts reflect, while nonetheless *not* suggesting that hatred — even "moral" hatred — is ultimately an adequate or final response to any situation, experience, or life. Why not?

At bottom, we do not say that it is so simply because it is inappropriate to the character of the God whose love moves to reconciliation by means of costly forgiveness. The paradigm case of refusing to be dominated by hatred, even in the face of the most severe of betrayals, is none other than that of the Triune God. This can be seen in God's struggle with Israel in Hosea 11. Even though God is "fiercely angry" at Israel's betrayal, God's "compassion grows warm and tender"; indeed, God indicates that what separates God from mortals is precisely the ability *not* to execute fierce anger, *not* to come in wrath but to forgive and make new. But though that may be the tendency of mortals, it is not inevitable; indeed, Christians have the example of the risen Christ, who returns to his judges, his betrayers, with a judgment that does not condemn but rather reconciles and offers new life.

Further, we should not recommend hatred as an adequate or final response to particular situations, experiences, or lives precisely because of its ossifying effects as a habit. We do not need excuses to hate, to desire vengeance, to return evil for evil; alas, they are deeply ingrained in a world where we almost inevitably diminish and destroy one another and ourselves. Murphy's and Hampton's cautions about the danger of moral hatred are significant, but ultimately they are insufficient. For they do not adequately describe the debilitating effects of the *habit* of hatred, even moral hatred.[33]

---

33. I am not sure quite how far to push differences of terminology between Hampton and myself on this issue, for in many respects I think her "moral hatred" bears fewer of the marks of "hatred" (certainly as she distinguishes it from "malicious" or "spiteful" hatred) than the terminology might suggest. Perhaps her "moral hatred" is much closer to my "prophetic protest" or "righteous indignation" than some of my

Of course, this does not mean that we necessarily ought to make people feel bad for their feelings of hatred, nor that we should acquiesce in situations of injustice by telling them simply either to forgive their enemies (hence, either directly or indirectly, urging them to repress their anger and hatred) or even that they must love them *now*. Neither does it mean that we should utter a therapeutic "I understand," which merely expresses our own feelings. Rather, we must seek to contextualize their feelings, in the first place, by seeking to develop habits of understanding and embodying God's forgiving and reconciling love prior to such situations (if possible) so that they can interpret the situation or experience or life in that context. Or, in the midst of lifelong situations of oppression, Christians can remind one another within Christian community and in proclamations and witness in and to the world of the larger horizons of God's forgiving and reconciling love.

More specifically, we can also work within situations and experiences marked by bitterness and hatred by focusing on the ways in which people's anger can issue forth in prophetic judgment (as in the prophets, as well as in the Psalms and Revelation, and in Jesus' parables); in action designed to further God's merciful justice; in learning to pray not only the imprecatory laments, but also those that end with a prospect for reconciliation (e.g., contrast Psalm 137 with Psalm 25), not only the consignment of enemies to destruction but also prayers of the Church for their salvation. Even at this early stage where hatred of the impenitent enemy or enemies is more real than love, however, there should always be a hearty awareness of, and hopefully (re-?)learning a desire for, the salvation of those toward whom we are indignant and those toward whom we are engaged in prayer and action.[34]

Hence, I am arguing that *even if* God may eternally punish some or many of us, and *even if* God may wreak a decisive vengeance against wrongdoers, we are not allowed to endorse hatred, moral or otherwise, as a

---

comments suggest. However, the decisive difference remains that she seems to think that "moral hatred" can be the appropriate *telos* of some judgments, whereas I do not think it ought to be so.

34. This last comment draws on a claim made by Blaise Pascal about polemics. In one of his *Provincial Letters* he contends that polemics and ridicule ought to be ruled by a love that "inspires a hearty desire for the salvation of those whom we attack." See Pascal, *The Provincial Letters*, tr. A.J. Krailsheimer (New York: Penguin, 1967) letter 11, p. 172. I am indebted to Jim Buckley for this reference. See the discussion of Pascal in chapter 1 of Buckley's *Seeking the Humanity of God* (Collegeville: Liturgical, 1992).

normatively good response to sin or wrongdoing. This is even true if the sinner or wrongdoer remains persistently impenitent. We are called to "love our enemies." Still, we ought to recognize that even this call, part of the way of life of forgiveness, may involve a phenomenally difficult struggle. We should not trivialize it as easily accomplished or suggest that it is always clear what such love entails, particularly in relation to the importance of accountability and punishment. So it is to such explorations that I turn in the next two sections.

Loving Enemies on the Path of Christian Forgiveness

Many of us tend to define our own lives more by whom we hate than by whom or what we love. This can be both because of resentment and hatred that arise from our encounters with, and perhaps our suffering at the hands of, real enemies; but we must also confront our temptations to *create* enemies as a way of preserving our own distorted identities or our presumptions of power.

However, Christians have tended to deny or repress either of these judgments. We have wanted to deny the reality of such hatred (or desires for revenge), believing that the call to forgive *requires* us to deny that reality in the name of love and forgiveness. This results in cheap grace with untransformed passions, thoughts, and actions. Hence, through a curious irony, which Nietzsche was quick to note, too many Christians (and others) have linked together a repressed hatred and an ideology of forgiveness. The results, unsurprisingly, are devastating for everybody concerned: for those who inflict suffering and those who suffer, and more broadly, for our communities and our politics.

By contrast, Christians ought to conjoin a clear recognition that there will be enemies, that is, people who are opponents of the crucified and risen Christ, with an acknowledgment that we are nonetheless called to love them. As I suggested in chapter 6, enemies are defined in the first instance by their unwillingness to live as forgiven and forgiving people, as people who seek to live in the light of God's reconciliation. They are people and political entities who seek vengeance rather than forgiveness, who seek to dominate and abuse rather than to repent and reconcile, who seek to repay violence with violence rather than with love, who seek vainglory rather than humility.

But if we fail to acknowledge truthfully who they are and what they are doing, then we cheapen forgiveness and, indeed, may perpetuate or exacerbate the cycles of violence and vengeance. The path of forgiveness cannot be authentic unless there is truthful moral and political judgment. Of course that means, in the first instance, acknowledging the senses in which all of us have been, and to some extent still are, enemies of God. That is what it means to repent daily, to continue to unlearn the patterns of sin and evil as we seek to become holy people.

But it is also not to lapse into a moral equivalence in which all of us are taken to be sinners and hence equally incapable of discernment or accountability. As I argued throughout Part II, we must exercise truthful judgment, but we must do so from the standpoint of those who have been forgiven, who know what it means to have been an enemy. And though it may be painful to acknowledge, it is important to recognize that there are those — sometimes those close to us — who nonetheless act as enemies toward us. As such, we must avoid the temptation to want to see only the good in others, particularly those who are close to us.

Even so, we are nonetheless called to *love* those enemies. That is, we are not permitted to allow our anger at those enemies to ossify into hatred, into a persistent desire for their diminishment or destruction. To do so would be to return to complicity in sin. That feelings of hatred and vengeance might surface and might be real is undeniable; but they need to be struggled against. For the habit of hatred and the desire for vengeance not only perpetuate the cycles of violence; they also constrict and thereby distort the vision of the hater.[35] And they tempt us to create enemies or to foster new fantasies about our already existing enemies so that we can feel better about ourselves. Most decisively, we are called to love enemies because that is what we have experienced as the enemies of God — a love that is capable of transforming enemies into friends. As Martin Luther King, Jr., suggested, "We must love our enemies, because only by loving them can we know God and experience the beauty of his holiness."[36]

35. This is one of the problems that afflicts Hazel Motes in Flannery O'Connor's *Wise Blood* (see chapter 5 above).

36. King, "Loving Your Enemies," in *Strength to Love* (Philadelphia: Fortress, 1963) p. 53. King's sermon is instructive at a number of points, though he makes forgiveness an instance within the task of loving enemies rather than setting the call to love one's enemies within forgiveness as a way of life. In one sense, this is simply an indication that King thought of forgiveness only as a word spoken or as a single, identifiable action; however, it might also have been an indication of his awareness of the persistence of brokenness that made reconciliation seem rather distant and loving enemies the more proximate possibility to be struggled for. This is a relatively early sermon, but King's

If we classify people simply as enemies, and indeed as enemies whom we are permitted to hate, then we prematurely condemn or abandon them. To be sure, there are extreme test cases of the judgment that we ought not to condemn or abandon any human being as beyond the scope of redemption (either God's redemption or our moral and political redemption). Hitler and the Nazis readily come to mind, as do a number of serial killers and (particularly as I write this) the people responsible for genocides in Bosnia and Rwanda. With such people and political entities it is certainly easier to make the case that they have "rotted" beyond any reclamation than it is to suggest that repentance and forgiveness are possible. Even so, if we condemn or abandon them we fail to recognize that, no matter how scarred their humanity, no matter how distorted their visage as a result of wounds inflicted or suffered (or self-inflicted), those enemies are human beings — and human beings created in the image of God and loved as children of God.

It is certainly true that many enemies have habits of domination, abuse, and violence that they refuse to abandon — or, even if they indicate a desire to unlearn them through new habits, they may have considerable difficulty in doing so. However, we must prepare ourselves for the possibility of their authentic repentance and for an openness to the prospect of a *new* humanity, of a trust in the Spirit who — by the power of the crucified and risen Christ — is making all things new. We do so by struggling and learning to love our enemies. As those who know what it means to be the prodigal children, so also we need to struggle to love our enemies by placing ourselves in the position of the forgiving parents.

At the least we learn to love them by giving up our desires for vengeance, by learning (through prayer — perhaps initially through the power of others praying for them in our stead, and through other practices) to wish them well. Such a wish might well include a recognition that one's, or one's people's, survival may require not being able, or even desiring, to be in those enemies' presence any more. We also earn to love them by engaging in lament, by prophetically calling them to account, by showing them an alternative way of life. Such an alternative form of power is found in Easter and Pentecost.

Unfortunately, we too often have difficulty in loving our enemies

---

doubts about the possibility of repentance by the "enemies" of the gospel, in this instance those who persisted in advocating racial separation, intensified toward the end of his life. More than thirty years later, in the midst of resurgent racism and renewed despair about the prospects for reconciliation on both sides, King's caution — and indeed his intensifying doubts — are prescient.

precisely because we are afraid they *might* repent. Such was Jonah's problem. Called by God to go and "cry out" against the people of Nineveh (enemies of the Israelites) for their great wickedness, Jonah flees for Tarshish. God sends him to the belly of a great fish, where Jonah, in great distress, seems to repent. So God calls him again to go to Nineveh, and this time he goes. Alas, they repent, hoping that God "will relent and change his mind," that God will "turn from his fierce anger" (Jonah 3:9). And God does reconcile with the Ninevites.

This makes Jonah quite angry. He was afraid that they would repent. He tells God that he fled at the beginning because "I knew that you are a gracious and merciful God, slow to anger, abounding in continual love, and ready to relent from punishing." And so, he concludes, "Lord, take my life from me. It is better for me to die than live" (Jonah 4:2-3). Jonah is unable to cope with the loss of his enemies, with the fact that his prophetic proclamation has actually produced repentance. He would rather die than face a gracious God and the Ninevites as potential friends. The story ends with the sharp contrast between Jonah, whose hostility is causing him to shrivel, and God, whose mercy reflects an expansive love.

By contrast, other people stand as a remarkable testimony to the redemptive power of loving enemies. Martin Luther King's struggles throughout the Civil Rights movement in the U.S. represent a powerful example, as do Archbishop Oscar Romero's struggles in the midst of divisions in El Salvador. There are also the countless witnesses of unnamed exemplars, people who have testified to the possibility and the power of God through their love of enemies who have often done horrifying things. Many of the stories are unknown; but others have been passed on.

For example, there is the tale of a remarkable Armenian woman in the early part of this century. The Armenian people have suffered horribly through the centuries, particularly in a Turkish-led genocide in the early part of the twentieth century. And yet from the Armenian Church comes the following story:

A Turkish officer raided and looted an Armenian home. He killed the aged parents and gave the daughters to the soldiers, keeping the eldest daughter for himself. Some time later she escaped and trained as a nurse. As time passed, she found herself nursing in a ward of Turkish officers. One night, by the light of a lantern, she saw the face of this officer. He was so gravely ill that without exceptional nursing he would die. The days passed, and he recovered. One day, the doctor stood by the bed with her and said to him, "But for her devotion to you, you would be dead."

He looked at her and said, "We have met before, haven't we?" "Yes," she said, "we have met before." "Why didn't you kill me?" he asked. She replied, "I am a follower of him who said 'Love your enemies.'"[37]

Geoffrey Wainwright's comment on this story is apposite: The story provides a "shining example of what Herbert Butterfield meant when he said that it is impossible to measure the vast difference that ordinary Christian piety has made to the last two thousand years of history."[38]

Another shining example is found in the story, told by Jon Sobrino, of a small card placed on the altar during a celebration of All Souls Day in a refuge in San Salvador.

> Around the altar on that day there were various cards with the names of family members who were dead or murdered. People would have liked to go to the cemetery to put flowers on their graves. But as they were locked up in the refuge and could not go, they painted flowers round their names. Beside the cards with the names of family members there was another card with no flowers which read: "Our dead enemies. May God forgive them and convert them." At the end of the eucharist we asked an old man what was the meaning of this last card and he told us this: "We made these cards as if we had gone to put flowers on our dead because it seemed to us they would feel we were with them. But as we are Christians, you know, we believed that our enemies should be on the altar too. They are our brothers in spite of the fact that they kill us and murder us. And you know what the Bible says. It is easy to love our own but God asks us also to love those who persecute us."[39]

It is worth noting that both of the contexts from which these stories come, the Armenian and Salvadoran peoples, have a rich, albeit tragic, awareness of the place of martyrs within the Christian life. Such people are all too aware that the call to love one's enemies is closely linked to the invitation to lay down one's life for the sake of others.

These stories, and others like them, should be told not in order to induce guilt among those who find it more difficult and more troubling to learn to love their enemies. Rather, they should stir our imaginations that

37. The story is told in Wainwright, *Doxology*, p. 434. He, in turn, indicates that he provides it as he heard it in an address by Dr. Peter Stephens in 1978.

38. Wainwright, *Doxology*, p. 433. The reference is to Butterfield's *Christianity and History* (London: Bell, 1949) chapter 7.

39. Jon Sobrino, "Latin America: Place of Sin and Place of Forgiveness," *Concilium* 184 (1986) p. 50.

are too often constricted by a phony "realism" about what is possible and what is impossible. They point toward the power of God's Spirit to make and remake human life, even in situations that might otherwise seem hopeless.[40]

The call to love our enemies is difficult; it compels us to face the truth about others and yet to struggle to love them. But we are called to do so precisely because the horizon of our life, the call to embody forgiveness, is so much broader than simply the absolution of individual guilt. Set in the context of a lifelong commitment to healing the brokenness of our relationships, to learning to live in communion — with God, with one another, and with the whole Creation — the call to love our enemies is a call to faithful witness to the God who refused (and refuses) to abandon humanity as enemies but sought (and seeks) to transform us into friends.

Further, the very claim that forgiveness aims not simply at resolving individual guilt, but more determinatively at healing the effects of original sin understood as ruptured communion, means that we cannot neatly divide issues of forgiveness and justice into the spheres of the personal and private and of the political and public. In modernity, such a bifurcation has become so widespread as to be almost a commonplace: Individual persons (or churches, understood as agglomerations of individuals) forgive, but states seek justice.[41] Such divisions perpetuate the myth that Christian forgiveness is an ethic of weakness and consolation, far removed from the harsh realities and machinations of political power. From such a perspective, forgiveness in general and "love of enemies" in particular may temper

---

40. Cornel West's powerful diagnosis of a hopelessness in "black America," which in fact could be extended much more broadly, suggests precisely the need for a theologically informed political imagination that can envision such practices as "loving enemies" in the midst of brokenness. The goal remains reconciliation, and these practices provide a context for struggling against hopelessness and despair about the current realities. See West's "Nihilism in Black America," chapter 1 of *Race Matters* (Boston: Beacon, 1993) pp. 11-20.

41. The causes of this bifurcation are complex, and cannot be discussed in any detail in this context. In one sense, the whole of this book is an attempt to challenge this bifurcation and to relocate ethics and politics within the larger and more comprehensive vision of Christian theology, a vision that extends back to Augustine and, I would argue, to Scripture itself.

The claim that individuals forgive, and states seek justice, is explicitly articulated in the closing chapter of Susan Jacoby, *Wild Justice*. But it also underlies perspectives influenced by Reinhold Niebuhr. See particularly his *An Interpretation of Christian Ethics* (New York: Harper and Brothers, 1935).

the demands of the political world; but they cannot challenge the means by which power is exercised.

By contrast, the difference between the Church and the state, or more generally the Church and the world, lies not in a division of labor between private and public, nor is it even a sharp division of space into the "sacred" world of spirituality and the "secular" world of politics. Rather, the decisive difference involves contrasting visions of the appropriate exercise of power and the ends toward which that power ought to be exercised.[42] Indeed, a Christian articulation of the politics of forgiveness and reconciliation, specified particularly in the vocation of loving enemies on the path of such reconciliation, ultimately challenges the assumption that secular states represent genuinely public political life. As Rowan Williams has argued, in reference to Augustine's *The City of God,*

> It is all very well to talk about the public realm, about justice and commonalty; but, empirically speaking, the means employed to make a *coetus* of persons more than a chance aggregate consistently subvert true common life. It does not greatly matter whether or not we decide to accord the *name* of *res publica* to this or that political order: the reality of common or public life is not there. Unity will always be something imposed from outside rather than growing from within: and so it comes about that states need enemies.[43]

Hence, from this perspective the Church, insofar as it practices the politics of forgiveness and reconciliation, more closely approximates the genuinely public sense of what it means to be human. And as the Body of Christ engages in such "public" action, its members are also called to embody throughout their lives the politics of forgiveness and reconciliation.

As such, Christians involved in "loving enemies" should not abandon the exercise of social and political power, when such power is available.[44]

---

42. For an instructive example of this argument, see Pope John Paul II's encyclical "Dives in Misericordia," *Origins* 10/26 (December 11, 1980) pp. 402-416. He argues that mercy, and more specifically forgiveness, are absolutely crucial if justice is to occur.

43. Rowan Williams, "Politics and the Soul: A Reading of *The City of God,*" *Milltown Studies* 19/20 (1987) p. 62. Williams's essay provides an important corrective to many readings of "political Augustinianism" and shows what is at stake in Augustine's understanding of the possibilities and limits of "civic virtue."

44. This suggests the necessity of rethinking issues about the so-called "Constantinian" turn in the Church's history. It is a mistake, I think, to presume that Christians

This is so even though Christians ought to be wary of the potential for corruption in exercising power and so should attend very carefully to the forms in which it is available and to what is required of those who wield it. On the other hand, many circumstances in which people are called on to "love enemies" involve disparities of social and political power in which there may be little recourse except to "pray for those who persecute you" and to struggle against the prospect of continued suffering.[45] But there are also circumstances in which Christians are (or could be) in positions of power — both in the Church and in the world — in which "loving one's enemies" involves determining whether punishment ought to be invoked for the sake of justice, truthfulness, and faithful witness to a vision of communal life, and if so, what kind of punishment. Such power can corrupt Christians, as it tragically all too often has; but abuses of power and the potential dangers of power ought not preclude Christians from exercising power for the sake of the gospel.

Throughout our lives, the goal of our habits of thinking, feeling, and acting must remain reconciliation, the possibility and the promise of new life neither bound by the past nor condemned to repeat it. Even so, the path of forgiveness, which aims at reconciliation, nonetheless requires a call that enemies become accountable, repent of their evil, and take responsibility for their actions (even if, or perhaps as, they begin the process of learning to accept forgiveness for those actions). Indeed, in the Book of Jonah the sign that the Ninevites repented of their evil was a willingness to don sackcloth and ashes, to adopt a stance of penance for their wrongdoing. In diverse settings, circumstances, and lives, our enemies may or may not repent (in either the short term or in the long term); but we need to emphasize accountability and responsibility, whether our enemies repent or not.

That is, we should not assume that forgiveness and accountability are antithetical or even that the embodiment of forgiveness precludes punishment.[46] This is particularly the case with enemies who persistently fail to

---

should never exercise social and political power; however, it is also a mistake to assume that Christians will invariably use social and political power to serve Christian ends. What we need is far more extensive analysis of the appropriately Christian exercise of power understood in relation both to church governance and to other contexts of social and political life.

45. See, for example, Karen Lebacqz's analysis of situations of sexual abuse in her essay, "Love Your Enemy: Sex, Power, and Christian Ethics," *The Annual of the Society of Christian Ethics* (Washington: Georgetown University Press, 1990) pp. 3-23.

46. That such is the case can be seen in the extraordinary action of John Paul II,

repent. But the foregoing insistence on *loving* enemies as a part of the path of forgiveness also suggests that this path will carry with it a distinctive vision of the prospects and limits of punishment — both in the Church and in other social and political contexts. If we rule out the possibility of vengeance and suggest that desires simply for retribution are inadequate, how should we think about the role of punishment within the practice of loving enemies, and more generally within the call to embody forgiveness?

Punishment and the Politics of Forgiveness

There is an extensive literature analyzing and recommending specific attitudes toward and uses of punishment in both ecclesial and secular political contexts. The issues are complex, and specific judgments about the wisdom of this or that practice often require careful deliberations involving a variety of factors. Obviously, my analysis here cannot do more than touch the surface of issues that, indeed, would demand fuller treatment in a separate book. Nonetheless, indicating the contours of the appropriate uses of punishment is necessary to understand my Christian vision of the politics of forgiveness.

People committed to living truthfully and also to living peaceably in communion cannot avoid the (regrettable) necessity of some forms of disciplinary — perhaps coercive — action. Minimally, such action is required as a way of clarifying through disciplined practices what are and are not appropriate attitudes, judgments, and behaviors within the community. Hence the importance of identifying those who are enemies of the truth, who refuse to participate honestly and faithfully in the deliberations about the good of the community's life. Every sustainable community must have boundaries; practices of forgiveness and reconciliation, and more specifically of loving enemies, are designed to prevent those boundaries from becoming barriers that wall the community off into a self-enclosed enclave.

As with any political community, a viable and visible Church cannot — and should not — avoid the exercise of discipline. More specifically, the Church typically will need to deploy disciplinary action, in at least some

---

who went to an Italian prison to offer forgiveness to Mehmet Ali Agca, the man who had tried to assassinate him. But the Pope did not think that his declaration "I forgive you" meant that Agca should be released from prison. This stands in remarkable contrast to some declarations of forgiveness that suggest that forgiveness involves a complete abdication of punishment.

instances, designed to induce repentance for the sake of eventual reconciliation. The crucial questions, however, are (1) what attitudes, judgments,
or behaviors are deemed to require such disciplinary action (deliberations
that must be ongoing, particularly when they involve exclusion or punishment), and (2) how that disciplinary action is to be carried out so as to
minimize its dangers and to maximize its potential for reconciliation. In
both cases, the understandings ought to be more explicitly articulated and
practiced within the context of the Church, for there it should be assumed
by all that there are shared commitments and practices that provide the
appropriate context for deliberating about these issues.[47] At the same time,

47. Obviously, there are also several questions begged in this formulation — given
that actual instantiations of the Church involve disputes about precisely what those
"shared" practices are (and not all churches share in the "same" practices), and that
there are sharp divisions about what constitutes sin (note the divisive disputes about
abortion, homosexuality, etc.), among other things. In the midst of divisions both
ecclesial (i.e., "church dividing") and social (i.e., racism), the South African Lutheran
bishop Manas Buthelezi refers to the importance of "taking up the cross" (Matthew
10:38) and "bearing one another's burdens" (Galatians 6:2):

> For me this means that the depth of Christian unity is to be prepared to be one
> with the other person after he or she has become a burden to us. . . . Christ has
> become one with that which caused him pain. Similarly to follow in Christ's
> footsteps means to be one even with that person who causes us pain, just as
> Christ has come to be symbolized by the cross that was a burden to him. As far
> as the racist is concerned, I take this to mean that I should try to be one with
> him in love, even if it is unilateral, unreciprocated love and to continue to minister
> to him even while he carves for himself a racist church. This is a hard thing to
> do. I believe that it is for this reason that it is called the taking up of the cross
> and bearing one another's burden.

("Church Unity and Human Divisions of Racism," in Eckehart Lorenz [ed.], *The Debate
on Status Confessionis* [Geneva: Department of Studies, Lutheran World Federation,
1983] p. 19. I am indebted to Michael Root for directing me to this passage.) Such a
passage suggests that, even in the face of horrifying social and ecclesial divisions, there
is nonetheless in the Church a clearer context for how the debates and disputes *ought*
to be discerned, and how authority ought to be exercised — despite the sadly tragic
character of actually existing ecclesial realities.

To be sure, the Church exists only through the ongoing struggles of debates and
disputes about what we are called to be and do and what ought to be rejected and
excluded; in this sense, the Church is always in the process of learning what it is called
to be and do. But such realities are different from the sad, tragic character of so many
contemporary realities, where the judgments are typically — the witnesses of Buthelezi
and others notwithstanding — severely lacking in theological reflection (and an awareness of the necessity of repentance).

however, my arguments in chapter 7 suggest that the craft of forgiveness can produce appropriate analogies (understood from within a Christian context) for responding to both questions in other social and political contexts.[48]

There is a broad spectrum in which conclusions are reached about what attitudes, judgments, and behaviors are deemed to require disciplinary action and perhaps coercive action. Some actions are relatively settled: To identify something as murder and someone as having committed the murder is already to specify that coercive action is necessary in order to testify, albeit negatively, to the community's valuing of each and every human life.[49] By contrast, there is considerable dispute about whether, for example, homosexual practice is a "sin" in ecclesial contexts or a punishable "wrong" in other social and political contexts. As a result, all communities require specific practices of discernment, deliberation, and debate, practices that must guard against assuming either that all judgments are continually "up for grabs" or that genuinely unsettled debates can be prematurely foreclosed through the deployment of discipline or coercion.

From the perspective of Christian theology, any disciplinary action, and more specifically any practice of punishment, always involves a tragic risk. It may be necessary and unavoidable; even so, there is the danger that those who are punished will learn *only* the infliction of (physical or psychic) pain and domination, however minimal or short-term. As John Milbank has argued,

> Augustine was one of the first fully to appreciate that memory can be strongest when compounded of the traces of suffering. Thus although a

48. In such contexts we cannot assume, even counterfactually (as with the "Church"), that there is a shared set of beliefs, judgments, or practices that can produce a commonly accepted authority (except in a pragmatic sense, as defined within the political community) sufficient to adjudicate the disputes. Take, for example, the issue of war: Christian theology and ethics have long assumed that the presumption is in favor of peace. Both pacifism and just war, as particular theories, are articulated within this assumption (this despite the fact that many contemporary attitudes toward war among Christians reflect neither of these positions). By contrast, in other social and political contexts, there is nothing to rule out of bounds "blank check" theories, or even — at least in principle — "theories" that assert the harshest realities of brute power regardless of questions about the "legitimacy" of those in power.

49. Of course, whether a particular action counts as a "murder" is often much more difficult to determine. Hence the distinctions that have been developed within various legal traditions about how to differentiate murder from other forms of killing.

punishment may be subordinate to essentially persuasive purposes which are at variance with worldly *dominium,* Augustine fails to see that the duration of punishment has to be an interval of such *dominium,* for the lesson *immediately* and intrinsically taught here must be the power of one over another, and it is always possible that the victim will learn only this lesson, and build up a resentment which prevents him from seeing what the punishment was really trying to point out. Punishment is always a tragic risk.[50]

Hence, even in situations where punishment may be necessary and unavoidable, we must seek to minimize its exercise and the spheres of its operation. Its purposes should *never* be to create, perpetuate, or exacerbate disparities of power and domination (though this has too often been the case); the goal must remain the hope of reconciliation and new life.

That is why an appropriately Christian stance toward punishment must occur within the larger horizons of the practices of forgiveness and reconciliation, and more specifically within an understanding of the injunction to love one's enemies. Such a stance requires that we take seriously that both the offenders and the victims are human beings — indeed, human beings created in the image of God. So they cannot be unalterably condemned or abandoned; on the view developed here, capital punishment is unjustified and unjustifiable, whatever its popularity or its relation to retribution, deterrence, or (more troublingly) vengeance.

However, this is not to endorse a purely "moral education" theory of punishment, nor more decisively an account that suggests that rehabilitation is the *only* purpose served by punishment.[51] There is an element of retribution in the account I am suggesting: As there is responsibility in the offenses that have been committed, so punishment for the offenders requires that they accept such responsibility. In requiring this, the community must determine what responsibility is involved and hence what punishment is appropriate. Such retribution is, at least in principle, separable from any feelings of hatred or desires for vengeance. It is the community's insistence that the offenders not be allowed to get away with the offense, and hence it signifies a defeat for the offenders. In such cases, they are instructed to recognize the legitimacy of their punishment through a restoration of

---

50. Milbank, *Theology and Social Theory,* p. 420.

51. In what follows I am indebted to separate reflections by Rowan Williams and Michael Ignatieff in a symposium on imprisonment in *Theology* 95 (March/April 1992) pp. 88-96 and 97-102.

imbalances in power. As Jean Hampton comments, retributive punishment "has a *telos,* but the *telos* is not so much to produce good as it is to establish goodness."[52]

Similarly, a stress on deterrence emphasizes that offenses affect the whole community and serves as a negative reminder of the crucial significance of its vision of social order. There is, in this sense, an exemplary character to the punishment, reminding others of the importance of avoiding those sorts of wrongdoing for the sake of goodness.

Even so, both retribution and deterrence theories assume that such punishment is in and of itself sufficient. They fail to recognize the tragic risks involved because they deal primarily with offenses as such and do not adequately attend to the situation of either the offended or the offender. Further, neither theory adequately attends to the necessity of healing the brokenness that has been created or exacerbated by the offense(s). Even worse, a stress on retribution sometimes lapses into a desire simply that the offender "get theirs"; and a stress on deterrence sometimes places a premium on what is desirable for the community to learn, even if it means "making an example" of this or that particular offender.

It might appear that my argument about loving enemies and maintaining the goal of reconciliation ought to lead me to endorse rehabilitative theories of punishment. Indeed, Christians have often adopted such theories and, at times, such practices (and have thus been accused of being soft on crime and of conflating the personal with the political). But a view that maintains reconciliation as the *telos,* the context in which punishment is to be understood and carried out, is *not* necessarily a view that punishment exists for the sake of rehabilitation. At least in part, we punish in order to convey judgments about what is and is not appropriate behavior. As the great philosopher of law H. L. A. Hart has observed, the reason for having punishments for murder is that we do not want people being murdered, not that we want to see murderers "cured."[53]

Rehabilitation theories rightly recognize that offenders do not cease being part of the society that is punishing them, or more generally that they do not cease being part of the human community. Further, they rightly recognize that the goal ought to be reconciliation achieved through the reform and repentance of the offender. But we should not punish people, particularly through legal sanctions, *only* until they repent or are reformed

---

52. Murphy and Hampton, *Forgiveness and Mercy,* p. 126.

53. Cited in Williams, "Penance in the Penitentiary," *Theology* 95 (March/April 1992) p. 91.

(or, even more troubling, until they are *con*formed to the standards of those doing the punishing). One important danger of doing so is that offenders will be "treated," as if they are ill, and thus, rather than inducing a greater responsibility through repentance, the offenders' ability to accept responsibility for their actions will likely be diminished. Some purposes of punishment may be carried out effectively even if the primary goal of that punishment, which is reconciliation, cannot be fully achieved because the offender fails to repent and be reformed.

In this light, it would appear that a Christian understanding of punishment ought to include elements of retribution, deterrence, and rehabilitation theories. More strongly, however, Christian understandings and practices ought to challenge the adequacy of even thinking in terms of such theories; the aim ought to be the reform of actual practices of punishment within the context of a Christian vision of forgiveness and reconciliation.[54]

As such, all of us — Christians and non-Christians alike — need to do some serious rethinking about the ways in which people currently engage in discipline and punishment — ranging from ecclesial patterns of discipline to coping with clerical misconduct to patterns in the U.S. of "locking people up" as virtually the only means we have of dealing with wrongdoing. It is particularly worrisome that in the U.S. we seem to continue to "punish" people long after their terms are up; once a convict, always a convict in our eyes.[55] To be sure, there are "hardened" offenders who require extended punishment; but Christians also need to probe our willingness to accede to modern practices of discipline and punishment whose purposes are, when clear, more menacing than encouraging.[56] In this sense, it is little

54. Duncan Forrester offers some important suggestions along these lines in his "Punishment and Prisons in a Morally Fragmented Society," *Studies in Christian Ethics* 6/2 (1993) pp. 15-30. Forrester summarizes the work of an ongoing group of Christians and others who have been studying ways to reform the Scottish penal system. As the members of this group talked with people involved in the system — from politicians to administrators to prisoners to guards and other staff — they began to realize that the standard "theories" of punishment not only are often disconnected from the actual realities of punishment, but that they mask and distort our awareness of the practices. Forrester notes that the group concluded that there is an urgent need to restore forgiveness and reconciliation as the *telos,* and thus the only justification, for undertaking punishment.

55. Victor Hugo's *Les Miserables* and its musical adaptation present a powerful vision of the nihilism that underlies Javert's commitment that Valjean's punishment is a lifelong mark. Javert cannot bear Valjean's forgiveness and so ultimately must kill himself.

56. For an important (and unsettling) account of the emergence of modern practices of punishment, see Michel Foucault, *Discipline and Punish,* tr. Alan Sheridan (New York: Vintage, 1977).

wonder that modern prisons seem to be doing little more than creating greater senses of despair among their inmates and greater fears about crime among the general population.

Whenever we undertake the tragic risk of punishment, we cannot abdicate the task of seeing those who have become enemies as human beings who need and deserve our love — a love that holds open the possibility of reconciliation. This should be primarily, and in an exemplary fashion, found in the Church's practices. As Milbank suggests,

> The Church, while recognizing the tragic necessity of "alien," external punishment, should also seek to be an *asylum*, a house of refuge from its operations, a social space where a different, forgiving and restitutionary practice is pursued. This practice should also be "atoning," in that we acknowledge that an individual's sin is never his alone, that its endurance harms us all, and therefore its cancellation is also the responsibility of all.[57]

The Church ought to seek ways to extend to other social and political contexts this practice of loving enemies on the path of forgiveness and reconciliation. For example, this has been done by a group of Christians in Scotland who have produced a series of proposals for consideration by the Scottish criminal justice system.[58] By engaging in these activities, Christians bear witness to a vision of punishment whose goal remains reconciliation but that nonetheless confronts truthfully and clearly the seriousness of sin and evil in our midst. When possible, Christians ought to work within established social and political contexts to enhance the prospects of reconciliation and, at the very least, to minimize the deleterious effects of punishment's pain and domination. But in states or other political contexts committed to little more than the exercise of *dominium*, we may have little hope but to resort to prophetic denunciation and the struggle to discern — in the power of the Holy Spirit — other possibilities of faithful and, hopefully, effective response.[59] This was one of the difficult struggles in which Dietrich

---

57. Milbank, *Theology and Social Theory*, p. 422.

58. See Forrester, "Punishment and Prisons in a Morally Fragmented Society," and also the report by Chris Wood, *The End of Punishment: Christian Perspectives on the Crisis in Criminal Justice* (Edinburgh: CTPI and St. Andrew, 1991). Significantly, the group concluded that "a Church that presumes to speak on such matters must take the principles it commends to society seriously in its own life" (Forrester, p. 30).

59. Can such possibilities of response ever include recourse to the intentional deployment of "violence" or "killing," however restrained as an extension of coercion

Bonhoeffer found himself engaged in the midst of Nazi Germany and in which people regrettably must be engaged now in situations around the world.

We Christians are enjoined to love our enemies, and I have suggested that this is a crucial practice on the path of forgiveness and reconciliation. Despite the importance of acknowledging the power of anger in the work of forgiving love, and despite the fact that some people seem worthy of our moral hatred, we are not permitted either to hate or to condemn our enemies. Soteriological decisions are God's, not ours; our task is to love even our enemies, remaining open to — and perhaps even hoping for — their repentance (even as we must continually repent) and for the possibility of reconciliation.

We ought not trivialize the difficulties entailed in learning to love our enemies; even reaching that far on the path of forgiveness and reconciliation, learning to give up desires for vengeance and to wish the other person well, may require considerable struggle. At the same time, however, we should not limit our imaginations of what God's Spirit can do by focusing on what is realistically "possible."

Learning to love our enemies involves personal as well as political judgments, and it is as applicable to our relations with others in small-scale human associations and in the Church as it is in other social and political contexts. We are most clearly enjoined to engage in the practice through our commitments in the Church; however, appropriate analogies can and must also be drawn for our engagements in the world.

Learning to love our enemies is, however, often a counter-cultural practice. Indeed, in many contemporary contexts, where people are habituated into — and in fact rewarded for — hating their enemies and desiring vengeance, Christians must offer a counter-habituation. It must involve learning the habits and practices necessary to resist the desire for revenge, and struggling to have those desires transformed by God's Spirit into desires for love.

Throughout the craft of forgiveness, and in our practice of loving enemies, we are involved in learning to become holy through seeking to

---

and perhaps even marked by a "love" of enemies and neighbors — even if, as Paul Ramsey suggested, it might be an "alien work of love"? Such a question raises large issues that cannot be resolved here; an adequate means of dealing with these issues would require treatment in a separate book.

heal broken relations. Given the persistence of sin and evil in our midst, that often involves difficult discernment in the power of the Spirit. However, it also compels us to ask one final question: Are there some people, who — at least in this life and in this world — are unforgivable? In the final analysis, what kind of story do — or perhaps should — we tell?

9 Is This a Story to Pass On?

Forgiveness, Holiness, and the Politics of Memory

IN HER HAUNTING NOVEL *Beloved,* Toni Morrison focuses on the heart-rending brokenness of slavery and its chilling aftermath. Set in rural Ohio several years after the Civil War, the novel chronicles the life of Sethe, a woman who escaped from slavery but is unable to escape from its heritage and its effects. Sethe is haunted by life on every level, from the destructive attacks on her flesh to the imprints of that abuse left on her soul. While a slave, she was been beaten and raped, separated from her husband and other loved ones, and treated like an animal. After she has struggled to flee the circumstances of her slavery with her children, Sethe sees some white men coming to take her back. Indeed, their arrival is described in apocalyptic terms: There are four men coming on horseback, and they plan to take her back on a borrowed mule. The ominous presence of evil is not hard to detect.

Sethe is unable to face a return to such a life; even more, she refuses to return her children to such a life. She wants to take them "through the veil, out, away, over there where no one could hurt them."[1] So, in order to prevent their return, Sethe kills her own infant child by slitting her throat. Once the men see this, they realize that they have no use for a deranged woman, and so they leave her alone. But the black folk in the community

---

1. Toni Morrison, *Beloved* (New York: Plume, 1987) p. 163. Further references will be given parenthetically in the text.

279

also are afraid of a woman who would kill her own child, and they leave her alone as well.

Sethe is haunted by her past, both by what has been done to her and by what she has done. Her past takes particular form in a young woman who appears out of nowhere and is first seen sitting on a stump. More specifically, the young woman seems to be the ghost of that child, Beloved. Sethe desperately wants to figure out how to love this girl, and it is clear that the girl wants to "be loved." But the effects of Sethe's past prevent her from being able to imagine any future, much less one different from the past. "To Sethe, the future was a matter of keeping the past at bay" (p. 42). But even that was no easy task. For Sethe knows that her brain is devious and that memories have a way of coming back whether we want them to or not. Indeed, the memories have a life of their own. So Sethe's life is marked by the endless yet unsuccessful task of trying to prevent those memories from working their way into her life. For Sethe, every day involved the "serious work of beating back the past" (p. 73).

A part of Sethe would like to die, except that she knows that death is "anything but forgetfulness." She is "suspended between the nastiness of life and the meanness of the dead" (pp. 3-4). The scars on her body and the distorted (and distorting) love that compelled her to kill and maim her children rather than see them returned to slavery have also scarred her soul. All of her energy is spent in trying to keep the past at bay; there are no other options, no sense of tomorrow. She has no room in her brain for the future, no time to imagine (p. 72).

Toward the end of the novel, the pain of that collapsed time comes home to Sethe. Her pain is identified to her by Paul D, an escaped slave whose own life is marked by physical pain and a scarred soul. He has, the narrator tells us, a "tobacco tin buried in his chest where a red heart used to be. Its lid rusted shut" (pp. 72-73). He tells Sethe, "me and you, we got more yesterday than anybody. We need some kind of tomorrow" (p. 273). But it seems that this sense of tomorrow is what Sethe, Paul D, and Beloved are condemned *never* to have.

On the next two pages, the concluding pages of the novel, the narrator contrasts a loneliness "that can be rocked" with a loneliness "that roams." Such roaming has no purpose, no narrative shape for the journey, no destiny to live for and move toward. And so, the narrator tells us, this was and is "not a story to pass on." Indeed, we are told this three times in those concluding pages (pp. 274-275). The cumulative effect of the novel and of this recurring phrase is a harrowing and haunting sense of the hells to which many people are condemned in *this* life.

In what sense, then, can we speak of forgiveness in relation to such horrifying evils and suffering, to such pervasive darkness, to such profound brokenness? Here we return to the themes of chapter 3 and ask whether forgiveness has been already, or is now being, eclipsed in the midst of such tragedy? Is it possible that even the holiness of Kolbe, the priest in Mac-Millan's *Orbit of Darkness*, is insufficient as a response to the evils of holocausts and genocides, slavery and poverty? Are there people who are — or ought to be — unforgivable? More generally, should the existence of such realities lead us to question whether there is a good and gracious, indeed, forgiving God who is worthy of worship?

In order to explore these questions anew, now on the far side of the constructive proposal developed in chapters 4 through 8, I turn to the question of forgiveness and evil in three interrelated steps. I do so first by exploring whether there may be some specific situations, people, or actions that ought to be understood as *unforgivable*. Specifically, I analyze Simon Wiesenthal's famous story *The Sunflower* and the symposium that follows the story. Then, in a second section, I take up the question, posed most poignantly by Ivan Karamazov in Fyodor Dostoevsky's *The Brothers Karamazov*, whether such evils are too high a price to pay for the world's harmony. That is, rather than trusting in God's forgiveness, should we not reject the goodness of God and instead simply express our protest and our outrage against God? Finally, I suggest the links between forgiveness and holiness as the Christian way of responding to, or, more appropriately, of living with, the painful memories and shattered hopes of our lives.

In each of the three sections of this chapter, I return to the phrase with which Morrison so powerfully focuses our attention: This is "not a story to pass on." In each section, I suggest a different way of understanding that phrase. I conclude by suggesting that, while there is no one reading that can determinatively override the others (at least on this side of the Kingdom, if the promises of God are to be fulfilled and shown worthy of our hope and trust), the most truthful way to live in this world is to embody the costliness of God's forgiveness through holy living.

This Is *Not* a Story to *Pass On*: Simon Wiesenthal's *The Sunflower*

In some sense, by the end of the chronicle of Sethe's life and of her encounters with Beloved, we reach the judgment that this is *not* a story to *pass on*. This is ironic, since the words come at the conclusion of the story, after it has, in fact, been passed on by the teller of the tale. Even so, there is a sense in which we reach this judgment despite the importance of telling the story and despite the lessons that must be learned from it. We do so because the memories are too painful for us to tell through the generations. We have to tell it, because we cannot forget it and because we cannot afford to forget it.

At the same time, however, it is *not* a story to pass on, because there is nothing positive to be gained from passing it on. We learn only the horrifying effects of slavery's past and their bearing on our identities in the present. Further, the story should not be passed on because some readers and hearers might as likely be inflamed with anger against Sethe as inspired to have compassion for her. As a result, we cannot avoid telling the story, but neither, at least in this sense, can we find the forgiveness that enables the healing of memories and the enabling of new life in the future.

Similar judgments have been offered about other horrifying evils. Many Jews have emphasized that we must "Never forget!" the Holocaust, a slogan that rings true to other people who have suffered intensely. At the same time, however, there is also the difficult task of learning to remember well. Simply insisting on the importance of remembering the past is not enough; we may need to tell about such events, situations, and lives, but to what purpose? Those who suffered from the evils, whose bodies continue to bear the marks of their suffering and whose souls have been numbed by pain, may actually be condemned to struggle with memories that have a life of their own, making each day's most serious task that of beating back the past.

Further, there is the danger that remembrance may become a form of vengeance. So, for example, in reflecting on contemporary Israeli politics, Amos Elon writes:

> I have lived in Israel most of my life and have come to the conclusion that where there is so much traumatic memory, so much pain, so much memory innocently or deliberately mobilized for political purposes, a little forgetfulness might finally be in order. This should not be seen as a banal plea to "forgive and forget." Forgiveness has nothing to do with it. While remembrance is often a form of vengeance, it is also, paradoxically, the basis of reconciliation. What is needed, in my view, is a shift in emphasis and proportion, and a new equilibrium in Israeli political life between memory and hope.[2]

2. Amos Elon, "The Politics of Memory," *The New York Review of Books* 40

Why does Elon think "forgiveness has nothing to do with it"? Presumably because what the Nazis did is *unforgivable*. George Steiner's perspective seems representative:

> Only those who actually passed through hell, who survived Auschwitz after seeing their parents flogged to death or gassed before their own eyes (like Elie Wiesel), or who found their own kin amid the corpses from which they had to extract gold teeth, a daily encounter at Treblinka, can have the right to forgive. *We* do not have that right. This is an important point, often misunderstood. What the Nazis did in the camps and torture chambers is wholly unforgivable, it is a brand on the image of man and will last; each of us has been diminished by the enactment of a potential sub-humanity latent in all of us. But if one did not undergo the thing, hate or forgiveness are spiritual games — serious games no doubt — but games none the less. The best *now*, after so much has been set forth, is, perhaps, to be silent; not to add the trivia of literary, sociological debate, to the unspeakable.[3]

In the wake of such judgments as Elon's and Steiner's, the question seems to be pressed with renewed urgency: Given the situations, experiences, and lives the Nazis (or white slaveowners, or Bosnian Serbs, or Oklahoma City bombers, or . . .) imposed and impose on our collective memories, how should we respond? Is this *not* a story, or more accurately, are these *not* stories, to *pass on?* Should we not be silent, even as we struggle neither to forget nor to remember? Or should we seek to remember well, recognizing that in such remembrance lies the possibility of both vengeance and reconciliation? Can we remember well without some form of forgiveness?

Such questions are at the heart of Simon Wiesenthal's struggle in his autobiographical tale *The Sunflower*.[4] Wiesenthal, an educated Jew, was caught in the web of the Nazi terror; as his tale begins, he is an inmate in

---

(October 7, 1993) p. 5. Earlier in the same essay, Elon comments on how people have used the claims of memory, and more specifically of remembering the Holocaust, in ways that prevent them from recognizing the legitimate suffering and claims to self-determinations of others — specifically Arabs (see pp. 3-4). Such an observation carries with it extremely important implications for how memories of victimization, when coupled with (perhaps newly found) political power, can create explosive (rather than redemptive) politics.

3. George Steiner, *Language and Silence* (New York: Atheneum, 1967) p. 163.

4. New York: Schocken, 1976. Further citations will be given parenthetically in the text.

a concentration camp in Poland. He is part of a work detail sent from the camp to do cleanup work in a makeshift hospital for wounded German soldiers in a building that was once the school that Wiesenthal attended. Along the way, Wiesenthal notices a cemetery for deceased Germans; he notices that each grave has a sunflower on it. For Wiesenthal, the sunflower signifies many contrasts between the fate of deceased Nazis and his anticipated fate and those of Jews like him: individual graves, decorated with sunflowers, or mass graves, unmarked and unmarkable? Continual connections to the living world or a loss of all such connection (see p. 20)?

On arriving at the hospital, Wiesenthal is ordered by a nurse, indeed a nun, to follow her into the building. He is taken down the hallways and brought into a room where he encounters a dying Nazi, a twenty-one-year-old SS man named Karl. Karl's body is wrapped in bandages, which cover even his eyes and head, and he is barely able to speak. Yet before he dies he wants to confess a crime that has been "torturing" his memory (pp. 32, 55), and more specifically he wants to confess to a Jew. He wants to confess his shame at having become a Nazi. Even more, he wants to confess a particular episode in which he has killed a family that was trying to flee a building crammed with hundreds of Jews, to which the Nazis had set fire. He could not get that family's faces out of his mind; he even covers his blinded eyes as he retells the episode to Wiesenthal. Indeed, Karl has suffered his mortal wounds in a later battle, a battle in which he could not bring himself to shoot another group of Jews, seeing instead the faces of that first family. As those faces prevented him from shooting again, a shell exploded by his side causing his blindness and, eventually, his death.

As Simon listens to Karl's story, he is simultaneously attracted to the authenticity of Karl and repelled by the horrifying tale he is telling. Indeed, Simon's thoughts continually return to the sunflowers, signifying the different worlds of dying Nazis and Jews. As Karl confesses, Simon does not leave; but neither does he speak. Simon has no doubt that Karl's confession reflects "true repentance"; Karl indicates that he wants to die "in peace" and that he has "longed to talk about [his crime] to a Jew and beg forgiveness from him" (p. 57). Simon is moved by Karl's repentance, yet he concludes that the contrast between the dying Nazi and the doomed Jew is too great; "between them there seemed to rest a sunflower. At last I made up my mind and without a word I left the room" (p. 58).

Yet Simon is troubled, indeed haunted, by questions about what he did or failed to do. When he returns to the camp, he asks his fellow inmates what they would have done. After the war ends, he takes the time to go to see Karl's mother, wanting to find out from her more about Karl's character. The mother's words confirm Simon's judgment about the truthfulness of Karl's confession and the sincerity of his repentance. Yet Simon is also troubled by the lack of remorse shown by most of the Nazis who were brought to trial after the war. And so, at the end of the tale, Simon continues to wonder: "Ought I to have forgiven him?" (p. 98).

He notes that there are many kinds of silence, and he wonders whether his own silence was perhaps more eloquent than words might have been. He also indicates that "only the sufferer is qualified to make the decision" concerning forgiveness. Even so, while his own eloquent telling of the tale seems to endorse Steiner's conclusion about the impossibility of forgiveness and the significance of silence, he also is haunted by the question of forgiveness. He is haunted, perhaps, by the sense that this is *not* a story to pass on, but that it nonetheless is a story that needs to be told if we are to be able to have a future that can remember the past well (and, thereby, not repeat the past's destructiveness).

Finally, then, Wiesenthal addresses a question to the reader of his tale: "You, who have just read this sad and tragic episode in my life, can mentally change places with me and ask yourself the crucial question, 'What would I have done?'" (p. 99). The question is posed to each of us, and in an extraordinary symposium that follows the story, thirty-two prominent intellectuals — Jews, Christians, and nonbelievers, poets and novelists as well as lawyers, rabbis, priests, and theologians — respond to the question. Not surprisingly, the responses reveal a wide variety of judgments, raise diverse themes and issues, and at times reflect substantial confusion about how the issues ought to be addressed.

Several of the responses focus, as does Wiesenthal's friend Josek in the story itself, on whether Simon would have a *right* to forgive Karl for offenses committed against other people. Only the victims, they assert, have such a right. Others focus on the dangers of "cheap grace," articulated perhaps most powerfully by Herbert Marcuse: "One cannot, and should not go around happily killing and torturing and then, when the moment has come, simply ask, and receive, forgiveness. In my view, this perpetuates the crime" (p. 170).

Perhaps the strongest objection to the prospect for forgiveness comes from Cynthia Ozick, who argues that forgiveness can "brutalize" just as vengeance does. Indeed, she suggests that "forgiveness is pitiless. It forgets the victim. It negates the right of the victim to his own life. It blurs over suffering and death. It drowns the past. It cultivates sensitiveness toward the murderer at the price of insensitiveness toward the victim" (p. 187). And so, she concludes, moral responsibility and the moral significance of just vengeance require that the SS man die unshriven, that he "go to hell" (p. 190).

Each of these responses has moral power and ought not to be glossed over. Ultimately, I do not think they are persuasive, at least not if one understands forgiveness as I have been suggesting in this book. However, in order to say how my account of forgiveness might bear on Wiesenthal's tale and thus to respond to the fear that this is *not* a story to pass on, we need to attend to some ambiguities within the story itself and within the circumstances of Wiesenthal's situation.

As several of the respondents make clear, the question Wiesenthal asks at the end of his story, "What would I have done?" or even the normative "what *should* I have done?" cannot be asked in the abstract. In the first place, as John Oesterreicher points out, an honest answer cannot suggest what I *would* have done, but only what I *hope* I would have had the *courage* to do (see pp. 176-177). Further, there are crucial differences in asking how Wiesenthal could have been expected to respond *at that time,* namely a time when he is virtually powerless as a man probably condemned to die a cruel death, and how he might have responded had the circumstances of power (and of attitudes toward the future) been different. At that time the sunflowers created worlds of difference; in different circumstances, perhaps after the war, perhaps in a different social and political environment, the worlds of Simon and Karl might not have been so different.

More decisively, however, we need to distinguish the question of what Wiesenthal, as a Jew, would or should have done from what "I" as a Christian would have to say. And even then, a further distinction must be pressed: between what a Jew might have said in that circumstance, what a Christian might (or, as I shall argue, should not) say *to* a Jew who was in that circumstance, and what a Christian might say in an "analogous" circumstance.

Wiesenthal is right to see in his own silence something significant. He may not have explicitly forgiven Karl, but neither did he explicitly refuse such forgiveness. His silence may have disappointed Karl, but surely it was more "redemptive" than some words he could have said in response.[5] Even

---

5. Such silence recalls Dietrich Bonhoeffer's suggestion that, in this time between the times, we need to have an appropriate sense of when nothing ought to be said. See the discussion in chapter 1 above and the discussion of "redemptive silence and speech" in chapter 6. Perhaps, in the spirit of the significance of touching people in the service of forgiveness and healing, Karl would have been less disappointed had Simon touched him; a brief clasping of the hand might have been appropriate. However, that might have been no less difficult or objectionable for Simon in that situation.

so, Milton Konvitz suggests — albeit with the benefit of time and distance from the event, and without judging the narrator — that "in this encounter the spirit of the Jewish tradition called upon the narrator to say to Karl" the following:

> I cannot speak for your victims. I cannot speak for the Jewish people. I cannot speak for God. But I am a man. I am a Jew. I am commanded, in my personal relations, to act with compassion. I have been taught that if I expect the Compassionate One to have compassion on me, I must act with compassion toward others. I can share with you, in this hour of your deep suffering, what I myself have been taught by my teachers: "Better is one hour of repentance in this world than the whole life of the world to come" (Avot, IV, 17). "Great is repentance, for it renders asunder the decree imposed upon a man" (Babylonian Talmud, Rosh Hashana, 17b). It is not in my power to render to you the help that could come only from your victims, or from the whole of the people of Israel, or from God. But insofar as you reach out to *me,* and insofar as I can separate myself from my fellow Jews, for whom I cannot speak, my broken heart pleads for your broken heart: Go in peace. (p. 160)

Such words are perhaps the best way, at least in Konvitz's judgment, for a Jew to transform redemptive silence into redemptive speech. Had Simon said these words, he would not have explicitly forgiven Karl, but he also would have showed compassion (and, hence, a refusal of vengeance) that signified the prospect of a future not bound by the destructiveness of the past.

What would, or should, a Christian say to a Jew who was in Wiesenthal's situation? Martin Marty is right to counsel silence. He writes, "Non-Jews and perhaps especially Christians should not give advice about Holocaust experience to its heirs for the next two thousand years. And then we shall have nothing to say. . . . Cheap instant advice from a Christian would trivialize the lives and deaths of millions" (p. 173). The same would hold for cheap advice that Christians not involved in the situation might offer to innocent sufferers anywhere, from Bosnians and Rwandans to contemporary Palestinians to victims of abuse and other violent offenses.[6] In such situations, we ought to recognize the importance of knowing what *not* to say.

6. Indeed, Elias Chacour indicated in conversation that one of the most difficult things for Palestinian Christians to hear is such "cheap, instant advice" from European and American Christians: "Why don't you just forgive the Israelis?"

Even so, Marty is also right to suggest that a Christian in an "analogous" situation ought to be searching for the possibility of grace, for the prospect of discovering and even creating signs of forgiveness. In some sense, this is what Konvitz was suggesting for Jews. But a Christian in a similar situation is empowered and even commanded to act for God in the process of forgiveness (or in determining that, if there is no repentance, the fullness of forgiveness must, contingently at least, be "withheld" for the sake of future reconciliation). This cannot be cheap grace, nor can it involve a trivialization of the victims, nor can it be an excuse to forget rather than remember.

Even so, a Christian might be encouraged to offer a response such as the following (an analogue to Konvitz's response):

> I cannot speak for your victims. However, I am called on to speak to you as a child of God, and as such I am empowered as a disciple of Jesus Christ to pronounce forgiveness in God's name. Indeed, I am commanded, in my personal relations, to act with compassion and forgiveness. I have been taught that if I expect the Compassionate and Forgiving God to have compassion on, and forgiveness for, me, I must act with compassion and forgiveness toward others. I see your repentance, and in that repentance I hear your genuine resolve to create a future that is not bound by the destructiveness of the past and to be able to die in peace. It is not in my power to render to you the help that could come only from your victims. Indeed, Christians are called to seek forgiveness and reconciliation not only from God but also in direct encounter with those whom we have offended. In this situation, you are not able to repair the damage that you have done, since your victims have died. There are, however, opportunities through which — were you to continue living — you might manifest your forgiven-ness, and the seriousness of your repentance, to others: through a willing acceptance of the justice of some sort of punishment (for the sake of retribution, deterrence, and rehabilitation), restitution to the victims' families, joining in the struggles against injustice and for reconciliation in other situations, and learning to show compassion and forgiveness with others whom you meet. I cannot speak for your victims — and, perhaps, I cannot even speak for myself — but in the name of God I embrace you, and I tell you: "Your sins are forgiven. Go in peace, to love God and your neighbor, and sin no more. May the peace of Christ be with you forevermore."

I recognize that such words may sound offensive to some victims; they are difficult to write, much less to say. Further, this is not advice I give to any innocent sufferers, much less an argument that Christians are *commanded* to say this (or something like this) in any specific situation. Among many issues, the craft of forgiveness requires a recognition of the struggles people have both in discerning the appropriate times, places, and contexts (including the disparities in power that may make any response problematic) in which redemptive silence and speech can be offered, and in developing the capacities whereby our words, emotions, and actions may be unified in a genuine desire for reconciliation.

Even so, I think words such as these do indicate the most appropriate response for Christians to make to situations even of extreme brokenness. They suggest a way of taking the past seriously, yet struggling to witness to the freedom that God has created for a new and renewed future. That is, our responses need to take seriously the ambivalence of wanting — but not being able — to forget, and of wanting — but not being able — to remember well.

In this sense, then, Christians ought to diverge from both Elon's and Steiner's suggestion that forgiveness is not a crucial issue in responding to situations like the Holocaust. Despite the power and insight of each of their accounts of the politics of memory, and the centrality of those who suffer, Christians have different resources on which to draw to suggest that forgiveness sets the context for a way of remembering the past for the sake of reconciliation. To be sure, Elon and Steiner are right to reject "cheap" views of forgiveness, including the tendency to equate forgiving with forgetting as well as the ways in which some accounts and enactments of forgiveness trivialize (or ignore) the victims and offer cheap grace. Yet, at least for Christians, the call to embody authentic forgiveness provides a lifelong context for remembering, not in a spirit of vengeance, but in the Spirit of the One who is making all things new.

In this sense, stories such as Sethe's and Wiesenthal's are nonetheless stories that can and should be passed on. They should be passed on by the communities who have suffered, for the sake of those communities and for us all. They should be because they show people who, despite their suffering, and despite their struggles, nonetheless have persevered. And, in that sense, they have provided a glimpse not simply of the horrifying evils of the past but also, at least analogously, of the life-giving power of the Spirit. In that sense, these are stories that can help us learn to remember well.

But is such remembrance possible, particularly for those who suffer? How might a Christian address Sethe, for whom the difficulty is precisely that she cannot avoid remembering the pain of slavery and, worse, cannot come to terms with her own act of "love" by which she killed her own child?

Or how might a Christian address Wiesenthal, for whom the memory of the concentration camps and of his own silence in response to Karl continue to haunt him rather than give *him* peace? These are perhaps the most troubling questions because they raise questions not so much about whether particular people can or ought to be forgiven but, indeed, whether even the Spirit is capable of making "all things" new.

That is, the Christian understanding of the Triune God presumes a narrative context, a context that begins with a peaceable Creation and is promised to "end" with the consummation of God's Kingdom in the endless harmony of praise and joy. But the rupture in the lives of people such as Sethe and Wiesenthal presents a challenge to beliefs that our stories, whatever they may be, can or should be located within a larger, comprehensive story of the Triune God. In other words, does the existence of horrifying evils and of the stories that remind us of those evils suggest instead that there is no coherent story, that there is no ultimate harmony — or that if there is such a harmony, Ivan Karamazov is right that "too high a price" has been paid for it?

This Is *Not a Story* to Pass On: Ivan Karamazov's Protest

A more radical rendering of Sethe's life and of the phrase that recurs in the conclusion of *Beloved* is to suggest that the real crisis is that hers is *not-a-story*. That is, it cannot be told in the normal narrative style of beginning, middle, and end. For there is no "end" for Sethe, either in the sense of a conclusion (even death will not bring "forgetfulness" or "healing") or in the sense of a *telos*, a future toward which she is moving. Instead, her life has been definitively ruptured through suffering and so she is condemned to an existence that defies the coherence of a story. Stories about her life can be presented, but they do not hang together in an overarching narrative. As such, her life challenges the presumption that God, and more specifically God's Spirit, is making *all* things new.

This more radical rendering can also be put more generally. The very goodness and graciousness of God are called into question not only by the existence of horrifying suffering but also by its pervasiveness. We cannot pass on "stories" such as Sethe's because they cannot be fit into a coherent story told from the standpoint of God's eschatological future. All we have, in their cases, are the chronicles of suffering endured and of memories "beaten back." In this sense, we might say that we ought to challenge the viability, and perhaps more determinatively the moral credibility, of God's forgiveness. Is our world such that we cannot envision Christian claims about the Triune God as a coherent story?

Such a question presents one version of challenges to belief in God, only not by doubting God's existence but by challenging God's goodness. Such a view challenges the coherence of Christian claims about God's forgiveness, about God's love, by suggesting either that a vision of the "future" of God's Kingdom is unintelligible (at least for those, such as Sethe, who have suffered horribly) or that the price of any harmony that is ultimately achieved in God's Kingdom is simply *too* costly.

As is well known, such a challenge is offered by Ivan Karamazov in his famous "Rebellion" in Fyodor Dostoevsky's *The Brothers Karamazov*. Ivan's problem is not that he does not believe in God. It is, rather, that he is troubled by the way in which God seems to rule the world; more specifically, he is horrified by the innocent suffering of children. Indeed, the fact that he is willing to grant that there is a God only heightens his difficulties, and makes his protest even more intense.

Ivan rejects any claim that there is a coherent story of a gracious, forgiving God that we can pass on. Ivan tells his brother Alyosha, a novice in a nearby monastery, about a number of stories of people who have suffered horrifying evils at the hands of others. He concludes these tales by offering the following extended protest to his brother:

> I absolutely renounce all higher harmony. It is not worth one little tear of even that one tormented child who beat her chest with her little fist and prayed to "dear God" in a stinking outhouse with her unredeemed tears! Not worth it, because her tears remained unredeemed. They must be redeemed, otherwise there can be no harmony. But how, how will you redeem them? Is it possible? Can they be redeemed by being avenged? But what do I care if they are avenged, what do I care if the tormentors are in hell, what can hell set right here, if these ones have already been tormented? And where is the harmony, if there is hell? I want to forgive, I want to embrace, I don't want more suffering. And if the suffering of children goes to make up the sum of suffering needed to buy truth, then I assert beforehand that the whole of truth is not worth such a price. I do not, finally, want the mother to embrace the tormentor who let his dogs tear her son to pieces! She dare not forgive him! Let her forgive him for herself, if she wants to, let her forgive the tormentor her immeasurable maternal suffering; but she has no right to forgive the suffering of her child who was torn to pieces, she dare not forgive the tormentor, even if the child himself were to forgive him! And if that is so, if they dare

not forgive, then where is the harmony? Is there in the whole world a being who could and would have the right to forgive? I don't want harmony, for love of mankind I don't want it. I want to remain with unrequited suffering. I'd rather remain with my unrequited suffering and my unquenched indignation, *even if I am wrong*. Besides, they have put too high a price on harmony; we can't afford to pay so much for admission. And therefore I hasten to return my ticket. And it is my duty, if only as an honest man, to return it as far ahead of time as possible. Which is what I am doing. It's not that I don't accept God, Alyosha, I just most respectfully return him the ticket.[7]

Ivan even gets Alyosha to admit that he could not countenance (nor would he think other people would countenance) providing the ultimate fulfillment and happiness of people if it required the torture of even one innocent child.

Alyosha's most definitive response is to suggest that Jesus Christ is the one, sinless being who can provide the necessary forgiveness. He says to Ivan,

you asked just now if there is in the whole world a being who could and would have the right to forgive. But there is such a being, and he can forgive everything, forgive all *and for all*, because he himself gave his innocent blood for all and for everything. You've forgotten about him, but it is on him that the structure is being built, and it is to him that they will cry out: "Just art thou, O Lord, for thy ways have been revealed!"[8]

Ivan, though, has anticipated this response; he counters it with the parable of the Grand Inquisitor.[9] Through the parable, Ivan seems to argue that, though freedom might be God's greatest gift to humankind, it has produced such tremendous suffering and confusion that most people would prefer the contentment of oppression to freedom. Jesus made a decisive mistake and a decisive misreading of humanity when he rejected the "temptations" in the desert (see Matthew 4:1-11) and chose instead to follow the path of the cross.

Ivan accepts that there is a God; he also believes that there are many

7. Dostoevsky, *The Brothers Karamazov*, tr. Richard Pevear and Larissa Volokhonsky (San Francisco: North Point, 1990) p. 245.

8. Dostoevsky, *The Brothers Karamazov*, p. 246.

9. Dostoevsky, *The Brothers Karamazov*, p. 246 and pp. 246-264.

stories that can be passed on. However, he does not think the story of the Christian God is one of them. Indeed, he rejects the claim that this God could produce a coherent story that ends with *any* version of "and they lived happily ever after." Ivan finds belief in God *morally objectionable* because the price of innocent suffering is too high for harmony, for human salvation. As a result, there is no easy answer to Ivan's protest, no quick recourse to the atonement of Christ or even to the promise of eschatologically produced harmony. Nor are there, at least for *this* objection, recourses to apologetic or theoretical attempts to justify God in relation to these evils.

Indeed, we are challenged by the multiple voices in *The Brothers Karamazov*, as well as in *Beloved*, to recognize that in some sense there is no one "answer" to the moral issues raised by their suffering and the evils that have been inflicted. Even more, there is a sense in which, both in form and in substance, Ivan's and Sethe's tales suggest that each one is *not a story* to pass on.[10] The most decisive version of this objection is that, as a result of the suffering that Ivan chronicles and Sethe endures, the tale of the Triune God is *not a story* to pass on.

How, then, ought we to respond? Before responding to the radical challenge that this is *not a story*, much less one to pass on, we need to return to the substance of Ivan's protest to explore its effects. Ivan objects that the "price" of innocent suffering is too high to "pay" for harmony. But his objection assumes either that someone such as God establishes a price that must be paid or that God demands the payment of such a price.[11] The Christian doctrine of God, as I have been explicating it, holds that God is pure self-gift, and that God's "costly" forgiving is enacted not through a transaction demanded by God, but through the painful embodiment of forgiving love — even to the point of Gethsemane, Calvary, and Emmaus. So we need to press whether Ivan's protest is, at least in the first instance, appropriate in its characterization of God.

Secondly, Ivan objects to Jesus Christ as the expression of God's forgiving because, Ivan suggests, he decisively misreads what humanity is

10. I have already commented on the substance of their tales; however, it is also significant to note that both tales contain significant challenges to the genre of "realistic narrative." For a provocative discussion of Dostoevsky's style, see Mikhail Bakhtin, *Problems of Dostoevsky's Poetics*, ed. and tr. Caryl Emerson (Minneapolis: University of Minnesota, 1984).

11. I am indebted to Nicholas Lash, who first enabled me to see this point in conversations on the topic of Ivan's rebellion. See also his discussion in *Believing Three Ways in One God* (Notre Dame: University of Notre Dame, 1992) pp. 116-117.

capable of embodying. So in his parable, the Grand Inquisitor takes the burden of God's gift on himself in order to "free" humanity from its freedom and for the contentment of slavery. The Inquisitor does so, even to the point of his own burden and even, it seems, his self-destruction. Yet it is significant that after the Inquisitor has addressed Christ, who stands in the dock as a prisoner, Christ does not respond to the charges.

> His silence weighed on [the Inquisitor]. He had seen how the captive listened to him all the while intently and calmly, looking him straight in the eye, and apparently not wishing to contradict anything. The old man would have liked him to say something, even something bitter, terrible. But suddenly he approaches the old man in silence and gently kisses him on his bloodless, ninety-year-old lips. That is the whole answer. The old man shudders.[12]

In this one simple act, the Inquisitor's "burden" is seen as an ignorance of the depths of Christ's mercy. Nothing more is said; nothing more need be said. As Nicholas Lash has eloquently described the effect of the kiss on the Inquisitor, "finding God's gift the dark and indecipherable burden we must bear turns out to be, in fact, just another variant in our endlessly ingenious capacity for egotism, which God's love makes light of."[13] Indeed, God's forgiving love makes "light" of the Inquisitor's egotism by refusing to accept the Inquisitor's terms of debate.

Similarly, the appropriate response to Ivan's protest is not to accept the terms in which it is formulated. It is an attack on theoretical attempts to justify God in the face of evil by focusing on its edifying effects. And, as such, it has considerable power. But the appropriate response to Ivan is the one that the prisoner offers the Inquisitor and that Alyosha offers Ivan at the conclusion of his parable: a kiss of peace. To be sure, Ivan's protest is not marked by an egotistic self-assertion so much as by a horror at seeing what happens to innocent children. Even so, Ivan's protest can collapse back into a self-justifying and self-righteous rebellion against the very possibility of forgiveness, of holiness, of love. Hence, the power of Alyosha's kiss.

More generally, then, we need to relocate the force of Ivan's protest from the sphere of theoretical theodicy to its pragmatic effects in responding to horrifying evils. As Kenneth Surin has suggested in a discussion of Ivan's protest, the decisive issue posed by horrifying suffering (like Sethe's or that of the children whom Ivan describes in "Rebellion") is twofold:

12. Dostoevsky, *The Brothers Karamazov*, p. 263.
13. Lash, *Believing Three Ways in One God*, p. 106.

First, we have to determine, "grammatically," whether or not things are such that it is inconceivable for the person *in extremis* to be in a position to speak of God as benevolent and gracious; or alternatively, whether we are in a position where we can somehow go on to imagine, and (far more crucially) to strive for, a form of life in which it will be possible to activate the concepts "divine love," "divine providence," and so forth.[14]

I have been arguing that the Christian faith does affirm the latter possibility through the life-giving work of Christ in the power of the Spirit. It does so through *our* embodiment of forgiveness in specific habits, practices, and disciplines that witness to the gracious and forgiving work of the Triune God. At the same time, however, I have suggested that it may be difficult — indeed, it may be contingently impossible — for any of us to *say* this as individuals directly to particular victims, particularly while they are still suffering.

That is, rather than *telling* victims and those who are suffering that they ought to forgive, or that they ought to believe in a good and gracious God, the first task of the Church — as people struggle to embody God's forgiveness in the pursuit of holiness — is to show solidarity with and compassion toward those who find themselves *in extremis*. Perhaps in some circumstances this can most eloquently be articulated in something representing a kiss of peace. Surin's own conclusion is instructive:

> I am suggesting that perhaps the only discourse which can do justice to the radicality of Ivan's challenge is one that can in principle be heard — but maybe not *spoken* to those who are victims — by a community that stakes its very existence on the memory of suffering, on an inarticulate speech of the heart, a speech which opened itself to the mystery of God, a divine mystery which makes present the mystery of healing. For to speak is to imply that healing is *experienced* as healing, whereas to hear in silence is to acknowledge that someone's hurt can be so great that it betokens the very absence of the experience of healing and thus of divinity itself. This hearing can only be undertaken in a spirit of inviolable solidarity with those who are afflicted.[15]

If we can learn to live with the silences, to recognize that which cannot be said and should not be carelessly spoken, then our speech will be more

14. Kenneth Surin, *Theology and the Problem of Evil* (Oxford: Basil Blackwell, 1986) p. 103.

15. Surin, *Theology and the Problem of Evil*, pp. 104-105.

spare and more richly charged with the redemptive power of the mystery of God.

Therefore, we need to cultivate the discernment of the Spirit, the One who enables us to recognize the habits of redemptive silence and speech. These habits involve our learning to distinguish diverse kinds of silence: from the silence of despair to the silence that nonetheless reflects a groaning — a quiet cry — for Creation to come to its fullness (see Romans 8:18-25) to the silence of contemplation in friendship with God and with one another. Further, these habits of redemptive silence and speech are culti- vated in the liturgy. After all, even if — and as — the Church learns to listen to the silences, it continues to "speak" God's forgiving love, God's peace, through its regular enactment of worship. More specifically, when the Church "says" the eucharist, it embodies the costly forgiveness of God for the sake of those who are silent and have been silenced.

The forgiven-ness of such eucharistic communities is manifest in solidarity with — and compassion toward — those who are afflicted and is embodied in practices of forgiveness and reconciliation. Such communi- ties offer an alternative rendering to the challenge that the tale of the Triune God is *not a story* to pass on. For the story of the Triune God, to which such communities witness, is not a narrative in which there is a simple beginning, middle, and end; rather, it is a story of God's self-gift in which God gives, and forgives, even to the point of the radical interruption that is the slaying and raising of Jesus Christ. But that interruption, which reverses our path of self-destruction and sets us on the path of re-turning to God through forgiveness and reconciliation, relocates our lives — and humanity's and indeed the Creation's destiny — in the eschatological work of the Spirit, who is making all things new. In this sense, the forgiving work of Christ in the power of the Spirit offers the decisive interruption in our world such that we can learn — in the power of that same Spirit — to envision God's future, to hope for it, and so to embody a faithful witness to it.

This Is *Not* a Story to *Pass* On: Producing Holy People

Despite — or more precisely, because of — these affirmations, the painful memories of Sethe endure, the difficult struggles of Simon Wiesenthal and countless others persist, and Ivan Karamazov's protest haunts us. We cannot afford to fail to acknowledge these pains and struggles, and even if we proclaim — albeit, at least in some circumstances, cautiously or even silently — that God's forgiveness bears no limits, we will do so authentically *only* if we confront the profound pain that many of our brothers and sisters (and perhaps we ourselves) have suffered and continue to suffer as a result of our pervasive brokenness, the ways in which we diminish and destroy one another and ourselves. That is, we cannot afford to "pass" on these stories; we need to confront them.

In the Gospels, Jesus does mention one unforgivable sin: blasphemy against the Holy Spirit (Matthew 12:32 and parallels). Though there is a long history of reflection on and speculation about what this means (and more precisely what makes the sin "unforgivable"), the answer seems to be relatively straightforward. This is so particularly when it is read in the larger context of Matthew's Gospel and, even more, of Jesus' ministry, death, and resurrection. The unforgivable sin is refusal to accept the forgiveness that God always offers. It is unforgivable because there is no way for us to accept forgiveness if we refuse to acknowledge our own need for forgiveness. Consequently, we quench the Spirit whose work is to enable us to embody forgiveness as we become holy in the light of Christ. Any sin can be forgiven, *if* we are willing to acknowledge the need for forgiveness as well as the need to forgive.

One decisive means by which we can fail to acknowledge our need for forgiveness is a desire to "pass" on stories of our own sin and evil — whether that for which we are directly culpable or that for which we are indirectly complicit. It is easier, and undoubtedly more pleasant, to put on rose-colored glasses and pretend that things are not so bad in our world and that "I" have never hurt or offended anyone else. But doing so is self-deceptive and self-destructive since we thereby fail to recognize the importance of Father Zossima's insight in *The Brothers Karamazov* that we are inevitably complicit in the sin and evil of the world. We cannot afford to "pass" on these stories and on a truthful rendering of our own stories, because it is only from engaging them that we will be enabled to sustain a truthful hope for our own forgiveness and reconciliation with God and with one another.

There are signs of a refusal to "pass" on these stories even in the texts themselves, to see a hope for the future even in the midst of death-dealing sets of memories and a tragic, suffering present. So, for example, Wiesenthal continues to wonder if perhaps some other response would have been more appropriate, if not words of forgiveness then at least a more hopeful or compassionate response.

More determinatively, Ivan's "protest" is not so much "answered" as responded to in the holiness of Father Zossima (whose story follows closely after the parable of the Grand Inquisitor) and, in the culminating sections of the novel, in the emerging holiness of Alyosha. Father Zossima takes on himself responsibility for his own sin and others' sin, and he manifests in his own life the pattern of Jesus' life, death, and resurrection. Dostoevsky seems to suggest that, while Ivan's tale is *not a story* to pass on, by confronting it (i.e., by not "passing" on it) in the manner of Father Zossima, the story of embodied forgiveness transfiguring people into holiness counteracts the force of Ivan's protest. That is, Father Zossima can confront Ivan's protest and Ivan's rejection of the story of the Triune God by embodying Christ's costly forgiveness in his own life and death.

And, perhaps most radically, even Sethe's tale — hopeless, in one sense, given the horrifying effects of the past — is set in a redemptive context. The epigraph to the novel ("I will call them my people which were not my people; and her beloved, which was not beloved") is from Paul's letter to the Church at Rome (9:25), which in turn quotes the same words from the prophet Hosea (2:23; 1:10). Both Paul and Hosea point to radical interruptions by which God creates something new out of a destructive past. In each case, the promised result is reconciliation and new life. In each case, such reconciliation and new life are promised despite the apparent "evidence" of circumstances in the present. This suggests that God's story cannot be told as a simple narrative but must be able to encompass the reversals in the story of Israel and the Church and, more determinatively, the transfiguring fidelity of God's promise that in Christ God was and is "reconciling the world to himself" (2 Corinthians 5:19). Such reconciliation comes only through an engagement with the past and the present in all of their joys and griefs, healings and woundings, friendships and betrayals.

Hence, even some of the most difficult texts, texts that challenge our belief that "this" — whatever it is — is a story to pass on, nonetheless bear within them glimpses of hope for redemption. In this sense, we cannot afford to "pass" on the stories of Sethe and of Wiesenthal and of innocent children suffering, or (to take other examples) of the pain of Palestinian mothers who have seen their children brutally tortured and killed as well as the desperate isolation of many people in our cities. Our witness to God will be most truthful and our forgiven-ness most hopeful if we do not shrink from facing the worst about ourselves and about the world in which we live. We do so neither in a spirit of humiliation (of ourselves or others) nor in the midst of a culture of victimization in which we always blame others while failing to take responsibility ourselves. Rather, we do so in the Spirit of truth, the Spirit who requires and inspires us to accept accountability for our lives and to manifest our forgiveness through ongoing repentance. And we do so in the Spirit of hope, the Spirit who promises that, indeed, God's future will bring the goodness of Creation to its promised consummation.

By not "passing" on these stories, but indeed confronting and telling them, we are able to absorb them so that they can be remembered well. We hope to absorb them so that the evils they reflect will not be passed on to others. Doing so may take time; indeed, it likely will take a long time. However, if Christians claim to worship not Christ *un*crucified but Christ crucified and risen, then we of all people ought to know that the past can be borne in hope — even if it takes a lifetime to learn how to do so well.

We see this hope embodied in holy people, for one of the signs of holiness is an ability to absorb sin and evil without passing them on to others. It is the ability to stop the cycles of sin and violence and vengeance through lives patterned after the life, death, and resurrection of Jesus of Nazareth. For it is in such patterning that people begin to discover the forgiven-ness and healing that is at the heart of our salvation and our communion with God, with one another, and with the whole Creation. There are numerous examples of such holiness; a brief listing might include such diverse modern saints such as Therese of Lisieux, Maximillian Kolbe, Dietrich Bonhoeffer, and Martin Luther King, Jr., as well as the great saints of the Church's memory such as Augustine of Hippo, Bernard of Clairvaux, Teresa of Avila, and John and Charles Wesley.

We also see this hope, perhaps less glowingly but nonetheless clearly and crucially, embodied in those communities of people who have refused to give in to counsels of despair but have — faithfully, hopefully, and even joyfully — witnessed to the redemptive power of God's forgiving and reconciling love. These include communities of Jesuits and Dominican priests and nuns, Latin American base communities, Wesleyan class meetings, L'Arche Houses, Catholic Worker Houses, and countless others whose names are less clearly recognized but are making impacts in people's lives.

One manifestation of the hope of the gospel and of our holiness is seen as we become people whose forgiven-ness is found not only in thanksgiving for a transfigured past but also in active, holy witness that embodies such forgiveness in relationships with others. At times this serves as a stimulus, a protest against any and all relationships that result in the diminishment or destruction of persons; at other times it serves as an occasion for the joyful celebration of reconciliation, and indeed the preparation of the "fatted calf" for an appropriate feast. Our refusal to "pass" on stories of horrific sin and evil should not make them occasions for despair, nor should they become occasions for morose or even somber acceptance. Christian forgiveness and Christian holiness ought to be manifested in the joy of the Holy Spirit, which comes from our friendship with God and with one another.

Perhaps the most appropriate way for us to cultivate communities and people of holiness is to focus on the day known as Holy Saturday, the worship known as the Easter Vigil.[16] It is the day poised between the destruction and death of Good Friday and the forgiveness and reconciliation of Easter Sunday, between our recognition of our own betrayals of Jesus (and our recognition that our betrayals of others are also betrayals of Jesus) and the judgment of grace that we receive from the risen Christ, restoring us to friendship with God and with one another and inviting us to an Easter feast.

In Wallace Stegner's novel *Crossing to Safety* the narrator describes an encounter with Piero della Francesca's painting of the resurrected Christ starting up behind the tomb. "That gloomy, stricken face permitted no forgetful high spirits. It was not the face of a god reclaiming his suspended immortality, but the face of a man who until a moment ago had been thoroughly and horribly dead, and still had the smell of death in his clothes and the terror of death in his mind. If resurrection had taken place, it had not yet been comprehended."

The narrator then describes how one of the characters, a woman who had endured much suffering, studied the painting: "She studied it soberly, with something like recognition or acknowledgement in her eyes, as if those who have been dead understand things that will never be understood by those who have only lived."[17]

The pain of suffering and death is awesome; their effects are often numbing. Even so, as we seek to locate our own forgiveness and pursuit of holiness in relation not only to our own sin and suffering but more determinatively to the world's sin and suffering, we ought to do so in the context of Christ's dying and rising. For the drama of Holy Week is an invitation to be among those who "have been dead" and can thus understand things inaccessible to those who "have only lived."

Even more, it is an invitation to keep the Easter Vigil, that ancient rite by which Christians mark the time between Jesus' death and his resurrection. And it is an invitation for which others can find appropriate ana-

16. For an insightful discussion of the significance of Holy Saturday, see Nicholas Lash, "Friday, Saturday, Sunday," *New Blackfriars* 71 (March 1990) pp. 109-119.

17. Wallace Stegner, *Crossing to Safety* (New York: Penguin, 1987) pp. 274-275.

logues. As George Steiner has recently suggested in *Real Presences,* Jews and others know analogues of the "long day's journey of the Saturday" between Good Friday and Easter Sunday. Jews and other non-Christians know the analogous effects of Friday: "of the pain, of the failure of love, of the solitude that are our history and private fate." And they know about Sunday, "the day of liberation from inhumanity and servitude . . . the lineaments of that Sunday carry the name of hope."[18]

As in the vigil, then, all people ought to be ever mindful of those forces that conspire in the production of sin and evil and death. At the same time, however, we ought — as forgiven and forgiving people — to be searching for, praying for, living for, and celebrating signs of God bringing about new life, signs of Easter, anywhere they can be found. We ought to cultivate communities of the Spirit whose holiness is manifest in practices of forgiveness and reconciliation. In so doing we ought to attend to the politics of memory, a politics that enables us to confront the past without being bound by it or condemned to repeat it.

Holy Saturday, along with the Easter vigil that marks that day, carries with it also a sense of the timeful character of the craft of forgiveness. It is indeed, in Steiner's terms, "a long day's journey." That was a day in which the disciples were undoubtedly dubious about the hope to which they had been called, and perhaps — as would be suggested by the Gospels' indication of how the disciples reacted to the news of Christ's resurrection on Easter Sunday — even close to despair and a fear-induced paralysis. Yet Easter did come, and so — eventually — did the inauguration of their new life as *forgiven* betrayers. So we ought to see the long day's journey of Saturday as a sign of encouragement in our struggles to embody the craft of forgiveness — from learning to live with the memories of the past to coping with feelings of resentment and desires for vengeance, to loving our enemies, and to becoming proficient exemplars of holiness through habits and practices of forgiveness and reconciliation.

More generally, the Easter Vigil also signifies a second sense of time, the time between the times of Christ's forgiveness through his cross and resurrection and the promised coming of the fullness of God's Kingdom in the power of the Spirit. In this time, we are called to be ever watchful. Let us be watchful for the ways in which we can embody the forgiving, transforming, and reconciling power of Easter in a world that all too often seems bent on finding new ways to crucify. That is no easy task, but it is

18. George Steiner, *Real Presences* (Chicago: University of Chicago, 1989) pp. 231-232.

the hope to which we have been called, and it is the promised truth on the basis of which we ought to stake our lives and deaths in fidelity to God's Kingdom. For what we have been given and forgiven, in the power of the Spirit of Jesus Christ, is the ability to live and die in such a way that we can trust in the triumph of God's grace. We do so even as we mark the Easter Vigil, longing for that day when we will see — and, we hope, live in — the "new Jerusalem" (Revelation 21:1-5a), where all will have been made new.

Index

Abuse, xi, 3-7, 45-46, 68, 71-72, 77, 85, 86, 89, 115, 150, 160, 174, 176, 178, 186, 190, 195, 199, 232, 244, 257, 260, 262, 264, 269, 279, 287

Accountability, xi, xvi, 121, 149, 154-156, 158, 168, 172, 231-232, 239, 242, 248, 252-255, 262-263, 269

Action, xii, 4-5, 16, 23, 27-30, 36-37, 42, 45, 72, 88, 90, 92, 95, 108, 110, 122-123, 125, 163-164, 185, 196-197, 218, 227, 229, 231, 233-234, 236-238, 248-250, 261-263, 269-272, 289

Adams, Marilyn McCord, 216-217, 225

Adultery, 62, 194

Amnesia, 176-178

Anabaptist Tradition, xvii, 17, 19, 182-183, 188, 202

Anger, 71, 107, 122, 132, 182, 197, 199, 226, 229-234, 241-251, 264, 277, 282

Anglican Tradition, xvii, 182-183

Anointing (see also Healing), 199-202

Anscombe, G. E. M., 218

Anthony, Abba, 128, 174

Apocalyptic, 179, 256-257

Apostasy, 194

Aquinas, St. Thomas, xiii, 85, 164, 210-211, 218

Arcane Discipline (see also Discipline), 28-32, 192, 228

Arendt, Hannah, 90, 97, 115

Aristotle, 209-211, 218, 227, 229

Asad, Talal, 164, 191

Athanasius, 119

Atonement (see also Cross; Jesus Christ; Trinity), 151-152, 155-157, 276, 293

Augustine of Hippo, St., 62-63, 79, 164, 169, 184, 219, 256, 267-268, 272-273, 299

Authority, 110-111, 186-190, 272

Autobiography, 44, 63-64, 169, 172, 187, 238

Bakhtin, Mikhail, 293

Balthasar, Hans Urs von, 120, 146, 215, 252, 254, 259

Baptism, 4-7, 20, 29, 38, 47, 89, 114, 125, 152, 156, 165-175, 176, 182-183, 187

Barth, Karl, 9, 118-119, 122-124, 128, 209-210, 220-224

Baxter, Michael, xvii, 179
Bernard of Clairvaux, 299
Bethge, Eberhard, 8, 24, 29
Berry, Wanda Warren, 67
Betrayal, 4, 63, 120, 129-130, 166, 173, 175-177, 235-236, 241-242, 244, 260, 298, 300-301
Bible Study, 13, 44-45, 89, 191, 224
Binding and Loosing (see also Reconciling Forgiveness), 182, 186, 192-194, 203
Bitterness, xi, 147, 179-182, 197, 200, 222, 231-232, 245, 247, 261
Blame, 37, 116, 194, 245-246, 298
Blasphemy against the Holy Spirit, 297
Bondi, Roberta C., 116, 174, 196
Bonhoeffer, Dietrich, xv, 7-34, 36, 39, 45, 52, 73, 90, 98, 104, 123, 145, 156, 165, 172-173, 185, 187, 192, 228, 259, 276-277, 286, 299
Bosk, Charles, 227
Bosnia, 264, 283, 287
Boundaries, 182-197, 201, 203, 270
Brakenhielm, Carl Reinhold, 215-216
Brokenness, xii, 5, 18, 28, 32, 49-50, 62-63, 117, 120, 126-127, 163, 176, 186, 196, 208, 213, 220, 230, 239, 246, 263-264, 267, 274, 278, 281, 289, 297
Brown, Peter, 234
Buckley, James J., xvii, 57, 132, 235, 261
Buckley, Michael J., 84
Bureaucracy, 40-42, 115
Buthelezi, Manes, 271
Butler, Bishop Joseph, 233-234, 247
Butterfield, Herbert, 266

Cahoy, William, 60
Capital Punishment (see also Punishment), 273
Cartwright, Michael, xvii, 137, 171
Chacour, Elias, 180-182, 241, 287
Character (see also Holiness; Saints),

xiii, 6, 37, 39, 57-58, 92, 103, 105, 125, 196, 202, 214-215, 218, 227, 237-238, 248, 255, 259-260, 285
Charry, Ellen, 117
Cheap Grace (see also Therapeutic Culture), 6-25, 28, 36, 39, 47, 89, 104, 136, 143, 150, 159, 165, 222, 226, 234, 253, 262, 285, 288-289
Chopp, Rebecca, 121
Church (see also Community, Christian), xii, xvi, 4-6, 10, 12, 16, 20-21, 25-26, 32-33, 36, 43, 46, 48, 63-67, 103, 117, 128, 131-133, 154, 156, 165-168, 171-172, 176, 183, 186-189, 195-197, 203, 216-217, 222-224, 230, 239, 253, 261, 268, 270-272, 276-277, 295-296, 298
Church Discipline (see also Reconciling Forgiveness), 19-20, 22, 166, 182, 189-190, 255
Class Meetings, Wesleyan, 168, 186, 299
Coles, Robert, 35-36, 38
Coles, Romand, 78
Communion, xii-xiii, xv-xvi, 5-6, 42, 47, 50, 59, 61-63, 66-67, 95, 103, 113-121, 124-127, 129-134, 136, 147, 154-155, 163-165, 169, 173-176, 183, 192, 194, 199, 202-204, 208, 219-220, 224-225, 230, 254, 267, 270, 299
Community, Christian (see also Communion), 10-33, 42-48, 51-52, 59, 65, 67, 111, 148-149, 154-157, 162, 163-168, 173-175, 178, 184-204, 207, 225, 227, 255, 261, 270, 299-301
Compassion, 45-46, 53, 58, 107, 232, 257, 260, 282, 287-288, 295-297
Cone, James H., 169, 172, 232
Confession (see also Reconciling Forgiveness), xvi, 10-11, 13-14, 16-22, 25-26, 28, 30-31, 38, 58, 159, 165, 183-186, 191, 198-199, 201, 284-285

Conflict, 81, 88, 180, 183, 192-196, 203

Conversion, 47, 63, 95, 127, 146-147, 157, 169, 201, 256, 258, 266

Costly Forgiveness, xii, xv, 5-25, 32, 36, 39, 47, 51, 59, 68, 72, 83, 91, 98, 104, 110, 113, 118, 121-122, 124, 163, 197, 230, 242, 253-254, 259-260, 281, 290-296, 298

Covenant (see also Communion), 106-107, 147, 195

Craft, xii-xiii, xvi, 13-14, 19, 21, 27, 72-73, 160, 196, 203, 207-239, 241-243, 247, 272, 277, 289, 301-302

Cranfield, C. E. B., 256

Creation, xii, 5, 61, 79, 83-84, 113-114, 118-120, 124, 126, 131-133, 149, 163-165, 173, 185, 203, 208-210, 219, 221-222, 230, 238-239, 241, 254, 290, 296, 299

Cross, 7, 17, 20-21, 24, 29, 68, 97, 102, 106, 111, 113, 123-124, 126, 155-156, 160, 190, 195, 254, 262, 271, 292-293, 296, 300-301

Culpability (see also Accountability; Guilt), 49-53, 59, 62-63, 102, 107, 145, 149-150, 154, 156, 235, 257, 297

Cunningham, David, xvii, 258

Dahmer, Jeffrey, 244

Dallen, James, 183

Daube, David, 108

David, King, 107

Davidson, Donald, 209

Death (see also Dying and Rising with Christ; Martyrdom; Suicide), 3-8, 22, 26, 76, 83, 85, 88, 90, 94, 97-98, 109, 126, 128, 137, 143, 155, 166, 180, 202, 246-247, 259, 280, 285, 297, 300-302

Depression, xvi, 72, 86-88, 168, 247

Derrida, Jacques, 78, 80, 212

Desire, 9, 21, 43-45, 47, 62, 71-72, 76, 79, 85-86, 93, 115, 119, 123, 171, 176, 191-192, 199, 219, 226, 231-234, 239, 242-251, 253, 257-264, 273-274, 277, 289, 297, 301

Despair, 19, 61, 72, 113, 122, 136, 155-156, 170, 172, 175, 177, 199, 267, 276, 296, 299-301

Deterrence, 273-275, 288

Diminution, xv-xvi, 4-7, 49, 59, 62, 73, 86, 90, 114-116, 120, 130, 151, 155, 168-169, 173-174, 203, 241, 246-247, 260, 297, 299

DiNoia, J. A., 222

Discernment, 27-29, 146, 157-158, 168, 173, 179-182, 188, 191-193, 196-197, 203, 207, 209, 223-224, 227-232, 234-235, 238, 263, 270-272, 276, 278, 289, 296

Discipleship, 7, 12-14, 17, 19, 22-25, 29-32, 39, 47, 62, 124, 166, 168, 173, 186

Disciplines, xiii, 5, 13, 17, 21, 25, 28-29, 32, 45, 163-164, 178, 184, 187, 189, 236, 270-272, 275, 295

Doctrine, 9, 43, 51-52, 186-188, 196, 201, 203, 224

Domination, xv, 72, 86, 92, 114-115, 148, 190, 262, 264, 272-273, 276

Donovan, Vincent, 178-179

Dorff, Elliot, 103

Dostoevsky, Fyodor (see also Karamazov, Ivan), 234, 281, 291, 293, 298

Dunfee, Susan Nelson, 60

Dunn, J. D. G., 110

Duquoc, Christian, 126

Dying and Rising with Christ (see also Baptism; Easter), 4-7, 17, 181, 300

Easter (see also Resurrection), 130, 175, 177-178, 180-181, 195, 221, 264, 300-302

Easter Vigil, 300-302

Eastern Orthodox Tradition, xvii, 182-183, 200-201

Eastwood, Clint (see also Munny, William), xv, 73

Eichmann, Adolf, 115
Eliezer the Great, 108
Eliot, George, 185, 226
Elon, Amos, 282-283, 289
Emotions, xii, 5, 42, 48, 50, 149, 163-164, 196, 218, 227, 229, 231, 233-237, 246-251, 261-262, 269, 289
Enemies, Love for, xvi, 14, 16, 20-22, 29, 47, 160, 194-197, 203, 230, 241-279, 301
Engel, Mary Potter, 60
Enlightenment, 7-8, 17, 37, 84, 211-212, 217
Eriugena, John Scotus, 253
Eschatology (see also Apocalyptic; Kingdom, God's), xii, 5, 15, 26-29, 32, 38, 57, 64-68, 112, 118, 124-126, 128, 131, 133, 136, 149, 154, 156, 163, 165, 167, 175, 189, 196, 203-204, 217, 230, 235, 237, 257-258, 290, 293, 296
Eucharist, 13, 29, 47, 89, 114, 156, 165, 175-182, 183, 198, 202, 266, 296
Evans, G. R., 183
Evil, xii-xiii, xv-xvi, 4, 6, 23, 27, 32, 52, 67-69, 72, 76, 81-91, 95, 98, 113, 114-117, 122, 126, 128, 131-132, 146, 155, 163-169, 174, 178, 190, 195-196, 203, 230, 233, 236, 239, 241-242, 246, 249, 255-257, 260, 269, 276, 278, 279-302
Excommunication (see Church Discipline)
Exemplars (see also Saints), xii, 13, 27, 33, 226, 228, 232, 265, 301

Father, God the (see also Prodigal Son; Trinity), 113-119, 125, 129, 132, 134, 155, 165, 203
Feil, Ernst, 11, 24-25
Finkenwalde, 12-13, 16, 18, 22, 24, 29
Footwashing, 202
Forgetting, xvi, 147, 177, 237, 280, 282, 288-290
Forrester, Duncan, 275-276

Fortune, Marie, 89-90
Foucault, Michel, 212, 225, 275
Fowl, Stephen, xvii, 4, 8, 117, 166
Friendship, xii-xiii, 5-6, 22, 44, 47-48, 63, 66-67, 76, 81, 112, 131, 135, 140, 145, 149, 164, 166-167, 174-178, 184, 196, 200, 203, 207, 211, 218, 228, 231, 254, 263, 265, 267, 296, 298, 300
Future (see also Life, New), 4-5, 23, 59, 90, 97-98, 125, 147, 149, 157, 167, 172-173, 175-182, 226, 237, 253, 279-302

Gethsemane, 293
Gift, 5, 47, 59, 80, 83, 95, 112, 113-115, 118-120, 167, 173-174, 177, 188, 199, 203, 230, 235, 237, 254, 292-294, 296, 302
Girard, René, 195
God (see Trinity)
Golding, Martin, 235
Goldstein, Valerie Saiving, 60
Good Friday, 120, 175, 177, 300-301
Goodness (see also Holiness), 81-82, 95, 108, 120, 185, 226, 241, 251, 255-257, 260, 263, 274, 281, 290-291, 299
Grace (see also Cheap Grace; Costly Forgiveness), 15-17, 38, 51, 56-59, 84, 97, 102, 106, 118-119, 124, 127-128, 135-137, 144-150, 158, 162, 168, 178-179, 195, 199-200, 221, 232, 253-255, 259, 264, 288, 290-291, 300-302
Grand Inquisitor, The, 292-294, 298
Gray, Madelein, 185
Greeley, Andrew, 3-7
Green, Clifford, 31
Gregory of Nyssa, 114
Guilt (see also Culpability), xii, xvi, 5, 18, 23, 25, 27-28, 32, 46, 62-63, 116-117, 122, 125, 138, 151, 154, 169, 176, 200, 213, 245-246, 250, 266-267

Gutiérrez, Gustavo, 22, 82-83, 84-85, 174-175

Haber, Joram Graf, 212-214, 233, 235-236, 248
Habits, xii-xv, 13, 32-33, 47, 49-50, 62-64, 66, 71-74, 76-77, 85, 88-90, 98, 114-117, 121, 126, 128, 131, 136, 144, 147, 149, 154, 156-162, 163-165, 183, 199, 203, 210, 225-239, 250, 258, 260-261, 263-264, 269, 277, 295-296, 301
Hampton, Jean, 213, 225, 246, 248-252, 260-261, 274
Harmony, 61, 82, 113-115, 281, 290-296
Harak, Simon, 85
Harnack, Adolph von, 7
Harrison, Beverly Wildung, 246
Hart, H. L. A., 274
Hatred, 10, 49, 64, 131, 180-182, 213, 233, 239, 241-252, 258-264, 273, 277, 283
Hatred, Moral, 248-252, 258-261, 277
Hauerwas, Stanley, xvii, 148, 194
Healing, 63, 82, 146-147, 163, 177-178, 181-182, 197-204, 213, 267, 274, 278, 282, 286, 290, 295, 298-299
Hegel, G. W. F., 106
Hell, 120, 243, 251-255, 258-259, 280, 283
History, 4, 28, 37, 62-63, 68, 72, 77, 85-86, 114-117, 119, 121-122, 126, 128, 130, 131, 147, 212-213, 228, 301
Hitler, Adolf, 8, 10, 12-13, 22, 24, 28, 32-33, 244, 264
Hobbes, Thomas, 78
Holiness, xii-xiii, xvi-xvii, 4, 13, 27, 32-33, 45, 49, 59, 64, 66, 73, 94, 96, 98, 121, 135, 147, 149, 154-156, 158-159, 162, 163-166, 171, 173, 175, 183-185, 191, 196, 203, 207, 217, 224, 227, 230, 237, 247, 253-254, 263, 277-278, 281, 294-302
Holocaust (see also Nazi Germany), xvi, 82, 103, 281-282, 287, 289
Holy Saturday, 120, 128, 254, 300-302
Holy Spirit (see also Trinity), xv, xvii, 21-22, 27, 29, 33, 51, 57, 66-67, 103, 112, 120, 124-125, 128-134, 135-136, 143-147, 149, 154, 157-158, 162, 163, 165, 167-168, 171, 173, 176-177, 182-184, 188-190, 193, 200-204, 207, 216-217, 220-224, 227-228, 232, 237-239, 259-260, 264, 267, 276-278, 289-290, 295-302
Homosexuality, 271, 272
Hope, 4-5, 55, 96-97, 109, 118, 127, 130, 132, 144, 155-156, 159, 165, 172, 174-182, 183, 194, 196-197, 203-204, 232, 251, 254, 256-259, 273, 277, 281, 283, 296-299, 301-302
Hopko, Thomas, 132
Hospitality, 103, 114, 161
Hugo, Victor, 275
Human Beings (see Nature, Human)
Humility, 173-174, 198, 212, 232, 244, 262
Hunsinger, George, 220-221, 223

Ignatieff, Michael, 115, 273
Imagination, 54, 87-88, 90, 122, 149, 186, 200, 241-242, 266-267, 277, 280, 295
Incarnation, 119-120, 124, 144
Injustice, 23, 26, 32, 69, 72, 83-84, 118, 190, 199, 231-232, 236, 246, 261, 288
Israel, Biblical, 84, 102-113, 117-118, 124, 133, 147, 253, 260, 298
Israel, Contemporary, 180-181, 282-283, 287

Jacoby, Susan, 244, 250, 267
Jennings, Theodore W., 39, 183

Jenson, Robert W., 167, 183

Jeschke, Marlin, 183

Jesus Christ (see also Trinity), xv, xvii, 4-7, 10-33, 51-52, 66, 68, 82, 84, 88, 90, 91, 94-95, 97, 101-113, 119-134, 135-137, 143-145, 149-150, 152-162, 165-166, 170-173, 175, 177-178, 181, 188-190, 195-196, 198, 200-204, 207, 214-217, 219-223, 231, 239, 249-255, 259-262, 264, 292-302

Job, Book of, 52, 82, 191, 198, 230

John of Patmos, 259

John Paul II, Pope, 89, 188, 268, 269-270

Jonah, 108, 264-265, 269

Jones, Arthur C., 172

Joy, 58, 83, 107, 120, 132, 168, 176, 222, 231, 290, 298-300

Judaism, xvii, 23, 38, 43, 101-113, 117-119, 121, 124, 133, 150, 155, 159, 209, 214-215, 244, 282-90, 301

Judgment, 11, 14-18, 21, 44, 47, 51, 53, 54-59, 97, 102-103, 106-107, 109, 119-127, 132-133, 135-137, 144-150, 158, 162, 171, 178-182, 185, 198, 221, 231-232, 235, 245, 247, 249, 252-261, 263, 272, 277, 300

Justice, xi, xvi, 26, 58-59, 62, 74, 89-90, 106, 118, 126-127, 180, 242, 244, 258, 260-261, 267-269, 288

Kant, Immanuel, 151, 217

Karamazov, Alyosha, 291-292, 294, 298

Karamazov, Ivan, xvi, 88, 151, 281, 290-298

Kasper, Walter, 117-118

Kenneson, Philip, xvii, 189

Kenosis, 119-120

King, Jr., Martin Luther, 232, 263-265, 299

Kingdom, God's, xii, 4-6, 10-11, 21, 30, 33, 47, 51, 56, 64-68, 83, 84, 90, 102-103, 105, 110-111, 119, 124-128,

133, 136, 144, 146, 149-150, 153-162, 163, 166-173, 175-177, 183, 194, 208, 230-232, 239, 247, 281, 290-291, 301-302

Kiss of Peace, 178-179, 294-295

Klassen, William, 256

Koenig, John, 197-198, 202, 236

Kolbe, Maximilian, 91, 104, 281, 299

Kolnai, Aurel, 212

Konvitz, Milton, 287-288

Kristeva, Julia, 87-89

Laments, 172, 191-192, 230-231, 242, 252, 259-260, 264

Language (see also Redemptive Speech), 29-32, 38-39, 47, 61, 78-79, 82-83, 113, 117, 122, 183, 190-193, 196-197, 220-224, 236-237, 289, 295-296

Lasch, Christopher, 44, 46

Lash, Nicholas, 68, 80, 133, 190-191, 293-294, 300

Lasserre, Jean, 9

Lear, Jonathan, 147, 225

Learning and Unlearning, xii-xiii, 5, 13-14, 17, 23, 49-50, 62-64, 66, 71-73, 76-77, 81-83, 85, 88, 90, 92, 96, 97, 131, 145-146, 148-149, 164, 175, 179, 224, 226-228, 230, 234-235, 238-239, 247, 261, 264, 269, 277

Lebacqz, Karen, 269

Lehmann, Paul, 66

Levinas, Emmanuel, 104-105, 110, 112, 126

Lewis, C. S., 236-237

Liberalism, Protestant, 7-10, 64-66

Liberation (see Life, New)

Life, New (see also Kingdom, God's), 4-5, 15, 17, 30-31, 51, 76, 88, 97-98, 103, 121, 124-125, 128-134, 137, 144, 156, 162, 166-169, 173-174, 183, 230-232, 235, 237, 260, 269, 273, 282, 298, 301

Lindbeck, George, xvii,

Lischer, Richard, 65
Long, Thomas, 41
Love (see also Communion; Enemies, Love for; Friendship; Gift; Trinity), xv-xvi, 5-6, 44, 47, 59, 61, 63, 72, 76, 84, 93, 95, 98, 114, 118-120, 124, 128, 130-131, 133, 147, 155, 160-162, 165-166, 168-178, 184, 203, 230, 233, 238, 241-278, 280-281, 289, 291, 293-294, 296, 299
Luther, Martin, 168
Lutheran Tradition, xvii, 13, 17, 19, 183, 188
Lying, 62, 71, 179, 195, 232

MacIntyre, Alasdair, 39-40, 43-44, 164, 209-210, 212, 218, 223, 226, 229
MacMillan, Ian, 91, 281
Maimonides, Moses, 159
Malcolm X, 232
Marcion, 106
Marcuse, Herbert, 285
Marion, Jean-Luc, 59, 114
Marsh, Charles, 11
Marshall, Bruce, 215, 223
Marty, Martin, 287-288
Martyrdom, 8, 24, 93-94, 96, 98, 266
Mary Magdalene, 130-131, 167, 177
Masai, 178-179
Maundy Thursday, 175, 177
McClendon, James William, 32, 193
Medicine, 201-202, 226-227
Memory (see Amnesia; Forgetting; Nostalgia; Remembering)
Mercy, 15, 28, 56, 89, 92, 97, 106-107, 119-120, 229, 253, 257-261, 265, 268, 294
Milbank, John, 69, 79, 80, 88, 113, 146, 165, 253, 272, 276
Minas, Anne C., 214-215
Montefiore, Claude, 161
Morrison, Toni, xv, 279, 281
Motes, Hazel, 137-145, 157, 159, 162, 263

Moule, C. F. D., 161, 179
Munny, William, 73-77, 85, 86, 90, 97
Murder, 73, 82, 86-88, 92, 94, 96-97, 120, 194, 236, 244, 266, 272, 274, 285
Murdoch, Iris, 81
Murphy, Jeffrie, 212-214, 216, 233, 243, 249-251, 260
Music (see also Singing), 113-115
Myers-Briggs Type Indicator, 40-42

Narrative, 63-64, 68, 82, 84, 143, 145, 147, 157, 159, 162, 163, 168-174, 176, 183, 184, 187, 190, 219-220, 233-235, 237-238, 279-302
Natural Law, 210
Nature, Human, 78-79, 95, 105, 110, 114-115, 119-120
Nazi Germany, xv, 7-8, 11-13, 22-33, 68, 80, 90-98, 115, 232, 244, 248, 264, 277, 282-290
Newman, Louis E., 109
Niebuhr, H. Richard, 157
Niebuhr, Reinhold, 267
Nietzsche, Friedrich, 14, 17, 78-82, 88-90, 97, 244-246, 248, 257, 262
Nostalgia, 176-178

Ochs, Peter, xvii, 118
O'Connor, Flannery, xv, 53-57, 65, 132, 137, 144-145, 147, 258, 263
Oesterreicher, John, 286
O'Hanlon, G. F., 215
Oklahoma City Bombers, 244, 283
Old Elizabeth, 169-174, 177
Ontology, 77, 81, 88, 242
Oppression, 7, 23, 67, 72, 84, 86, 96, 116, 120, 125-127, 155, 169, 172, 174, 176, 188, 198, 230-231, 260-261, 292
Ordination, 19, 182, 185-187
Origen, 256
Ozick, Cynthia, 285

Packwood, Robert, 46

Palestinians, 180-182, 241, 287, 298

Particularity, 11, 84, 90, 95, 114, 127, 130-132, 135-137, 143-145, 147, 149, 157-158, 162-164, 167-168, 173, 175-176, 178, 185-186, 193, 207-239

Pascal, Blaise, 261

Past, xii, 4, 37, 63, 74-75, 83, 88, 90, 125, 127, 130, 146-147, 149, 151, 157, 167-168, 172-173, 175-182, 183-185, 213, 228, 234, 237, 253, 269, 279-302

Pastoral Care (see Psychology)

Paton, Margaret, 215

Patton, John, 199

Paul, St., 4, 36, 157, 166-168, 179, 182, 198, 231, 253, 255, 298

Peace, xii, 5, 21, 26, 69, 76, 79, 81-84, 88, 97, 113, 129, 165, 178-181, 191-192, 194, 203, 230, 249, 256-257, 270, 272, 288, 290

Penance (see Confession; Reconciling Forgiveness; Repentance)

Pentecost, 264

Peter, St., 130-131, 167, 169, 177, 182

Philosophy, 112, 150-151, 153, 210-215, 217-220, 224-225, 229, 252

Piper, John, 257

Plantinga, Cornelius, 71

Plaskow, Judith, 60

Politics, xiv, xvii, 7, 9, 26-27, 31, 33, 36, 38, 42, 46, 60, 64, 66, 68, 77-80, 83, 89, 109, 114, 190-191, 208, 219, 225, 239, 242-244, 248-251, 255, 262-264, 267-278, 279-302

Poschmann, Bernhard, 183

Possession, 5-6, 17, 33, 47, 58-59, 62-63, 114, 191

Power, xvi, 6, 80, 87, 89, 93, 95, 97, 115-116, 127-129, 148, 150, 164, 183, 190-192, 196, 228, 231, 239, 242-246, 262, 267-270, 272-274, 286, 289, 302

Practices, xii-xiii, xv-xvi, 4-5, 13, 17, 21-22, 27-33, 38-39, 45-53, 63-64, 66-67, 71-72, 76-77, 87, 89-92, 95, 98, 103, 126-127, 129, 131, 135-136, 140, 143-147, 149, 151, 154-162, 163-204, 207-208, 217, 222-226, 234, 236-239, 250, 264, 271-277, 295-296, 301

Prayer, 13, 20-21, 29-31, 63, 92, 94, 170, 191-192, 195, 197-204, 217, 236, 253, 255, 259, 261, 264, 269, 301

Preaching, 11, 13, 16, 20, 125, 191

Pride (see also Self-Abnegation), 18, 30, 47, 59-60, 63, 155, 185-186, 190, 224, 294

Privatized Forgiveness, 6-8, 10, 13, 19, 38-40, 42-44, 49-50, 89, 187, 267

Prodigal Son, Parable of, 16, 58-59, 64, 74, 102, 118, 121, 264, 299

Prophetic Protest, 4, 30, 148, 155, 165, 171-172, 174, 182, 189, 231, 242, 246, 255, 260-261, 264, 276, 299

Protestantism (see also Liberalism, Protestant), 143, 182-183, 200

Psychology, xiii-xv, 14, 17, 31, 35-36, 39, 42, 48, 58, 65, 67-68, 89, 147, 178, 225

Punishment (see also Capital Punishment), xi, xvi, 107, 195, 229-230, 239, 242-245, 247, 252-254, 258, 261-262, 269, 270-278, 288

Raboteau, Albert J., 171, 189-190

Racism, 62, 116, 177, 195, 232, 264, 271

Rahner, Karl, 185

Ramsey, Paul, 277

Rape, 236, 241, 244, 250, 279

Reconciliation, xii, 5-6, 15, 20, 29, 38, 42, 53, 76, 82, 90, 107, 109, 113, 126-127, 132-133, 146, 148, 154-155, 159, 163, 165, 178, 180-197, 200, 203, 213, 219, 222, 230, 232, 235, 237-238, 241-242, 245, 249, 252,

255-262, 267-269, 271, 273-277, 282, 288-289, 296, 298-299, 301

Reconciling Forgiveness, 165, 182-197, 241-242

Redemption (see also Jesus Christ), 29-30, 83, 120, 135, 137, 139-140, 143-144, 151-152, 154, 157, 193, 196, 251, 253, 264-265, 283, 286, 296, 298-299

Redemptive Speech (see also Silence), 183, 190-194, 196-197, 203, 224, 228, 231, 286, 289, 295-296

Rehabilitation, 244, 273-275, 288

Remembering, xii, xvi, 4, 147, 149, 175-182, 190-192, 197, 203, 237, 272-273, 279, 302

Reparation (see Restitution)

Repentance, xi, xvi, 5-6, 13-16, 19-21, 27-28, 31-33, 37, 42, 45, 47, 49-53, 58-59, 67, 72, 102-103, 105, 107-108, 110, 117-118, 121-123, 125-126, 135-162, 165-169, 171, 173, 179-182, 192, 194-195, 198, 201, 203, 213, 224, 227, 231-232, 235, 239, 241-242, 244, 248-250, 253-258, 261-265, 269-271, 274-278, 284-285, 287-288, 299

Repression, xvi, 96, 177-178, 234, 244-247, 261-262

Resentment (see also Anger; Bitterness), 231, 233-234, 245-248, 262, 273, 301

Responsibility, 17, 28, 45, 50, 104, 115-116, 121, 126, 147, 153, 185, 187-188, 208, 231, 238, 254, 269, 273-275, 285-286, 298

Restitution, 108, 110, 127, 151, 154

Resurrection (see also Dying and Rising with Christ; Life, New), 4-7, 11, 29, 97, 102-103, 109, 111, 113, 124-129, 155, 175, 181, 190, 195, 221, 254, 293, 300

Retribution (see also Punishment), 242-251, 258-259, 270, 273-275, 288

Rieff, Philip, 42-43

Roberts, J. Deotis, xviii, 172

Roberts, Robert C., 48-49, 218, 232

Roman Catholic Tradition, xvii, 17, 19, 65, 143, 182-183, 185, 187-188, 200

Romero, Archbishop Oscar, 265

Root, Michael, 271

Rottedness, 248-252, 264

Rwanda, 244, 264, 287

Sacraments (see also Anointing; Baptism; Confession; Eucharist; Reconciling Forgiveness), 11, 14, 16-17, 143, 166, 171, 173, 176, 182, 186, 200-201

Sacrifice, 102, 107-111, 118-119, 125, 133, 152, 157, 175-176, 178, 214, 247

Saints (see also Exemplars), 27, 92, 196, 199, 228, 299

Salvation, 102, 107, 109, 119, 123, 243, 251-255, 258-259, 261, 277, 293, 299

Sanders, E. P., 106, 110

Scapegoating, 176, 182, 190, 195

Scarry, Elaine, 199

Secular Parables, 26, 209, 220-225

Self-Abnegation, 18, 47, 59-60, 155, 186, 190

Self-Deception, 17-18, 50, 57, 59, 67, 77, 131, 168, 172-173, 177, 185-186, 199, 228, 297

Self-Giving (see Love)

Self-Righteousness (see Pride)

Sermon on the Mount, 65-66, 195, 255

Sethe, 279-282, 289-290, 293-294, 296, 298

Shame (see also Self-Abnegation), 60, 116, 186, 200, 222, 250, 256-257, 284

Sickness, 198-199

Silber, John R., 151

Silence, 26, 30, 183, 190-194, 196-

197, 203, 224, 228, 231, 283, 285-287, 289-290, 294-297

Simpson, O. J., 46

Sin, xii-xiii, xv-xvi, 4-7, 11, 13-33, 38, 42, 45-47, 49-52, 54, 57-69, 71-91, 98, 105, 107-109, 113-117, 120-128, 130-131, 136-137, 139, 143, 146-162, 163-204, 208, 214, 219, 230-232, 236, 238-239, 241-242, 245-253, 261-263, 267, 271-272, 276-278, 288, 297-301

Singing (see also Music), 92, 94, 95, 172, 191

Slavery, xvi, 62, 169-172, 189-190, 244, 279-283, 289

Smedes, Lewis, 48-53, 57, 59, 60, 68, 90, 231

Sobrino, Jon, 63, 266

Soloveitchik, Joseph B., 159

Somebodiness, 169, 171-172

Speyr, Adrienne von, 183

Stalinism, 68, 115

Stegner, Wallace, 300

Steiner, George, 283, 285, 289, 301

Stendahl, Krister, 257

Stout, Jeffrey, 211

Strawson, Peter, 217

Styron, William, 87

Suffering, 3, 24-25, 31-32, 62, 72, 82-85, 87, 90, 94, 98, 116-117, 128, 155, 170, 172-175, 197-199, 229, 231-232, 236, 244-246, 257, 262, 264, 269, 272-273, 281-282, 285, 288-298, 300

Suicide, 72, 87, 91, 94-95, 247, 275

Surin, Kenneth, 84, 294-295

Swinburne, Richard, 137, 151-158

Tamez, Elsa, 175

Taylor, Charles, 212

Techniques, xiii, 37, 40-43, 50

Teresa of Avila, 299

Therapeutic Culture, xv, 35-53, 57-69, 89, 116, 128, 187, 261

Therese of Lisieux, 299

Thomas, John Christopher, 202

Thurian, Max, 183

Tilley, Terrence, 84, 185

Time, xiii, 13, 85, 128, 131, 133, 159, 163, 168, 178, 181, 183, 196-197, 199, 201-203, 233-239, 250, 280, 286, 299-302

Torture, 82, 84, 86, 94, 259, 283, 292, 298

Traditions, xvi, 207-239

Tragedy, 115, 227, 230-231, 272-274, 276, 281, 297

Trinity (see also Father, God the; Holy Spirit; Jesus Christ), xi-xvii, 5-7, 21, 33, 38, 51-52, 56-57, 61-68, 81-84, 86, 88-89, 91, 95, 97-98, 101-134, 149, 153, 155, 163-165, 176, 185, 196-197, 200-204, 207-211, 213, 215-225, 230-231, 238-239, 251-262, 267, 290-302

Trust, 72, 76, 181, 183, 190, 193, 242, 244, 281, 302

Truth, 11-12, 17, 22, 45, 62, 67, 129, 131-132, 138-141, 153, 163, 177-178, 182, 183, 187, 189, 194, 199, 203-204, 220, 222-224, 267, 270, 291, 298, 302

Truthfulness, xii-xiii, xvii, 11, 17-19, 22, 32, 47, 58, 62, 67, 129, 131, 164-165, 168, 172-174, 177-178, 182-183, 187, 190-191, 194-195, 199, 203, 222-224, 228, 231-232, 237, 246-247, 263, 267, 269-270, 276, 281, 297-298, 302

Tugwell, Simon, 200

Turpin, Ruby, 53-59, 60, 64, 147, 232

Tyler, Anne, 226, 233-234

Unforgivableness, xvi, 73, 77, 105, 194, 208, 239, 243, 278, 279-302

Unforgiving Servant, Parable of the, 121, 162, 195, 212-214, 218, 249

Unintentional Sin, 102, 107-108, 214

Universality, 117-118, 127, 131-132, 135-136, 144, 163-164, 207-239

Valliere, Paul, 119-120

Vengeance, xi, xvi, 21, 71, 74, 77, 85, 107, 117, 120, 122, 125, 176, 178, 226, 233-234, 237, 239, 242-263, 270, 273, 277, 282-283, 285-287, 289, 299, 301

Victimization, 4, 42, 45-46, 48, 62, 64, 67, 75, 85, 104-105, 114, 116-117, 122, 125-127, 149, 166, 169, 174, 177-178, 187, 199, 242, 285, 298

Violence (see also Abuse), xi, xv-xvi, 3-8, 23-33, 45-46, 52, 62, 68-69, 71-98, 107, 113, 114-115, 117, 120, 122, 125, 127, 136, 150, 155, 160, 168-169, 173, 178, 190, 199, 201, 221-222, 233, 242, 247-248, 262-264, 276-277, 287, 299

Virtues, xiii, 167, 211-212, 218, 232, 237, 244-245, 250

Voltaire, 19

Wainwright, Geoffrey, 125, 175, 254, 266

Walls, Jerry L., 252

War, 188, 272, 276-277

Watson, David Lowes, 186

Wedemeyer, Maria von, 23

Wesley, John and Charles, 299

Wesleyan Tradition, xvi-xvii, 168, 183, 186, 202, 299

West, Cornel, 267

Westphal, Merold, 81-82, 245

Wiesenthal, Simon, xv, 104, 281-290, 296-298

Williams, Delores, 169

Williams, Rowan, 45, 63-64, 85, 120-122, 125, 127, 129-132, 148, 176-177, 268, 273

Wilson, Edward O., 78

Wolterstorff, Nicholas, xviii, 230

Wood, Chris, 276

Wood, Ralph, xvii, 54-56

World (see also Creation), xvi-xvii, 6-7, 10-15, 24-30, 47, 49, 51, 58, 67-69, 72-73, 75-84, 87-91, 96-97, 104, 106, 109, 111, 114, 116, 119-134, 143-144, 146, 148, 153-154, 157, 163-167, 169-170, 172-174, 185, 192-193, 196-197, 199, 201-203, 208-210, 219-225, 227, 238-239, 241, 250, 260-261, 268-269, 277-278, 281, 284, 287, 291-292, 296-302

Worship, 30, 38, 84, 109, 112, 191, 215, 281, 296, 299-300

Wounds, 72, 125, 146, 182, 191, 201, 245, 264, 284, 298

Wrath, 56, 106-107, 247, 254-258, 260

Wright, N. T., 109, 111-112

Wuthnow, Robert, 44-45, 47

Yeago, David, xvii, 111-112

Yoder, John Howard, 188, 192-193

Yom Kippur, 107-109

Zacchaeus, 102, 148

Zerbe, Gordon, 256-258

Zizioulas, John, 114, 132

Zossima, Father, 297-298